Feeding Mars

HISTORY AND WARFARE
Arther Ferrill, *Series Editor*

FEEDING MARS: Logistics in Western Warfare from the Middle Ages to the Present   John Lynn, *editor*

THE SEVEN MILITARY CLASSICS OF ANCIENT CHINA
Ralph D. Sawyer, *translator*

FORTHCOMING

THE HUNDRED YEARS WAR FOR MOROCCO: Gunpowder and the Military Revolution in the Early Modern Muslim World   Weston F. Cook, Jr.

THE CHIWAYA WAR: Malawians in World War I
Melvin E. Page

HIPPEIS: THE CAVALRY OF ANCIENT GREECE
Leslie J. Worley

THE HALT IN THE MUD: French Strategic Planning from Waterloo to Sedan
Gary P. Cox

ON WATERLOO
The Campaign of 1815 in France by Carl von Clausewitz
Memorandum on the Battle of Waterloo by the Duke of Wellington
Christopher Bassford, *translator*

THE ANATOMY OF A LITTLE WAR: A Diplomatic and Military History of the Gundovald Affair, 567–585
Bernard S. Bachrach

WARFARE AND CIVILIZATION IN THE ISLAMIC MIDDLE EAST   William J. Hamblin

ORDERING SOCIETY: A World History of Military Institutions   Barton C. Hacker

Feeding Mars

Logistics in Western Warfare from the
Middle Ages to the Present

EDITED BY

John A. Lynn

Mershon Center Series on
International Security and Foreign Policy

A Member of the Perseus Books Group

All rights reserved. No part of this publication may be reproduced or transmitted in any form or by any means, electronic or mechanical, including photocopy, recording, or any information storage and retrieval system, without permission in writing from the publisher.

Copyright © 1993 by Westview Press, Inc. A Member of the Perseus Books Group

Published in 1993 in the United States of America by Westview Press, Inc., 5500 Central Avenue, Boulder, Colorado 80301-2877, and in the United Kingdom by Westview Press, 36 Lonsdale Road, Summertown, Oxford OX2 7EW

Library of Congress Cataloging-in-Publication Data
Feeding Mars : logistics in western warfare from the Middle Ages to the
  present / edited by John A. Lynn.
    p. cm. — (History and warfare)
  Includes bibliographical references and index.
  ISBN 0-8133-1716-9 — ISBN 0-8133-1865-3 (if published as a paperback)
    Logistics—History.   I. Lynn, John A. (John Albert), 1943–
II. Series.
U168.F44   1993
355.4'11'09—dc20   92-27652
                                                                    CIP

Printed and bound in the United States of America

∞ The paper used in this publication meets the requirements
   of the American National Standard for Permanence of Paper
   for Printed Library Materials Z39.48-1984.

10   9   8   7

Contents

Preface vii
Acknowledgments xi

PART ONE
The Historiography of Logistics

1. Logistics and the Aristocratic Idea of War
   Edward N. Luttwak 3

2. The History of Logistics and *Supplying War*
   John A. Lynn 9

PART TWO
Medieval Logistics, 400-1500

Medieval Introduction 31

3. Byzantine Logistics: Problems and
   Perspectives, *Walter E. Kaegi* 39

4. Logistics in Pre-Crusade Europe,
   Bernard S. Bachrach 57

5. Naval Logistics in the Late Middle Ages:
   The Example of the Hundred Years' War,
   Timothy J. Runyan 79

PART THREE
Early Modern Logistics, 1500-1815

Early Modern Introduction 103

6. The Logistics of Warfare at Sea in the Sixteenth Century:
   The Spanish Perspective, *John F. Guilmartin, Jr.* 109

7   Food, Funds, and Fortresses:
    Resource Mobilization and Positional Warfare
    in the Campaigns of Louis XIV, *John A. Lynn*   137

8   Logistical Crisis and the American Revolution:
    A Hypothesis, *John Shy*   161

PART FOUR
Modern Logistics, 1815-1991

    Modern Introduction   183

9   The Misfire of Civil War R&D,
    Robert V. Bruce   191

10 Forging the Trident:
    British Naval Industrial Logistics,
    1914-1918, *Jon Tetsuro Sumida*   217

11 "Deuce and a Half":
    Selecting U.S. Army Trucks,
    1920-1945, *Daniel R. Beaver*   251

12 War Plans and Politics:
    Origins of the American Base of
    Supply in Vietnam, *Joel D. Meyerson*   271

    Bibliography of Logistics from
    the Ancient Greeks to the 1980s,
    George Satterfield   289

About the Book   309
About the Contributors   311
Index   313

Preface

Mars must be fed. Today his tools of war demand huge quantities of fuel and ammunition. The soldiers and sailors who practice his craft need food, clothing, and equipment. All these must be produced, transported, and distributed to contending forces if they are to begin or continue the contest. No one can doubt the importance of feeding Mars in modern warfare, and it takes no great effort to recognize that it has always been a major aspect of large-scale armed struggle.

Yet despite its undeniable importance, surprisingly little has been written about it. The literature of warfare is full of the triumphs and tragedies of common soldiers or the brilliance and blundering of generals, but the tedious tasks of supply attract few readers. They have little to do with those aspects of military history that have made stories of warfare a popular genre ever since tribesmen huddled about the fire boasting of their feats in battle. Logistics lacks the drama of combat. It can be expressed on balance sheets no more exciting than shopping lists; movement is not measured by the dashing gallop of charging cavalry but by the steady plod of draft horses.

The fact that military historians have not given logistics its due may be explained by the fact that their audiences have not wished to be bothered by such details; Edward Luttwak advances this argument in Part One of this volume, that devoted to the history of logistics. At this time, there is really only one cross-national study with a broad time perspective. That is, of course, Martin van Creveld's *Supplying War: Logistics from Wallenstein to Patton*, published in 1977. In selecting this topic, van Creveld displayed keen judgment. And by getting to the question first, van Creveld earned the conqueror's right to set the terms of the debate. Consequently, the essays in this volume can hardly avoid being part of a dialogue with *Supplying War*. For this reason, Part One will also deal directly with van Creveld's important work, presenting and commenting upon his hypotheses and methods.

This volume is meant not to replace or invalidate van Creveld or other important works, such as James A. Huston's study of U.S. logistics, *The Sinews of War: Army Logistics, 1775-1953*. A collection of essays such as this cannot offer a complete and consistent reinterpretation of the history of logistics. Such was never our goal. Instead, by supplementing, qualifying, and criticizing existing views, these contributions will add to our understanding of logistics in war. In the process, the chapters presented here will establish the importance of certain issues not touched upon before and throw some existing conclusions into question; rather than establish a new orthodoxy, they will, if successful, encourage the historical study of supply in warfare.

Focus and Organization

Since this volume is a collection of essays by many authors with diverse interests and approaches, the contributions cannot be easily forced into a common pattern with a single, tightly defined focus. True, this collection concentrates on aspects of the way in which fighting forces acquired the wherewithal to fight, from food to ammunition. However, even such an emphasis is not a simple matter, since it involves questions of production, administration, and transportation.

There are aspects of supply that the authors have not discussed, in particular the mobilization of a society's resources by civil authorities through taxation and credit. Books on state finance could fill libraries, whereas studies of logistics across time are rare. To deal once again with the field of war finance would have dissipated the efforts of the contributors. It would have distracted them from little-discussed questions of supply and burdened them with the need to discuss material that has already received a great deal of attention.

The focus of this volume in time, place, and subject matter resulted from both the design of the editor and the expertise of the contributors. It is exclusively western, which we take not as ethnocentrism but as a comment on the state of knowledge in western and non-western military history. After Part One on the history of logistics, the volume proceeds with three additional parts, each defined by time period—medieval, 400-1500; early modern, 1500-1815; and modern, 1815-1975. The medieval part is most concerned with the capacity of medieval states and technology to maintain forces in the field or at sea. The early-modern part emphasizes the procurement and shipment of supplies. And the modern part deals with questions raised by the Industrial Revolution: research and development, organization of war production, creation of modern transport, and the organization of a modern logistic administration.

Each of the three parts begins with a short introduction, not intended to provide a complete mini-history of logistics but rather to set the stage for each era by discussing some basic theme or themes of historical logistics relevant to the time period. These introductions are intended to help readers change gears as they move through the volume and to introduce each of the contributions.

The Roles of Logistics

While logistic needs have changed over the centuries, logistics have always exerted tremendous influence on strategy and operations, even if this influence has not always been obvious to those who would restrict the study of war to the chess game of planning or the bloody contest of battle. Rommel agreed when he stated, "In fact, the battle is fought and decided by the quartermasters before the shooting begins."[1]

Obviously, the modern military's appetite for supply precludes any major operations without proper logistic support, but the dependence on logistics is not simply a present-day phenomenon. Naval operations have relied on ships carrying their own supplies with them since the first war-fleets went to sea, and these supplies have often been drawn from central depots and arsenals. Such is the nature of naval warfare. True, armies could and did take many of their provisions from campaign areas; however, this necessity also determined the actions of armies. They might have to stay on the move to feed themselves and their horses off local resources, or they might have to occupy territory not for its strategic value but only in order to sustain the war effort by exploiting its resources. When armies developed extensive logistic infrastructures during the seventeenth century, this did not liberate strategy from logistics but tied them even closer together. In any case, then and now, campaigns that cannot be supplied because the resources are either not available or cannot be transported to the navies or armies that need them are doomed to delay and defeat.

Less apparent than the strategic significance of logistics are its links to questions of political development. The mobilization of resources for war has been a major factor in shaping the modern state. Of course, this is a much broader phenomenon than logistics alone. It includes the need for states to tap financial resources through taxation and credit and the need to organize the production of war materiel. Logistics has been part of this formula, particularly when the ability to draw upon resources in remote campaign areas eased the strain on governments at home or, on the other side of the coin, such demands imposed especially onerous burdens on local areas. Brian Downing has argued that early modern European states that fought their wars without oppressively burdening subjects with taxes and other levies preserved their old representative institutions and consequently developed liberal governments. Those states that were compelled to draw heavily from their own peoples and had to impose their demands by force turned to more authoritarian forms of government.[2] William McNeill also explains the rise of command economies in the modern world as a by-product of war pressures.[3]

The ways in which mankind has chosen to feed Mars have had consequences of profound importance. As such they should be of concern to historians who study either the conduct of war itself or war's impact on government and society. We, the authors of these essays, present them to our readers in the hope that these contributions will lead to a greater understanding of the role played by logistics in history.

John A. Lynn
University of Illinois at Urbana-Champaign

Notes

1. Rommel in Martin van Creveld, *Supplying War* (Cambridge: 1977), p. 200.
2. Brian Downing, *The Military Revolution and Political Change in Early Modern Europe* (Princeton: 1991). See as well Charles Tilly, *Coercion, Capital, and the European States, AD 900-1900* (Oxford: 1990), and David Kaiser, *Politics and War: European Conflict from Phillip II to Hitler* (Cambridge, MA: 1990).
3. William H. McNeill, *The Pursuit of Power* (Oxford: 1982).

Acknowledgments

Many individuals and organizations contributed to the creation of *Feeding Mars*, and I would like to formally thank them. Bernard Bachrach and Geoffrey Parker first proposed the idea to me of a series of essays devoted to the history of logistics. That idea became the third conference of the Midwest Consortium on Military History, held at the University of Illinois at Urbana-Champaign in October 1990. At this scholarly meeting, the chapters in our volume first saw the light of day as papers. During the conference, Dan Beaver devised the organization of the volume as it now stands, and even the name of our volume became an item of discussion. Ed Luttwak finally christened it *Feeding Mars*. Those who participated in our conference but whose names do not appear on the list of authors added much by their comments. William Maltby, Richard Mitchell, Williamson Murray, Robert Johannsen, Peter Maslowski, and Edward Coffman all helped to sharpen our arguments and hold the authors to their tasks.

Of course nothing would have happened without generous financial support from a number of sources. The lion's share came from the College of Liberal Arts and Sciences at the University of Illinois at Urbana-Champaign. Other Illinois units that contributed include International Programs and Studies and the Department of History. In addition, we received funds from the Mershon Center at the Ohio State University. In fact, this book takes its place in the Mershon series on International Security and Foreign Policy.

Both the original conference and the process of turning the papers delivered at it into chapters required a great deal of organization and effort. Luckily, I received invaluable help from the Program in Arms Control, Disarmament, and International Security at the University of Illinois. In particular, Merrily Shaw, assistant to the director, and Mary Anderson, administrative secretary, took over many of the necessary tasks. It is hard to conceive of how I could possibly have undertaken this project without their help.

The people at Westview Press have also given me the kind of enthusiastic backing and professional assistance every author wants. I would like especially to thank Peter Kracht and Michelle Asakawa.

For her contributions as conference host and personal editor, as well as for her all-round support, I would like to express my gratitude to my wife, Andrea Lynn.

Lastly I must single out for special thanks my great friend and colleague Geoffrey Parker, Charles E. Nowell Distinguished Professor of History at the University of Illinois. His constant support in this project turned wishes and plans into reality.

J.A.L.

PART ONE
The Historiography of Logistics

1

Logistics and the Aristocratic Idea of War

Edward N. Luttwak

Considering the chapters presented in this collection, one must immediately ask oneself how it could be that the many questions raised by the authors were not raised long before, for they are such *interesting* questions. To know how armed forces acquired their weapons and vehicles, how troops were fed in garrison or on the march, how horses were kept in fodder or motor-vehicles in fuel, and how ships were provisioned or air forces kept flying is both intriguing in itself and also of great importance in explaining the course of events.

Indeed, to the modern reader, the very fact that pre-modern political entities with their embryonic state bureaucracies, scant technical means, and inflexible economies could supply armed forces at all raises a whole host of fascinating questions. How could the needs of armed forces—which almost invariably dwarfed those of all contemporary civilian institutions—even be calculated with any approximate accuracy? How could the required equipment and supplies be gathered, purchased or produced in the absence of any similar civilian undertakings on any comparable scale? And how could supplies be stored and transported on that disproportionate scale in the absence of today's technical means, from refrigeration to motor vehicles? These are all questions that historians should have been eager to answer long ago.

Yet in the vast literature on military history, from ancient narratives to the most modern writings, from works of impeccable scholarship to those only intended to entertain a popular readership, the means by which armed forces were equipped and supplied in peace and war are quite often simply ignored or, at best, treated only in fragmentary fashion. Amidst the detailed recitation of tactical moves that one finds in battle accounts, the moment may be reached when this or that formation is said to have been overcome not by the enemy but by its own lack of food, fodder, fuel or ammunition; or else one may read that troops hard-fighting till then were defeated, because they were faint with hunger or maddened by thirst; or, to the contrary, an abundance of supply may be noted but without any explanation of how the feat was achieved. Likewise, amidst elaborate accounts of war operations on a larger scale, short asides may tell us that this or that maneuver was shaped by the need to await supplies, secure routes of resupply, or find supplies on the spot—or to the contrary, that it was well-sustained by ample supplies, again without explanation. And in historiography written on a still larger scale—amidst the exposition of the imputed causes of the war or wars—about the magnitude and kind of the military forces raised by each side and about the manner and outcome of the larger operations undertaken, one routinely finds only cursory introductory or parenthetical comments on how the armed forces as a whole were equipped and sustained and on how any particular part of them was supplied in the field, or perhaps remained unsupplied.

Against such historiography it is obvious that in historical reality, the equipment and supply of armed forces could hardly be an activity merely episodic, incidental or parenthetical. On the contrary, it was necessarily a continuing effort of central importance. As such, it was often the objectively limiting factor on what was done at each remove, and yet more often, no doubt, it was the most pressing concern of protagonists great and small that duly influenced their conduct.

The obvious reason for this systematic divergence between the historiography of war and its actual history is that the latter must reflect ineluctable material realities, while the former has tended rather to reflect the prevailing literary conventions. For, of course, military historiography is no different from any other historiography in its origin as a branch of literature and as such is subject to literary norms and priorities. Of these, the first is the writer's need to entertain readers or at least attract their attention, if only to gain thereby opportunities to admonish, instruct, or justify—those being the classic motives of pre-commercial (and pre-publish-or-perish) writing. To be sure, the literary conventions of military historiography have varied much over time. But it may safely be said that within them generally, whatever is dramatic easily displaces what is merely important. And while the grand strategy of war or its politics and, even more, its operational and tactical levels, have always been eminently suitable for dramatic exposition, that was not the case when it came to descriptions and analyses of how armed forces were variously funded, equipped and supplied.

To be sure, *modern* historiography is supposed to be a branch of scholarship and not literature, and as such its aim must be to successively uncover better truths by applying the scientific method to the evidence, rather than to entertain, first of all. More generally, modern historiography, military or not, is supposed to be fully emancipated from literary concerns and conventions. But in reality their influence has lingered on, and especially so perhaps in the case of Anglo-American military historiography—which has only most recently been rescued from the antiquarians, official analysts, regimental pietists, and purveyors of battle stories to schoolboys of all ages that long had the subject almost to themselves. Certainly after the catastrophic massacre of the First World War, the discipline became unrespectable in academia, and among intellectuals in general. War being seen as murderous stupidity and nothing more, it was not deemed a fit subject for scholarship. In universities on both sides of the Atlantic, dedicated military history positions were very rare, and separate departments unknown. Hence historians burdened with that label could only secure appointments with relative difficulty, even though as authors they always found ample readerships.

There has been no vast increase in the teaching employment of military historians as such—hardly possible given the recent condition of English-speaking universities in general, and of their history departments in particular. But works on military history now crowd academic reading lists, and the specialization no longer disqualifies candidates for posts in "general" history. Historiography itself is the beneficiary of this rehabilitation, for it is no longer distorted by a willful disregard of its military dimensions.

That only modern "scientific" military historiography can accommodate the study of military logistics is obvious enough, for only within it is the important given its due as compared to the merely dramatic.

But there is also a more fundamental reason why the study of logistics is an eminently modern endeavor. For it is entirely characteristic of the modern mentality to find the subject itself very interesting, while it was evidently much less interesting to our pre-modern predecessors. The historiography of logistics, of course, deals with the question of *how* war was prepared and supplied as opposed to why it was fought, what battles and campaigns were fought, and why they were won or lost. And as Braudel's huge success shows most clearly, such "how-questions" attract particular attention in our managerial and technological age, when readers are more apt to identify with managers, engineers, producers and consumers than with field commanders, soldiers or warriors. It stands to reason that readers so eager to discover how bread was baked and distributed in the peaceful urban commerce of the seventeenth century should find it yet more interesting to discover how it could be supplied to armies on the move, overcoming much greater managerial and technical challenges.

It was not so before the modern era. We may assert categorically that Thucydides and all his emulators of classical antiquity included lengthy speeches while excluding any sufficient account of how food, fodder and weapons were procured because the contemporary reader wanted his history books to be written in that way. And that was true thereafter as well until the spread of industrialization engendered the birth of the modern by altering the composition of society. Almost by definition a member of the elite himself—and as such quite likely to have some personal role in politics, diplomacy or war—the pre-modern reader had substantive reasons to be much interested in the political, diplomatic and military reasoning embodied in the speeches, and just as, if not more, interested in the techniques of persuasion of the "diplomatic" speeches, as well as the techniques of exhortation of the pre-battle speeches.

From the *condottieri* of the Renaissance to Patton, notable practitioners of war have strongly commended the study of military history as a guide to tactics, operations and strategy; and we know that exactly the same advice was current in other cultures (sixteenth century Japanese warlords made much of their translated Chinese classics). However, the evidence that tactics, operational methods or strategies learned from the written word were actually applied in war is notoriously inconclusive in most cases. But there is no doubt at all that entire paragraphs of both the diplomatic and exhortation speeches contained in classic texts were much re-used—for there was of course no barrier of differing real-life circumstances to impede the application of written words into spoken words as there was between mere words and real-life action. Thus the speeches in Thucydides and all such were the most *practically* useful parts of their entire texts for their pre-modern elite readers.

Beyond classical antiquity and throughout the pre-modern era, military historiography continued to be not merely literary in character but also in a loose sense aristocratic, inasmuch as it was mostly written by elite practitioners or writers close to them for a primary intended readership likewise composed of elite practitioners, Thucydides, Polybius, Tacitus, and Cassius Dio, but also their Renaissance and later successors such as Montecuccoli and Frederick the Great and indeed some of their twentieth-century emulators (one thinks of the Manstein and Guderian memoirs), were all political or military leaders or both who naturally wrote for readers who would share their aspirations, if not their achievements. Undeniably, for each of them in his own time, logistics were as much a precondition of war and indeed of politics as they are now, but they were not an *aristocratic* concern except in the broadest sense. The army must be led, exhorted and commanded ... but the supplies merely follow (*l'intendance suive*), procured by grubby sutlers whom one does not have at one's dinner table (which they provision) and for whom one does not write one's books—for even if they read, it is not their good opinion that one courts by writing.

While the class that would have been interested to read about logistics was not a reading class at all until the modern era, the class that did the writing thus regarded logistics as undignified, the province of its social inferiors. In that regard, it is suggestive that Ammianus Marcellinus, who wrote the most about logistics among all classical authors, was also almost alone among them in not being in any sense a patrician, but rather a distinctly non-aristocratic professional soldier and bureaucrat. Just as he himself dealt with supply during his career, he also wrote of supply. By contrast, Thucydides, Polybius, Tacitus and all others such until our own times in the case of hopelessly reactionary figures (e.g. Manstein—who despised Hitler for including the resources of the Ukraine in his theater-strategic calculations) would quite automatically rely on members of the merchant class or their official equivalents (or even their uniformed equivalents) to accomplish every aspect of logistics, from the prior calculation of needs, to the acquisition of funds, to procurement, processing, transport and distribution.

How far that mentality could extend beyond all reason is perhaps best exemplified by Rommel, whose entire North-African campaigning was conditioned by the exiguous capacity of ports that he never even thought of trying to augment, that being evidently a matter too lowly to deserve his attention. He focused instead on the properly aristocratic pursuits of theater strategy, operational art and tactical leadership (he was even willing to personally lead a convoy of supply trucks... but only on a heroic crossing of the enemy front line, whereas he was quite unwilling to attend to logistics in their everyday form, prosaic but decisive). Needless to say, any American theater commander in Rommel's place would have promptly made it his business to turn the parameter of port capacity into the desired variable by according the necessary priority to the required engineering means (which even the Third Reich could have spared, even for a secondary front). And the example of Rommel, incidentally, shows that one need not claim an aristocratic genealogy to have an aristocratic mentality.

The military historiography here presented, therefore, represents another large step in the modernization of the subject by focusing on the managerial and technological questions that are the most relevant for our own meritocratic age, and that this reader for one also finds supremely *interesting*. Precisely because the vast spread of cases here studied from Byzantium to Vietnam immediately evokes many other cases of obvious interest still unstudied, it may be hoped that beyond its own considerable achievement, this work will also stimulate further progress in the field.

2
The History of Logistics and Supplying War

John A. Lynn

In the opening chapter of this volume, Edward Luttwak argues that military historians failed to award logistics its rightful place in the drama of war until the coming of our own technocratic age. Before the second half of the twentieth century, problems of supply may rarely have received the attention they deserved, but in 1977 Martin van Creveld published *Supplying War: Logistics from Wallenstein to Patton,* a volume that marked a milestone in the writing of military history. Although van Creveld has published several books since *Supplying War* appeared, it remains his most important contribution. By this intellectual tour de force he shifted logistics from a supporting role to center stage, convincing soldiers and scholars alike that throughout modern history, strategy has rested upon logistics. Luttwak would add that the audience was finally ready to hear such arguments, so that van Creveld's success lay both in his arguments and in his timing. In any case, *Supplying War* rates as one of those rare volumes that so dominates a subject that anyone attempting to advance knowledge in the field must confront it.

However, while van Creveld has set the terms of the debate, he has not closed it. He has made a career of being outspoken and controversial, so he could not be surprised to find that his work is both read and criticized. In a sense, his work could hardly escape being flawed, at least in detail. The very fact that the subject had been relatively neglected by historians necessarily meant that at the time when he wrote *Supplying War* there was a limited body of historical literature upon which van Creveld could draw. Pursuing such broad goals while drawing upon such a thin literature was bound to create problems.

Thus, *Supplying War* serves as both background and baseline for this present volume, and it is impossible to begin without a critique of this notable book. Whatever its strengths or weaknesses, if considered as a call for further research on historical logistics, *Supplying War* has succeeded admirably.

Van Creveld's Thesis

Van Creveld's thesis begins with a definition of logistics as "the practical art of moving *armies* and keeping them supplied."[1] From the start, then, he restricts himself to land warfare and ignores the vital question of naval logistics. Not only does he allow himself this idiosyncratic exclusion, but it soon becomes apparent that he wants to examine only campaigns in Europe and, during World War II, North Africa. Non-Western wars, U.S. conflicts before 1942, and the Pacific theater in World War II fall outside his scope. By defining his subject matter in these terms, he makes his discussion not only more manageable but more malleable as well.

Stripping his theme down to the basics, van Creveld announces: "By and large, the story of logistics is concerned with the gradual emancipation of armies from the need to depend on local supplies."[2] Or another way to say it is that over time armies became more bound by supply lines that linked them with depots in the rear. He proposes an interpretation of the nature and timing of this process that differs from a kind of orthodoxy that has grown up among military historians. As is the case in so many debates between historians, the controversy comes down to a struggle between the two interpretive poles of change and continuity. In the case of logistics, the orthodox view stresses change and van Creveld stresses continuity.

Traditionally, military historians have argued that during the seventeenth century supply sank to the level of pillage and plunder in the Thirty Years' War. After mid-century, stronger, more centralized states, epitomized by the France of Louis XIV (1643-1715), developed the administrative tools and mobilized sufficient resources to supply their armies on a far more regular basis. Magazines disgorged their food and fodder to armed forces tied to them by supply lines depending on wagons and river craft. From the second half of the seventeenth through the late eighteenth centuries "umbilical cords" of supply bound armies.

With the French Revolution and Napoleon I (1799-1815) this picture changed fundamentally, first for France and later for its foes. Revolutionary armies demonstrated that they could maneuver without paying much heed to regular supply, and in any case the confused and inept government did not support its armies adequately. Napoleon made a virtue of necessity and relied upon his army to forage for its needs and so liberated it from the tyranny of supply lines. His regiments now marched across the map of Europe as no forces had before, winning decisive victories as much by movement as by battle. None other than the great Clausewitz stressed this transformation.

Finally, the Industrial Revolution brought about a revolution in logistics during the nineteenth century which brought a return to supply from the rear. The major European land powers, most notably Prussia, harnessed the railroad to haul men, equipment, and supplies over distances and at speeds never before possible. What was possible became necessary, and armies soon depended on regular supply from the rear. In the Austro-Prussian War and the Franco-Prussian War, railroads became lifelines. World War I simply intensified this dependence on depots and mechanical means of transportation. While it debuted in World War I, it was during World War II that the truck revolutionized logistics by providing a new and highly mobile link between the railhead and the army in the field.

In contrast to the orthodoxy, Martin van Creveld argues that the continuity of methods of supply, 1625-1914, overshadowed what change there was. Beginning with the Thirty Years' War, he describes how the armies of Wallenstein and Gustavus II Adolphus of Sweden (1611-1632) both lived off the country. He then asserts that the subsequent armies of the late seventeenth and eighteenth centuries were also not really bound by any "umbilical cord" of supply and instead relied on the campaign area to furnish a great deal of their supply. This was made possible by the balance of supplies needed. Ammunition use was so modest that, except in the case of a siege, a field army could pack all the ammunition it would require in its wagons. Fodder and food were the real issue. Horse-drawn armies consumed great quantities of fodder, but this could be cut in the fields as the army passed. Food too could be found in local farms and warehouses. Only when an army stopped long enough to devour local resources did it require supply from the rear. Thus, it was nothing but the contemporary predilection for siege warfare that made magazines and convoys necessary for an army's survival.

Napoleon regained mobility not by revolutionizing supply but by abandoning sterile siege warfare. Van Creveld implies that the armies of the seventeenth and eighteenth centuries could also have engaged in Napoleonic maneuvers had military leaders at the time possessed the imagination to transcend the artificial rules of siege warfare and thrust for the enemy's vitals rather than just beat him about the arms and shoulders. As for the great Napoleon, van Creveld sees him functioning as much like Wallenstein. The French capacity to achieve rapid mobility by foraging for supplies was simply a higher form of what was already done before.

By the mid-nineteenth century, European railroads may have revolutionized mobilization for war, but they did not fundamentally alter supply on campaign. They proved to be excellent at transporting troops and supplies to jump-off points in the first stages of campaigns. Rail transport allowed the Prussians to assemble far larger forces along their frontiers in less time than ever before in 1866 and 1870. However, once those armies began to advance, horse drawn wagons connected them to the railheads, which could be relocated forward only slowly and with difficulty. Fast marching armies still drew the lion's share of their supplies from the land over which they advanced in a manner essentially similar to that employed in the Thirty Years' War. Van Creveld's chapter on the Schlieffen Plan in 1914 maintains that even the opening offensive of World War I required German soldiers to get their sustenance from the campaign zone. Only the static trench lines and massive bombardments on the western front finally tied armies permanently to supply depots.

It took the massive use of trucks to liberate armies from these bonds. Thus, only in World War II could supplies keep pace with advancing armies, which became totally dependent on supplies carted up from the rear in long cavalcades of trucks. The balance of supplies required by the new mobile armies had also changed. No longer were fodder and food the primary items. As horses disappeared, so did the need for fodder. Modern forces became entirely dependent upon timely resupply of ammunition and fuel, since modern weapons consumed huge quantities of these items. Compared to ammunition and fuel, food sank to relative insignificance as a percentage of total supply needs.

Interestingly enough, as the supply bases for armies expanded in the twentieth century, the relationship between movement and supply reversed itself. Earlier armies could supply themselves more easily on the move than when they stopped, particularly since fodder was easiest to harvest in fresh pastures. In contrast, during the twentieth century, armies became more easy to supply in base areas and more difficult to supply on the move, since nearly everything had to come up from the rear.

Van Creveld's emphasis on an army's capacity to fend for itself in the field ties in with another of his hypotheses. He criticizes the value of detailed military planning. Napoleon's march to the Danube in 1805 was improvised and successful; his advance on Moscow was planned with great care and failed miserably. Von Moltke the Elder won in 1870-71 because the Prussians adapted and fended for themselves; von Moltke the Younger's version of the Schlieffen Plan failed in 1914 despite mountains of staff work. The supply effort in Normandy kept men fed and tanks fueled in 1944 not because the planning worked, but because improvised exertions and effort overcame the shambles on the beaches. Later, as Patton surged forward, he was frustrated by logistics planners who posited consumption rates far higher than they really were and, on the basis of this error, argued that he lacked the supply and transportation to continue his aggressive attack.

The conclusions stressed by van Creveld are not all his own, nor does he claim that they are. The emphasis on living off the country by early modern armies as opposed to supply from the rear and the fact that the need to forage for fodder in the field determined the areas and months of the year that could support campaigns are well known enough.[3] His near complete denial of the "umbilical cord" of 18th century supply and his interpretation of Napoleon seems to be more original with him. His argument that the railroad was of limited logistic use during the Prussian campaigns of the mid-19th century had already been developed previously by Dennis Showalter in *Railroads and Rifles*.[4] And he was certainly not the first to criticize the Schlieffen Plan on the basis of its logistic shortcomings.

There is much that is laudable in van Creveld's scheme, some that is not, and some methodology that must be considered questionable. His exclusion of naval warfare and American experience is at least idiosyncratic and probably warps some of his conclusions. His emphasis on the fact that armies lived off the country for certain categories of supply, primarily fodder, rings true, but the related assertion that field armies placed little reliance upon supply from the rear before the twentieth century is highly questionable. And his use of sources and statistics leaves an informed reader knashing his or her teeth from time to time.

Fundamentals of Transportation at Sea

In excluding naval warfare from his definition of logistics, van Creveld accepts an archaic idea. Jomini also limited logistics to armies, but in twentieth-century military terminology, and particularly since World War II, logistics has encompassed war at sea. Granted, in taking on such a major topic over the course of more than three centuries, van Creveld has to be selective in his choice of experience. But the responsibility is his if his selection biases his conclusions, and the exclusion of naval logistics does. Had he examined naval logistics, he certainly would have had to at least modify his statements concerning the shortcomings of war planning.

The character of naval logistics differs distinctly from that of land warfare. For one thing, the physics of ships contrasts sharply with that of wheeled vehicles. While the question of transportation is not the sole issue at stake in studying logistics, it is basic, and sea transport enjoys tremendous advantages. Water literally carries the cargo itself. At sea, vessels maintain their momentum because of greatly reduced friction and because water's level surface means that vessels need not fight the force of gravity. These factors, plus the fact that the size of ships need not be scaled to the width of a roadbed, allow vessels to be of a size and weight far, far in excess of land vehicles.

Naval warfare has always operated by different logistic parameters. If many of the complications and concerns of logistics on land have been irrelevant at sea, such as the need for fodder, armies have also enjoyed ways of living off the country that have been unavailable to navies. For much of history, an army could be dispatched with the expectation that it would fend for itself, but a fleet had to be supplied from the outset or its crews would suffer and its mission fail. All food, ship's stores, ammunition, and fresh water, a supply that armies could find on the spot, had to be collected, inventoried, and shipped aboard, with the only chance of resupply being rare stops at ports of call. Granted, in the age of sail, the energy to drive a ship did not have to be stored or found. But with the arrival of steam power, vessels had to lay in stocks of coal as well. This was made possible by the large carrying capacity of the ships, increased by the adoption of iron and steel hulls. The need to carry all requirements from the outset of a voyage meant that logistics at sea reached a high level of administrative complexity and efficiency long before this was achieved in land warfare. Therefore, naval logistics have always required a great deal of advance planning, for necessary stores that were not on board could not be created from thin air.

The great fleets assembled as early as the sixteenth century, such as the Armada, demanded a logistic sophistication and completeness that would not be essential for armies until the twentieth century. Moreover, whenever armies took to the sea for transport or amphibious operations they had to accept the same parameters that operated for navies. This was no small matter, from William's invasion of England in 1066 to Gallipoli in 1915 to Inchon in 1950. Therefore, the inclusion of the logistics of warfare at sea in van Creveld's discussion would have muddied the waters of his thesis. It would not have been so easy for van Creveld to criticize the foibles of planners and praise the logistic improvisations of field commanders if he had considered the successful U.S. central Pacific campaign of 1942-1945, especially when contrasted with the failure of the German onslaught to defeat the Soviet Union in 1941.

His condemnation of planning rings truest in the period from the mid-nineteenth century to World War I, when general staffs were still relatively young and had yet to comprehend fully the promises and limitations of the tools of transport that the Industrial Revolution had just fashioned. The greatest logistic feats 1915-1945 involved maritime shipping and naval power—the harnessing of war production in the United States and the transport of its deadly bounty across the Atlantic and the Pacific. Seventeen million measured tons of cargo and 1.6 million army troops were shipped to the United Kingdom in preparation for Overlord; they did not arrive through a fit of absence of mind.[5] This could not have been accomplished without considerable planning. When van Creveld criticizes the logisticians who hampered Patton by stating that their calculations were in error, he obscures the point that these pusillanimous bureaucrats had an abundance of material in the first place precisely because earlier phases of planning had succeeded. Consequently, van Creveld's attack on planning is to my mind the least important and the least interesting of his arguments.

Exclusion of American Wars and the Evaluation of Railroads

Just as van Creveld's exclusion of naval logistics colored his conclusions, so his failure to discuss the American Civil War allows him to say things he could not have said with such authority if he had considered the American experience. This is particularly important in his statements about the operational value of railroads in the nineteenth century.

During the European wars 1866-1871, railroads proved to be excellent at concentrating troops and supplies for the opening campaigns in record time.

However, as van Creveld correctly argues, once armies advanced from the railheads they outpaced their horse drawn transport. As late as the German attack of 1914, horse transport still linked armies to supply, and the slow pace of those wagons and the lack of fodder for German horses contributed to the failure of the Schlieffen Plan.

While his argument that railroads were unable to supply moving armies until the twentieth century may ring true in a European context, it must be sharply modified if the experience of the American Civil War is taken into consideration. The Austro-Prussian and Franco-Prussian were short wars that were decided by aggressive mobile campaigns at the outset of each war. The first lasted seven weeks, and the decisive battle was fought less than four weeks into the conflict. The second lasted ten months from the declaration of war on July 19, 1870, yet the decisive field campaigns were over in the first seven weeks, even if Parisian resistance went on through January. In sum, the campaigns were rapid-moving and brief, too brief for generals to adapt to and exploit the full potential of steam power.

In contrast, the four years of the American Civil War saw railroads and steam-driven river transport in much more key roles. To point to the fact that railroads could not adequately support the Schlieffen Plan does not erase the fact that they were essential to Sherman's 1864 advance on Atlanta fifty years earlier. While he moved forward along the tracks from Chattanooga to Atlanta, trains linked him with his depots to the rear which were stocked by river and rail transport. Railroads also brought ammunition resupply right up to the Union army at Antietam during the night of 17-18 September 1862. In addition, the Civil War employed railroads and river transport to supply fodder for horses, making the Union and Confederate armies the first that escaped the need to periodically change camps simply to find new fodder for their horses.

The Complexities of Living off the Country

But accepting van Creveld's exclusion of naval logistics and American experience, we still run into problems. An essential part of van Creveld's thesis is his emphasis on self-supply by armies, on their capacity to live off the land right up into World War I. The fact that armies campaigned over areas inhabited by populations who stocked food to feed themselves and grew fodder to feed their animals made it possible for armies to sustain themselves by drawing upon these supplies. Living off the country, with both its advantages and disadvantages, was critical to operations and strategy in land warfare for the first 290 years covered in *Supplying War*; only the last 30 years witnessed a dependence on supply from the rear. So goes the argument.

Considering how important the concept of "living off the country" is to van Creveld, it is surprising that he did not explore it with much care. He employs the term primarily as a contrast to the tedious process of forwarding supply from magazines, depots, or army ovens. Making careful distinctions between the different practices covered by this umbrella term reveals both a variety of methods and an important development over time, a development of which van Creveld may be unaware.

Actually, since most of this variety and development occurred in the early modern period, 1625-1815, van Creveld may simply have ignored the changes because they fall outside the time period that is his real interest. Van Creveld seems a bit ambivalent about the real focus of his work. The title of *Supplying War* announces that it deals with *Logistics from Wallenstein to Patton*, a period of 320 years. However, the introduction redefines his concern as the "study of logistics and its influence on strategy during the last century and a half." However, he is at his bravest, perhaps his most outrageous, in his initial two chapters, which cover the first 190 years, 1625-1815. Van Creveld might respond that it is unfair to take him to task on this "background" material; however, those pages serve not simply as background but as the foundation for his edifice, and weak foundations are apt to bring the whole building down. Even if the first chapters interest van Creveld least, they still cover the most ground and offer the most strident breaks with traditional interpretations.

There is no question that early modern armies counted on exploiting the wealth and materiel of areas they occupied. But they did it in many ways, and some had nothing to do with supporting armies on the march by foraging, the primary variety of living off the country that occupies van Creveld.

Because of the weight and bulk of fodder, particularly green fodder, horse-drawn armies had to gather it on campaign, at least before the advent of railroads. Forage parties in search of fodder operated with relative speed, collecting in a matter of hours food that could immediately be given to the army's horses. This is no small consideration, for if we make the not too farfetched analogy that fodder was fuel, forage being to horses what gasoline is to trucks, then a horse-powered army could readily find its fuel supply on the land as it marched. Only when an army was stalled by engaging in a siege or at the very beginning or end of a campaign would it rely on the dry fodder stored in magazines. But granting the undeniable need to live off the country in terms of fodder for animals does not dismiss the need for an army to sustain its human element with other kinds of supply laboriously brought up from the rear.

The crux of variety and change in methods of supply lay not in the supply of fodder as much as in the supply of food. Here we witness an evolution away from a crude form of foraging to a reliance on more regular supply utilizing certain other methods of "living off the country" and finally a return to foraging, though of a rather different sort, as practiced by the armies of Napoleon. Certainly, the late Middle Ages witnessed campaigns in which armies as a whole foraged for their sustenance. The sixteenth century brought attempts at the creation of more regular supply systems; however, these all too often broke down owing to administrative and financial inadequacy. As late as the Thirty Years' War armies still depended upon seizing much of their own food in the field. The horrors of that war precipitated a series of military reforms, most notably in France, which stressed regular means of supply through magazine and convoy. Thus, armies during the great wars of the late seventeenth and eighteenth centuries turned away from foraging for foodstuffs and relied more on other methods.

One way to utilize the resources of the local area was simply to pay troops and allow them to purchase their bread from local sources. This method was employed before the nineteenth century by garrison troops and often by soldiers in winter quarters. However, reliance upon pay gave rise to serious abuses, particularly when it was a question of trying to pay troops on campaign. Problems arose not only when pay was late or insufficient, as it often was, but when the food supply could not meet the needs of too many soldiers concentrated in too small an area, so that even if the men had coins in their pockets, there was not enough to buy. Either case left soldiers little other recourse but pillage, another, though extremely inefficient method of self-supply. For these reasons, the notion of paying soldiers who then purchased their own food gave way to direct supply of the food to the soldier by state agents or private contractors.

A more regular form of extortion forced towns, cities, and entire districts to foot the bill and supply food for a passing or occupying army. This was an old system which crystallized during the Thirty Years' War as "contributions." Under the threat of force, civil authorities agreed to provide money and goods to the general of the threatening army or to officials of the ruler he served. Towns who refused to pay ran the risk of being sacked and burned. Early modern armies from Wallenstein to Napoleon depended on contributions to support their actions. However, after the Thirty Years' War, contributions often simply shifted the burden of maintaining an army from regular taxes raised at home to war taxes imposed on the populations of occupied territory. As such, contributions might not affect the day to day operations of the logistic system. To the extent that contributions were used to stock magazines which maintained the soldiers by more regular means—that is, by depots, army ovens, and convoys—the raising of contributions really does not fit the category of "living off the country" as van Creveld defines it. When European generals and statesmen of the period 1660-1789 spoke of making war feed war, they were primarily concerned with imposing contributions.[6]

The *étapes* system provided another method of supplying troops with food that they need not drag behind them. Through *étapes*, troops on the march drew their food from local markets or depots at set intervals along their route. The term "*étapes*" originated in the word for market. In the earliest form, troops on the march notified local officials in advance of the day they would arrive and the amounts of food that would be required. These authorities then set up a market at which soldiers or commissaries bought what was needed. Such a system provided for the march of troops in Italy and along the Spanish Road in the sixteenth century. By the mid-seventeenth century, the French had established military routes within their own borders to move detachments of anything from a small band of recruits to several regiments. Administrative decree set stops along these routes at which local authorities or private contractors supplied the troops directly, without the soldiers having to pay for their food.

Moving by *étapes* freed troops from carrying their own supplies; however, it required a great deal of administrative preparation. Such troops did not forage for food along their way, since they knew it would be waiting for them each evening at the end of their march. Historians make much of Marlborough's quick advance from the Low Countries to the Danube in 1704 as an example of how troops could live off the country. It will be noted that his army did not depend on forage parties but on a form of *étapes*, organized in friendly and neutral territory and dependent on the willing or forced cooperation of local authorities. In this advance, all the British soldier needed was money to purchase the supplies brought to him, and the wonder of Marlborough's march is that the money was at hand. It is worth noting that rather than providing an example of what kind of mobility all armies might have had, the unique character of this advance demonstrated that such a means was really outside the possibility for other armies that lacked the ready cash, and that meant just about everyone else.

Marlborough's march to the Danube in the 1704 campaign is often compared to Napoleon's advance on Ulm in 1805. On the surface they look rather similar, but in fact they depended on radically different methods of supply. Napoleon did not swing his army from the Rhine to the Danube by moving units in an *étapes* system. Had he tried to do so, the administrative efforts for such a large force would have probably been beyond his means and certainly would have compromised the secrecy he so much desired. Instead, Napoleon returned to foraging.

Napoleon's version of foraging differed from the undisciplined pillage of earlier days; it was designed to be as controlled as such a system could be. He dispersed his corps along a broad front and advanced in such a manner as to maximize the area from which they could draw their supplies. Each day along the march, forage parties brought in what they could, feeding the soldiers catch as catch can. While individual soldiers might loot when they could, the driving motivation behind the foraging by Napoleon's troops was the commander's desire for mobility, not the individual soldier's quest for food or lust for booty. In fact, as will be shown, the Napoleonic practice of foraging made very different assumptions about the common soldier than were held before the French Revolution. Importantly, unlike marauders of the Thirty Years' War, the grand armée did not dissolve into a mob.

By increasing mobility while maintaining the integrity of the military units, Napoleon's army gained in military effectiveness from its ability to forage when on the march.

The point of this discussion is that while "living off the country" was always important, that phrase masks a good deal of variety and evolution. It is fair to say that while living off the country was pursued as a desirable method of supply in one of its several forms, 1625-1815, after then it became a method of supply of last resort—something one did when regular supply broke down. The return to self-supply 1866-71 by the Prussians came because the link between railhead and army broke down. Despite von Moltke the Younger's plans, the great wheeling maneuver of 1914 similarly left troops stranded. This change from self-supply as a matter of choice to a matter of necessity imposed by failure is one that van Creveld would have done well to bring out, but he did not. After all, as much as anything else, the failure of regular supply and the recourse to living off the country between 1866-1914 sustains his skepticism toward military planning.

Some Problems with Numbers: The Need for Magazines

In trying to demonstrate that armies could and did live off the country van Creveld reveals a problem with his methodology—the way he handles numbers. He makes it a point to state that he will rely on "concrete figures and calculations, not on vague speculations," which would appear to lend authority to his conclusions.[7] But if numbers, percentages, and mathematics were to be the crux of his argument, he should have been more careful using them.[8]

He rightly points out that for field armies on campaign, the green fodder that kept the horses in the field had to be harvested locally, because carting it great distances was prohibitive. Consider that a supply wagon pulled by four horses carried about 1200 pounds. Since each of its four horses consumed about 50 pounds of green fodder each day, the team ate 200 pounds per day.[9] Therefore, during a round trip three days up from a depot and three days back, the horses would require their entire load for themselves and have nothing to deliver. Obviously, this would simply not work. Dry fodder simplified the problem, since it weighed only about 20 pounds per horse per day; however, an army in the field had to depend on green fodder most of the time, at least until the mid-nineteenth century when railroads could ship in dry fodder from hundreds of miles away. Fodder could be found locally, and since it required no processing other than cutting it in the fields, it could be easily "produced" by troops on campaign.

So far so good, but any attempt to evaluate supply must distinguish between food for men and fodder for animals. By lumping supplies together and simply speaking of weights and percentages of the total, van Creveld does violence to this necessary distinction. Food was another matter from fodder, and for a

European army on campaign, bread was the most critical item. It could not just be found, it had to be manufactured. Grain might grow in the fields, but it had to be cut, threshed, ground, and baked before it could be eaten as bread. The need to turn grain into bread meant that wheat or flour seized on campaign would not in itself be enough to feed an army on the move.

Let us examine a scenario van Creveld himself presents to prove his point. An army of 60,000 requiring 90,000 bread rations per day is to march 100 miles at a rate of 10 miles per day.[10] Such an army will require 600 tons of flour to feed itself on its ten-day march. Parties from the army will forage 5 miles to either side of the route of march, meaning that they can draw on 1,000 square miles. Van Creveld assumes a population of 45 per square mile and that the inhabitants have stored away 6 months' worth of flour, yielding a total of 7,000 tons available to the army. So he argues the army will have plenty of bread to eat.

But this is a case of historical slight of hand. Consider the figures another way. Given that forage parties will roam five miles in each direction, they will cover an area 10 miles square, that is 100 square miles, from which the army can draw each day. Now according to his calculations this area has squirreled away 700 tons of flour, and the army needs only 60 tons per day. So far so good, but raw flour is not the problem; it must be baked into bread before it will be edible. With a population density of 45 people per square mile, there will only be 4,500 inhabitants in 100 square miles; therefore, the capacity of village ovens in the area will only be sufficient to bake bread for approximately this number of consumers. Even if the ovens burned night and day to double their output, they would still only produce 10 percent of the bread required by the army. Consequently, within the parameters set by van Creveld himself, his army would not thrive but starve.

He cannot rescue himself by simply changing the scenario to add that the army could bring its own ovens along. Portable ovens existed, but they took time to set up, two days in the case of French army ovens ca. 1700.[11] The problem of setting up and breaking down the ovens meant that the only way to use them efficiently was to establish a bank of them and then supply an advancing force with convoys shuttling back and forth from the ovens. At this point we are back to the limitations imposed by regular supply from the rear—exactly what van Creveld claims to have avoided in his example.

In fact, to the extent that large armies required bread, they usually had to supply it via magazines and army ovens. His own example does not demonstrate van Creveld's point but the rather different one that baking capacity limited movement as much as did the availability of grain.[12] Another, far more careful study of logistics by G. Perjés argues just this and concludes that seventeenth-century armies had to be supplied with bread from the rear.[13] Since *Supplying War* is a work of synthesis, we ought not to fault him for not having mastered all the campaigns or eras of warfare from original sources. However, he is open to criticism for misusing the very sources he refers to in order to strengthen his case. His use of Perjés's important work is so selective that it leads one to question whether van Creveld simply chose to omit what did not suit his thesis.

During the late seventeenth and eighteenth centuries, the dependence on magazines and supply convoys even on campaign was no chimera; it was very real. And it was not simply a product of siege warfare. The military correspondence of the time is filled with concerns for magazines and supply convoys. Consider the French offensive of 1672 that began the Dutch War. Louis XIV had accumulated enough grain for 200,000 rations a day for a full six months in seven magazines.[14] Six months covered the entire campaign season. The campaign of 1672 certainly saw a dramatic French advance, but no great siege. In 1697, a year in which the French again undertook no major siege in Italy, they took steps to send grain enough from Burgundy to maintain an army of 30,000 for an entire campaign or one of 60,000 for over three months.[15] A century later, the maintenance of regular supply from the rear was considered necessary. In 1792, the Duke of Brunswick limited his advance because of the necessities of convoys and bread. His army did take Longwy and Verdun along the way, but each siege lasted but a day or two. It could justly be claimed that the plodding formalities of Prussian supply saved the revolution from his invading host as much as did victory at the Battle of Valmy.

Some Problems with Numbers: The New Logistic Needs

Another example of a case in which van Creveld uses figures in a misleading way concerns his discussion of the way in which supply requirements evolved over time. He correctly points out that in warfare before the Industrial Revolution, food and fodder posed the greatest problems for armies on campaign. In contrast to the very pressing need for forage, until the mid-nineteenth century, and perhaps until World War I, ammunition consumption was low enough that an army could carry a campaign's worth of it in its wagons without requiring resupply except in the case of a siege. However, ammunition requirements soared in World War I, when massive artillery bombardments consumed great stocks of munitions, and machine guns spit out thousands of rounds in short order. In addition to this rise, the need for fuel rose with the use of motor transport and then armored fighting vehicles. Petroleum eventually liberated armies from horse power; however, fossil fuels also bound navies and armies to supply bases.

Van Creveld makes a good point, but then he stretches it and in doing so forgets other important logistic needs of a modern army. Consider his statement that from the advent of trench warfare in World War I, ammunition requirements increased greatly: "Whereas, even as late as 1870, ammunition had formed less than 1 percent of all supplies, . . . in the first months of World War I the proportion of ammunition to other supplies was reversed, and by the end of World War II subsistence accounted for only eight to twelve percent of all supplies."[16] While all these facts may be true in the narrow sense, the statement is misleading. The sentence implies that the percentage of food in supply tumbled while that of ammunition dominated. In fact the percentage of food remained about the same as it had been for armies of the eighteenth century. Consider the case of U.S. Army supply in World War II as revealed in Table 2.1, which shows pounds shipped per day per man. Food stood at 10-11

Table 2.1 U.S. Army Supply in World War II (in pounds shipped per man per day)

	Food	Ammo	Fuel	Cloth ing	Constr. material	Totals
Ground troops, Europe	7.17	3.64 (5%)	11.40 (17%)	0.43	7.28	66.80
Addition for Air Forces		4.41	13.40			
TOTAL Europe	7.17 (11%)	8.05 (12%)	24.80 (37%)	0.43 (.6%)	7.28 (11%)	66.80
Ground troops, Paciific	6.71	5.14 (8%)	10.80 (16%)	1.00	11.90	67.40
Addition for Air Forces		3.47	11.08			
TOTAL Pacific	6.71 (10%)	8.61 (13%)	21.88 (32%)	1.00 (1.5%)	11.9 (18%)	67.40

Source: Robert W. Coakley and Richard M. Leighton, *Global Logistics and Strategy, 1943-1945*, vol. 2 (Washington, DC: 1968), p. 825.

percent of supplies shipped to American GIs. Van Creveld earlier credits food at about 18 percent of the supplies needed by an early modern army circa 1700. However, his calculations were flawed; he assumed too few mouths to feed and the use of dry fodder for horses rather than the green fodder usually employed on campaign. If we rework his calculations, the weight of food falls to 10 percent of an army's daily need, just what it was for U.S. forces over two centuries later. The rest of supply for the early modern army went to fodder.[17]

To return to the figures for World War II: ammunition did not soar above food requirements but ranked *below* them at only 5-8 percent of the amount shipped for ground forces. Granted, if one includes air force requirements the figure climbed to 12-13 percent, but van Creveld did not figure in air forces, so why should we? So while there is no question that ammunition rose in importance, it did not dominate supply as van Creveld implies, at least when measured for U.S. forces. Fuel was more significant, reaching 16-17 percent for ground forces, and 32-37 percent if air force requirements are figured in. But if we compare petroleum fuel with the fuel of the horse drawn army, fodder (33.3 pounds per day per man and 90 percent of supply for an early modern army), modern fuel declined in weight and percentage![18] The most important

The History of Logistics and Supplying War

hole in van Creveld's calculations, however, is the fact that he missed construction materials, which rivaled or surpassed ammunition as measured by weight per man per day and approached the figures for fuel. Construction materials shipped stood at 11-18 percent, making the point that a modern military must create its own infrastructure to operate effectively. So the picture concerning food, ammunition, and fuel is not quite as van Creveld paints it, and the needs of modern armies in the field are more varied than van Creveld portrays. Again, the figures for U.S. consumption of ammunition, food, and construction material were available in works cited by van Creveld, but he overlooked them or chose not to present them.[19]

The problem with such errors in the interpretation and/or explanation of statistical material is not simply that they in themselves are wrong or misleading but that the errors throw the author's entire use of figures into question. The existence of such questions does not invalidate van Creveld's other conclusions, but it does cast a shadow of reasonable doubt. Such shortcomings are particularly disappointing in a work which announces that it will be rigorous in dealing with statistics.

The Need to Consider More Than Figures

A lack of concern for subjective factors in warfare accompanies van Creveld's emphasis on numbers. He becomes the ultimate bean counter, even if his way of counting beans looks more like a shell game from time to time. It is as though logistics is simply a question of moving beans from here to there, but that is not always the case. There are other factors, and in one case at least an unwillingness to take those factors into consideration leads van Creveld to take the wrong road.

In his discussion of Napoleonic logistics, van Creveld argues that there was essential continuity between the armies of Louis XIV and those of the emperor. And since continuity rather than change typified early modern logistics, the armies of the Sun King could have been as rapid as those of Napoleon if only they had possessed the imagination, and if they were not so mesmerized by siege warfare. However, van Creveld overlooks two important factors that constrained Louis's actions far more than did any strategic myopia: limited war aims and the nature of his soldiery.

Typically, rulers of the late seventeenth and eighteenth centuries were not out to exterminate each other. They struggled over territory and limited advantages. Even Louis XIV pursued surprisingly defensive goals after 1675. He certainly never aimed at European hegemony as did Napoleon. Consequently, he had little need of Napoleonic maneuvers. His most dramatic effort came in 1703-4, and even then the advance of French troops into Germany was designed to bring peace, not topple the Hapsburgs or seize their lands for France. However, even if Louis had seriously wanted to carry out some vast Napoleonic scheme, he could not have done so, and neither could his successors. He simply lacked the kind of soldiers who could have carried out a Napoleonic campaign, or at least contemporary commanders had good reason to feel that such men were not to be found.

Living off the country, in the sense used when discussing Napoleon's advance in 1805, would have proved very dangerous for an *ancien régime* army. Before 1789, officers believed their soldiers to be men with little honor. Unsupervised detachments would either turn to pillage, as they had with such gusto during the Thirty Years' War, or desert, as they did in large numbers in every war. Consider the judgment of St. Germain, French minister of war 1775-77, who dismissed his rank and file as "the slime of the nation," or Frederick the Great's constant concern over desertion.

More basically, to princes and generals of the era 1648-1789, the notion of living off the country was less likely to raise the promise of mobility than it was to conjure up the specter of mutiny. Failure to provide guaranteed supply from the rear opened the door to the dissolution of the entire army. Uncertain supply almost inevitably brought with it a degree of suffering. Foraging might go well, but it might not. The professional soldiers of the *ancien régime* had little attachment to any cause or to the army itself. As such, they were not expected to bear up well when they went unfed or unpaid. During the sixteenth, seventeenth, and early eighteenth centuries, mutiny threatened those commanders who did not pay or feed their armies. Geoffrey Parker counted over 45 mutinies involving the Spanish Army of Flanders between 1572 and 1607.[20] Such soldier rebellions continued sporadically during the seventeenth century. In 1647, elements of Turenne's Army of Germany, which had not been paid, mutinied when ordered to march to the Low Countries.[21] With the crisis of supply that attended the cruel winter of 1709-10, a number of French garrisons mutinied.[22] Soldiers viewed obedience as the quid pro quo for pay and food; when the state reneged on its part of the bargain, this released the soldiers from their obligation.

The French Revolution changed this formula, and officers expected the men in the ranks to feel a greater sense of duty, to their *patrie*, to the new regime, and to their comrades. A new contract based on national loyalty replaced the old one based on money payment. As such, they could be called upon to suffer if necessary. Supply often broke down miserably during the wars of the French Revolution, yet the troops did not mutiny. In 1794, when Jourdan marched 40,000 men from the Army of the Moselle to Charleroi in order to join elements of the Army of the North, his men literally starved, but they arrived in good spirits. The new citizen soldiers did not rebel.[23] This question of motivation and expectation, of *mentalités*, brought a real watershed in logistics. Grumble he might, but the new soldier bore temporary hardship and kept to his tasks. So would the Prussians of 1866-71 and 1914.

Napoleon could cut loose of regular supply sources in 1805 because he had confidence that his troops could forage for themselves without deserting or rebelling if food became scarce. Napoleon could abandon careful logistic administration for a time to achieve mobility. This was in contrast to Marlborough, who moved swiftly in 1704 not by disregarding the details of supply but by a great and effective feat of superior administration. His letters and agents preceded the army, made sure markets awaited the troops, and guaranteed that they would have money in their pockets to buy supply. Of course, it should be noted, as van Creveld correctly points out, that even Napoleon still had to depend on regular supply much of the time. After Ulm fell, he did everything to organize supplies shipped by the Danube River, and even then he need the stores he captured in Vienna. Still, Napoleon could exploit opportunities through superior mobility not simply because he was a bolder strategist but because he could trust his soldiers.

An emphasis on the possibilities of the new kind of soldiery is fairly traditional; it goes back to none less than von Clausewitz himself. Van Creveld rejects it out of hand in his own quest for originality. Clausewitz argued that war was a question of will, and that strategy had to aim at that will. Since, as van Creveld so correctly argues, logistics is a determining factor in strategy, can we safely exclude questions of the will when we examine matters of supply?

Conclusion

While many of the comments expressed above have been critical, they do not, nor are they intended to, undermine the importance of *Supplying War*. The existence of some flaws in fact or in conception does not necessarily negate the value of an entire work. Certainly this is the case with van Creveld's book. As a body of challenging hypotheses, *Supplying War* is important and valuable. Its very controversial nature makes it a call to arms; it focuses attention on the subject of logistics and demands more research on the role that logistical factors have played in warfare over the ages. In fact, this volume of essays is evidence of the influence van Creveld has had in stimulating further research, since there probably would be no *Feeding Mars* if *Supplying War* had not appeared.

Notes

1. Martin van Creveld, *Supplying War: Logistics from Wallenstein to Patton* (Cambridge: 1977), p. 1.

2. Ibid., p. 182.

3. So well known are they that they even appear in an encyclopedia article that van Creveld cites. *Encyclopedia Britannica*, 15th edition, vol. 14 (Chicago: 1970), pp. 239-47B, "Logistics," by R. M. Leighton. Van Creveld cites the 1973 edition, p. 232 and note on p. 279. It is also interesting that van Creveld begins his book with the same quotation from Jomini that Leighton employs at the start of his article.

4. Dennis Showalter, *Railroads and Rifles: Soldiers, Technology, and the Unification of Germany* (Hamden, CN: 1976). While Showalter's book appeared before *Supplying*

War, van Creveld probably did not have time to use it in his work. Instead, van Creveld cites Showalter's dissertation "Railways and Rifles: the Influence of Technological Developments on German Military Thought and Practice, 1815-1865" (Ph.D. diss., University of Minnesota, 1969).

5. The figures were taken from Appendix D-5, "Troop and Cargo Flow to the United Kingdom for Overlord, January 1943-July 1944," in Robert W. Coakley and Richard M. Leighton, *Global Logistics and Strategy, 1943-1945*, vol. 2 (Washington, DC: 1968), p. 838.

6. See John A. Lynn, "How War Fed War: The Tax of Violence and Contributions During the *Grand Siècle*," *Journal of Modern History* 65, no. 2 (June 1993).

7. Van Creveld, *Supplying War*, p. 3; and again he refers to these words on p. 236.

8. The way he describes army growth in the opening paragraph of Chapter 1, van Creveld, *Supplying War*, p. 5, is a classic misuse of figures. He flies back and forth from the size of individual field armies at a particular battle to forces arrayed on a front during wartime to the entire force of a state's army in such a fashion that he leaves the reader spinning. This is comparing apples, oranges, and rutabagas.

9. G. Perjés, "Army Provisioning, Logistics and Strategy in the Second Half of the 17th Century," *Acta Historica Academiae Scientiarum Hungaricae* 16, no. 1-2 (1970), pp. 16-17, states that green fodder should be calculated at 25 kg, or 55 pounds, per horse per day. He also figures a ration of dry forage at anything between 8 and 11 kg but estimates a reasonable ration at 10 kg, or 22 pounds. Van Creveld, *Supplying War*, p. 24, allows a dry ration of 20 pounds and green forage at twice that weight. Just to have a nice round number I will figure green fodder at 50 pounds per day per horse.

10. Van Creveld, *Supplying War*, p. 34. This use of an army of 60,000 requiring 90,000 rations and including 40,000 horses would seem to come from the discussion in Perjés, "Army Provisioning," a work cited in van Creveld's notes. It is probably Perjés who showed van Creveld the way to Puységur. It is a shame that van Creveld did not take Perjés whole, because Perjés comes to very different conclusions.

11. François Nodot, *Le munitionnaire des armées de France* (Paris: 1697).

12. The importance of ovens and mills is highlighted by a French directive of 1636 designed to make it as difficult as possible for the attacking Spanish armies to continue their advance: "Tell all the generals to send out before them seven or eight companies of cavalry in a number of places with workers to break all the ovens and mills in an area stretching from their own fronts to as close as possible to the enemy." in Patrick Landier, "Guerre, Violences, et Société en France, 1635-1659," (Doctorat de troisième cycle, diss., Université de Paris IV, 1978), p. 86.

13. Perjés, "Army Provisioning."

14. Louis XIV, *Oeuvres de Louis XIV*, Grimoard and Grouvelle, eds., vol. 3 (Paris: 1806), p. 117.

15. Archives departementales, Côte d'Or (Côte d'Or), C 3676, June 1697. Calculations are based on a sack weighing 200 pounds. Nodot, *Le munitionnaire*, pp. 4-5, stated that a standard grain sack held 200 pounds and would supply 180 rations. Nodot is an extremely valuable source for all the details of supplying an army with bread. Perjés, "Army Provisioning," p. 7, figures a sack at 165 pounds.

16. Van Creveld, *Supplying War*, p. 233.

17. Van Creveld, *Supplying War*, p. 24. He makes a number of mistakes in these calculations, judged from his own discussion. First he figures that "a typical army of Louvois's day" numbering 60,000 troops required only 60,000 rations. Later, p. 34, he

uses the more realistic figure that such an army needed 90,000 rations, a figure derived from the contemporary Puységur. He also calculates the bread ration at two pounds, when it was, in fact 1.5 pounds for the French. At least he is consistent in this mistake. His own calculations then add up to 120,000 pounds of bread, to which he adds 60,000 pounds per day of other food. He then estimates the number of horses at 40,000 — a figure from Puységur — and assumes they will eat dry forage on campaign weighing 20 pounds a day per horse or 800,000 pounds per day for the entire army. This weight would be correct for dry fodder, but on campaign it was far more common for horses to consume green fodder, and a horse required 50 pounds of it per day. But employing van Creveld's calculations of these figures of 180,000 for food and 800,000 for fodder means that food stood at 18 percent of the army's needs. But if we adjust for the larger number of mouths to feed, the lesser weight of bread, and the heavier weight of green fodder, the following results:

225,000 pounds of food per day (90,000 x 1.5 =
   135,000 pounds of bread + 90,000 pounds of other
   foodstuffs [60,000 pounds for 60,000 men;
   therefore 90,000 pounds for 90,000 mouths]
2,000,000 pounds of fodder per day (40,000 horses x 50
   pounds of green fodder per day
2,225,000 pounds total

So by these calculations, food composed 10 percent of daily consumption of an army on campaign feeding green fodder to its horses.

18. Appendix A-5, "Maintenance Requirements, European and Pacific Areas, World War II," in Coakley and Leighton, *Global Logistics and Strategy*, p. 825. As the text explains, "The term maintenance requirements as used here may be construed to mean all shipments to the theater for use by the Army except for initial equipment."

19. He cites James A. Huston, *The Sinews of War: Army Logistics, 1775-1953* (Washington, DC: 1966), in his bibliography. The figures I use from *Global Logistics and Strategy* are available in a brief form on page 495 of Huston. Interestingly, van Creveld did not use the more complete *Global Logistics and Strategy*.

20. Geoffrey Parker, *The Army of Flanders and the Spanish Road, 1567-1659: The Logistics of Spanish Victory and Defeat in the Low Countries Wars* (Cambridge: 1972), 185 and table on pp. 290-92.

21. Jean Bérenger, *Turenne* (Paris: 1987), pp. 245-51.

22. These included the garrisons at Quesnoy, Arras, Mons, St. Omer, Tournai Nassau, Valenciennes, and Cambrai, *Mercure historique et politique*, XLVI (January 1709): 91-119; Service Historique de l'Armée de Terre, Archives de Guerre (AG), A^{1}2149, #249-54, 256, 258 in Claude C. Sturgill, *Marshall Villars and the War of the Spanish Succession* (Lexington, KY, 1965), p. 82.

23. Jean-Paul Bertaud in *La Révolution armée* (Paris: 1979) argues that the army eventually became politicized because of its alienation from the government of France. But its involvement in the coups d'état of 1797 and 1799 was a very, very different phenomenon than the mutinies of the seventeenth and eighteenth centuries.

PART TWO

Medieval Logistics, 400-1500

Medieval Introduction

Warfare shaped government and society during the Middle Ages, and in no other period was logistics more basic to military operations or did supply emerge more clearly as a weapon of war in itself. Considering this importance, it comes as some surprise that we lack a general study of medieval logistics to compare with those focused on the ancient world, modern Europe, or U.S. forces. The essays in this part attempt to partially fill that gap.

Evolution of Government and Its Military Capability

Any consideration of warfare in the Middle Ages must take into account the evolution of government authority during that epoch. Of course any examination of a period covering more than a millennium is bound to uncover considerable variety. While medieval historians still debate over the extent and capacity of central government institutions then, it is safe to say that they did not match those of imperial Rome or of the absolute monarchies of the early modern period. That being said, rulers and ruling bodies varied tremendously in their power and abilities over the span of the Middle Ages, 400-1500. As a whole, the period traced a pattern of decline, divergence, and development. Since logistics is closely related to the effectiveness of political and economic institutions, change in these aspects of medieval life certainly influenced the ways in which military forces were created and sustained.

Of course, any generalizations concerning the decay of Roman practices in the medieval West must be tempered by a recognition of the greater stability of the old eastern Roman lands, the Byzantine Empire. While it too suffered from destructive invasions, loss of territory, and economic crisis, it experienced a less dramatic deterioration in government power and reach than that which occurred in the West. In fact, the preservation of much of the old Roman tradition in the East helped to buffer the empire's decay in the West by providing a model or at least a myth that Germanic monarchs sought to emulate.

In his article here, Walter E. Kaegi demonstrates the formidable nature of Byzantine logistic feats. Clearly the Byzantines developed a government capable of large scale military operations. Their accomplishments were extremely impressive, since Constantinople maintained armed forces which totaled some 150,000 men under Justinian I (527-65) and still contained as many as 120,000 by the 840s. These numbers exceeded those of the largest western European armies until the seventeenth century. In accomplishing this task, Byzantines enjoyed a Roman inheritance more firm and more intact than did their counterparts in the West. However, this served only as the foundation for continual evolution. Byzantines faced and overcame serious logistic difficulties, particularly in their campaigns against the Sassanid Persians during the early seventh century. In desert campaigns, their forces could not count on living off the country or buying supplies but had to ship food and fodder. Eventually, Byzantines made use of permanent warehouses, or magazines, to supply troops along the frontier. Kaegi concludes that Byzantine logistics did not function with great efficiency; however, the system performed well enough for the relatively passive status quo power that Byzantium became.

If we change our focus to the West, the traditional picture drawn by historians sees a far more profound decay of Roman institutions than occurred in Byzantium. First, a series of internal crises, wars, and invasions eroded central authority as the old western empire broke up into a series of Germanic kingdoms. These new rulers were not simply destructive, however, and they often recognized that they had an interest in preserving what they could of the Roman inheritance. Roads and fortifications would obviously be of military use, not least in terms of movement and logistics. Of less obvious utility, perhaps, but still of value were old Roman administrative and military practices and boundaries.

Second, the Roman inheritance diminished with time, and authority and military organization fragmented further to rest on the most local level. Higher strata of political and military authorities existed but were less firmly rooted and less effective than those found on the spot. At this point, feudalism produced the bulk of the armed forces that could be rallied by the prince or his barons. While dating the expansion of feudalism can be risky, the period 900-1100 serves as a reasonable indication of the high water mark of feudalism. This is not to say that major military, and thus logistic, efforts were not possible at this time. Perhaps the most notable were William's conquest of England and the first crusade, although both occurred at the very end of this period, and it can be debated how much the forces involved in either enterprise were held together by feudal bonds. In any case, even at the darkest moments, some economic and political miracles defied the general deterioration, most notably the Republic of Venice.

Third, the consolidation of national monarchies in the high Middle Ages produced new political and military institutions which rivaled and then surpassed those of a smaller and weaker Byzantium. To some degree, the new western organizations grew from Roman survivals, but to a greater extent they evolved as practical responses to the challenges of the Middle Ages. The major states of the modern world emerged in the last centuries of the medieval period:

powerful Spanish monarchs reconquered the Iberian Peninsula; English kings seized Wales and threatened to add much of France to their domains; and France emerged as a rich, unified, and great state on the Continent. States relied more and more on reliable paid troops, calling out feudal arrays only to supplement and bulk up the professionals. By the last quarter of the fifteenth century, Louis XI (1461-83) tried to maintain a standing peacetime army in excess of 20,000 in France, although this gambit proved to be an expensive and short-lived venture, well ahead of its time. Still, it demonstrated that much had changed—that European governments were developing a new political, fiscal, and thus logistic, capacity to feed, cloth, and arm their forces. At sea, Europeans developed the naval technology to launch the first explorations of the globe.

Writing of pre-Crusade Europe in his essay, Bernard S. Bachrach challenges this traditional picture by insisting that rulers in the pre-Crusade period displayed greater ability and achieved greater military feats than usually believed, and that these feats demonstrated superior logistic capacity. Roman inheritance was more substantial and enduring than usually believed. Roman fortified cities continued to be military and political centers well into the Middle Ages, though they were now occupied by German counts and dukes. Early medieval rulers took care to keep their walls in good repair, a considerable public works project in itself. The maintenance of old fortifications and the construction of new ones demonstrated an administrative ability that could be translated into logistics. Roman strategic conceptions also remained alive, argues Bachrach, including the use of great walls such as Offa's Dyke and other strategic barriers. Medieval burgs were constructed precisely to facilitate movement and maintain forces on the march. Efforts in Saxony and England displayed coherent systems of garrisons using the services of local landholders. Surveys of population and production which extended Roman administration provided a basis for logistic decisions practices. Charlemagne carried out large scale operations against Saxony which bear witness to abilities in supply and transportation of a considerable scale. William the Conqueror's invasion of England required shipping men, horses, and a huge amount of supplies in over 700 vessels—a logistic feat of note. Pre-Crusade Europe may not have equaled the skills of Rome or of late medieval Europe, but neither was it without capable organization and administration.

Feudalism and Supply

The military history of the Middle Ages is thus still a matter of controversy on the most basic level, and some new synthesis seems still off in the future. Whatever that synthesis might be, it must take account of the fact that not only was logistics basic to warfare in the Middle Ages, but questions of supply shaped society itself. This second point is enshrined in the single word "feudalism," which for our purposes we will reduce to the grant of the use of land and its products in exchange for military service. Along with the grant of land, or lands, went the delegation of political and personal authority over those who worked the soil. This is not an all inclusive definition to be sure, since feudalism involved more; however, it covers the element that concerns us. In its origins feudalism was a matter of military compensation and maintenance, and since the feudal contract became a foundation of western society and government, it provides a stark example of the great consequences that can flow from seemingly pedestrian questions of supply.

An important constant of pre-industrial logistics was the necessity of armies in the field to draw at least a substantial percentage of their sustenance from the area they campaigned over—in short, to live off the country during wartime. However, at least by the seventeenth century, peacetime standing armies were paid and sustained directly by central authority. Feudalism represented a simpler and more primitive system. It provided a way in which armed forces could be maintained essentially by living off the country even during periods of peace, when Mars was at rest. Feudalism allowed the long-term maintenance of military forces at minimal cost to the prince whose purse contained little hard currency. It allowed the man at arms to feed himself, his family, and his retainers off the produce from his own fields and from what peasants gave him in manorial dues. In addition, he maintained his arms and horses, all without cash payment. Feudalism, therefore, provided for the creation and maintenance of a force in being.

The Use of Supply as a Weapon

While peacetime logistics gave feudalism its value, wartime logistics hindered its effectiveness. Not only was a feudal military force generally dispersed, but when it assembled for campaign it did so only for relatively brief periods, usually 40 days, determined not by strategic necessity but by feudal contract. A knight and his retainers were usually to supply their own food while on campaign. In fact, a feudal contract might stipulate the amount of food to be brought to the field. Characteristically, medieval armies did not have elaborate logistic arrangements to maintain themselves on campaign and often turned to pillage and plunder. Since the logistics of medieval warfare was so precarious, it is not surprising that supply became a weapon, both in offense and defense.

Supply figured heavily in positional warfare, i.e., the attack and defense of fortresses and fortified towns. Certainly a major factor in late medieval warfare was the distinct advantage enjoyed by static defenses. Fortifications of earth, wood, and stone posed formidable obstacles to medieval armies. Even when methods existed to batter down or undermine walls, these techniques were difficult, time-consuming, and easily thwarted. Storming the walls was very costly in manpower, so a small garrison could likely keep attackers at bay. It is no wonder that plans for defense emphasized fortifications. The medieval military commentator de Balsac advised a prince threatened with invasion to "withdraw all livestock from the frontier and a broad swath into the interior of his country and to place all food supplies from the countryside in strong places so that the enemy might not find anything when they came to lay siege and ride about in strength."[1] Interestingly, this statement by de Balsac relates fortifications to logistics by using their walls to deny necessary supplies to the attacker.

The difficulty and cost of storming stone fortifications in the late Middle Ages meant that besieging armies preferred to starve out their foes. But this took time, often more time that the agreed yearly service owed by knights. A castle that could hold out longer than the term of service owed by soldiers in the attacking army could well survive to see the enemy force melt away. Garrisons were understandably reluctant to forsake their defenses, and armies stalled to conduct a siege would find it difficult to supply themselves or even keep their feudal elements in the field.

If supply worked as a weapon for the defense, the offense turned the concern for future production and wealth to its own advantage. Attackers tried to compel defiant garrisons to come out from behind their walls by wreaking unacceptable havoc to the surrounding countryside. While carrying out this destruction, the attacking army lived as best as it could off the spoils seized from the surrounding area—at least while they lasted. However, if the method failed, it rapidly became impossible for the besieging army to continue the siege as well, since it had destroyed the very means of its own existence.

The most rapacious technique of destruction combined with living off the country during the late Middle Ages was the *chevauchée*, or ride, undertaken by an advancing army. This was a destructive raid, meant to lay waste an enemy's territory, feed the attackers, and provide them with booty. Again, it also spared the attacker the cost of sieges and might draw a reluctant foe into the field of battle. The English raised it to its peak in the fourteenth century. English *chevauchées* were undertaken by substantial forces but of sizes small enough to feed themselves on the move effectively. In 1339, Edward III led 5,550 men, and in 1435 John Fastolf counseled Henry VI to send out two parties of 3,000 men each. The *chevauchée* led by the Black Prince in 1355 advanced 900 km in a period of less than two months, at an average pace of 15 km per day. This included having to stop along the way to seize several major towns.[2]

The *chevauchée* demonstrates in the starkest relief the degree to which logistics and operations were bound together in the Middle Ages. Supply did not simply allow the army to fight; supply was itself a sword. The logistics of feudalism and siege warfare provided one, but certainly not the only, reason why monarchs preferred to replace feudal forces with hired professionals when they could.

The Technology of Transportation

To say that supply was a particularly vulnerable chink in the armor of medieval warfare is not to say that military forces were devoid of all logistic finesse. Bachrach refutes such negative assertions even for the early Middle Ages. An examination of the technology of transport establishes that the medieval world surpassed the ancient world in important regards and provided some of the basic tools for the modern era, on land and on sea. The most apparent advances in land transport between the Neolithic period and the nineteenth century had more to do with the draft animals than the carts themselves. The medieval innovations of horse collars and horseshoes stand out as the most important. The most significant improvement in the vehicles themselves was probably the introduction of the pivoting front axle, also a medieval innovation.

But the greatest capacity for transport during the Middle Ages came on water, not on land. Since seas and rivers provide vessels an unimpeded surface which does not require the building or maintenance of highways and bridges and which is not made unusable by mud, it was and remains easier to carry goods by water. Since medieval government and the medieval economy lacked the authority and wealth to maintain a great road system, water transport was even more important than it would be in the early modern or modern periods.

Timothy J. Runyan contributes to our knowledge of late medieval maritime logistics during the Hundred Years' War. He documents the considerable effort required to assemble the fleets that transported and sustained English forces in France. Royal officials cobbled together mighty fleets by temporarily summoning, or "arresting," ships from port towns. It was cheaper for the king to call upon the merchant fleet to supply the vessels he needed than to build a large royal armada, although once his fleet was mobilized the king took on the expense of maintaining and paying the crews. To the throng of ships commanded from the ports, the king added his own more modest number of vessels. The fleets ran the gamut from the rare ship of over 1000 tons to those of under 100, with an average size of about 170 tons. Just as ships were "arrested" from ports, custom and law allowed the monarchy to compel sailors to man them. The greatest feat of maritime transport was the carrying of entire armies and their equipment to France; however, English troops still relied upon supply from England even after they had landed. Royal purveyors bought in markets at home; sheriffs identified and stocked supplies. Foodstuffs were then staged locally, carted to ports, and shipped. The effort to assemble, maintain, and employ fleets required a notable administrative effort, an effort that left a paper trail exploited by Runyan to tell his tale.

Conclusion

Despite the controversies that surround the historical interpretation of medieval warfare, the central importance of logistics remains clear. Methods of supply not only filled the cook pot of the medieval warrior but served as his sword and shield. Medieval logistics probably required a level of sophistication and effort that would surprise modern readers. The rewriting of medieval military history may even demonstrate that only in understanding the maintenance of military forces can historians explain the patterns of medieval society and government.

Notes

1. Philippe Contamine, *War in the Middle Ages*, trans. Michael Jones (Oxford: 1984), p. 220.

2. *Ibid.*, pp. 215, 222-28.

3

Byzantine Logistics: Problems and Perspectives

Walter E. Kaegi

This essay explores the challenges of supply faced by Byzantium as it conducted campaigns against a formidable array of enemies in a variety of circumstances over the course of a millennium. Although one may quibble about dates, the most reasonable point for the beginning of Byzantine logistics was the creation of a seat of imperial government at the former city of Byzantium, now renamed Constantinople, by Emperor Constantine I in 330. That act created a new set of strategic realities with important effects on military transportation and communications; it marks the beginning of the early Byzantine period (A.D. 330-610). The seventh century brought a transition to the middle Byzantine period (610-1025), a distinctly different era in logistics, as the empire readjusted to enormous territorial losses to the Muslims, Avars, and Slavs, and to a lesser extent, to some of the Germanic kingdoms (especially to the Visigoths and Lombards). The principal scope of this essay is the early and middle Byzantine periods, because in the final or late Byzantine period (1025-1453), and especially after 1300, the empire faced diminishing strategic depth and multiple threats, which made its logistical situation a nightmare for anyone attempting to construct a viable defense of the empire.

Byzantine logistical theory and practice must be pieced together from disparate writings and records, since the Byzantines did not see logistics as a distinct branch of military experience with its own literature. No one simple Byzantine word for logistics exists, although there are terms like *touldon* for baggage train. But there was a classical Greek word for it—*logistike*, in the sense of "calculations," which are what logistics is. Hence Latin *logista*, from Greek *logistes*, one who calculates. But the term, although extant in very classical Greek authors and therefore available to Byzantine word purists, is rarely encountered in Byzantine texts, if at all, perhaps because of considerations of stylistic vocabulary. Logistics existed, of course, and has always existed in some form, but my impression is that logistics is a problem of more concern to modern military planners than to Byzantine ones, although one must explain the limits of such a statement. One must use sources other than narrative histories to understand Byzantine logistics.

While Byzantines wrote of supplies, baggage, wagon trains, camps, bases, and provisions, they did not speak of logistics *per se* as the science of calculations for planning military supply. Their military manuals include references to the above details, and in their list of problems with which generals should be familiar they include ones that involve logistics, but they do not speak of that abstract term or concept in itself. In addition, surviving records on older campaigns probably helped the Byzantines to calculate the logistical needs of contemporary campaigns. The Roman heritage of military treatises and histories of campaigns was of limited value to the Byzantines because opponents and conditions had changed. Nevertheless, broad familiarity with earlier examples was probably of some value in trying to calculate needs and avoid mistakes. Yet there was probably no systematic searching among Roman precedents for their relevance to specific logistical challenges faced by Byzantines. More importantly, they would forge their own solutions to the specific problems they encountered.

The Parameters of Byzantium's Logistical Challenges

The Byzantine Empire, as a glance at a map will underscore, depended upon transportation by water as well as by land. The logistical nerve center of the empire was Constantinople, but it could not exercise that function without domination of the waterways of the Dardanelles, Sea of Marmara, and the Bosphorus.[1] Those vitally important waterways really needed only ferry-type transport ships, but they were indispensable. For reaching her extensive island possessions and Italy and the Crimea, the Byzantine Empire also needed larger seaworthy shipping, and for the modest navigable rivers, the Danube, and early in her history, the Nile and Euphrates, she needed riverboats. Because of the rugged topography of the Greek mainland and Anatolia, water transportation was the most reliable, if slow, way to reach many localities. So water transport was employed to move imperial troops as well as to ensure transportation of their supplies.

Where possible it was better to send supplies by sea, as the cost of overland transportation for bulky items was very high. It was difficult for Byzantium's opponents during most of her history to penetrate to the Dardanelles and Bosphorus, but such penetration would in fact have resulted in the paralysis of her logistical system with its central requirement that the government be able to shift troops and supplies at will between Europe and Asia while simultaneously attempting to deprive others, whether external or internal foes of the government, of the ability to do likewise. Given the importance of the

Dardanelles, Bosphorus, and Sea of Marmara, the Byzantines built both shipping and coastal defense fortifications to dominate those waterways and to give the capital the flexibility to shift troops and warships in the direction it chose. Naval strength was important for holding on to Egypt, North Africa, and Italy, and points along the Black Sea.[2] But except for the Danube, rivers were not important for transporting men and material after the loss of Egypt and northern Syria in the seventh century.

Byzantium's other principal logistical nightmare was a two-front war at the furthest ends of its frontiers, namely, simultaneously on its eastern and northern frontiers, respectively: near the Caucasus, northern Syria and Upper Mesopotamia; and in the Balkans at the Danube or Balkan mountains. That nightmare became a reality several times in the long history of the empire: most notably, in 626 and again later in the seventh century when Avaric and Slavic invasions and raids in the Balkans coincided with the Islamic conquests in western Asia and North Africa; in the late eleventh century, when Norman pressures on Byzantine southern Italy and the Balkans coincided with the Seljuk breakthroughs in Anatolia; and in the middle of the fourteenth century when the empire faced the rise of Serbia and its thrust toward Thessalonica while the Ottomans expanded in western Anatolia and then, in 1354, crossed into the Balkans as well.

At the same time, the Byzantine Empire was a vast land-based power with lengthy logistical lines. Any understanding of Byzantine logistics requires some regard for distances, more specifically the problems of distances within the empire in different directions from the capital. The most direct routes to the frontier with the Muslims in the eighth through early tenth centuries were more than six hundred to eight hundred kilometers long, while to the Armenian regions of the eastern frontier the distance was more than 1300 kilometers. From Constantinople west to the Danubian frontier in the early seventh century was another six hundred and more kilometers. If we assume that soldiers moved at approximately sixteen to twenty kilometers per day, with baggage trains moving even more slowly, then we can say that the speed of transportation was predictably very slow, whether by land or sea. Of course the use of expensive mounted couriers or fire signals or mirrors could accelerate communication of information.

Several frontiers involved special logistical challenges. The most complex logistical systems—because of the seriousness of the external threat, the length of the exposed frontiers, the need to supply large numbers of Byzantine forces for positional and mobile warfare, and because of the absence of self-sufficiency of some kinds of local provisions and equipment—were those for Upper Mesopotamia and the defense of Syria (where supplies of food, wood for construction and fuel were inadequate), the Danube (inadequate supplies of pay, food, weapons, mounts, and clothing), and the overseas backup for whatever Byzantine presence there was in Italy (repeated problems of procuring adequate soldiers' pay and food because of corruption, distances and poor communications with Constantinople). The Byzantines could not easily support troops on the Sava River or in what is now western Serbia.[3] The weather created almost impassable transportation bottlenecks in the spring and winter, especially in the East, in the mountains of Armenia. There were always grave dangers for supplies in mountain passes (not only because of inherent challenges of tortuous terrain but also because of time-honored efforts of one's foes to try to cut off supplies by blocking or ambushing or even annihilating supply trains in transit through the perilous passes); hence much discussion of this in military manuals.

Water routes helped in the transport of men and supplies to the edges of Anatolia, but there were limits. Ships could bring troops to the periphery of Anatolia, but the topography rose in elevation very sharply a few kilometers inland, creating more hurdles to goods than to men being moved into the interior. The Anatolian Plateau required its own land-based logistical system rather than much reliance on ship-transferred supplies at the hard-to-reach ports on its perimeter. Pack animals, not wheeled vehicles, were essential for transporting goods and supplies from any ports through the surrounding heights to the interior.

Because the size of armies is an important variable in systems of logistical support, it is necessary to note briefly the changing strength of the Byzantine army from period to period. In the age of Justinian I, the total army probably was inferior to its reputed paper strength of 150,000. By the reign of Heraclius in the early seventh century, on the eve of the emergence of Islam, total Byzantine armies were somewhat smaller; the largest operational forces may have reached 30,000 or more, while the total army may have hit 113,000 to 130,000, plus indeterminate numbers of barbarians, especially Arabs. For the late eighth century, one scholar estimates 80,000 total troops, a number which he believes rose to 120,000 by 842. By the fourteenth century the size of the army fell to a few thousand.[4]

Byzantine logistics had to function in an environment of shrinking population, financial and technical knowledge. To some extent, the empire had the opportunity to utilize late Roman structures and infrastructures, but the problem was that those were often too costly to maintain and repair in the face of declining material and human resources. This affected the logistical situation as well. Because the empire's generals and ministers had to skimp, it was necessary for them to modify procedures and institutions adapted from their relatively more bountiful Roman military heritage. They had to do more with less. It was impossible to conduct warfare on a scale comparable to that of the Roman Empire in the fourth century. But this transformation happened gradually: late Roman logistics imperceptibly changed into Byzantine logistics. Older Roman logistical vocabulary survived in part, but transliterated or transformed from Latin into Greek for record-keeping. No unique Byzantine ideology affected or energized the conception and implementation of logistical services. The eastern provinces of the empire experienced a scaling down of the size of armies and their supplies from the fifth through the beginning of the seventh century, in accordance with these changing realities. This, not style or technology, was the critical characteristic that distinguished Byzantine from Roman logistics.

The relative lack of resources meant that the empire did not rely on massive fortifications with commensurably large garrisons and provisions to match. Instead the emphasis was on minimal (and lighter and more mobile) defenses, with a minimum of commitment to the piling up of massive supplies of provisions and arms. Thus quantitative superiority was never the dominating principle behind the wars that the Byzantines waged. Their writers tirelessly argued, perhaps with excessive confidence, that craft and intellectual acumen could overcome numerical adversity, so there never was even a theoretical predilection to seeking overwhelming numerical superiority in provisions and weapons or personnel to ensure victory.[5]

The late Roman praetorian prefecture had been unable to handle the logistics of the empire very well. It was in charge of baking and distributing bread for troops on land or sea. Its officials calculated the needs of the troops and accordingly instructed local provincial and municipal officials to collect and distribute the necessary quantities of provisions (wine, vinegar, grain, cheese, meat) to the soldiers. Often the local officials cheated and profited on the transaction or interfered with procuring the full amounts. The cumbersome *annonae*, or military rations or ration shares or taxes in kind, provided a means for procuring provisions, but this practice was subject to corruption and wastage. Rations in kind had been the foundation of supplies in late antiquity, but practices were modified in the seventh century and became essentially transformed by the middle Byzantine period.[6] The seventh century experienced the greatest single crisis of Byzantine logistics, in fact, its very experiences (e.g., Avaric and Slavic invasions and settlements in the Balkans, and Muslim conquests of Syria, Palestine, Egypt, Upper Mesopotamia, Armenia, and North Africa) caused the creation of a substantially modified system. It was extremely difficult for the government to support more than 15,000 expeditionary troops of reasonable quality in the field. Byzantine armies rarely exceeded that in the middle period and were smaller in the final centuries of the empire.

There were no important innovations in transportation by the Byzantines. Likewise there was no Louvois or Le Tellier, that is, no single Byzantine creative genius or reformer in logistics. There was no Byzantine military revolution in tactics, operations, or logistics. Byzantine techniques and practices worked well enough to permit the empire to preserve much of its territory for centuries, but the conservatism of its leaders discouraged the kind of inquiry and readiness to adapt to change that was imperative for long-term survival. Pack animals were important for transport, in fact much more important than wagons. There were special problems procuring pack animals and making sure they reached the distant eastern frontiers. They receive extensive mention in a treatise on imperial expeditions from Constantinople to the eastern frontier.[7] The old Roman post system broke down sometime in the seventh century, and maintenance of other infrastructure, such as milestones, probably broke down too. Roads slowly were transformed into routes or tracks, and others fell into disuse and sometimes became overgrown with vegetation. Loss of much of what had been the Roman Empire reduced the resources but also shortened lines of communication.

Availability of natural resources affected logistics. The scarcity of water was a principal problem in parts of the East and Southeast, but not in Europe. In fact, the need for drinking water was necessarily a principal factor to calculate in operations in the empire's East, as well as in lengthy naval expeditions. Lack of timber in parts of the East required bringing some wood along for certain military purposes, especially for siege operations.

Logistical Problems

The Byzantines inherited Roman traditions of the camp as the military base, although this was adapted to the realities of an era different from that of the legionary.[8] The authors of manuals stressed the need to locate camps near supplies of water. Military manuals also gave much discussion to the problem of the placement of supplies and the related camp near scenes of battle and how to guard the supplies and the baggage train. There is an extensive literature on this, however unglamorous. An objective in warfare was the seizure of such supplies and their bases. The manuals contained some attentiveness to problems of provisions before the engagement. They include warnings to keep some several days' supplies of food and other provisions some distance from the battlefield in the event of a defeat and the need to retreat. Troops before battle were expected to have an extra day's rations on hand in the event of victory so that they could engage in more effective pursuit. Military manuals included descriptions of how to protect the supplies of the troops. They also warn to try to prevent foragers from being ambushed while gathering provisions on campaign. While these manuals avoid many details, the tone of references about provisions is one of caution and prevention or reduction of risk. But the exhortations of the manuals is not the same as the methods and procedures for calculating logistical needs, which no extant manual explains.

The problem of the procurement of weapons is not given much attention in the literature. Soldiers had to present weapons and mounts for inspection to demonstrate that they were fit. Specific districts might be ordered to produce weapons such as arrows. Muslims, according to one Muslim treatise, admired the quality of Byzantine spearheads. The Maurice *Strategikon* states that the commanding officers are responsible for arming and equipping soldiers and that the commanding officer of a *meros* (7000 men approximately) should determine needs and purchase arms and equipment during the winter season.[9] The precise procedures for doing this, however, are not described in any detail whatever; neither are we told whether, as was likely, the procedures involved some fiscal bureau of the government, i.e., the praetorian prefecture.

Moreover, the Byzantine military manuals, unlike the memoranda of Constantine VII, say nothing about how to calculate those needs.[10] Leo VI in his *Tactica* (ca A.D. 900) ordered that soldiers be armed and equipped by their officers during the winter season. Leo VI also described the kinds of wagons required for carrying arrows and stipulated that units also should have a hand-mill. Soldiers' tools included hammers and axes for siege machines, pitch, bread, bows, pack animals to be able to go ahead without wagons,[11] and twenty or thirty pounds of biscuit is to be placed at a distance for emergency use.[12] Leo VI warns that above all, before embarking on expedition into enemy territory, make certain that you have supplies and fodder for the animals in case the enemy has devastated the territory and has left nothing to consume.[13] Maurice, *Strategikon*, also warns to hobble the oxen who pull wagons before battle so they do not attempt to dash away frightened and thereby disturb men and horses.[14] He advises testing the water in enemy territory by first trying it on the prisoners.[15] Maurice also warns to destroy the forage for the enemy when they are strong in cavalry.[16] He also stresses that troops should carry enough rations, a day's worth, so that they need not break off operations for their lack.[17] There is always the question, however, how much the manuals represent realities instead of the ideal. All of this underscores that logistics was an object of imperial foresight and concern.

The Byzantine military manuals provide some of the best sources for understanding how supply systems functioned, even though many gaps and puzzles remain. There are reports of warehouses near the eastern frontier at several points in the seventh century, and again reports of these in the tenth century. These warehouses were for military purposes, to contain ready supplies for the army, including grain and fodder. They appear to be located where defensive or offensive action tended to repeat itself, that is, in problem areas of the frontier such as Armenia and Upper Mesopotamia in the seventh century. There is no evidence that they existed everywhere.[18] Archaeological evidence has not been probed for information on logistics. It may someday give evidence on warehouses and supply ships, but it is unlikely to solve many other obscure questions concerning logistics. Sigillography may help, however.

Logistics was intimately intertwined with the tax system and fiscal administration in the early Byzantine period. Although connections cannot have been completely severed in the middle period, one simply does not hear about it much. In the early Byzantine period a number of governmental ministers were identified with mismanagement and corruption in the handling of logistics, most notably, the praetorian prefect John the Cappadocian in the reign of

Justinian.¹⁹ There are no reports of sensational scandals about this in the middle Byzantine period, although the reasons remain unclear. The principal catalyst for change in the seventh century was the leadership's realization that the empire and its army faced a fiscal crisis that was equally a logistical crisis.

Procurement of supplies disrupted prices and the civilian economy in specific regions where large numbers of troops were temporarily concentrated for operations in the fourth century at Antioch in the reign of Julian and in Anatolia in the late sixth century, ca 575. Probably there were other cases that remain unreported and unknown.²⁰

Another complex and obscure logistical problem is the nature and role of the camps and their probable roles in logistics in the early period, including the *praefectus praetorio vacans*. This was an improvisation to help with problems of logistics.²¹ However the creation of such positions did not solve recurring deficiencies.

Byzantine emperors ceased to campaign in person from the death of Theodosius I in A.D. 395 until the reign of Heraclius, in A.D. 612 or 613. In those intervening years one may assume that emperors had no firsthand knowledge of logistical problems, except any recollections of their own from military service prior to rising to the throne. What they learned from oral or written reports of others, however, is hard to judge and may have been extensive. How Heraclius actually altered the practice of logistics is unclear. After the resumption of campaigning in the field by emperors the likelihood of emperors' knowing and understanding something of logistics probably vastly improved and may explain in part the reduction in instances of military unrest because of grievances concerning logistical problems. That does not mean that logistical problems ceased to exist, but at least emperors might have had some personal familiarity with them and with the personnel who might solve them and understand just how important and critical such problems might be and how their solution might affect the outcome of military operations. Mistaken judgments concerning logistical problems in the intervening years may have derived, at least partially, from the lack of emperors' experience with such issues.

The empire benefited from interior lines in conceiving and acting on its strategy. Its foes' logistical problems were different and depended more on flexibility and mobility. Byzantium's defense-in-depth was a mobile one in theory, but it was, in reality, a cumbersome mobility.

The foe with the most sophisticated logistical system in the early Byzantine period was of course the Sassanian Persian Empire, but until the seventh century, it could not support lengthy expeditions into Byzantine territory. Until the Crusades, most other foes of Byzantium lacked staying power in long expeditionary campaigns. The Byzantines took advantage—at least they tried to— of the logistical problems of their enemies to defeat them without taking maximum casualties in doing it. The Byzantines preferred a strategy of exhaustion and delaying tactics to cause their opponents to wear themselves down and expose themselves to attack. These strategies involved many assumptions about logistics, in particular that both the Byzantines and their opponents, the invaders, commanded only limited provisions.

One may speculate concerning how well emperors and their advisers understood and appreciated logistics. Justinian I neglected it in his extensive operations in the middle of the sixth century. Logistical problems had been objects of fear ever since the debacle against the Vandals in the reign of Leo I in the late fifth century. The imperial advisers wisely avoided overstraining logistics and so eschewed major expeditions to penetrate or conquer areas north of the Black Sea. The Byzantines could not have supported their troops there. Likewise they could not have penetrated further into North Africa. Limits on logistics became understandably intertwined with limits of finances and manpower. Therefore it is doubtful whether one can calculate approximate percentages of total military costs that were attributable to logistics.

The Byzantines were far from infallible in their logistical calculations. If anything, in a world without mass production they tended to underestimate needs for supplies and manpower and draft animals. These problems derived usually from political decisions to push on irrespective of realistic calculations. However, such decisions were not made by the bureaucrats, who tended to be cautious although very possibly corrupt. The government tended to become overstretched in its commitments to military expeditions. But these miscalculations were exceptions, however costly ones.

Presumably military commanders had some idea about how changing weather conditions affected transportation and rates and security of communications, but prediction and information may well have been very primitive except for cases in which friendly barbarians, deserters, and scouts could provide more accurate information.

There were, however, some advantages to being a very old bureaucratic empire, especially with respect to logistics. Most Byzantine military expeditions took place in regions where the Byzantines had some previous experience. We have no precise knowledge of how long older records and plans were kept, but some knowledge survived of aborted as well as unsuccessful military expeditions and invasions. That does not mean that the results of earlier experiences were always communicated to those who were responsible for planning and calculating the needs for the latest military operations. There probably was no systematic culling of surviving materials, but some traditions and reports survived, accurate or inaccurate as they might be. And conditions could and did change. Obsolete knowledge and stereotypes could be dangerous. Incautious planning could result in disastrous logistical problems in the Balkans, in North Africa, in Sicily, and of course in western Asia. Even for major expeditions, the regions involved were ones where the empire, at some point in its lengthy past, had conducted operations. Even though the enemy leaders, structure, and conditions might have changed very much since the last experiences, one was not taking expeditionary forces into wholly unknown regions.

Because during much of the middle and late Byzantine periods the empire's logistics generally involved calculations for defensive operations, which lay within the empire's borders, the logistical needs were being calculated for regions and personnel that should have been well known to the responsible bureaucrats. That should have been a much less daunting challenge than calculating for major offensive expeditionary campaigns. Much of the relevant calculations involved planning for the collection and stockpiling of adequate supplies of grain at predictable exposed frontier regions which the enemy traditionally attacked. In the early period they included the frontier region in Upper Mesopotamia and parts of Armenia. Logistics in support of a defensive strategy assumed slow-moving warfare. There was danger of damage to the empire's own agriculture and property. There were also complex issues involved in billeting troops with the empire's subjects.

In the early Byzantine period, logistics in many peripheral regions involved assumptions about heavy logistical support and information from allied peoples. Thus there was a need for and an expectation of aid from friendly Arab tribes in logistics across the desert between Syria and central Mesopotamia, or again for operations east of the Dead Sea. Aid from friendly peoples in the Caucasus was indispensable for successful military operations there. The logistics in the Caucasus were complex and difficult. It was necessary to have special provisions to support troops in Thrace and, in the early period, in Upper Mesopotamia. In both regions money was not enough. One needed to ensure the availability of sufficient supplies of food for men and fodder for animals. The upper Euphrates River was always logistically important for the Byzantines and for their foes as an invasion route.

Very little information exists except for incidental references in narrative sources about how well and in what detail there was communication and cooperation between the military and bureaucrats in coordinating calculations for supplies and in actually articulating military, that is, strategic and operational planning. There was potential for friction between individuals, there was potential hostility to bureaucrats, especially eunuchs, on the part of military commanders and their soldiers.

Byzantine bureaucratic or political control of the armies depended in part on exploiting the dependency of the armies on logistics. Therefore bureaucrats appointed by the fisc were not directly responsible to military field commanders but to bureaucrats in Constantinople (not unlike the military intendants of the seventeenth-century French army who exercised some watchful control over royal generals).[22] Such bureaucrats controlled money and supplies and the records, including the invaluable muster lists of the units. It is uncertain how Byzantine bureaucracies maintained or attempted to ensure quality control of supplies. In some instances (bad bread on naval expedition to Africa in 533), they clearly failed to achieve that aim.

During the middle Byzantine period the so-called theme system was an essential part of the military structure for land and maritime operations. Within each theme (army and its military district), the military commander, often called *strategos*, commanded the troops, but the *chartoularios* was in charge of the muster list and the *protonotarios* was in charge of weapons and supplies and money. The last two officials really were responsible for the logistical side of each theme's organization.[23] Little study has been done concerning the unspectacular *protonotarios* of the theme. But no archives survive from any theme, although we do have many lead seals from various themes. These were used to authenticate and seal documents. The disintegration of the theme system by the end of the tenth century, together with poorer documentation, makes it difficult to understand how the government handled logistical procurement and planning after AD 1000.

The potential liability of the empire's subjects for physical labor in support of the logistical needs of its armies is beyond the scope of this essay. There was a loose group of taxes called *angareia* (loads or burdens) that could be used for military support. How did the emergence of the Byzantine theme "system" change Byzantine logistics? The government still remained responsible for supporting, that is, supplying, troops while on expeditionary campaign.[24] One knows even less about the logistical support system for elite mobile expeditionary armies called the *tagmata*, or imperial guard units of the eighth and ninth centuries. Muslim geographical texts claim that Byzantine soldiers were expected to bring along their own food for campaigning (one source cites the types of food). That could only have been the case for campaigns of limited territorial scope. For long-distance, that is, expeditionary, campaigns it would have been necessary for the government to ensure adequate provisions.

As one rereads the appendix to the tenth-century emperor Constantine VII's *Book of Ceremonies*, it is clear that two other officials are prominent when the emperor campaigns in person in the tenth century: the count of the imperial stable and the *logothete* of the flocks.[25] They are in charge of horses and pack animals and are the principal officials concerned with quartermaster responsibilities when the imperial household is involved in a major military campaign.[26] But such cases do not mean every military campaign, because the emperor did not always campaign in person. At the less elevated level, it was the protonotarioi of the themes who prepared the local supplies for an expedition, probably conforming to their inherited role from the long since disappeared praetorian prefecture of the late Roman Empire.

Evaluations

In general, the logistical system of the empire was cumbersome and relatively inefficient in the early period. In later centuries the empire was smaller and poorer and could no longer function as it had in its earliest centuries. One wonders how fully the empire's leaders and their advisors even understood the empire's logistical needs. There was no unified budget or cross-referenced master lists for supplies.

Consistent with Byzantium's character as a venerable bureaucratic empire, its leaders tended to handle normal logistical situations satisfactorily; they were able to draw on their extensive experience to manage those tasks adequately. The empire's leaders tended to be risk-averse. Their caution reduced the number of major risky aggressive campaigns with their attendant problems of logistical overextension. Their inclination to avoid risky wars and to preserve or alter only modestly the *status quo* probably contributed to the empire's longevity. It was the unforeseen and rapid changes and challenges that were extremely difficult for Byzantium to handle. The empire was insufficiently flexible to react or adapt quickly enough to major new challenges for which her historical experiences offered no easy lessons.

How much of a difference did logistics make in the history of the empire? By the late period, the Venetians appear to have developed a logistical system well suited for themselves. The Ottomans had little to learn from Byzantine logistics, which were reduced to insignificance by the time of the emergence of the Ottomans. However, the Byzantine Empire's logistical system did not function impossibly badly, because the empire survived for a very long time. Yet it was a system for passive retention for an essentially status quo power, rather than an aggressively expansionistic one (even though it did temporarily recover Bulgaria in the late tenth century, as well as many of the Taurus passes and some of northern Syria at the same—late tenth/early eleventh century—period.)

Changes in Byzantine logistics occurred for a number of reasons: major changes in the financial resources of the empire and its consequent ability to finance its logistics; changes in the enemies of the empire and their ways of fighting; supposed changes in technology, but these were not great in that period; and changes in administrative structure of the empire and its localities/provinces. Yet the logistical problems of the fourth and fifth centuries were far different from those of the tenth and eleventh centuries, which in turn were far different from those of the fourteenth. Byzantine logistics did not remain static.

Throughout most of its history the Byzantine Empire was not engaged in major expeditionary campaigns beyond its borders, so most of the logistical operations and challenges of the empire involved operating within familiar borders or once familiar borders and routes of the empire, where there should have been records and standard practices and traditions and memories of how to conduct logistical operations. Those traditions may have been an impediment as well as an asset. But the greatest dangers were not necessarily the unfamiliar ones, as much as the fact that Byzantium was pressed on two separated fronts simultaneously or eventually, and this simply put too much financial strain on the limited resources of the government and its subjects. Strategically, the Byzantines were normally conservative, trying to hold on to what was their own or to recover what had once been part of the Roman Empire. Concerning such areas there were many traditions and records, in theory, if one knew how and had the time and willingness to investigate older records. But that does not mean that there were no challenges to Byzantine logistics. Everything was far from being smooth and easy.

Speed was primarily of essence in cutting off raiders in such a defensive empire. The logistical system was slow and cumbersome, but the empire could live with that. It counted on the slowness of logistics and travel and communications to help contain and discourage its enemies during the first seven centuries of its existence, when it still possessed some territorial and strategic depth. Older traditions had sometimes spoken of the advantages or indeed the necessity of a lightning strike against a foe in central Mesopotamia, but normal reality was slow campaigning and slow logistics. This normally allowed time to recoup, to reflect, and to react.

In the early period, it was extremely difficult for the empire to maintain logistical support and communications with its small garrisons in North Africa, scattered over a long irregularly guarded perimeter, and in Spain and the Balearics and Sardinia and Sicily. That defense was not sophisticated but involved a modest holding operation with the minimum of troops. Such was the general defense at the end of the early period: defenses stretched very thin, with ever less complex logistical systems being able to be supported. Moreover, private shipping was declining in the sixth and seventh centuries and so was probably less reliable and frequent to aid the government in carrying materials and men and provisions for the Byzantine troops. The condition of local civilians, moreover, was deteriorating, so they were less likely to be able to supply the Byzantine troops easily from their own resources. At the same time, the financial and demographic base for supporting the Byzantine in the West was declining.

Weaknesses in central procurement and tax revenues required more emphasis on local self-support in the matter of military and civilian provisioning and the procurement of military supplies. The old state arms factories (*fabricae*) cease to be mentioned, although it was still necessary to have weapons and shirts (formerly provided by the Comitiva Sacrarum Largitionum or Count of the Sacred Largesses) for the troops.[27] Yet problems of provisioning never brought the total decentralization of everything or reduction of everything to centrifugal forces.

The passage of a large army was probably usually much more of a burden than an economic benefit for Byzantines, just as it had been earlier for subjects of the Roman Empire. There was too much requisitioning and billeting. Despite hortatory references in legal codes to the need for sparing the civilian population of the empire, the passage of soldiers was a hardship because of the inadequate logistical system. But the government never developed sufficient transport to convey all of the necessary supplies. It necessarily resorted to various expedients that reduced themselves to requisitioning.

It was not realistic to expect to find requisitionable supplies in extensive quantities on the borders of the empire, for those regions were topographically rough and only lightly inhabited, with little arable land. Probably much territory was overgrown with vegetation, where the rainfall permitted it. In such areas the soldiers needed to have the government plan for its supply system and not just expect the troops to forage successfully for themselves. Probably efforts to accumulate adequate provisions for major campaigns tended to tip off the enemy about impending campaigns.

Muslim geographers emphasized the need to take into account the condition of vegetation in planning expeditions into Byzantine territory. Thus raids in the late winter, late February and early March, were to last only twenty days because of the need to return to Muslim territory so that the horses would again find good grass. Muslims believed that the winter weakened the Byzantines and their mounts, a strange counterpart to the Byzantine assumption that Arabs and Persians were enervated in the cold weather! Spring campaigns could last thirty days, while summer ones were to last sixty days because of the availability of fodder. Logistical assumptions are fundamental in these calculations.[28] The authors assume that except in the summer, there was only a limited supply of fodder available for the mounts of the raiders.

Arabic sources are the most important extant ones on the logistics of the principal sophisticated foes of the Byzantines in the middle period, the Muslims of the Umayyad and Abbasid caliphates. The Bulgars and Slavs and Avars and Magyars had no sophisticated logistical support systems, nor did the Rus or Carolingians. The logistical challenges for the Muslims were formidable, involving distances, weather, disinformation, and danger of hostile action by the Byzantines.

The Byzantines inherited a legacy of poliorcetic traditions. But the conduct of sieges required sophisticated logistical preparations and support. Most Byzantine-conducted sieges took place on the empire's eastern or southeastern frontiers, where there were more cities and sophisticated fortresses. Exceptional sieges in the Balkans did take place, however, such as those of Silistra (Dorystolon, in Bulgaria) in the late tenth century. Logistical organization was indispensable for sieges.

The Byzantine government wanted its central imperial authorities to control logistics in order to maintain and increase imperial authority. They did not want to decentralize logistics for fear that this could result in centrifugal tendencies within the empire that would be harmful to the empire and the reigning dynasty. It was dangerous, in the eyes of the government, to delegate authority for logistics to those who might turn against the government and perhaps also against the specific faction who controlled the government.

It appears that the Byzantines failed to develop proper logistical support for their armies and border garrisons after the Byzantine reconquest or reoccupation of those regions in the east in the eleventh century. That is one of the several reasons for the collapse of Byzantine armed resistance at the moment of the Seljuk invasions in the eleventh century. Logistical problems of defending those remote areas were not given serious study and serious resources. Muslim geographers provide the fullest information, however imperfect, about conditions in those frontier zones. The Byzantine sources about logistical conditions in those areas are very poor indeed. The Byzantines required much more complex and comprehensive logistical infrastructure if they expected to expand very much beyond what they had already conquered. That was not impossible, but it required much planning and resolve, which they apparently never accomplished. Their older systems would have been inadequate.

Any attempt to evaluate the overall effectiveness of Byzantine logistics should take into account the longevity of the empire. The system cannot have been all bad, because like other aspects of the Byzantine military system, it contributed in part to the empire's lengthy survival without so overstraining the capacities of the empire's subjects that it brought on collapse and permanent breakdown. That does not mean that the system would necessarily have worked well elsewhere, or that it was without problems. Yet it evidently was not impossibly deficient. The Byzantines, for the most part, did learn in fact to live and fight within their means. There is no evidence that the Byzantine logistical experience heavily influenced other states' military institutions and planning. Their institutions for logistics did not appear to be very excellent to others and so they, in contrast to some other institutions, did not become a Byzantine legacy to others.

Notes

1. A. Philippson, *Das byzantinische Reich als geographische Erscheinung* (Leiden: Brill, 1939); E. McGeer and A.P. Kazhdan, s.v. "Army," *Oxford Dictionary of Byzantium* (Oxford: Oxford University Press, 1991), pp. 183-185.

2. Hélène Ahrweiler, *Byzance et la mer* (Paris: Presses Universitaires de France, 1966).

3. Walter E. Kaegi, "The Capability of the Byzantine Army for Military Operations in Italy," to be published in volume ed. by Antonio Carile, *Teodorico e i Goti tra Oriente e Occidente* (forthcoming, Università di Bologna).

4. Estimates for the reigns of Justinian and Heraclius are my own revisions from Walter E. Kaegi, *Byzantium and the Early Islamic Conquests* (Cambridge University Press, 1992), pp. 39-41. For 780 and 842: use with caution Warren Treadgold, *The Byzantine Revival 780-842* (Stanford: Stanford University Press, 1988) Table I, p. 353. But for criticisms, see also, R.-J. Lilie, "Die byzantinischen Staatsfinanzen im 8./9.

Jahrhundert und die *stratiotika ktemata*," *Byzantinoslavica* 48 (1987), pp. 49-55. Mark Bartusis, *The Late Byzantine Army* (Philadelphia: University of Pennsylvania Press, 1992), pp. 247-53, 262-65.

5. Walter E. Kaegi, *Some Thoughts on Byzantine Military Strategy* (Brookline, MA: Hellenic College, 1983).

6. Walter E. Kaegi, "Variable Rates of Change in the Seventh Century," *Tradition and Innovation in Late Antiquity*, ed. F.M. Clover and R. S. Humphreys (Madison: University of Wisconsin Press, 1989), pp. 191-208; Walter E. Kaegi, "The *Annona Militaris* in the Early Seventh Century," *Byzantina* 13 (1985), pp. 591-96. See Kaegi, *Byzantium and the Early Islamic Conquests*, pp. 35-38. Praetorian prefecture: A.H.M. Jones, *Later Roman Empire* (Oxford: Blackwell, 1964), pp. 448-62; L.E.A. Franks, "The Fiscal Role and Financial Establishment of the Praetorian Prefects in the Later Roman Empire" (Ph.D. diss., Christ's College, Cambridge University, 1971). For a reconstruction of the disappearance of the pretorian prefecture, see John Haldon, *Byzantium in the Seventh Century* (Cambridge: Cambridge University Press, 1990), pp. 195-207; cf. Jean Durliat, *Les finances publiques de Dioclétian aux Carolingiens, 284-889* (Sigmaringen: Jan Thorbecke, 1990); cf. S.J. Barnish, "Taxation, Land and Barbarian Settlement," *Papers of the British School in Rome*, n.s. 54 (1986) 185-95.

7. Constantine VII, "What Should Be Observed When the Great and High Emperor of the Romans Goes on Campaign," in *Three Treatises on Imperial Military Expeditions*, ed. trans. John Haldon (Vienna: Verlag der Österreichischen Akademie der Wissenschaften, 1990), lines 75-139, 185-187, 286, 347-419, on pp. 98-103, 106-107, 112-113, 116-121.

8. Pseudo-Hyginus, *Des fortifications du camp*, ed. trans. Maurice Lenoir (Paris: Belles Lettres, 1979).

9. Maurice, *Strategikon*, 1.2 in *Das Strategikon des Maurikios*, ed. George Dennis and trans. E. Gamillscheg (Vienna: Verlag der Akademie, 1981) p. 76, and in Maurice, *Strategikon*, ed. George Dennis (Philadelphia: University of Pennsylvania Press, 1984), p. 12. Hereafter, these two editions will be referred to simply as Dennis-Gamillscheg and Dennis.

10. Other than a reference in Leo VI, *Tactica*, 6.2, in Jacques Paul Migne, *Patrologia cursus completus: series graeca*, 161 vols. (Paris: 1857-), 107:721, to the need for about thirty to forty arrows per soldier plus an adequate number of bowstrings, and two spears. See also Maurice, *Strategikon*, 1.2 (Dennis, p. 12). Regarding officers equipping soldiers during winter see Maurice, *Strategikon*, 1.2 (Dennis, p. 14).

11. Leo VI, *Tactica*, 6. 28-29, in Migne, *Patrologia cursus completus*, 107:730; also in Maurice, *Strategikon*, 12B.6 (Dennis-Gamillscheg, pp. 422-23; (Dennis, p. 139)

12. Leo VI, *Tactica*, 10. 13, in Migne, *Patrologia cursus completus*, 107:790; on baggage train see entire section 10. Maurice, *Strategikon*, Book 5 (Dennis, pp. 58-60).

13. Leo VI, *Tactica*, 17. 36, in Migne, *Patrologia cursus completus*, 107:922.

14. See Maurice, *Strategikon*, 12B.22 (Dennis, p. 161) on hobbling oxen; see 5.2., 3 (Dennis, p. 58-59) on leaving reserve horses in camp away from the battlefield to avoid confusion.

15. Maurice, *Strategikon*, 9.3 (Dennis, p. 99-100).

16. Maurice, *Strategikon*, 7 pr. (Dennis, p. 64).

17. Maurice, *Strategikon*, 7.10 (Dennis, p. 67); cf. 7.13 (Dennis, p. 68).

18. Walter E. Kaegi, "Annona Militaris in the Seventh Century"; Walter E. Kaegi, "Variable Rates of Change in the Seventh Century," in F.M. Clover and R.S. Humphreys,

Tradition and Innovation in Late Antiquity (Madison: University of Wisconsin Press, 1989), pp. 191-208.

19. Procopius, History of the Wars, 3.13.12-24, in Loeb Classical Library, vol. 2 (Cambridge, MA: 1954), including bread problems but also ones of good drinking water 3.12.23-24.

20. Glanville Downey, "The Economic Crisis at Antioch under Julian the Apostate," Studies in Roman Economic and Social History in Honor of Allan Chester Johnson, ed. by P.R. Coleman-Norton (Princeton: Princeton University Press, 1951), pp. 312-21; P. de Jonge, "Scarcity of Corn and Cornprices in Ammianus," Mnemosyne, Ser. 4, 1 (1948), pp. 238-45; Kaegi, Byzantine Military Unrest, pp. 64-88.

21. On all of this see J. Karayannopoulos, "Byzantinische Miszellen," in Studia in Honorem Veselin Beshevliev (Sofia: Academy, 1979), pp. 490-91; Walter E. Kaegi, "Two Studies on the Continuity of Late Roman and Byzantine Military Institutions," Byzantinische Forschungen 8 (1982), pp. 98-113, and "Late Roman Continuity in the Financing of Heraclius' Army," XVI. Internationaler Byzantinisten-Kongress, Akten = Jahrbuch der Österreichischen Byzantinistik 32/2 (1982), pp. 53-61; and some criticisms of them by Paul Speck, "War Bronze ein knappes Metall? Die Legende von dem Stier auf dem Bus in den 'Parastaseis' 42," Hellenika 39 (1988), pp. 3-17; N. Oikonomides, "Middle Byzantine Provincial Recruits: Salary and Recruitment," Gonimos: Neoplatonic and Byzantine Studies Presented to Leendert G. Westerink at 75, ed. by John Duffey and John Peradutto (Buffalo: Arethusa, 1988), pp. 121-36, and Kaegi, Byzantium and the Early Islamic Conquests, p. 34. But Haldon, Byzantium in the Seventh Century, pp. 201-7, 220-32. See R. Scharf, "Praefecti praetorio vacantes: Generalquartiermeister des spätrömischen Heeres," Byzantinische Forschungen 17 (1991), pp. 223-33.

22. Douglas C. Baxter, Servants of the Sword: French Intendants of the Army (Urbana: University of Illinois Press, 1976).

23. Kaegi, "Two Studies," esp. pp. 98-111, and N. Oikonomides, Listes des préséances byzantines (Paris: CNRS, 1972), pp. 314-15, 341, 364. R.-J. Lilie, "Die zweihundertjährige Reform," Byzantinoslavica 45 (1984), pp. 27-39, 190-201; Haldon, Byzantium in the Seventh Century, pp. 208-53.

24. N. Oikonomides, "Middle Byzantine Provincial Recruits: Salary and Recruitment," Gonimos: Neoplatonic and Byzantine Studies Presented to Leendert G. Westerink at 75, ed. by John Duffey and John Peradutto (Buffalo: Arethusa, 1988), pp. 121-36.

25. Constantine VII, "What Should be Observed When the Emperor Intends to Go on an Expedition," in Haldon, Three Treatises, line 53, on pp. 84-85; Oikonomides, Listes, pp. 338-39.

26. Constantine VII, "What Should Be Observed When the Great and High Emperor of the Romans Goes on Campaign," in Haldon, Three Treatises, lines 59-60, 69-74, 75-84, 314, 333-335, 353-354, 411, on pp. 96-99, 114-117, 120-121.

27. Roland Delmaire, Largesses Sacrées et Res Privata. l'Aerarium Impérial et son administration du IVe au VIe siècle (Paris: Collection de l'École Française de Rome, 121; Paris: Boccard, 1989). S. James, "The fabricae: State Arms Factories of the Later Roman Empire," Military Equipment and the Identity of Roman Soldiers. Proceedings of the Fourth Roman Military Equipment Conference, ed. J.C. Coulson. BAR International Series 394 (Oxford: BAR, 1988), pp. 257-331.

28. M.-J. De Goeje, ed., Bibliotheca Geographorum Arabicorum (Leiden: Brill, reprint 1967), 6: 200.

4

Logistics in Pre-Crusade Europe

Bernard S. Bachrach

A careful examination of the major handbooks of medieval military history, even the relatively recent ones by Verbruggen and Contamine, ostensibly ignore the logistic infra-structure which undergirded long-term military policy when they discuss the art of war in pre-Crusade Europe. Indeed, the reader of these works is encouraged to believe that between the fall of the Roman Empire in the West and the later Middle Ages, the military in western Europe was dominated initially by bands of half-naked barbarians who raided in an undisciplined and erratic search for booty while living off the land whose inhabitants were incapable of developing a cogent strategy to provide for the common defense. This barbarian phase, which saw the invasion of the Muslims, Vikings, and Magyars destroy the primitive successor states of the Roman Empire, was followed, we are led to conclude, by a so-called "feudal" epoch in which bandit magnates on horseback looted and terrorized the countryside while exploiting defenseless peasants from crude wooden motte and bailey strongholds which dotted a landscape rent by anarchy.[1]

Immense military projects sustained by various governments in the kingdoms of pre-Crusade Europe, such as Offa's Dyke, Charlemagne's effort to build a Rhine-Danube canal, and the Danevirke, are given passing mention more as curiosities than as the surviving material evidence for the development of highly sophisticated logistic systems capable of sustaining grand strategies of a most complicated kind. In a similar vein, scholars have ostensibly ignored the logistic system which enabled Charlemagne successfully to pursue a "thirty years war" in Saxony or which made possible William of Normandy's conquest of England. In this paper I will survey some impressive military accomplishments in pre-Crusade Europe in an effort to adumbrate the logistic organization which enabled them to be undertaken. The thesis of this paper is that "logistics science" in the early medieval world was the heir of the late Roman military establishment.

The Late Roman Background

The military history of Western Europe well into the twelfth century and beyond was dominated by the physical remains of the later Roman empire. The art of war for at least six centuries was thoroughly conditioned by imperial military topography, which was composed in large part of an interrelated complex of fortifications, roads, bridges and ports. These were built or rebuilt during the hundred or so years following the invasions and civil wars of the third century in order to sustain a strategy of defense in depth against the prospect of future invasion and required an immense and sophisticated logistic system to create and sustain.[2]

During the era of reconstruction in the fourth century, essentially ca. 275-375 A.D., the Roman emperors, generally with the support of the provincial governments in most of the western half of the empire, undertook to build or refurbish many hundreds of fortifications among which the *urbes, castra,* and *castella* were the most important. Detailed records of the way in which imperial resources were organized in order to carry out these projects do not survive to any significant degree. Thus, in order to grasp the order of magnitude of the logistical infra-structure created during the later Roman empire to sustain these defensive operations, it is necessary to examine the surviving monuments.[3]

The largest and most important class of fortifications built by the Romans was the *urbs* (sometimes called the *civitas*), which served as the capital of a district. The district somewhat ambiguously was also called the *civitas*; later these districts came to be called *pagi* (sing. *pagus*). The imperial government saw to the fortification or refortification of several hundred *urbes* or *civitates* in the western half of the empire. Almost 100 of these were in what is now France.[4]

The *urbes* of the later Roman Empire were centers of imperial military administration. They served as major bases for troop concentrations and as depots for supplies. The *civitas* was the basic unit of local government, and the *urbs* was the capital or headquarters for the officials who administered the region both politically and militarily. It was in the late Roman *urbes* that the largest concentrations of population were to be found, where industries such as textile manufacture, arms production, and glass making were centered. When the church came up from underground in 313 as a result of Constantine's Edict of Toleration, ecclesiastical administration was based in the *urbes*.[5]

The size and form of the *urbes*, as delineated by the defenses built between ca. 275-ca. 375, varied greatly but generally were conditioned by the socio-economic state of the city following the crash of the third century and its topographical idiosyncrasies. Table 4.1 provides some of the vital statistics for a sample of fourteen urbes from the west and southwest of France which fairly represents the many hundreds which scholars have studied. This includes Perigueux, which was quite small with a perimeter wall of only 955, meters and Poitiers, which was large with a perimeter wall almost three times longer. The area enclosed within the walls of the *urbes* also differed greatly from one *civitas* to another with an average for the sample provided here of just under twenty-four hectares.[6]

TABLE 4.1 Sample *Urbes*

Name	Perimeter in meters	Area in hectares	Number of towers
Agen	1,300	10	?
Angers	1,200	9	?
Angouleme	1,400	14	35?
Bordeaux	2,350	32	46
Bourges	1,830	26	45
Limoges	1,100	11	?
Nantes	1,600	16	9
Orléans	1,100	9	8
Perigueux	955	5	24
Poitiers	2,600	42	70?
Rennes	1,200	9	4
Rouen	1,600	16	34
Saintes	2,175	27	40
Tours	1,100	9	20

Source: Bernard S. Bachrach, "Early Medieval Fortifications in the 'West' of France: A Revised Technical Vocabulary," *Technology and Culture*, 16 (1975), P. 547. Reprinted with permission.

Although the *urbes* differed markedly in size, shape, population and wealth, they did display remarkable uniformity with regard to their defensive characteristics. For example, the perimeter walls tended to stand about ten meters in height and were about five to six meters thick at the base. The lower courses of the walls up through the four or five meter mark consisted of huge uniformly cut stones that were about a cubic meter and that averaged about a ton in weight. The upper courses of the walls were generally constructed from much smaller blocks of carefully cut and faced stone. The foundations of the walls often extended five or six meters beneath the surface of the ground and generally were constructed of huge stones similar to those at the base of the wall. This deep foundation made it exceptionally difficult for sappers to undermine the defenses.[7]

A second common characteristic shared by the defenses of the *urbes* was the extensive use of towers to strengthen the perimeter walls. In general, the towers were spaced at about twenty meter intervals along the walls and extended often as much as five or six meters out from them. The towers' semicircular structure made them more resistant than a flat wall to attack by a battering ram, while the protrusions from the walls provided overlapping "fields of fire" for the defenders' missile weapons. Elaborate systems of gates and gate towers guarded the "weak places" in the wall and frequently moats are found surrounding the entire *urbs* or parts of it.[8]

Continuity with the Early Middle Ages

Each of the political leaders in Rome's successor states who tried to rule even a relatively small area in Western Europe such as Anjou or the Bordelais, much less a substantial part of what today is France, England, Italy, or Spain, had to make a policy decision of immense importance. Either he had to develop a logistic system to undergird a grand strategy which sought to maintain and control the erstwhile imperial fortifications which dominated the countryside, of which the *urbes* described above were only the most formidable, or see to it that these great piles of stone and mortar were rendered indefensible.

Throughout Western Europe, the military decision-makers in Rome's successor states consistently organized the logistic structures which permitted them to invest important manpower and material resources in maintaining and improving the physical infrastructure of the erstwhile imperial defensive system. For example, within the *urbs* the *arx*, or *praetorium*, which served as the citadel for the Roman garrison, usually was preserved to provide a defensible home for the medieval count or duke and his military household.[9] Indeed, in conjunction with the maintenance of various segments of the late Roman defensive system in various areas, arrangements were made to ensure the ability of the state to control ports, roads and bridges so that these could be used by friendly forces and closed to enemy forces. In order to preserve these military assets, rulers throughout western Europe developed a logistical infrastructure based upon the systematic use of corvée.[10]

The success of early medieval rulers in developing the logistical system to maintain imperial fortifications is clearly demonstrated by the fact that the Roman *urbes* remained secure centers of military and civil administration. The *civitas* remained the basic unit of local government and the *urbs* was the capital for the count or duke who headed both the civil government and the military administration in the Visigothic, Frankish, Ostrogothic-Lombard, and Anglo-Saxon kingdoms of Spain, Gaul, Italy, and Britain (with some variation), respectively. The militarily secure nature of the urbes is also evidenced by the fact that they remained the center of ecclesiastical organization; the bishop had his cathedral within the walls of the *urbs*.[11]

The monumental military architecture of later Roman origin which dominated Europe's medieval landscape, although built of stone to the best standards of the late antique world, needed consistent care because of the ravages wrought by nature and by the incidents of war. We catch a glimpse of the logistic system developed by the Ostrogothic ruler Theodoric the Great (d. 526) to maintain the scores of fortifications scattered throughout his *regnum* through the letters of his Latin secretary and close advisor, Cassiodorus. Thus, for example, the latter addressed a letter "to all Goths and Romans" in which he put forth the view that "most worthy of royal attention is the rebuilding of ancient cities, an adornment in time of peace, a precaution in time of war." Cassiodorus went on to echo Vegetius when discussing the importance of keeping the fortifications in good repair before they are needed when he wrote, "it is expedient to execute works of this kind in times of peace rather than during war."[12]

In order to sustain the work of maintaining the fortifications, a logistic system was created in which functionaries were employed on a regular basis and crews of professional construction specialists were kept on the government payroll. With regard to the former, Cassiodorus wrote on behalf of Theodoric to Sabinianus, who headed a large *officium* charged with keeping Rome's walls in defensible condition:

> We are very anxious to keep the walls of Rome in good repair, and have therefore ordered the [people dwelling in the district of the] Lucrine port to furnish 25,000 tiles annually for this purpose. See that this is done and that the cavities which have been formed by the fall of stones may be roofed over with tiles and thusly preserved....[13]

These types of taxes in kind placed a considerable burden on the population of a city. Thus, rulers often tried to prevail upon civic spirit rather than upon the harshness of levies. For example, Theodoric ordered: "if anyone has in his fields stones suitable for the building of walls let him cheerfully and promptly produce them. Even though he will be paid very little he will have his reward as a member of the community and thus he will also benefit." To the count of Sura, Cassiodorus relayed the order "have the blocks of marble which are everywhere lying about in ruins wrought up into the walls by the hands of the work crews that I am sending to you." To Arles following the siege of 508, Theodoric sent money "for the repair of the walls and old towers" and work crews of specialists to carry out some of the more technical work.[14]

While the need to keep the defenses in good repair was widely recognized, the vagaries of government were known to put pressure on the defense budget. This then resulted in what might appear to have been emergency measures. For example, in 584, the Merovingian king, King Chilperic, learned that several *urbes* which had recently been captured by his forces were likely to be the object of a counter-attack in the near future. Thus he sent *nuntii* with orders to his *duces* and *comites* commanding them to make sure that the walls were in good repair.[15]

On occasion, it even came about that the Roman defenses were improved by the heirs of the empire. For example, during the later sixth century, Mummolus, a high ranking military officer of Gallo-Roman origins serving in the army of the Frankish king who ruled Burgundy, prepared to defend the *urbs* of Avignon to withstand a siege. However:

When he first entered the *urbs*, he noted that a small part of it was undefended by the Rhone river. Thus he took measures to have a channel led from the river to protect the entire part of the wall that had been exposed. Moreover, before this was done he had very deep pits dug in the bed of the channel.[16]

Gregory of Tours, a contemporary, explains that the pits were dug so that anyone wading into the channel in hopes of crossing on foot would easily slip into the unseen pits and drown because of the weight of his armor or simply because he could not swim.[17] It is perhaps equally interesting that Gregory did not feel it necessary to comment upon the fact that a labor force was easily assembled by demanding the corvée for the work and that Mummolus' engineers had solved a difficult problem in hydraulics which had apparently eluded the Roman builders. Military technology in early medieval Europe is consistently underestimated by modern scholars.[18]

The pattern of maintaining the physical infrastructure provided by the massive building efforts of the later Roman Empire was by no means limited to the preservation and improvement of the *urbes*. Vast numbers of lesser strongholds, i.e., *castra* and *castella*, not to mention various types of *refugia, podia, rochae* and military camps, also called *castra*, which were far more numerous than the massive *urbes*, were kept in use. The *castrum* at Dijon, built ca. 275 by the emperor Aurelian, enclosed ten hectares and has been well studied because its archaeological remains are so thoroughly in accord with a description written by Gregory of Tours more than three centuries after its construction. Gregory wrote:

> It is a fortified place with very strong walls built in the middle of a plain.... On the south is the river Ouches...on the north another and smaller stream which enters one gate and surrounds all of the fortifications with its peaceful flow.... Four gates face the four quarters of the world and thirty-three towers guard the circuit walls. These towers are made of squared stones to a height of twenty feet and above they are constructed of smaller stones. The total height of each tower is about thirty feet and they have a thickness of fifteen feet.[19]

The continued use of late Roman fortifications is surely remarkable, and it should be emphasized that at least some of these likely were in place before the Roman conquests north of the Alps. For example, during the later sixth century, Gregory of Tours calls attention to Chastel-Marlhac, a *castrum* which "was naturally fortified" and originally may have been a Celtic hill fort. Gregory writes:

> [It] was surrounded not by man made walls but by cliffs that were a hundred or more feet in height which were hewn into walls. In the middle was a large pool of water which was fine for drinking and in another part there were springs that were very full and ran through the gate of the fortification. The defenses enclose

such a great defensive perimeter that the inhabitants within the walls cultivated the soil and harvested substantial crops.[20]

Side by side with the old fortifications, new ones were also built. Thus, for example, Bishop Desiderius of Cahors (d. 655), an expert in the Roman law and one-time treasurer to King Dagobert I, not only commanded that a great deal of work be done to keep the *urbs* of Cahors in defensible condition and oversaw its completion but also saw to the construction of *castella*. Near the river Lot, he built a fortified ecclesiastical enclave strengthened by "four towers of wondrous size." His military construction work was summarized by a biographer in the century after his death: "Wisely building up the defenses and sweating over his work with great labor he fortified churches, houses, gates, and towers in the circuit of the walls and ordered these to be kept secure and solid for the future." In these activities the bishop acted as an agent of the government, and the magnitude of his accomplishment only hints at the sophisticated logistic system he developed to carry out these important military projects.[21]

The combination of new and old fortifications, Celtic and Roman among the latter, is perhaps best illustrated by the efforts of Alfred the Great (d. 899) to defend the kingdom of Wessex. Asser, a Welsh bishop who served at Alfred's court, praised the king for the "cities and towns which he had restored and the others, which he had built where there had been none before."[22] Thus, for example, Alfred utilized the great Roman walled city (*urbs*/*civitas*) of Winchester and Iron Age forts such as Chisbury. In addition, new fortifications were constructed such as that at Eshing. The older fortifications were, in some cases at least, significantly repaired, restored or modified at what appears to have been a considerable outlay of both human and material resources.[23] In all, Alfred saw to the readying of thirty-three strongholds which were established to control the routes within Wessex while at the same time creating a defense in depth for the kingdom and its environs.[24]

A document drawn up during the reign of Edward the Elder but before 914, called the "Burghal Hidage," provides a glimpse of the sophistication of the administrative system which met the logistic demands of Wessex's defensive system after the initial building and rebuilding of fortifications had been accomplished. Briefly, the perimeter defenses of the thirty-three fortifications were measured or surveyed. Then income-producing landed resources, presumably close to each stronghold, were listed and assessed so that the returns from one hide of land were delegated to each member of the garrison, who in turn was required to defend and keep in repair one quarter-pole of wall, i.e., 4.25 feet. The very high quality of this administrative work is illustrated, for example, at Winchester, where 2,400 hides were allocated for the support of the garrison required to defend a perimeter wall that measured 9,954 feet. The margin of error was less than one percent in providing the logistic support to sustain a force of 2,400 fighting men. [25]

The development of a massive and sophisticated logistic system to support both the defensive and offensive strategies of various states in pre-Crusade Europe was not confined within the former borders of what had been the later Roman Empire. Charlemagne, for example, understood very well the logistic limitations inherent in the use of pack animals and ox or horse drawn vehicles. Thus he saw that it was worthwhile to establish fortified depots and lines of supply that were defended by strongholds in frontier areas.[26] This *desideratum* was recognized by the late Roman military writer Vegetius, whose *De re militari* was, as observed above, very popular during the early Middle Ages.[27]

The spread of Roman military ideas regarding the need to maintain sound logistics beyond what had been the borders of the empire is well illustrated by the efforts of the Saxon ruler of *Francia Orientalis*, King Henry I (919-936). The Saxon peoples on the northeastern frontier of the Carolingian empire were little unified before Charlemagne conquered the region and introduced substantial numbers of settlers from the West. The Saxons also had demonstrated no ability to provide the logistical basis needed to sustain their fortified strongpoints in the face of sieges or to provide adequate supplies for their field armies. Under King Henry, however, a concentrated effort was made to protect Saxony from Magyar raids by building a defense in depth based upon strategically located strongholds and reinforced with a mobile field force.[28]

Widukind, the premier Saxon chronicler of the period, describes in noteworthy detail various aspects of the means by which Henry provided for the logistic sustenance of this new system. Concerning the garrison he writes:

> Henry...chose one from every nine farmer-soldiers (*agrari milites*) and required that they live in burgs in order to build small dwelling places [within the fortifications] for the other eight members of the unit (*confamiliares*) and in order to receive a third part of their produce and keep it in the burg. The eight men were to sow and to harvest the grain [from the land] of the ninth man [stationed in the burg].[29]

This effort undertaken by Henry to build a coherent system of fortifications in Saxony, which had both regular garrisons and an efficient system of supply based upon service by landholders and a tax on their produce, has more than a passing resemblance to the efforts made in contemporary Anglo-Saxon England by Alfred the Great and Edward the Elder. Both systems likely owed much to earlier efforts—such as the *centenae* in Rome's successor states, which were based upon an imperial model—either through marginal continuities in localized areas or through the surviving written records. In addition, Western relations with Byzantium during the later ninth and tenth centuries were well developed, and Byzantine authorities, like their imperial antecedents, used farmer-soldiers extensively.[30]

The extensive use of fortifications in post-Carolingian Europe required the mobilization of substantial resources to provide the logistical underpinnings to build these assets in the first place and subsequently to maintain both the physical structure and their garrisons. The military building efforts of Fulk Nerra, count of the Angevins (987-1040), for which he has gained in modern times the sobriquet "le grand bâtisseur," are of central interest. The Angevin heartland had a rural population of at least 60,000 with a density of about 25 persons per square kilometer. With a labor force drawn from this population Fulk saw to the building of at least thirty stone towers of monumental proportions in the course of his reign. In order to carry out this work of the initial construction of the towers only (curtain walls, expansion of the fortifications, and repairs are not included), Fulk needed to keep a force that averaged 140 men on a work site every day of the year and laboring approximately ten hours per day.[31]

At first glance this seems to be a rather nominal figure because the number is rather small. Yet, to provide yearly wheat equivalent calories to sustain these workers at an absurdly low figure of two kilograms of unmilled wheat per worker per day, it was necessary to provide more than 100,000 kilograms of unmilled wheat. This obligation, in turn, required the true wheat surplus provided by more than 460 agricultural workers from more than 2,700 hectares of average arable land. In short, it required somewhat more than 3.2 agricultural workers to sustain each fully employed construction worker for a year.[32]

It is obvious that no society can long survive, much less prosper, as was the case in the Angevin state during this period, if the agricultural and construction work forces were composed solely of laboring males without dependents. Indeed, once we consider that the population in this region was increasing during this period, we must assume an average minimum nuclear family size of 4+ persons. The average agricultural work under these conditions, it should be made clear, could sustain a family of 4+ persons through gardening, hunting, and gathering and thereby more than double the caloric equivalent that was provided through the cultivation of the six hectares of arable land, which was the normal agricultural holding. However, the situation with regard to full-time construction workers poses a different problem, and it appears highly unlikely that the dependents of masons, lime burners, and smiths were able to grow or gather the food required for their sustenance. Thus, it seems likely that the surplus produced by at least four and perhaps even more than four agricultural workers was required to provide the wheat-equivalent calories needed to sustain each construction worker and his dependents.[33]

For purposes of a comparison, it may be observed that the surplus produced by at least twelve agricultural workers was required to provide the wheat-equivalent calories needed to sustain a mounted warrior and his horse (with oats for the latter). In this context, it is of some interest that Fulk Nerra sustained a force of mounted warriors which was divided into two basic units. One served in his military household and the other was scattered throughout the garrisons deployed in the strongholds of the Angevin state. The total mounted force sustained by the government is estimated to have numbered between 2,000 and 3,000 effectives.[34]

This brief survey of some of the great military projects undertaken in pre-Crusade Europe provides an opportunity for us to gain some insight into the otherwise not very well documented area of the logistic systems which undergirded these efforts. These few examples could be multiplied manifold not only for the areas and periods discussed above but for both Spain and Italy, which have been conspicuously neglected. However, before going on to examine in some detail some of the surviving written documentation which early medieval decision makers had at their disposal to keep track of logistic demands, I want to look at two additional efforts of a somewhat different character, Offa's Dyke and Charlemagne's Rhine-Danube canal, which both enable us, from archaeological evidence, to grasp the order of magnitude of supply systems commanded by these monarchs.

By the later seventh century and probably a good deal earlier, it was believed in Britain that Hadrian's wall and the Antonine wall were built during the early fifth century, the first without imperial aid and the latter with support from Rome, or so we may infer from Bede's remarks on the subject:

> Having, indeed, freed the Britons for a while from heavy pressure, the Romans advised them to build a defensive wall from sea to sea....The islanders constructed such a wall...but because they lacked engineers they built of earth rather than of stone....[35]

Then, according to Bede, the enemy was again successful, so the Roman government advised the Britons and helped them to build

> a strong wall of stone in a straight line directly from sea to sea....This celebrated and still conspicuous wall was constructed with the combined resources drawn from both the public and private sectors of society and the assistance of the Britons. The wall is eight feet wide and twelve feet in height and as one can see today it ran directly from east to west.[36]

In short, Bede was sure that the government of fifth-century Britain, either with or without help from Rome, commanded the logistic infra-structure to carry out substantial building projects for military purposes. His frame of reference for this confidence, shall we call it the early medieval capacity for the organization of such resources, i.e., logistic expertise, was very likely the famous Danevirke, an enormous earthen rampart which cut the Jutland peninsula off from the mainland. The first and most impressive phase of the Danevirke was completed ca. 737, just two years after Bede's death, and undoubtedly had been begun at least a decade or so earlier.[37]

Bede was dead more than two decades when Offa (775-796), a contemporary of Charlemagne, became king of Mercia and, according to the Welsh prelate

Asser, "built a great wall ["vallum magnum"] from sea to sea between Britain (i.e., Wales) and Mercia."[38] This *vallum*, or Offa's Dyke as it has come to be called, is almost 150 miles in length and stretches from the estuary of the Severn in the south to Basingwerk on the Dee in the north; it effectively separates England from Wales. The earthen rampart of the wall rises about 25 feet from ground level and is fronted by a ditch of about six feet in depth. The entire wall and ditch complex averages about sixty feet in width. At least some parts of the rampart were surmounted by a stone wall, and this may have been the case through much of the distance north of Basingwerk. However, in those places in which the rampart was not surmounted by a stone wall, it is likely that it was topped by a wooden palisade. Seen in historical perspective, Offa's Dyke is longer than the combined distances of the Hadrianic and Antonine walls, which were built during the *flourit* of Roman imperial power. Thus, Offa may be thought of as commanding logistic assets for the building of monumental fortifications of the same order of magnitude as those available to the government of Roman Britain during the acme of imperial power.[39]

It is perhaps appropriate to bring this brief examination of the physical evidence for the sophistication of early medieval logistics to a close with Charlemagne's efforts to build a canal connecting the Rhine to the Danube River. As is well known, Charlemagne's canal-project failed, and the linking of the North Sea to the Black Sea by a continuous water route was not to be realized until 1846, when King Ludwig I of Bavaria succeeded where his more illustrious predecessor had not. However, what requires our attention here is not the fact that Charlemagne failed but that he had the imagination, logistic infrastructure, and skilled engineers to undertake a task which modern specialists agree was within his grasp.[40]

Charlemagne's effort to build the canal is relatively well documented by a combination of written sources and archaeological, topographical, geodetic and hydrographic research. In short, during a period of about ten weeks in the autumn of 793, Charlemagne put a minimum of 6,000 workers to digging a carefully surveyed trench that was intended to connect the Rezat, a navigable affluent of the Regnitz-Main-Rhine river chain, with the Altmühl, an affluent of the Danube in the neighborhood of Weissenburg about equi-distant, 75 km, from the old Roman cities at Regensburg to the east and Augsburg to the south.[41]

From the remains, it is established that the entire project was to be about 1,400 meters in length, 30 meters in width and up to six meters deep in the center of the channel. The workers were expected to move, counting the carrying over scaffolding, some 780,000 cubic meters of earth at a rate of 0.3 cubic meters per man hour. Modern estimates, which are perhaps a bit too high, suggest that the work site had to be supplied with some 1,200-1,500 tons of grain, about 1,000-1,200 oxen and 2,000 to 3,000 pigs to provide approximately 4,000 calories per day for each worker over the course of the ten week period of labor. Incidentally, the canal project did not fail for lack of workers or supplies but because the autumn of 793 was exceptionally rainy and not only was it often difficult if not impossible to dig but the sides of the canal were undermined by the downpours.[42]

The efforts described above, and these, it must be emphasized, are but a small fraction of what was done, should make it clear that the successor states of the Roman Empire in the West were not peopled by half-naked barbarians who some anthropologically minded social scientists believe can be profitably compared with the non-literate natives of sub-Saharan Africa or of the North American continent. Nor is it useful to think of a so-called "feudal age," which often is alleged to have followed the dissolution of the Carolingian Empire, as dominated by illiterate bullies who built primitive wooden stockades atop earthen mounds and won their putative aristocratic life-style by brutally exploiting a thinly scattered population of lice-covered serfs.[43]

The military culture of pre-Crusade Europe was firmly built within the contours, both physical and psychological, that had been established in the later Roman Empire. Early medieval government, in which the military played a substantial role, was thoroughly based upon the use of written documentation, and, in addition, those men in decision making capacities at the higher levels understood that one could learn from books how to gain advantages.[44] More explicitly, the rulers of the period, like their late Roman predecessors, were constantly gathering information, having inventories made and bringing them up to date. The appropriate behavior for a government in this regard had been set out clearly in Luke 2:1, as it reads in the Vulgate: "there went out a decree from Caesar Augustus that all the world should be taxed, so that the entire world may be surveyed." *Domesday Book*, completed in 1086 by the agents of William the Conqueror, is only the most impressive surviving record of this type of survey from pre-Crusade Europe.[45]

At various times during the early Middle Ages, rulers carried out massive surveys not only of public lands but of the resources of the church and of laymen with the intention of establishing relevant information concerning their logistic base in men and materiel for military operations. For example, the Merovingian ruler Dagobert I (d. 639) ordered that the *faculatates* of all monasteries in his realm be inventoried and that half be placed at the disposal of the state (*res publica*) for the support of the military and for the civil administration. The monks, though aggrieved, are said to have acquiesced to the king's policy for the good of the *res publica* and its defense. However, when Dagobert attempted to raise the state's share to two-thirds, the monks resisted.[46] Dagobert's efforts were not novel, nor did the apparent opposition of the monasteries retard future rulers from making similar efforts. Thus, in 751, Peppin I, the first of the Carolingian kings, ordered all church property, not only that belonging to the monasteries, to be described and divided.[47]

The survival rate of the statistical sources, as James Westfall Thompson called them more than a half-century ago, is poor.[48] However, this should hardly be thought surprising or evidence for a lack of interest by contemporaries in such documents, since these surveys not only were severely time-limited in their application but they were inscribed on valuable parchment which could be and was easily reused.[49] Among those great surveys, conventionally called polypytchs, which were likely the main vehicle by which Charlemagne and his successors required their subjects to record various of their resources, that done by Abbot Irmino of Saint-Germain-des-Près (811-29) is the most complete.[50] This document makes clear that about half of the monastery's income from its estates went to sustain the Carolingian army. Indeed, the survey includes exceptional detail down to the number of eggs and chickens owed to the army for its logistic support.[51] These figures are of the same order of magnitude as those recognized by Archbishop Hincmar of Rheims, who observed, albeit grudgingly, that about two-fifths of the church's income legitimately went for the support of the military.[52]

Charles the Bald, king of *Francia Occidentalis* and emperor (d. 877), had a wide variety of surveys made during his reign. For example, on the large scale in 869, "he sent letters to the bishops, abbots and abbesses of his realm so that they would have *breves* drawn up and sent to him...which described the number of households (*mansi*) that were to be found on their *honores*." He followed up this order to the religious hierarchy with another to his major lay administrators. Thus, the *vassalli dominici*, i.e., royal agents of the central government analogous to the *agentes in rebus* of the later Roman Empire, were to have *breves* drawn up concerning the households established on the *beneficia* held by the counts. The latter, who were the primary secular civil and military administrators of Charles' kingdom at the local level, were to have established *breves* of the *beneficia* held by *vassalli* in their respective *civitates*.[53]

This survey required many thousands of returns and concerned, or so it would appear, only lands held in beneficial tenure. Thus, for example, the private property of those who were required to comply with the king's orders was not to be inventoried in this survey. The order of magnitude of the statistical data which Charles the Bald's bureaucracy was expected to process in this one instance may perhaps be gauged from a mere summary of the survey compiled at Charlemagne's order for the monastery of Saint Wandrille by Abbot Landric and Count Richard in 787. This inventory, done only ninety years earlier, described 4,278 *mansi*, of which 2,551 were held in beneficial tenure.[54] Should it be assumed for heuristic purposes that the ratio of beneficed to non-beneficed *mansi* at Saint Wandrille represented a norm, then Charles' survey of 869 would have enregistered about 60% of the *mansi* controlled by the great lay and ecclesiastical magnates of his realm.

At the same time that Charles the Bald issued orders for the massive survey discussed above, which was to be completed within the space of only one year, he sent out requisitions for a much smaller project, i.e., the building of a *castellum* at Pitres. The previous year he had stopped at Pitres, come to the conclusion that a *castellum* was needed there, ordered the ground to be surveyed and the number of feet of wall each landholder in his kingdom would be responsible for building.[55] Thus in 869, he sent out the orders that each unit of 100 *mansi* (obviously such account groups were already in existence as evidenced by the calculations made the previous year) was to provide one free worker (*histaldus*) for the *castellum*-project and also from each account-unit of 1000 *mansi* one cart with two oxen was to be provided.[56]

When the Carolingian army went to war under Charlemagne and his successors, as it did virtually every year, troops were summoned from throughout the empire to fight in whatever region they might be needed.[57] Indeed, a particular theater of operations such as Saxony, where Charlemagne fought for some three decades, was well in excess of a thousand kilometers distant from some recruitment areas. For example in 806, Charlemagne planned to campaign on the Saxon frontier against the Sorbs and thus sent out summonses to the major lay and ecclesiastical officials throughout the empire to join the host which would muster at Strassfurt on 18 June.[58] In order to comply with this summons, an important Carolingian religious functionary such as Abbot Fulrad of Saint Quentin, who received one of these summonses, had to be ready with his contingent of levies and ox carts of supplies to leave his monastery some 800 kilometers west of Strassfurt no later than 15 April and perhaps even a week or two earlier. Although Fulrad could expect to have access to "fodder wood and water" for his logistic needs while traveling within the Carolingian empire for at least four months (two months to Strassfurt and two months for the journey home), he either had to haul or to purchase the grain and other food supplies that were required for the men and horses of his contingent during the journey to and from the muster. In addition, Fulrad had to haul or have some other assured means of obtaining the supplies that he needed for a campaigning season in Saxon territory for three months.[59]

The logistic problems that were imposed upon men with command responsibilities such as Abbot Fulrad were immense, and Charlemagne took cognizance of these. Under normal conditions for an offensive campaign, i.e., *expeditio*, close to home, which should not be confused with the requirements of local defense in which the regulations governing the *lantwehr* were enforced, each manse was expected to provide an able bodied fighting man for the host. When the theater of operations was distant from the region of recruitment, then the obligations were lighter. Thus, for example, when a contingent raised in Frisia was needed on the Spanish frontier, the region was required to supply fewer effectives than if Saxony were the theater of operations.[60]

We can see some of the specifics of Charlemagne's appreciation of these problems with regard to the campaign of 806 mentioned above. Thus, for example, when the monastery of Saint Wandrille had to carry out Charlemagne's orders for a campaign such as that in 806, which was preceded by a journey of almost 1000 kilometers, it was not required to make sure that one fighting man was provided for each of its 4,278 manses.[61] Rather, the manses were grouped in units of five, and only one fighting man was to be provided from each such group.[62] The abbot of Saint Wandrille therefore had to be sure that a contingent of about 850 to 860 effectives appeared at Strassfurt on 18 June to meet the obligations owed by the monastery.

We can even gain some insight into the order of magnitude of Saint Wandrille's baggage train for this campaign. Each fighting man was required to have a minimum of three months of food and six months of clothing dating from the muster on 15 June at Strassfurt. If an allotment of two kilograms of unmilled wheat, the daily average caloric minimum for a moderately active man, is assumed to have been the basic ration, then the contingent from Saint Wandrille would have had to have hauled something in excess of 75 tons of grain to meet the three month or ninety day requirement. This load of basic rations would have required in excess of 150 ox carts, each drawn by two oxen and having a capacity of about 500 kilograms.[63]

However, before trying to calculate the order of magnitude of a baggage train such as that required by a contingent from Saint Wandrille for operations on the Saxon frontier against the Sorbs, it should be made clear that a multiplicity of equipment was required as well. Thus, for example, in the summons for 806, mentioned above, Charlemagne required that each contingent was to have in its ox carts "axes, planes, augurs, boards, spades, iron shovels, and the other equipment for the army."[64] This rather vague requirement, like that for each fighting man having sufficient clothing for six months of campaigning, placed the onus for making correct calculations on each of Charlemagne's responsible officials. Failure was met with very stiff penalties.[65] Thus, if the number of carts were increased by only 15% in order to meet the hauling requirements adumbrated above, a total of at least 165 vehicles and some 200 oxen were needed. This calculation includes a small number of extra beasts to be used as substitutes in case some of the original teams were lost as a result of accidents.

Such a baggage train, integrated into a line of march that included some 850 effectives, likely would have extended in excess of two kilometers over the old Roman roads from the region east of Paris to the banks of the Rhine. Beyond the Rhine, travel obviously was far more complicated and the potential for hostilities increased. In addition, if the line of march included food animals, e.g., sheep and cattle to be slaughtered along the way, as appears to have been normal, and also food for the journey to and from the muster, i.e., a supply of grain rations for some four months, the contingent may have had a line of march of some five or six kilometers.[66] In any given year, Charlemagne might have more than 50,000 effectives operating in offensive actions on the frontiers of the empire and beyond.[67]

As we bring this study to a close, some mention of the logistic underpinning of the most impressive of the major military operations in pre-Crusade Europe,

William of Normandy's conquest of England, deserves some attention. In order to make these observations manageable, I will focus primarily on the month from ca. 4 August to ca. 4 September 1066, when the duke had the command responsibility for provisioning about 14,000 men and from 2-3000 horses of the best type in an encampment of some 280 acres on the shores of the Gulf of Dives.[68]

However, before we focus on this problem, a few observations concerning the building of William's invasion fleet and especially of his horse transports—all largely done de *novo*—will cast some light upon how a society in pre-Crusade Europe coped with the immense demands placed upon it for a war of conquest. Ships capable of transporting large numbers of very valuable war horses—William took from two to three thousand across the Channel—*in battle ready condition* were unknown in northern Europe since the invasion of Britain by Julius Caesar some eleven centuries earlier. Thus, with the aid of Normans from southern Italy and Sicily, William obtained designs for Byzantine horse transports and the naval architects to lay out the skeletons for these craft. In addition to being easier and faster to construct than the clinker-built ships traditionally used in northern Europe, the Byzantine method, which was already well developed almost a century earlier, made it possible, once the skeleton of the vessel was constructed, to use ordinary carpenters to complete the work. Thus, perhaps with some exaggeration, Baudry of Bourgueil, a contemporary, observed that carpenters were called from all over the world and they turned from building houses to constructing ships.[69]

William oversaw the completion of some 700 vessels, including about 200 horse transports, in less than eight months, the recruitment of the army, the provisioning and payment of these forces prior to 4 August, the journey to Saint-Valery-sur-Somme, the channel crossing, the landing at Pevensey with its fortification and provisioning, the march to Hastings, the fortification and provisioning of the latter, the battle itself, and finally the logistics of the post-battle period, including the siege of Dover, until William's rather hurried coronation in London on Christmas Day 1066.[70]

William's command responsibilities at Dive-sur-Mer during the month under consideration required approximately 4,000 tons of foodstuffs to feed the men and horses, i.e., each day the men required 28 tons of unmilled wheat grain and 14,000 gallons of clean fresh water if they were fed only on cold mush and water. The horses required between 12-18 tons of grain, 13-19.5 tons of hay, 4 to 5 tons of straw and 20,000 to 30,000 gallons of fresh water each day. Some additional requirements include 36,000 calf-skins for tents, 8,000-12000 horse-shoes, and at least 75,000 nails or about 8 tons of iron that previously had been forged by skilled workers into shoes and nails. Just to keep the horses in shoes in camp required at least 10 blacksmiths, each working a ten-hour day every day to do the job. Finally, William's sanitation squads had to clear some two to three million pounds of horse manure from the camp in the course of the army's stay at Dives.[71]

To conclude, pre-Crusade Europe saw military decision-makers develop sophisticated logistic systems to provide vast human and material resources to maintain old Roman fortifications and to build new ones. These logistical systems were needed to sustain grand strategies which established elaborate systems of defense in depth as well as extended fortified frontiers. Networks of roads and bridges were maintained to keep the defenses operative through effective means of transportation and communication. Detailed inventories were compiled to provide the statistical data which made it possible to levy resources and manpower in order to build and maintain these monumental projects. The troops needed to man the defenses were levied and extensive material support was allocated to sustain both these garrisons and also to provide for mobile field forces. Military expenditures in pre-Crusade Europe consumed a major part of the society's surplus productive capacity. The planning was detailed and produced a defensive infra-structure whose ruins still dominate the landscape in parts of Western Europe.

Notes

1. For generations the basic handbooks have been Hans Delbrück, *History of the Art of War: Within the Framework of Political History*, vol. 3, *The Middle Ages*, trans. Walter J. Renfroe (Westport, Conn.: 1982), from the 1923 ed. of *Geschichte der Kriegskunst im Rahmen der politischen Geschichte* (the third volume was reprinted in 1964 with an important introduction by K. G. Kramm); Ferdinand Lot, *L'Art militare et les armeés au Moyen Age et dans la Proche-Orient*, 2 vols., (Paris: 1946); and Charles Oman, *History of the Art of War in the Middle Ages*, 2 vols., 2nd ed., (1924 repr. New York: 1964). More useful but not entirely superceding the above are J. F. Verbruggen, *The Art of War in Western Europe during the Middle Ages, from the eighth Century to 1340*, trans. Sumner Willard and S.C.M. Southern (Amsterdam-New York: 1977). This originally appeared as *De Krijgskunst in West-Europa in de Middeleeuwen* (Brussels: 1954). The translation adds a treatment of the eighth century whereas the original began in the ninth. Unfortunately, Verbruggen's very valuable notes were omitted from the translation. Of basic importance is now Philippe Contamine, *War in the Middle Ages*, trans. Michael Jones (Oxford: 1984).

2. Basic background with a fine treatment of the literature is Edward N. Luttwak, *The Grand Strategy of the Roman Empire from the First Century A.D. to the Third* (Baltimore: 1976).

3. The fundamental survey is now Stephen Johnson, *Late Roman Fortifications* (Totowa, N.J.: 1983).

4. H. von Petrikovits, "Fortifications in the North-Western Roman Empire from the Third to the Fifth Centuries A.D.," *Journal of Roman Studies*, 61 (1971), pp. 178-218.

5. For the background on the cities see A.H.M. Jones, *The Later Roman Empire, 284-602* (Norman, Okla.: 1964), 1:712-66.

6. Adrien Blanchet, *Les enceintes romaines de la Gaule* (Paris: 1907); and Bernard S. Bachrach, "Early Medieval Fortifications in the 'West' of France: A Revised Technical Vocabulary," *Technology and Culture*, 16 (1975), pp. 539-49, and p. 547 for the chart.

7. Johnson, *Late Roman Fortifications*, pp. 31-54; R. M. Butler, "Late Roman Town Walls in Gaul," *Archaeological Journal*, 116 (1959), pp. 25-50.

8. Johnson, *Late Roman Fortifications*, pp. 38-44.

9. See, for example, Bachrach, "Early Medieval Fortifications," pp. 44-45.

10. Greg., *Hist.*, Bk. VI, chs. 11, 19; Bk. IX, ch. 31 (*Gregorii episcopi Turonensis, Libri Historiarum*, ed. B Krusch and W. Levison, *Monumenta Germania Historica, Scriptores rerum Merovingicarum* [Hannover: 1951], I.1), provides some useful examples.

11. Despite the important pioneering work of Helen Cam, *Local Government in Francia and England* (London: 1912), this subject has not received the attention it deserves.

12. Cassiodorus, *Variae*, Bk. I, chs. 28, 13, respectively (ed. Th. Mommsen, *Monumenta Germania Historica, Auctores Antiquissimi* [Berlin: 1894], XI); and Vegetius, *De re militari*, ed. Carl Lang (Leipzig: 1885), Bk. IV, *praef.*

13. Cassiodorus, *Variae*, Bk. I, ch. 25.

14. *Ibid.*, Bk. I, ch. 28; Bk. II, ch. 7; Bk. III, ch. 44, respectively.

15. Greg. *Hist.*, Bk. VI, ch. 41.

16. *Ibid.*, ch. 26.

17. *Ibid.*

18. For example, this topic is virtually ignored by Contamine, *War in the Middle Ages*, pp. 3-29, and the bibliography pp. 317-19. See, however, *Mappae Clavicula: A Little Key to the World of Medieval Techniques*, eds. Cyril Smith and John Hawthorne in Transactions of the American Philosophical Society (1974), pp. 68-70, concerning lead arrows for setting fire, fire arrows, battering rams, various types of incendiary mixtures, and anti-incendiary measures.

19. Greg. *Hist.*, Bk. III, ch. 19; Johnson, *Late Roman Fortifications*, pp. 84-86, with a diagram.

20. Greg. *Hist.*, Bk. III, ch. 13; note how this echoes Vegetius, *De re militari*, Bk. IV, ch. 1, regarding the distinctions between natural and manmade defenses. Gregory's description goes on to emphasize many of the characteristics for an effective fortification as enumerated by Vegetius, Bk. IV, chs. 2-8 *passim*. Cf. Ross Samson, "The Merovingian Nobleman's Home: Castle or Villa?" *Journal of Medieval History*, 13 (1987), p. 293.

21. *Vita Desiderii Cadurcae urbis episcopi*, chs. 9, 16-17, ed. B. Krusch, *Monumenta Germania Historica: Scriptores rerum Merovingicarum*, 4 (Hannover and Leipzig: 1902). For the role of the bishop as a government official see Jean Durliat, "Les attributions civiles des éveques mérovingiens: l'example de Didier éveque de Cahors (630-655)," *Annales du Midi*, 91 (1979), pp. 237-54.

22. *Asser's Life of King Alfred*, ed. W. H. Stevenson (Oxford: 1904), ch. 91. Note the similarity to Vegetius, *De re militari*, Bk. IV, ch. 1, while praising the emperor. Of great value is the commentary and translations of Asser by Simon Keynes and Michael Lapidge, *Alfred the Great: Asser's Life of King Alfred and Other Contemporary Sources* (London: 1983), pp. 223-75.

23. Bernard S. Bachrach and Rutherford Aris, "Military Technology and Garrison Organization: Some Observations on Anglo-Saxon Military Thinking in Light of the

Burghal Hidage," *Technology and Culture,* 31 (1990), pp. 3-4, with the literature cited there.

24. Richard Abels, *Lordship and Military Obligation in Anglo-Saxon England* (Berkeley-Los Angeles: 1988), p. 71.

25. An edition and translation of the Burghal Hidage is provided by A.J. Robinson, ed., *Anglo-Saxon Charters* (Cambridge: 1934), pp. 246-9. Also useful is D. Hill, "The Burghal Hidage: The Establishment of a Text," *Medieval Archaeology,* 13 (1969), pp. 84-92; with the general observations of Patrick Wormald, "The Ninth Century," in *The Anglo-Saxons,* ed. James Campbell (Ithaca, N.Y.: 1982), pp. 152-53. Bachrach and Aris, "Military Technology and Garrison Organization," pp. 1-17.

26. Bernard S. Bachrach, "Animals and Warfare in Early Medieval Europe," *Settimane di Studio del Centro Italiano di sull'alto medioevo* (Spoleto: 1985), XXXI, pp. 716-26; and Bernard S. Bachrach, "Charlemagne's Cavalry: Myth and Reality," *Military Affairs,* 47 (1983), pp. 181-87.

27. For Vegetius' views see *De re militari,* Bk. III, ch. 8, and the discussion by Bernard S. Bachrach, "The Practical Use of Vegetius' *De re militari* during the early Middle Ages," *The Historian,* 47 (1985), pp. 239-54. For Bede's knowledge and use of Vegetius see Charles W. Jones, "Bede and Vegetius," *Classical Review* 46 (1932), pp. 248-49..

28. D. Schafer, "Die *agrarii milites* des Widukind," *Sitzungsberichte der königlich preussischen Akademie der Wissenschaften,* xxvii (1905), pp. 569-77; E. Sander, "Die Heeresorganisation Heinrichs I," *Historisches Jahrbuch,* lix (1939), pp. 1-26; Karl Leyser, *Medieval Germany and its Neighbours, 900-1250* (London: 1982), pp. 11-42, where the military organization is reviewed with an emphasis on the development of cavalry but no apparent effort to connect this with the strategic hard points of the burgs is made. Concerning the latter, see especially pp. 15-21. Much work remains to be done on this very controversial topic and it is hoped that my doctoral student, Mr. Edward Schoenfeld, will solve some of the outstanding problems in his forthcoming Ph.D. dissertation on Saxon military organization.

29. *Die Sachsengeschichte des Widukind von Korvei,* I, 35, eds. H.-E. Lohmann and P. Hirsch, *Scriptores Rerum Germanicarum* (Hannover: 1935).

30. For the Anglo-Saxons see Abels, *Lordship and Military Obligation,* pp. 69-79. For general introductory purposes see Leyser, *Medieval Germany,* pp. 103-37; and on more specific topics see *Occident et Orient au Xe siècle. Actes du IXe congrès de la Société des Historiens médiévistes de l'Enseignement supérieur Publique,* Dijon, 2-4 juin 1978, Publications de l'Université de Dijon, 57 (Paris: 1979). Concerning the Byzantine military see Arnold Toynbee, *Constantine Porphyrogenitus and His World* (London: 1973), pp. 224-322; cf. John Haldon, *Recruitment and Conscription in the Byzantine Army, ca. 550-950* (Vienna: 1979). Alexander C. Murray, "From Roman to Frankish Gaul: 'Centenarii' and 'Centenae' in the Administration of the Merovingian Kingdom," *Traditio,* 44 (1988), pp. 59-100, is of importance here, but the full consequences of his observations have yet to be established.

31. Bernard S. Bachrach, "The Cost of Castle Building: The Case of the Tower at Langeais, 992-994," *The Medieval Castle: Romance and Reality,* ed. K. Reyerson and F. Powe (Dubuque: 1984), pp. 46-62 For background see Bernard S. Bachrach, "Angevin Campaign Forces in the Reign of Fulk Nerra, Count of the Angevins (987-1040)," *Francia* 16.1. (1989, appeared 1990), pp. 67-84; Bernard S. Bachrach, "The Angevin Economy, 960-1060: Ancient or Feudal?" *Studies in Medieval and Renaissance History*:

ser. 2, 10 (Vancouver: 1988), pp. 3-55; Bernard S. Bachrach, "Neo-Roman vs. Feudal, the Heuristic Value of a Construct for the Reign of Fulk Nerra, Count of the Angevins (987-1040)," *Cithara*, 30 (1990), pp. 3-30; and Bernard S. Bachrach, "Geoffrey Greymantle, Count of the Angevins (960-987): A Study in French Politics," *Studies in Medieval and Renaissance History*, ser. 2, 7 (Vancouver: 1985), pp. 3-67, esp. pp. 19-20.

32. Bachrach, "The Cost of Castle Building," pp. 51-52. cf. Charlemagne's canal and William of Normandy's encampment discussed below.

33. *Ibid.*

34. Bachrach, "Angevin Campaign Forces," pp. 73-79.

35. Bede, *Eccl. Hist.*, Bk. I, ch. 12 [*Bede's Ecclesiastical History of the English People*, ed. Bertram Colgrave (trans, hist. intro. and notes) and R.A.B. Mynors (Latin text) (Oxford: 1969)]. The reader will take note of some differences in my translation.

36. *Ibid.*

37. James Graham-Campbell, *The Viking World* (New York: 1980), pp. 208-9. This monumental military architecture built in northern Europe should not be thought to have been lacking in Roman influence. One may note, for example, that the great Viking camps of the later tenth and early eleventh centuries were surveyed according to measurements by the Roman foot. See, for example, Peter Sawyer, *The Age of the Vikings*, 2nd ed. (New York: 1972), pp. 132-35.

38. *Life of Alfred*, Bk. I, ch. 12.

39. Cyril Fox, *Offa's Dyke* (London: 1955), has now been substantially undermined by a series of articles authored by David Hill, "The Inter-Relation of Offa's and Wat's Dyke," *Antiquity*, 48 (1974), pp. 309-12; "Offa's and Wat's Dykes: Some Aspects of Recent Work," *Transactions of the Lancashire and Cheshire Antiquarian Society*, 79 (1977), pp. 21-33; and "The Construction of Offa's Dyke," *Antiquaries Journal*, 65 (1985), pp. 140-42. A good general treatment is to be found in Patrick Wormald, "The Age of Offa and Alcuin," in *The Anglo-Saxons*, ed. James Campbell (New York: 1982), pp. 120-21.

40. A basic review of the literature accompanied by improved calculations is provided by Hans Hubert Hofmann, "*Fossa Carolina* Versuch Einer Zussammenschau," in *Karl der Grosse*, Helmut Beumann, ed. (Dusseldorf: 1965), 1:437-33.

41. *Ibid.*, pp. 444-46.

42. *Ibid.*, pp. 449-51.

43. Many of those influenced by anthropologists have focussed on legal history as, for example, Steven White, *Custom, Kinship, and Gifts to Saints* (Chapel Hill: 1988). In this context the failure to give due weight to the written culture of the West is of paramount importance. See below note 50. With regard to the scruffiness of "feudal society" see the highly tendentious and often simply misguided efforts (especially his abuse of archaeological evidence) by Robert Fossier as discussed by Bachrach, "Neo-Roman vs. Feudal," pp. 18-20.

44. A basic and vital study is Rosamond McKitterick, *The Carolingians and the Written Word*, (Cambridge: 1989). Regarding the use of books see Bachrach, "The Practical Use of Vegetius' *De re militari*," pp. 239-54; and cf. Alexander Murray, *Reason and Society in the Middle Ages* (Oxford: 1986 corrected), pp. 110-37, who unfortunately seems to believe that the 12th century was the beginning of something new in the West in this context.

45. Two useful recent studies on the topic are John Percival, "The Precursors of Domesday: Roman and Carolingian Land Registers," in *Domesday Book: A Reassess-*

ment, ed. Peter Sawyer (London: 1985), pp. 5-27; and R.H.C. Davis, "Domesday Book; Continental Parallels," in *Domesday Studies: Papers Read at the Novocentenary Conference of the Royal Historical Society and the Institute of British Geographers, Winchester 1986*, ed. J. C. Holt (Woodbridge: 1987), pp. 15-39. It is Davis (p. 15) who calls attention to the citation from Luke. It is necessary that we recognize that all of the "models" for government, the military, and other aspects of "ancient" ways of "doing business" were part of the reality with which the people of the Middle Ages lived on a daily basis.

46. See *Miracula Martini Abbatis Vertavensis*, ch. 7, ed. Bruno Krusch, in *Monumenta Germania Historica, Scriptores rerum Merovingicarum*, 3 (Hannover: 1896). Bernard S. Bachrach, "Fulk Nerra's Exploitation of the *Facultates Monachorum* ca. 1000," in *Law, Custom, and the Social Fabric in Medieval Europe: Essays in Honor of Bryce Lyon*, ed. Bernard S. Bachrach and David M. Nicholas (Kalamazoo: 1990), pp. 29-49, where this text is described in detail. Thomas Head, *Hagiography and the Cult of Saints: The Diocese of Orléans, 800-1200* (Cambridge: 1990), pp. 217-26, strengthens the case for the view that Letaldus of Micy was working from an authentic Merovingian text but does not weaken the case for Fulk Nerra's activities.

47. *Annales Guelferbytani, an.* 751; *Annales Alamanici, an.* 751; and *Annales Nazariani, an.* 751 all in *Monumenta Germania Histocica, Scriptores*, ed. G. Pertz (Hannover: 1826); and Davis, *Domesday Book*, pp. 18, 30.

48. "The Statistical Sources of Frankish History," *American Historical Review*, 40 (1935), pp. 635-45, was a pioneering study which relied heavily on German scholarship of a particularistic orientation. Unfortunately, Thompson's work has been largely forgotten as evidenced by its absence from the articles cited above in note 46.

49. Regarding parchment see McKitterick, *The Carolingians and the Written Word*, pp. 138-41; and concerning the severe time limitations on such documents see Bernard S. Bachrach, "Some Observations on the Military Administration of the Norman Conquest." *Anglo-Norman Studies*, ed. R. Allen Brown, VIII (Woodbridge: 1985), pp. 19-21.

50. Auguste Longnon, *Polyptyque de l'Abbaye de Saint-Germain-des-Près* (Paris: 1886-1895), 2 vols. For the general background on these documents see Robert Fossier, *Polyptyques et Censiers* (Turnhout, Belgium: 1978), which unfortunately is severely flawed as made clear by Walter Goffart, "Merovingian Polyptychs: Reflections on Two Recent Publications," *Francia*, 9 (1982), pp. 55-87.

51. See, for example, the excellent discussion by Jean Durliat, "Le polyptyque d'Irminon et l'impot pour l'armée," *Bibliothèque de l'Ecole des Chartes*, 141 (1984), pp. 183-201.

52. Hincmar, *De Ecclesiis et Capellis*, ed. W. Gundlach in *Zeitschrift für Kirchengeschichte*, 10 (1989), p. 135, where the share going to the fighting men denoted as casati is put at one-fifth of the total. However, Janet Nelson, "The Church's Military Service in the Ninth Century: A Contemporary Comparative View?" *Studies in Church History*, 20 (1983), p. 124, makes a good case for the total military obligation of the church as much closer to two-fifths.

53. *Annales de Saint Bertin*, ed. Felix Grat, et al. (Paris: 1964), an. 869.

54. *Gesta abbatum Fontanellensium*, 45, ed. S. Loewenfeld [*Monumenta Germania Historica, Scriptores rerum Germanicarum* (Hannover: 1886)]. See also Davis, *Domesday Book*, p. 31.

55. *Annales de Saint Bertin*, an. 869.

56. *Ibid.*, an. 869.

57. Bernard S. Bachrach, "Charlemagne's Cavalry: Myth and Reality," *Military Affairs*, 47 (1983), p. 181, n. 1, provides a substantial bibliography. I am currently working on a monograph tentatively entitled "Charlemagne and the Armies of the Carolingian Empire."

58. *Cap. reg. Francorum*, ed. Boretius, no 75.

59. Bachrach, "Animals and Warfare," pp. 716-26.

60. The best study remains F. L. Ganshof, *Frankish Institutions Under Charlemagne*, ed. and trans. Bryce and Mary Lyon (Providence: 1968), pp. 59-68, 151-161, but much work is required.

61. See, above, note 59.

62. Ganshof, *Frankish Institutions*, pp. 154-55, nn. 14-19, provides a list of documentary references. Ganshof's interpretation of these requires revision.

63. Bachrach, "Animals and Warfare," pp. 716-26.

64. *Cap. reg. Francorum*, ed. Boretius, no. 75.

65. Ganshof, *Frankish Institutions*, pp. 160-61, nn. 64-73, provides references to the relevant texts.

66. Bachrach, "Animals and Warfare," pp. 716-23.

67. The treatment of military numbers for this period has been revolutionized by K.F. Werner, "Heeresorganisation und Kriegsführung im Deutschen Königreich des 10. und 11. Jahrhunderts," *Settimane di Studio del Centro Italiano sull' alto Medioevo*, 15 (Spoleto: 1968), pp. 791-843, which also treats the Carolingians in detail. Werner's arguments have been accepted by Contamine, *War in the Middle Ages*, p. 25; and by Bachrach, "Angevin Campaign Forces," pp. 72-73, with some upward revisions.

68. Bachrach, "Military Administration of the Norman Conquest," pp. 2-5.

69. Bernard S. Bachrach, "On the Origins of William the Conqueror's Horse Transports," *Technology and Culture*, 26 (1985), 510-17; 521-31. *Les oeuvres poétiques de Baudri de Bourgueil (1046-1130)*, ed. Phyllis Abrahams (Paris: 1926), lines 335-6.

70. Bernard S. Bachrach, "On the Origins of William the Conqueror's Horse Transports," *Technology and Culture*, 26 (1985), 505-31; and Bachrach, "The Military Administration of the Norman Conquest," pp. 1-25.

71. Bachrach, "The Military Administration of the Norman Conquest," pp. 11-18, where unfortunately some errors of arithmetic were made. These have been corrected above. R.H.C. Davis, "The Warhorses of the Normans," in *Anglo-Norman Studies*, ed. R. Allen Brown, X (Woodbridge: 1988), p. 80, noted some of these errors but his own arithmetic introduced additional errors. See also R.H.C. Davis, *The Medieval War Horse* (London: 1989), p. 79. This book introduces some new and useful information based upon the study of wild horses but unfortunately repeats too many old errors as well. See my review in *Journal of International History*, XIII (1991), pp. 347-48. Although John Gillingham, "William the Bastard at War," *Studies Presented to R. Allen Brown*, ed. Christopher Harper-Bill, Christopher Holdsworth and Janet Nelson (Woodbridge: 1989), p. 156, would seem to have reservations regarding my reconstruction of the logistics on various points of detail, he observes "on the general point, he must be absolutely right."

5

Naval Logistics in the Late Middle Ages: The Example of the Hundred Years' War

Timothy J. Runyan

The conflict between England and France which we know as the Hundred Years' War dominates the political and military history of late medieval Europe. This epic struggle resulted from a complex combination of factors focused around the dynastic claim to the French throne by England's King Edward III and the attempts of the Valois monarchs, whom the English regarded as usurpers, to control France and prevent the union of the two thrones by conquest. While the roots of the conflict extend to an earlier age, the war began in 1337 and continued until 1453. Before its conclusion, most of the other states of western Europe became involved, and Spain actually served as a theater of conflict. Because the struggle was waged primarily on the Continent, English fleets faced the formidable task of transporting and disembarking thousands of knights, squires, archers, soldiers, and support personnel for over a century. Indeed, a key factor in the success or failure of these assaults was the naval and logistical support provided by the English navy to its army. Thus, the experience of the English in the Hundred Years' War provides a good illustration of naval logistics in late medieval warfare.

Assembling a Fleet

Obviously, the English king had to have a fleet in order to transport the men and materiel necessary to fight a cross-Channel war. Tradition enabled the monarch to requisition ships and sailors for service in the same way that he was able to call soldiers to his command. The soldiers were summoned by feudal levy, by calling up the *fyrd,* through hired military service as mercenaries, or through the later contractual system of indenture.[1] While these systems were in general use for the army and occasionally for the navy, sailors were often recruited in a less formalized manner. Throughout the fourteenth century, the king's sergeants-at-arms traveled about the kingdom with commissions to arrest and take for military service men and ships from the various ports they were assigned to visit. Ships within the specified tonnage and approved as seaworthy were taken into the king's hand by the sergeants for royal duty.[2] No limit was set on the period of arrest, but the wages of the mariners and captains were paid by the crown at standard rates.[3] The wages were not unreasonable, although the loss of profits in freight by a ship which was removed from commercial service made the loss much greater to the owners of the vessel as well as to the masters and mariners who generally benefited from the safe delivery of the cargo and their share of the profits.

Along with these general commissions of arrest which applied to the kingdom at large were the contributions made to the raising of the fleets by the Cinque Ports.[4] This ancient confederation originally consisted of Hastings, Romney, Hythe, Dover, and Sandwich. These "head ports" were the original chartered seaports which were provided with liberties and exemptions from various taxes and obligations in return for their provision of ships and men for royal service. At various times throughout the period, these original five ports absorbed as associate members over thirty separate maritime communities. The best known of these are the ports of Winchelsea and Rye, which had become attached to Hastings before 1190. The portsmen were an important part of the commercial and military fabric of the realm and behaved as a political unit in defense of their common privileges.

The arrangement between the crown and the Cinque Ports was that the latter would provide fifty-seven ships for fifteen days service annually. The ships were fully manned and equipped for military service. The Cinque Ports exchanged their services for royal liberties allowing them freedom from tolls, port customs, suit to the shire and hundred, jury duty, and the grant of certain special favors. The extent of these liberties shows that the crown anticipated considerable returns in assistance when it called upon the portsmen. It also reflects the extent to which the monarchy would go to secure a fleet capable of transporting the instruments of war across the Channel.[5]

The liberties enjoyed by the Cinque Ports and the reciprocal benefits which were provided to the king contributed a considerable amount to the fighting force at sea. However, the limitations of time, service, and numbers meant that the king had to look beyond the Cinque Ports in order to be assured of a fleet at sea on a more regular basis. Once the ports completed their annual required service, the king was forced to work out an arrangement *eo tempore* for their continued military service. In the periods of protracted war with the French and their Castilian allies, both on land and at sea, this meant the utilization of all of the ports and shipping of the realm to maintain a standing national fleet that could carry the war to the enemy.

The core of a king's fleet existed before the demands of the Hundred Years' War required a royal navy. As early as the thirteenth century there were royal clerks in charge of the king's ships (*naves regis*). Richard the Lion Heart probably left John the nucleus of a fleet, the remnant of his crusading ventures. He seems to have taken a considerable interest in shipping while active in the east on the Crusades, although he is surely not the author of the famous Laws of Oléron, a set of maritime regulations supposedly brought by Richard from the East to become the basis of maritime law on the Atlantic coast. Nevertheless, there was a greater amount of naval activity in the thirteenth century, and the creation of an administrator to supervise the king's ships clearly attests to this. The keeper of the king's ports and galleys, later known as the clerk of the king's ships, was the first administrator of the embryonic English navy, and the records of these clerks help to explain the logistical demands of fighting the Hundred Years' War.[6]

Final responsibility for the navy was entrusted to the king's admirals. An early reference to this office is found in a Gascon Roll of 1295, which describes a certain Bernard de Sestas as admiral of the Bayonne fleet and captain of its ships and mariners.[7] Over the next few years the term reappeared, and by 1303 the explicit reference to Gervase Alard as *admirallus flote nostre navium* was the most unqualified reference to an admiral.[8] Even though the title was in use, we cannot proceed to the assumption that all of the attendant powers of an admiralty were in existence. He was still only a *magister* or *capitaneus* in practice until the mid-fourteenth century. Only after the 1340s did the office become specialized to the point of pertaining only to naval service and acquire legal jurisdiction over all ships and men within the admiralty. An admiralty court was instituted to serve as the adjudicator of maritime disputes, and the powers of the admiral were expanded. The two or three admirals in charge of waters north, south, or west of the Thames were consolidated in 1360. John Pavely, prior of the Hospital of St. John of Jerusalem in England, became the forerunner of the Lord High Admiral by his appointment to the consolidated position of admiral of all of the king's fleets in that year.[9]

The duties of the admiral were spelled out in the early years of Edward's reign in a unique document—the *Fasciculus de Superioritate Maris*.[10] Drawn up in 1339 by three ecclesiastics, including the chronicler Adam Murimuth, the *Fasciculus* dealt with current piracy disputes with the French and Flemish, discussed the legal powers of the admirals and even constructed an argument to reinforce the English monarch's claim to be the sovereign of the seas. Neighboring France and Flanders did not think too much of these pretensions as sovereign of the waters they regularly plied, and the French suggested sarcastically in 1322 that those who claimed such broad powers ought to do a better job of enforcing them. For instance, when was justice going to be rendered for the latest case of English piracy on peaceful French merchantmen?[11] The issue was beyond debate after 1337 and the outbreak of the Hundred Years' War, but the *Fasciculus*, unsurprisingly, pushed forward English claims to a sovereignty of the seas. The idea never passed from the minds of Edward III or his citizens. In 1350 we find Parliament reasserting this dominion over the waters on behalf of Edward. A great victory at sea had been won (L'Espagnols sur Mer) and a consequence was the opportunity to reclaim a part of the royal domain and reaffirm that the seas were ruled by the English crown.[12]

What types of vessels were arrested for the royal fleet? Any ships fit for service in the royal expeditions were invariably sought out and arrested by the king's agents. They went after vessels in good condition and of the specified size (tonnage) demanded by the king's writ. Generally, the writs called for larger ships, those of a hundred tons or more. Later, if the large vessels were not forthcoming, the order might encompass all ships over fifty tons or even twenty.[13] Clearly, this depended upon the scale of the campaign and the success of the royal agents in arresting ships.

While this method enabled the king to assemble a fleet, both for fighting and for transport, crown dependence upon the merchants and their ships to serve as a royal navy was quite costly for the merchants involved. It can be argued that the shipowners did all right in turning their vessels over to the king. They were paid for the use of their ships, compensated for damages they sustained, and the crews were reasonably well paid—the masters at 6d. per day and the mariners at 3*d*. per day. But this is a hard case to prove. Compensation for damages incurred while in royal service was spotty, and whether the vessels ever came up to the original standard cannot be proved. In the Brittany campaign of 1341-43, for example, many ships were employed to carry troops and supplies. There were considerable losses due to the bad weather, and the king and council by their *"grante bonte and grace especiale"* made payment to the shipowners for damages. Within a nine-month period about £1,000 was paid to owners of forty-five ships.[14] The money was not distributed evenly; the three owners of the *Bartelmeu* of Fowey, for example, received £120 in 1344.[15] This was a great deal of money for the time, and we know that a galley of 120 oars could be built in 1294 for £205.[16] There are very few references to compensation paid for damages to ships while in royal service. Out of thousands of sailings by royal order, in the fourteenth century there were fewer than a hundred instances of compensation for damages and no examples of compensation to the owner of a ship which was either captured or destroyed.[17]

It is not surprising, then, that there were some who objected to this method of raising fleets and avoided the arrest orders. The only way to manage this was to avoid ports where agents were seeking ships for the king's service or to refuse the order (unless one already had an exemption). Refusal of the royal arrest order was a serious offense, and we cannot know how successful captains and owners may have been in avoiding ports where they might be arrested. Most shipowners and masters complied with the crown and allowed the arrest of their vessels. Others did the same but quit royal service the moment their assignment was completed. Some quit a little too early, and the king called this desertion.

What happened in several cases was that the shipowners submitted to impressment and carried the victuals or troops to the port of disembarkation and then bolted, usually for Gascony, to pick up a paying cargo for the return voyage to England. The most notable case was in 1342-43, when over two hundred ships left Edward III in France. The king faced hostile forces and had few ships left to ferry his armies home or to safety if things went badly for him. Edward was furious and issued orders for the arrest of the deserters and the confiscation of their ships.[18] Most of these orders were later canceled, since he needed the services of the ships and men.[19]

Nonetheless, it was a risky business for a shipowner to have his vessel taken into royal service. Naturally there were complaints, and a conference held in London in 1344 between the king and some merchants no doubt touched on this point.[20] Desertions occurred again in 1346, reflecting the failure of the crown to come to terms with this problem.[21] In spite of the flaws in the system, however, the king was not prepared to expend the resources necessary to build his own fleet. A mercantile fleet existed, and by ancient custom he had the right to use it. The cost to him was the cost of wages, victuals, tontight (payments to shipowners based on tonnage in the 1380s), and occasional compensation to shipowners for damages to vessels. Impressment of merchant vessels was much cheaper to the crown than the construction of ships from scratch and avoided the maintenance and storage problems which accompanied ownership. Nonetheless, tension continued between the crown and the shipowners and should make clear the further complexities of warfare at sea in an age before the organization of standing fleets.

Types of Ships

In spite of protests by shipowners, Edward III managed to assemble and operate a fleet during the first phase of the Hundred Years' War. A recent computer-assisted study of 1,291 English ships operating during this important phase of the war, 1337-1360, generated some interesting data about ships and mariners involved.[22] The list of vessels includes 965 which are not identified by type. The remainder are identified by type as follows: 1 buss, 2 flunes, 2 galiots, 2 hulks, 3 doggers, 3 lodships, 5 crayers, 5 spinaces, 6 galleys, 7 carracks, 12 barges, 12 nefs, 13 tarites, 19 boats, 46 ships, and 187 cogs. This last vessel, the very important cog, constitutes 57 percent of the 325 vessels identified by type. Working vessels such as barges only constitute 3.7 percent of those identified, and balingers are not even mentioned in this survey.[23]

A number of observations can be made about these numbers but nothing can detract from the impressive number of cogs which are noted here. The fourteenth century saw the emergence of the cog as the standard vessel for transport and war. Fortunately, a cog was recovered at Bremen, Germany, and is undergoing conservation. The Bremen cog is 23.5 meters long and seven meters in the beam and is rated at 130 tons. Cogs reached three hundred tons in the fourteenth century.[24] Few records of the building of these large single-masted vessels exist, but their regular occurrence in the records certainly indicates that many were constructed at this time.[25] The common use of the cog with its broad deck and high freeboard made unnecessary the addition of protective battlements if the ship was primarily intended to carry victuals, horses, or even troops, but not to fight at sea. Galleys represent an exception and deserve a special comment.

The long history of the use of galleys in the North extends back at least to Roman times. While the great sailing ships of the fifteenth and sixteenth centuries became the mainstays of the sea routes, galleys and other oared ships continued to be used in the North and by northerners abroad. One of the last great galley builders in medieval England was Edward I. In 1294, Edward ordered the port towns to construct twenty galleys for use in his war with the French. The towns were to pay for the construction of the galleys and then turn them over to the king.[26] This very ambitious project would have provided the crown with the maneuverable force it needed to oppose the French with their array of foreign allies and large fleet of galleys. In calms the galleys could be used to place the English in advantageous fighting positions. Edward was thinking war at that time because the galleys were not as useful to English merchants, who preferred larger cargo carriers dependent upon wind, not expensive oarsmen, for propulsion. Many of Edward's galleys were not completed, and accounts of construction exist for only eight of the twenty vessels. The crown built few ships, and from the late thirteenth century onward, a galley was a less preferable choice of ship to build.

Some observations about the nature of ship construction and design are appropriate. The construction of larger ships, those of four hundred tons and above, continued after *ca.* 1400 culminating in the *Gracedieu,* of about 1,400 tons, which was begun at Southampton in 1416.[27] There were problems with the large ships, as one might expect. Many ports and docks were unable to accommodate the huge vessels. In fact, it has been argued that by the late fifteenth century smaller ships of about two hundred tons or less were very popular and more useful than the larger vessels. This occurred not because of a decline in mercantile activity, but because of the greater accessibility and utility of the smaller vessels. Even the Dutch freighted smaller trading craft for most of their runs to the Baltic in the mid-sixteenth century. The average size was estimated at 170 tons. What becomes apparent is that the relative number of ships of about two hundred tons or less remained stable owing to their ability to maneuver in the harbor and dockyards, and because they were affordable. Many of the ships were owned by merchants, some by nobles, clergymen, or others. It is also true that ship design had altered enough so that the crown began to build ships of a strictly military character.[28]

It is generally assumed that when royal ships were not in service they were hired out to merchants to turn a profit, a share of which would be returned to the king. While this is perfectly reasonable, little evidence exists to confirm that this was the practice before the fifteenth century. Instead there are accounts of the king's ships laid up in Ratcliff or elsewhere to be refurbished or repaired and of the costs of storage with a skeleton crew.[29] Likewise, there is little evidence of lease contracts between merchants and the crown in the fourteenth century. If the king owned many galleys, the failure to find such leases would be understandable. But he did not, and this suggests that the practice of leasing royal ships to merchants was not employed as regularly as has been suspected. This also suggests that maintenance costs for a royal fleet were quite large, since the ships were not earning their keep but only serving the purposes of the crown.

There is more evidence of the leasing of royal ships during the fifteenth century. For example, William Catton, keeper of the king's ships, put out to hire most of the royal fleet in 1414. Ships were hired out to merchants who used them to carry wine from Bordeaux, to sail to Newcastle for coal and to Danzig for pitch, tar, and timber. The practice proved very lucrative and over £2,000 was earned on the freight charges.[30] Clearly it was advantageous to hire out the ships if such a large return could be generated and the risk of loss or damage could be tolerated. These ships paid for themselves and offset the dock charges that would have mounted up if they had stayed in port. The key factor in all of this, of course, is that there was very little hostility on the seas in 1413-14. When war erupted again and an expedition was launched in 1415 which ended at Agincourt, the navy was officially accounted for by the treasurer for war and not the clerk of the king's ships. Over £12,000 was released from the exchequer for the repair of ships and for men's wages.[31]

We should not be surprised that the king did not seem overly concerned with the economic advantages of his fleet during peacetime. The royal ships were the personal property of the monarch and their utilization was very much a matter of his personal whim. Perhaps the best expression of this is the fact that the royal fleets were sometimes sold off to pay the king's debts. The sale of ships in 1377 on Edward III's death and again in 1422 after the death of Henry V are examples of this practice. The arguments in King's Council in settling the will of Henry V do not suggest any concern for the safety of the realm as a consequence of the sale of the royal fleet. Perhaps the Council assumed that sufficient ships could be arrested if needed by royal right and that the security of the state was thus not imperiled by the sale. They did keep six of the largest and most useful ships as the nucleus of a fleet, including the huge *Jesus, Holyghost, Trinity Royal,* and *Gracedieu.* The *Gracedieu* was lost in the Hamble River where she was struck by lightening and burned in 1439.[32] Her remaining timbers can still be examined at very low tides.

Thus, the crown had little need to build ships or to maintain a fleet since, as we have seen, it could depend upon the mercantile fleet to be available for conversion to military duty. While such a conversion is impossible in the modern navy, it was practicable in the fourteenth century because of the purpose for which ships were required and the materials needed for their construction. The single-masted merchantmen could be converted to military use simply by some extensive carpentry work. The cost of refitting and carpentry work necessary to make a mercantile vessel fit for war was modest in most instances, and not all ships were fitted out with castles fore and aft to serve as fighting platforms. The addition of castles atop the mainmast and on the fore and rear decks completed the basic requirements. Since naval battles usually turned out to be land battles fought at sea, there was no great problem in equipping the vessels for war.[33] The use of cannon would require additional restructuring of the ship, but though available, they were not adopted at sea for some time. Bows, arrows, lances, fine swords, and heavy objects dropped from the top-castles were the usual weapons.

Most ships used for naval operations and transport, then, were impressed merchant ships which may or may not have been refitted for service. In fact, of the 1,291 ship entries noted in the study above, only thirty-one are identified as "king's ships"—vessels purpose-built for warfare with fore- and rear-castles and fighting tops. Some 98 percent of the vessels were privately owned and were no doubt refitted for war at sea, undergoing extensive carpentry work to make them fit as horse and troop transports or men-of-war, as indicated by exchequer accounts in the Public Records Office, where notice of payments to ship carpenters is made. Most entries, however, are for the repair and refitting of vessels already designated as king's ships.

A final observation drawn from the ship survey of nearly 1,300 vessels concerns the home ports of the vessels. The survey was broken down into home ports and from this the number of vessels from individual ports or regions can be analyzed. In this instance only a few comments are relevant to the conduct of the war. Most noticeable is the clear emergence of ports from north of the Thames to the Humber and the southwestern coastal towns as important suppliers of ships for trade and war. Registrations from the principal members of the Cinque Ports (Dover, Romney, Hythe, Hastings, and Sandwich) produced only eighteen ships, twelve of which were from Sandwich. Other members, Rye with ten ships and Winchelsea with thirty-two, clearly rank with or above their associates. London listed thirty-five vessels.

In the survey of 1,291 entries, the number of English vessels whose home ports are noted has been reduced to 467 for comparative purposes. Of the 1,291 vessel entries, 316 are not identified by home port and 271 are foreign vessels. Also, home ports which listed only one or two vessels were removed from the survey (237 vessel entries), leaving the number of vessels at 467. This is an arbitrary selection but one which helps allow a relative comparison of the home ports of the ships.

The home port from the southwestern coast with the largest number of references was Dartmouth with seventy-one. Bristol provided twenty-nine vessels, Southampton twenty-two, Fowey fourteen, and Exmouth nine. Plymouth supplied eight, and dozens of smaller ports added vessels. This survey of the larger southwestern ports provides a count of 153 vessels. This is 153 of the 467 English ships listed from home ports which contributed 3 or more vessels. It represents 33 percent of the total.

On the North Sea coast along East Anglia to the Humber, Great Yarmouth provided fifty ship references, the largest number from one single port (although some few of these may refer to Yarmouth on the Isle of Wight). King's Lynn accounted for thirty vessels, Kingston-upon-Hull twenty-nine, Ipswich eighteen, Little Yarmouth another four, and Harwich eleven. This sample totals 142 ship listings. These 142 vessels coupled with the 153 from the southwest coast total 295 of the 467 listed, or 63 percent of the total. A large portion of the remainder come from small ports which supplied only a few vessels each.

A number of conclusions may be drawn from this data, but of particular note is the large number of ships from the Southwest and from along the coast between the Thames and the Humber. While these regions are adjacent to London and the Cinque Ports, they clearly overshadow both in the number of registrations of vessels. Recruitment of ships for war would obviously need to concentrate heavily in these regions. In fact, many of the corresponding entries for the king's sergeants-at-arms sent to impress ships for royal use are directed to these coastal regions, but no systematic study of their activities in this regard has been made. But since, as we have seen, only thirty-one vessels of nearly 1,300 surveyed are identified as king's ships, there was a constant need by the crown to find and arrest ships for naval service.[34]

The attention given to the identification and preparation of fleets is justified because of the need to understand how fleets were assembled for expeditions to France and elsewhere. The use of merchant vessels in the conduct of war came at a price to the commercial interests of the crown and the merchants, since the ships were removed from commercial use for long periods of time. The king's alternatives were to hire a mercenary fleet, as the French did, or to build and man a standing navy of considerable size. Neither option was acceptable. This returns us to the earlier discussion of the composition of English fleets in the war.[35]

Manning the Fleet

If we may turn from the question of ship types to the question of manning and the impressment of shipping, a few comments are in order. The first recorded minutes of the Proceedings of the King's Council in 1337 were on the subject of the arrest of shipping. Admiral Sir John Roos was to survey all ships arrested for the King's service from the Thames northward and to get them to Orwell. He was to certify in chancery the number of ships over thirty tons and the number of men they required for double shipment (double complements of soldiers and sailors), together with a list of the ship's names and masters.[36] While this action in the first year of the Hundred Year's War may not seem all that significant, other events of Roos' admiralty and this period are significant and shed light on the preparation of fleets for war.

While arrest orders for ships were effective and fleets were quickly raised in 1337 and after, the arrest of mariners provided some problems. Early in June of 1336 there was a "mutiny," or at least a refusal to work, by mariners impressed in Wales to serve the king. They refused to sail unless paid in advance, indicating clearly that there were problems in receiving wages while in royal service. The crown's response was that there was no precedent for this but that a subsidy might be granted (and was), but *not* as wages. A deliberate effort was made to avoid the establishment of a precedent.[37]

In 1337 it became increasingly difficult to arrest men for royal expeditions. Admiral Roos issued orders for the arrest of a man who was ordered to equip himself as a man-at-arms and to be at Orwell on the appointed date or face imprisonment as a rebel—not an unusual sort of order save that in this case the man turned out to be an attorney. No doubt in "shock," the lawyer immediately fired off a petition to the crown claiming that he owned no land or tenement and had never borne arms before. He described himself as "un apprentiz de la court de la nostre seigneur le roy et attorne" and further claimed that his clients would suffer by his absence (in fact, the way he put it, their injury arose from his being an attorney). The king considered the matter and ordered the admiral to cancel the summons.[38]

The cancellation of the summons was not an unjustified special favor given to a man of the law. Men were frequently impressed for no good reason. However, men were not normally impressed for sea duty unless they had some maritime experience or were from a port town. In May of 1336 the impressment of men in Norwich was stopped on their appeal because Norwich was not a maritime town.[39] There are other instances when men with no maritime experience were taken and later executed by royal writ. There are also suggestions that some men bought their way out of service once impressed. In 1314 two masters with orders to bring twenty-eight ships to the king for his campaign in Scotland were upbraided for having wasted time, purveying victuals that they did not pay for, indiscriminately signing on men of no sailing experience, and receiving fines from those who did not want to make the journey.[40]

Protection of the population from such abuses took no organized form, although some benefits may have resulted from the complaints of merchants through Parliament. The Commons represented the shipowners in the 1370s on several occasions. In 1373 the shipowners petitioned the king that the lengthy arrest of shipping was injurious to shipowners who wanted and should receive payment from the time of the arrest until the end of royal service rather than only during the period of actual service. All too frequently they claimed that ships were arrested months in advance of a royal expedition and that this prevented them from carrying on any trading activity. The response was that the king would only take ships when needed and that payments would be made as usual. The Commons then petitioned that shipowners be compensated for rigging and stores expended in royal services as had been ordered in Parliament four years earlier. The king denied that such a pledge had been granted.

One could go on enumerating the many cases of conflict involving men and ships over their service to the crown. In the end the ancient privileges of arrest and impressment were maintained with little change. Ships continued to be arrested on a large scale and converted to naval use by making the necessary changes to the vessels. Also, the men continued to be gathered from wherever they could be found by the arresting officials—admirals, masters, clerks, sergeants-at-arms, or other deputies. The ships were arrested and seized (*arrestandis et capiendis*, the manuscripts state) and the most able mariners were elected (*eligendis*) for service. The necessary quota of men was found, and double shipments were recruited for the expeditions. The system was not without its problems as we have noted, but it did prove a satisfactory alternative to the creation of a large standing navy owned and maintained by the crown.[41] The Commons did make some impact on the process by its attacks on purveyance and in the institution of the Navigation Acts in the 1380s. But these alterations were slight. The wholesale selling of the royal fleet in 1377 and again in 1422 emphasizes the dependence of the monarchy upon the merchant marine. Indeed, galleys and barges aside, merchantmen were the English men-of-war until the use of cannon demanded the construction of purpose-built ships.

Merchantmen as Transport Ships

Merchant ships also served in an important logistical capacity as troop carriers and victuallers of armies operating abroad. No real conversion was necessary to put them into service, save the construction of stalls to hold the horses ferried across in great quantities for use by the knights. Warfare in the age of chivalry required the transport of horses and armor as well knights and squires. This was not a new feature of medieval warfare. However, the English fighting in France also faced the element of amphibious operations, where ships served as landing or attack craft as well as transports.

A much earlier instance of mounted warriors charging directly from ships is recorded in accounts of an amphibious assault on Crete in 960. The troops rode their horses directly onto the beach using landing ramps. The Muslim defenders were startled by this tactic. An estimated four hundred ships took part in the maneuver, and if that is true, then several thousand horses were involved.[42] In 1061, the Normans invaded Muslim Sicily from Calabria in *nefs* (ships of no specified type) with 440 knights and as many as twenty-one horses per ship. The assault on Byzantium in the Fourth Crusade included unloading horses through hatches in the hulls of ships.[43] Galleys were best suited to this maneuver because of their shallow draft and oar power, which allowed controlled beaching.

The transport of horses by ship also meant added administrative work. Since compensation was promised by the crown for horses lost or killed in the war, each animal was appraised by a military leader and a royal official. Compensation was based on this appraisal.[44]

Loading horses onto a ship was a difficult matter. Many types of ships were used during the fourteenth and fifteenth century. Large sailing vessels such as cogs with their high freeboard (the distance from the top of the hull to the water line) created special problems. Horses could not be loaded directly onto the main deck save by special docking facilities, or unloaded at a port that lacked them. Holes cut in the hull acted as doorways approached by special gangways made for the loading or unloading. Some gangways were thirty feet long and five feet wide, but most were fifteen to twenty feet in length. If we note that in theory each knight had four horses, each squire three and every mounted archer two, we can quickly grasp the transport problem.

While a number of solutions could be employed to load and unload horses, the best option was to use ships altered to accommodate horses with appropriate gangways. For every crossing, hurdles of about seven feet by four feet were constructed to form stalls used to separate the horses. Boards, racks, ropes, canvas, metal rings, nails, and large empty wooden tuns were also used for this purpose.[45]

Horses were difficult to transport by sea partly because ships needed to be purpose-built or altered to accommodate them, but also because of their dietary needs and the physical strain they suffered. It was not customary to ship horses by water in the Mediterranean before 1123. When they were shipped, it was essential that the animals had fresh drinking water. But even with food and water, horses did not always travel well, as Richard the Lion Heart discovered on the Third Crusade. His *destriers* reached Cyprus after a month at sea without once lying down. They were prevented from doing so by canvas slings fixed under their stomachs to protect them. As a result, when they disembarked the horses were so stiff and dizzy it took a season for them to recover.[46] Problems of transport doubtless encouraged some men-at-arms to arrange for the purchase of horses after they crossed the Channel. Horses were purchased on arrival for the Black Prince's expedition to Gascony in 1355. Those who purchased horses abroad had them appraised and marked by the constable of Bordeaux so that they might claim compensation in case of loss.

The Problem of Supply

Compounding the problems associated with acquiring and transporting horses during a cross-Channel war was the equally pressing need to acquire and transport supplies and victuals. English harbors were frequently crowded with ships preparing for military expeditions, while the adjacent towns were swollen with mariners, soldiers, and others preparing to depart. The burden on the port towns was considerable, but so was the opportunity. Profits rolled in while the value and importance of the town grew. The most common complaint by shipowners and merchants was the lengthy delays before an expedition was under way.

As with horses, supplies and victuals were sometimes obtained after the army arrived in enemy territory. In large measure the principle that an army must live off the land applied. An English army in France, Spain, or elsewhere could not depend entirely upon the supply link back to the home country to provide food and other needed provisions. Daily supplies were collected from the local population by force if in hostile territory and by payment if in friendly territory. Since the local farmers and residents usually had no love for the invading army in either case, men were sent out to seize or pay for needed victuals. This required not only an organized body of men to do this work on a daily basis, but also the men, horses, carts, and wagons needed to transport the victuals to the camps.

For the most part, however, supplies were gathered at home through a practice known as purveyance and transported to the army by sea. Purveyors were men sent out by the crown to purchase victuals and equipment needed for royal purposes, including military expeditions. They were appointed by letters patent explaining what they were charged to do and the source from which payment would be made on goods purveyed. Their advantage in the marketplace was the right to buy goods in advance of competing buyers. Purveyance was never popular, and the demands on the realm were often beyond the capacity of some areas to provide. Sometimes this difficulty was acknowledged. When Rutland's representatives, for example, attested that they could not provide the victuals assessed them for the 1346 expedition, an understanding crown reduced their wheat quota by half.[47] Others complained that the sheriffs or their agents spared the rich in purveying victuals while the poor were compelled to pay.[48] A 1362 statute spelled out abuses in the system of purveyance, which was an unpopular practice in peacetime as well as during war.

In England, the sheriffs did much of the work in identifying victuals for military use. They also collected and sometimes transported supplies to a staging port or even directly abroad. To accomplish their task, the sheriffs or the receivers of victuals to whom they often surrendered their quotas needed men, containers, and transportation. Wooden tuns had to be purchased and transported to corn mills or elsewhere for loading. Goods sometimes had to be transported on wagons, but the placement of collection centers along navigable rivers and other waterways simplified the task of transporting supplies to points of embarkation. Hoists and other dockside equipment further simplified the work of collecting, warehousing, and dispensing the victuals as needed.

The supply of troops by sea became particularly important in the case of besieged port towns like Calais. Between 1347 and 1361 food was purveyed for the defense of the town. Estimates exceed £14,000 per year for the price of food alone. This is in addition to other goods carried by merchants and sold in Calais. The principal items purveyed for Calais were wheat, malt, oats, beans, peas, and beef and bacon carcasses. Because of its strategic importance, Calais was exempted from the occasional prohibitions on the export of corn from England. Merchants were regularly granted permission to transport corn, usually to Calais, and were promised prompt payment.[49]

The enterprise was so vast that for the 1346 campaign in Yorkshire alone ten mounted men were employed for fifteen days to purvey supplies, buy and collect victuals, and deliver tallies (promises of payment) or money to the suppliers. The supplies moved to Hull from seven collection points. Corn was ground at mills nearby, packed into eighty tuns, and moved to Hull. Seven men worked for eight days to provide the necessary transportation.[50] Similar efforts were routine at Yarmouth, London, Dover, and Sandwich, where troops frequently gathered for the crossing to France.

Control of the Channel

Assembling a fleet, refitting the ships to transport troops and horses, impressing the sailors to man the fleet, and gathering the necessary supplies was of little use to the English, however, if their fleet could not control the English Channel. After the outbreak of war in 1337, the English coastal towns were in great fear of raids and of even a general French invasion. In 1338-39, the south ports were hit by raiding parties, and the ports of Sandwich, Hastings, and Portsmouth were partially burnt. Folkstone, Dover, Thanet, and the Isle of Wight were harassed and even Southampton was damaged. Many ships were lost through these attacks, and shipping was badly interrupted. A major invasion was planned by Philip of Valois in 1339, and the port of Sluys on the Flemish coast was the assembly point for the vessels which would transport the armies to England. Nature intervened on behalf of the English, however, and the fleet was scattered and disbanded after a severe storm in October.[51] The following summer another large fleet was assembled at Sluys for the purpose of destroying the English at sea and preparing the way for an invasion force. Instead, Edward III commanded an English fleet that decisively overcame a combined French, Castilian, and Genoese flotilla. The victory was one of the greatest of the war and the first important one—coming six years before the great land battle at Crécy where the longbow worked to such advantage. What is important to notice about Sluys is that Edward commanded from aboard his flagship in person and directed the destruction of the larger enemy force, and in doing so, he helped determine the future course of the war. Had the English lost at Sluys and not been able to carry the war to France, there may not have been a Crécy, and the scene of battle might havé centered more on the Channel or perhaps even in England.[52] Such a heretical thought, though far from our minds, certainly was a possibility to contemporaries. By sailing boldly to Sluys and defeating the enemy in his preparatory stages before the scheme for the defeat of the English could be effected, however, Edward certainly altered the location, if not the tenor, of the fighting in the first phase of the war.[53] His action also meant that, for a time at least, the English could safely transport the troops and supplies necessary to fight the land war on the Continent.

During the next decade, few naval engagements of any significance occurred, and the Channel was busy with the activities of troop transport, victualling, and trade. Parliament was kindly disposed toward Edward after the victory at Sluys and provided him with considerable grants for the war effort. The ships which had served in the sea fighting were returned to their mercantile pursuits. What strikes us about the return of these vessels to mercantile practice is the ease with which they were converted from military to commercial use, and vice-versa. The practice of royal arrest and reliance upon the merchant marine depended upon the nature of the commercial ships and the ease with which they could be refitted for military purposes.

However, sporadic conflict in the English Channel and elsewhere between the French and their allies and the English continued. In fact, undeclared warfare at sea is the best description of the state of naval and mercantile relations between these parties extending back at least to the reign of Edward I at the turn of the century. Merchants frequently pirated or were pirated with the excuse that the other parties were the enemies of France or England. Truces seem to have been conveniently forgotten, and suits to the crown were often the recourse.[54] These appeals remain our record of these piratical raids. They were, in effect, crimes of convenience with convenient excuses generated to justify plundering. The admiralty was called upon to patrol the coasts and Channel against enemy ships and pirates on several occasions, but its effectiveness is difficult to estimate. While occasionally discouraged, the merchants never lost their desire to risk the journey. The prospect of profits was too great an enticement to fourteenth-century merchant venturers.

The solution achieved at some point in the late thirteenth or fourteenth century to help abate this problem was the introduction of convoys. These were especially successful in the English wine trade routes to Gascony. Larger fleets of merchants often escorted by royal ships filled with men-at-arms could deter individual raiders or even small pirate fleets.[55] For protection, the transports were usually armed by the assignment of a squadron of armed men and archers to sail with the ships and defend them from attack. The crew must have assisted in the fighting, and their added numbers meant that the vessels represented a considerable military challenge to pirates or enemy ships. The English ships generally sailed in convoy for added protection on both mercantile and military missions. The wine carriers to and from Bordeaux regularly traveled in convoy during the war to defend against French and Castilian men-of-war or pirates. The threat from the latter was often enough in itself to encourage the arming of ships or at least the safety of numbers. But not all merchants could afford or were prepared to wait for the cumbersome process of gathering a fleet at a designated port, awaiting royal escorts to join them and then sailing a prescribed course to Bordeaux or elsewhere. Many shipowners preferred to push on with their trade and risk encounters with French merchants *cum* pirates. The same held true for the French, although they were not as active in the trade of wine or wool, which was so important to the English economy.

It is perhaps convenient to rethink at this point the value of seaborne commerce to the royal economy. Customs accounts and extant shipping records leave no doubt that the English trade in wine and wool was a major source of crown revenue.[56] The interruption of this trade and thus a resultant decline in customs revenue was a matter of serious consequence to the treasury, and therefore to Edward's ability to wage war unless this revenue could be replaced in other ways.[57] So-called control of the seas, therefore, is a meaningful term for this period if limited to a definition which signifies the capacity of seaborne commerce or the transport of troops to continue to move unobstructed by pirates or enemy fleets. We are frequently told that such control was in the hands of the English after 1340, when they won the great battle of Sluys. Careful review of the records, however, reveals quick retaliation and raiding by the French. The ports on the southern coast of England were raided as they had been in the 1330s, and attacks on the routes to Gascony in the Bay of Biscay continued.[58]

It is true that major expeditions were launched in the 1340s against the French coasts by large flotillas, but such expeditions did not require command of the seas. It would have taken an equally large flotilla of several hundred ships to intercept the English expeditions of 1342-1343 and 1346. While we focus on the resultant victories on land at Crécy in 1346 or Poitiers in 1356, we must not lose sight of the logistical achievement involved in moving men, horses, and supplies to the Continent which made these English victories possible. Again, the French retaliated, and the three great English victories of the early phase of the war were soon forgotten when conditions soured and a truce was signed at Brétigny in 1360, much to the dissatisfaction of the English.[59] The truce was followed by a peace which lasted to 1369; this lengthy interruption of the war resulted in the conflict being shifted south into Iberia and back onto the seas, where royal standards were replaced with the banners of merchants and pirates.[60]

Conclusion

During the Hundred Years' War of the fourteenth and fifteenth centuries, the English encountered much the same logistical challenges that have confronted all nations at war throughout history. The primary task facing the English was the transportation of troops, supplies, and in this case, horses to the theater of action. To accomplish this task, the English kings had to assemble and man a fleet of ships, refit the ships for fighting or transport, gather supplies and victuals at embarkation points, then ensure the safe passage of their fleets across the Channel. Some of the methods they used were unpopular, particularly the arrest of merchant ships and the practice of purveyance, both of which tended to have a detrimental effect on the English economy. Because of tradition and a reluctance to consider alternatives, however, such practices persisted throughout the war. And in spite of the ultimate costs, the methods used by the English to meet the logistical necessities of their war with France enabled them to win the victories that came to be celebrated by later generations of Englishmen— Sluys, Crécy, Poitiers, and Agincourt.

Ironically, the English won the major battles but lost the war. They were driven from Gascony and all other continental possessions save the seaborne supplied port of Calais, where logistical support and fierce resistance kept the city in English hands for a century. The survival of English Calais serves as a final comment on the seafaring ability of English naval forces and the important part they played in logistical support.

Notes

1. See Michael Powicke, *Military Obligation in Medieval England* (Oxford: 1962) and A. E. Prince, "The Indenture System Under Edward III," *Historical Essays in Honour of James Tait*, eds. J. G. Edwards, V. H. Galbraith, and E. F. Jacob (Manchester: 1933), pp. 283-97.

2. Walter de Harewell was a sergeant-at-arms ca. 1348-52 and illustrates for us the activities of these men. He moved from port to port during most of his tenure of office. Public Records Office (London; hereafter PRO), Exchequer of Receipt, Issue Rolls, E. 403/344 m.3, for travel to the west country; E. 403/353 m.10, for travel to Gascony with a small ship; E. 403/347 m.27, sent to arrest ships at Plymouth; E. 403/355 m.38, E. 403/356 m.34, sent to Cornwall to arrest ships.

3. The usual rate per diem was 6*d.* for a master or constable, 3*d.* for a mariner, and 1*d.* for a ship's boy. Added to the wages was a *regard* as an added bonus. These were often considerable and no doubt encouraged reluctant seamen to risk dangerous voyages. In time they became an expected part of the pay.

4. For a complete history, see K. M. E. Murray, *The Constitutional History of the Cinque Ports* (London: 1935).

5. For a discussion of the Cinque Ports and their acquisition of privilege and maritime enemies, see F. W. Brooks, "The Cinque Ports," *The Mariner's Mirror* 15 (April 1929), pp. 142-91; "The Cinque Ports' Feud with Yarmouth in the Thirteenth Century,"

The Mariner's Mirror 19 (January 1933), pp. 27-51; and the chapter on the Cinque Ports in his *The English Naval Forces, 1199-1272* (London: 1932).

6. See, for instance, the account of Thomas de Snetesham, PRO, E. 372/203 m. 38, and William Clewar, E. 372/209 m. 47.

7. R. G. Marsden, ed., *Select Pleas in the Court of Admiralty, I. The Court of Admiralty in the West A.D. 1390-1404 and the High Court of Admiralty A.D. 1527-1545*, vol. 4 (London: The Selden Society: 1894), pp. xii-xiii.

8. *Calendar of Patent Rolls (1301-1307)*, p. 131 (hereafter *CPR*).

9. Thomas Rymer, ed., *Foedera*, 10 vols. (The Hague: 1739-45), 3:i, 199. The commission was dated 26 March 1360.

10. PRO, Chancery Miscellanea, C. 47/14/15. For a description of the manuscript, see Marsden, *Select Pleas*, p. xxx.

11. Thomas Rymer, ed., *Foedera*, 4 vols. (London: Record Commission: 1816-69), 2:475. The letter was dated 17 February 1322.

12. *Rotuli Parliamentorum*, ed. J. Strachey, et al., 6 vols. (London: 1783; Index, 1832), 2:311. (Hereafter *Rot. Parl.*)

13. See, for example, the 1340 arrest order for ships of over twenty tons following earlier requests for larger vessels. *Calendar of Close Rolls (1339-41)*, pp. 422, 370. (Hereafter *CCR*.) See also Timothy J. Runyan, "The Organization of Royal Fleets in Medieval England," in T. J. Runyan, ed., *Ships, Seafaring, and Society: Essays in Maritime History* (Detroit: Wayne State University Press, 1987), pp. 45 ff.

14. PRO, E. 101/24/9(b), mm. 1-45; E. 101/24/8.

15. PRO, E. 101/24/9(b), m.16.

16. R. J. Whitwell and C. Johnson, "The Newcastle Galley, A.D. 1294," *Archaeologia Aeliana*, 4th ser., vol. 2 (1962), p. 145.

17. The bulk of the total is the forty-five ships noted above (n. 14). Others may have been compensated, but I have not found the manuscript sources to verify payments.

18. See the complaint in a commission to Admiral John de Montgomery on 30 May 1343, ordering him to arrest the deserters. *CPR (1343-45)*, p. 92. See also *CCR (1343-46)*, pp. 128-34 and Rymer, *Foedera* (Hague ed.), 2:iv, 126.

19. For the cancellations, see *CPR (1343-45)*, pp. 108-09; *CPR (1341-43)*, p. 663 *passim*.

20. Rymer, *Foedera*, 3:i, 4. For complaints in 1348, see *CCR (1349-54)*, pp. 550-51 and *Calendar of Inquisitions Miscellaneous (1348-77)*, pp. 5-7.

21. PRO, French Roll, C. 76/23 m.21.

22. The project was CMS/SAS based with a program designed to record entries of a ship's name, home port, size, owner, master, whether or not the vessel belonged to the king's fleet, crew size, general information concerning its activities, the source of the reference, and additional information. It should be clear to the reader that this data is not without problems of purity. Included here and in the following discussion of home ports, all references to ships come from the *Calendar of Close Rolls* and *Calendar of Patent Rolls* for this period. In some instances a ship may be entered more than once. There are many *St. Marys*, for instance, and it is not always possible to tell if the *St. Mary* with no master, size, or home port given is the same ship as, say, the *St. Mary* of Lynn, which was ordered to join the king's fleet at Southampton under the command of William Alfen (*CCR, 1350-54*, p. 52). My survey is not comprehensive enough to date to eliminate such repetitions and ascertain the exact number of discrete vessels among the 1,291 entries. Given this significant caveat, I

believe the analysis to be of value, but only if considered in a broad context. The reader should be well aware of the frailty of the numbers and percentages noted in the following pages for these reasons. By way of further example, there are fifty-seven entries for ships named *La Nicholas*. This is understandable, since St. Nicholas was the patron saint of sailors. But it is not possible to determine how many discrete vessels there were named *La Nicholas*. For their assistance with the design of the computer program and compilation of ship references, I would like to thank Daniel Morris, William Harris, and Claudia Benko.

23. On ship types from contemporary references, see B. Sandahl, *Middle English Sea Terms*, 3 vols. (Uppsala: 1951-1982) and R. W. Unger, *The Ship in the Medieval Economy* (London: 1980), chapter 4. For the significance of certain ship types, see J. W. Sherborne, "English Barges and Balingers of the Fourteenth Century," *The Mariner's Mirror* 63 (May 1977), pp. 109-14. More extensive work on ship types from illuminations is included in the essays by C. Villain-Gandossi, *La Méditerranée aux xiie - xvie siècles: relations maritimes, diplomatiques et comerciales* (London: 1983).

24. On cogs, see S. Fliedner, *The Cog of Bremen* (Bremen: 1972); D. Ellmers, "The Cog of Bremen and Related Boats," in *Medieval Ships and Harbours in Northern Europe*, ed. S. McGrail (Oxford: 1979), and Unger, *The Ship in the Medieval Economy*, chs. 4 and 5. For the history of the ship, see Romola and R. C. Anderson, *The Sailing Ship: Six Thousand Years of History*, rev. ed. (New York: 1963); G. S. L. Clowes, *Sailing Ships: Their History and Development as Illustrated in the Collection of Ship Models in the Science Museum*, 5th ed., 2 parts (London: 1932); Bjorn Landstrom, *The Ship* (New York: 1961); August Jal, *Archeologie Navale*, 2 vols. (Paris: 1840).

25. See, for example, the ship list in PRO Chancery Miscellanea, C. 47/2/35 mm. 4-5. There is an account of the building of a ship in the early fifteenth century in W. J. Carpenter Turner, "The Building of the *Holy Ghost of the Tower*, 1414-1416, and Her Subsequent History," *The Mariner's Mirror* 40 (November 1954), pp. 270-81.

26. C. Johnson, "London Shipbuilding, A.D. 1295," *Antiquaries Journal* 7 (1927), pp. 424-37; J. T. Tinniswood, "English Galleys, 1272-1377," *The Mariner's Mirror* 35 (October 1949), pp. 276-315.

27. *CPR (1416-22)*, p. 84; PRO, E. 364/57 for the building accounts; Susan Rose, "Henry V's *Grace Dieu* and Mutiny at Sea: Some New Evidence," *Mariner's Mirror* 63 (Feb. 1977), pp. 3-6.

28. This is persuasively argued by G. V. Scammel, "English Merchant Shipping at the End of the Middle Ages: Some East Coast Evidence," *Economic History Review*, 2nd ser., 13 (1961), pp. 327-28. For the Dutch carriers, see A. E. Christensen, *Dutch Trade in the Baltic Sea About 1600* (Copenhagen: 1941), p. 94.

29. Cf. the cog *Thomas* was in for repairs at Ratcliff from 22 February 1344 to 21 November 1345, then sailed with a crew of 97 to Normandy and spent from 26 October 1345 to 17 March 1346 in harbor, with a crew of four men and a page. PRO, E. 101/24/14/4 m.1.

30. PRO, E. 364/54 and for the particulars of the account see E. 101/44/24. See also Susan Rose, *The Navy of the Lancastrian Kings: Accounts and Inventories of William Soper, Keeper of the King's Ships, 1422-1427* (London: Navy Records Society, 1982), p. 35.

31. PRO, E. 364/59; Rose, *Navy of the Lancastrian Kings*, p. 36.

32. For the sale of ships after 1377, PRO, E. 364/12 m.G. For the sale of Henry V's fleet, see C. F. Richmond, "The Keeping of the Seas During the Hundred Years' War,"

History, 49 (1964), pp. 283-98 and Rose, *The Navy of the Lancastrian Kings*, pp. 52-55 and Appendix IV.

33. Gangways were necessary to load the horses onto the ships and hurdles to separate them into stalls. See the order for carpenters and these items. *CCR (1339-41)*, p. 505.

34. Some of the royal expeditions required hundreds of vessels. The king's fleet at the Battle of Sluys was estimated at between 147 and 330 ships by five chroniclers: The *Chronique de London depuis l'An 44 Henry III jusque à l'An 17 Edward III*, ed. J. Anngier, 38 (London: Camden Society, 1844), pp. 26-27 says 300 ships; *Chronicon Monasterii de Melsa*, ed. E. A. Bond, Rolls Series, 3 vols. (London: 1866-68), 3:44 says 200; Geoffrey le Baker, *Chronicon*, ed. E. M. Thompson, Rolls Series (London: 1889), p. 68 and Adam Murrimuth, *Continuatio Chronicon*, ed. E. M. Thompson, Rolls Series (London: 1899), p. 105 both claim 260 ships; the low estimate of 147 is made in *Chronicon de Lanercost*, ed. J. Stevenson (Edinburgh: 1839), p. 333. Edward III's own estimate was 190 ships, noted in a dispatch to his son, the Black Prince. Archives of the City of London, Register F, fol. 39. Over 220 ships were involved in the 1342-43 expedition to Brittany. *CPR (1343-45)*, p. 92. Estimates for the 1346 expedition to Normandy range up to 1,000 ships, cf. Thomas Walsingham, *Historia Anglicana*, ed. H. T. Riley, Rolls Series, 2 vols. (London: 1863-64), 1:267-68. For an estimate of 400 ships, see *Chroniques de J. Froissart*, eds. S. Luce, G. Raynaud, L. and A. Mirot, *Société de l'histoire de France*, 14 vols. (Paris: 1869-1966), 3:355.

The very high number of 738 ships was given for the transport of 32,000 men to the siege of Calais in 1347. British Library, Harleian MS 246, f. 12b and MS 3968, f. 130; British Library, Cotton MS Titus F, 3, f. 262.

35. For further information on the preparation of fleets, see Runyan, "The Organization of Royal Fleets in Medieval England," pp. 37-52.

36. N. H. Nicholas, *A History of the Royal Navy*, 2 vols. (London: 1847), 1:215; *Rotuli Scotiae*, ed. D. McPherson, et al., 2 vols. (London: 1814-19), 1:478-79. (Hereafter *Rot. Scot.*)

37. Rymer, *Foedera* 2:941.

38. *Rot. Parl.*, 2:96; Nicholas, *Royal Navy*, 2:176.

39. *Rot. Scot.*, 1:419.

40. Nicholas, *Royal Navy*, 1:404-05.

41. See Timothy J. Runyan, "Ships and Mariners in Later Medieval England," *Journal of British Studies* 16 (Spring 1977), p. 3ff.

42. John H. Pryor, "The Transportation of Horses by Sea During the Era of the Crusades: Eighth Century to 1285 A.D.," *The Mariner's Mirror* 68 (1982), p. 10. See also Pryor's revised views in "The Naval Architecture of Crusader Transport Ships and Horse Transports Revisited," ibid. 76 (August 1990), pp. 255-73 and "The Crusade of Frederick II, 1220-1229: The Implications of the Maritime Evidence," *The American Neptune* 52, no. 2 (Spring 1992), p. 114, n. 7.

43. Pryor, "Transportation of Horses," p. 21.

44. H. J. Hewitt, *The Black Prince's Expedition of 1355-1357* (Manchester: 1958), p. 33.

45. H. J. Hewitt, *The Organization of War Under Edward III, 1338-62* (Manchester: 1966), p. 79.

46. Pryor, "Transportation of Horses," pp. 14-15.

47. Hewitt, *Organization of War*, p. 58.
48. *Ibid.*, pp. 58-59.
49. *CCR (1354-60)*, p. 223. This promise was made in 1355 when the two armies were in France. See S. J. Burley, "The Victualling of Calais," *Bulletin of the Institute of Historical Research* 31 (1958), pp. 49-57.
50. PRO, E. 101/25/16, the account of William Kelleseye, receiver of victuals.
51. A plan for the invasion of England was drawn up by the French in 1339 and was later captured by the English. It is in the British Museum, Harleian MS 3836, and printed in Travers Twiss, ed., *Black Book of the Admiralty*, 4 vols. (London: 1871-76), 1:420, and in the chronicle of Robert de Avesbury, *De Gestis Mirabilis Regis Edwardi Tertii*, ed. E. M. Thompson (London: 1889), p. 205. The account of the storm is found in Henry Knighton's *Chronicon*, ed. J. R. Lumby, 2 vols. (London: 1889-95), 2:13-14.
52. Froissart provides us with a fairly extensive account of the battle in *Chroniques de J. Froissart*, 2: 34-40.
53. Edward ordered his sergeants to arrest ships over thirty tons and to impress mariners before he took the fleet to Sluys. *CCR (1339-41)*, pp. 370, 422. Fifty ships under Robert de Morley, admiral to the north, joined Edward's fleet at sea. Walsingham, *Historia Anglicana*, 1:227; Adam Murimuth, *Continuatio Chronicarum*, ed. E. M. Thompson (London: 1889), p. 105. For Morley's appointment as admiral, see F. M. Powicke and E. B. Fryde, *Handbook of British Chronology*, 2d ed. (London: 1961), p. 128.
54. For notice of the *Cristemasse*, pirated by men of Bristol, see *CCR (1337-1339)*, p. 88. Simon de Rathby, master of the *Escumer*, was recorded plundering and murdering merchants off the Isle of Wight, *CPR (1343-1345)*, p. 388. The *Tarete*, bound for Flanders, was robbed and boarded by members of the king's fleet. Edward III agreed to compensation and held responsible the owners and masters involved. *CPR (1340-1343)*, p. 538.
55. For example, ships were escorted to Bordeaux. PRO, Exchequer Accounts, Issue Rolls, E. 403/555 m. 44.
56. See Robert L. Baker, *The English Customs Service, 1307-1343: A Study of Medieval Administration*, Transactions of the American Philosophical Society, N. S. 56, pt. 6 (Philadelphia: 1961), Appendix 1 for wool exports. For the volume of trade and revenues, J. H. Ramsay, *A History of the Revenues of the King of England, 1066-1399* (Oxford: 1925) gives a breakdown of income sources. For information on expenses at this time, see M. M. Postan, "The Costs of the Hundred Years' War," *Past and Present* 27 (April 1964), pp. 34-53. For naval implications, see J. W. Sherborne, "The English Navy: Shipping and Manpower 1369-1389," *ibid.* 37 (July 1967), pp. 163-75. On the wine trade, see M. K. James, "Fluctuations in the Anglo-Gascon Wine Trade during the Fourteenth Century," *Economic History Review*, 2d series, 4 (1951). For wool, see T. H. Lloyd, *The English Wool Trade in the Middle Ages* (Cambridge: 1977).
57. For financial implications, see the work of E. B. Fryde, including his "Materials for the Study of Edward III's Credit Operations: 1327-1348," *Bulletin of the Institute of Historical Research* 22 (1949), pp. 105-38 and 23 (1950), pp. 1-30.
58. Before the Battle of Sluys, the French had considered a full-scale invasion of England (see n. 51 above). In July 1342 an English fleet commanded by the Earl of Northampton lost four ships to a Spanish fleet while crossing to Brittany. PRO, E. 101/24/8; 9 (6), m. 26; Knighton, *Chronicon*, 2:27-28.

59. The settlement followed the disastrous campaign of 1359-1360. On the treaty, see J. LePatourel, "The Treaty of Brétigny 1360," *Transactions of the Royal Historical Society*, 5th ser., vol. 10 (London: 1960), pp. 19-39; P. Chaplais, "Some Documents Regarding the Fulfillment and Interpretation of the Treaty of Brétigny," *Camden Miscellany*, 3d ser., vol. 19 (1952).

60. This activity is noted by P. E. Russell, *The English Intervention in Spain and Portugal in the Time of Edward III and Richard II* (Oxford: 1955), esp. chs. 1 and 11.

PART THREE

Early Modern Logistics, 1500-1815

Early Modern Introduction

The crucible of the early modern period created a new world alloyed from several historical elements and melded by the fires of warfare. Three of those elements of the Western experience require discussion here. First, maritime and naval supremacy allowed the Portuguese and Spanish, followed by the Dutch, English, and French, to explore and colonize the world, raising Europe to global predominance. Second, on the continent of Europe, warrior princes forged bureaucratic, centralized governments which provided the pattern for the modern state. Third, at the end of the period a series of political revolutions, attended by bloody wars, presented the world with new democratic republics, which would become models for the future. Armed force played important roles in all three of these developments, and the task of supplying fleets and armies shaped and was shaped by the these monumental processes.

Maritime and Naval Logistics

A growing chorus of historians claim that the early modern era witnessed a military revolution, although they debate the scope, timing, and influence of the phenomenon.[1] Just how the label "military revolution" will fare over the next decade of historiographical controversy no one can tell. One aspect which is sure to retain its central importance, however, is the sixteenth-century marriage of the maritime technology of the European sailing ship with the large artillery pieces born of the gunpowder revolution in the sixteenth century. The fighting ships that issued from this match provided the means with which Europeans explored the globe, dominated the seas, and planted their settlements. Certainly this process involved more than naval might, yet if naval might was not a sufficient cause, it was a necessary prerequisite of European expansion.

The tremendous advances in maritime technology made during the late Middle Ages provided the foundation for the work of the sixteenth century. Both ship size and sophistication grew during the 1500s. The first massive fighting vessels, such as Henry VIII's *Mary Rose* and *Great Harry*, were too large—the latter at 1000 tons displacement—and so unstable as to be nearly useless at sea. They bore an impressive number of cannon, but relatively few large pieces. The *Great Harry* bristled with 184 guns, but only 43 were of heavy caliber. It was not such unwieldy vessels that laid the keel of European naval supremacy but the more handy and at first smaller galleon mounting only heavy guns in broadside batteries close to the waterline. This archetype of the new war vessel first appeared in the 1620s at only 250 tons, but naval builders mastered the style and doubled the size of the galleon by the 1580s. Three galleons of the English fleet that opposed the Armada weighed in at 800 tons or more. The number of big guns increased with the size of the ships. The *Elizabeth Jonas*, launched in 1559, carried sixty four; the *Sovereign of the Sea*, 1627, carried 104 guns, although this later vessel was in fact too large to maneuver well at sea.[2]

The weight and power of cannon massed on ship far surpassed that used in land warfare. Single ships carried far more guns than did entire armies. French forces at Ceresole in 1544 and at Rocroi in 1622 both put only 20 cannon in the field. In fact, even modest ships mounted as many guns as did the walls of major fortresses. Ath, for example, claimed only 32 cannon in 1697; and Briesach in 1703 was defended by only 82 pieces. Even the number of guns boasted by the largest fortresses were not much by naval standards. At Lille in 1708, during the greatest single siege of the War of the Spanish Succession, a garrison of 16,000 French with 159 cannon held out for four months against a besieging force of 35,000 men with a siege train of 120 cannon and 80 large mortars. At Beachy Head in 1690 the French fleet totaled 4,646 cannon against a combined British and Dutch fleet armed with 3,696 guns. With such a concentration of such power, European fleets swept the seas.[3]

Obviously the dominance of European fleets required the ability to supply those fleets, whose crews consumed tons of biscuit, salt meat, beer, wine, and water and whose guns required great quantities of shot and gunpowder. This is the subject of the essay by John F. Guilmartin, Jr.. He reminds us that the administrative sophistication of logistics at sea far surpassed that of logistics on land. Vessels could not live off the land; they could not find at sea supplies that had not been shipped aboard, had been consumed, or had gone bad. The skills of commissaries, private and royal, were developed in supplying galleons and galleys. Guilmartin examines the kind and quantity of stores required and the way in which they were manufactured, stockpiled, registered, and loaded.

Certainly the ability and competence the Spanish displayed was great, particularly when viewed in an early modern context. By the end of the century they could mount an expedition on the scale of the Spanish Armada, which included 125 ships, bristling with 2,431 guns and carrying 27,000 men.[4] The capacity to marshal war material is revealed in even higher relief by the ability to launch great fleets of galleys in the Mediterranean. With their need for rowers, galley fleets matched armies in the numbers of mouths to feed. At Lepanto in 1571 the opposing fleets together totalled 400 vessels with as many as 160,000 men, the largest mass of humanity at any battle of the sixteenth century.[5]

Artillery, Siege Warfare, and Supply

Artillery not only gave naval vessels their power, but Geoffrey Parker theorizes that it shaped the entire military revolution. Parker goes so far as to ascribe the growth of armies to the spread of the new style of fortresses—designed with low walls, broad ditches, and angled bastions in what he terms the *trace italienne*.[6] Whether or not his contention that artillery and the new style of fortifications created great armies, there is no question that such forces appeared. The wartime strength of French forces multiplied about fivefold over the course of the seventeenth century, hitting 400,000 by the 1690s, at least on paper.[7] Swelling muster rolls contributed to the formation of absolutist governments, which alone commanded the political authority and the administrative capacity to mobilize the resources required by such gargantuan forces.

Obviously such great armies generated a logistic challenge of unprecedented magnitude. This challenge surpassed even Louis XIV's capacity to supply his armies simply from state coffers. As already pointed out, early modern armies tried to make war feed war as much as possible. Most obviously they foraged for fodder where they campaigned, so a campaign on enemy land saved the subjects of the prince whose army could fight across the border. But there were other means of tapping local resources as well, including the levying of contributions, or war taxes, on occupied populations.

Martin van Creveld argues that the siege warfare so prevalent during the period prior to the French Revolution posed nearly insolvable problems for early modern armies, which he insists could only supply themselves adequately on the move. Van Creveld believes that siege warfare alone made magazines and supply lines necessary and that it was somehow a lower form of combat than maneuver warfare. For him, the concentration on fortresses was somehow artificial and unnecessary. In his essay, John A. Lynn suggests that there was another side to the relationship of siege warfare to supply and, in doing so, turns van Creveld's argument on its ear. For Lynn it is not so much that siege warfare made regular supply necessary but that early modern methods of supply compelled armies to rely on fortresses and fortified lines. Fortifications served essential roles both in maintaining forces by regular supply and in fostering or limiting an army's ability to live off the country. Fortresses contained magazines and protected lines of communication, but they also determined access to resource areas. To Lynn, the control of the countryside through fortresses and fortified outposts and lines was an essential aspect of logistics in the early modern era, a time when there were ever more soldiers and horses to feed.

The Techniques of Regular Supply and Transportation

In the need to support the expanded forces of the seventeenth century, armies developed better mechanisms of collecting and distributing supplies.

Le Tellier and his son Louvois, who served as war ministers for Louis XIV during a period of nearly fifty years, 1643-1691, developed a system of military magazines stockpiling all sorts of war's necessities. Primarily they held grain for bread and a certain amount of dry fodder to feed the horses when green fodder was scarce, as at the opening of the campaign season. For example, in preparation for the French offensive of 1672, Louvois bought and stored enough grain for 200,000 rations a day for the full six months of the campaign season.[8]

To supply an army required not just stores but a transportion system. To facilitate supply from the rear, armies added what would be today termed "organic" transport. For French forces this was supplied by private contractors, or *munitionnaires*. Circa 1700, the wagons, grouped under "captains" responsible for twenty-five wagons each, held about four times the daily bread ration for the army they served. With such a wagon train an army could function at a two day march from its ovens for some time or, in special situations, it could stock up and move a bit farther before reestablishing its ovens.[9] Temporary ovens could also be erected at an army's camp and the supply wagons used to haul flour, which was a much more efficient system. When need arose, military administrators requisitioned peasants and their carts to meet the army's needs.

John Shy discusses just how important such a transportation system could be to the fate of armies, and to the fate of the American Revolution. As citizen-soldiers of the revolutionary epoch, the Americans who fought could be expected to bear considerable hardship, but they could not be expected to survive without food. Yet continual breakdowns in the supply of Continental forces drove them to starvation. Shy writes in sharp contrast to American historians who blame the suffering of the Continental army on the corruption of particular officials, the lack of unity among the states, or the weakness of Congress. Shy explains the logistic shortcomings of revolutionary forces as an unhappy but unavoidable consequence of the lack of proper transport in the fledgling United States.

While European armies benefited from both their own organic supply trains and the ability to requisition peasant carts, the Americans fell short. The sparse population of the new world limited the amount of cartage available to the forces of the rebellious colonies. Even though the new land was rich, it depended mostly on east-west river transportation, which did not serve the military needs of an army that maneuvered mostly on a north-south axis. Population tended to be so dispersed over the countryside that passing armies could not simply draw their supplies easily where they were. In addition, when the army took up winter quarters, it lacked the transportation infrastructure to bring in supplies from a sufficiently broad area to maintain the soldiers without causing hardship to civilians. Supplies rotted in warehouses while soldiers starved. Shy reminds us that supply was more than simply eating on the move while on campaign. Armies had to winter too, and in such cases, living off the country became difficult or impossible. Shy provides an unusual but convincing example of the necessity for "umbilical cords" of supply in the eighteenth century.

Concluding Remarks

Western logistics in the early modern period fueled armed forces as they spread European dominance across the globe, as they grew and fostered the evolution of stronger bureaucratic states, and as they fought in the great revolutionary struggles that ended the era. As such, logistics can be viewed as more than simply the handmaiden of strategy. During the period 1500-1815 logistics provided the supporting cast for the great dramas of Western, even world, history.

Notes

1. On the thesis of the military revolution see Michael Roberts, *The Military Revolution, 1560-1660* (Belfast: 1956); Geoffrey Parker, *The Military Revolution: Military Innovation and the Rise of the West, 1500-1800* (Cambridge: 1988); and Jeremy Black, *A Military Revolution? Military Change and European Society,* 1550-1800 (Atlantic Highlands, NJ: 1991).

2. Parker, *Military Revolution*, pp. 90-92, 99.

3. Gaston Bodart, *Militär-historishes Kriegs-Lexikon, 1618-1905* (Vienna and Leipzig: 1908), pp. 112, 121, 132, and 158.

4. Colin Martin and Geoffrey Parker, *The Spanish Armada* (London: 1988), pp. 44-45. This is the strength of the Armada as it neared England after five ships had dropped out. See as well pp. 62-63 for a full muster.

5. Parker, *Military Revolution,* p. 89.

6. See the discussion of Parker's thesis that the *trace italienne* drove military expansion in John A. Lynn, "The *trace italienne* and the Growth of Armies: The French Case," *Journal of Military History* 55, no. 3 (July 1991), pp. 297-330.

7. John A. Lynn, "Recalculating French Army Growth During the Grand siècle, 1610-1715," *French Historical Studies* (forthcoming).

8. Louis XIV, *Oeuvres de Louis XIV*, Grimoard and Grouvelle, eds., vol. 3 (Paris: 1806), p. 117.

9. See François Nodot, *Le munitionnaire des armées de France* (Paris: 1697) for a description of the organic transport, the *équipages des vivres,* army ovens, and all the details of formal bread supply. At two days' distance from the ovens, the wagons had to make a four day round trip; therefore, the train had to deliver four days' rations to feed the army while it made the next circuit to the ovens and back to the army. Martin van Creveld, *Supplying War* (Cambridge: 1977), p. 19, interprets the army wagon train as "designed not so much to carry provisions from the rear as to accompany the army in the field as a rolling magazine with a few days' reserves." This is flat wrong; as far as I can see this can only come from a careless reading of Louis André, *Michel Le Tellier* (Paris: 1906), pp. 451-54, or from a misinterpretation of the term "rolling magazine" as employed by R. M. Leighton in his article "Logistics" in *Encyclopedia Britanica*, 15th edition, vol. 14, (Chicago: 1970), pp. 239-47B.

6

The Logistics of Warfare at Sea in the Sixteenth Century: The Spanish Perspective

John F. Guilmartin, Jr.

Few nations and periods present more inviting opportunities and daunting challenges to the military historian than sixteenth century Spain. As the fifteenth century entered its final quarter, Spain—more properly the united kingdoms of Aragon and Castile—was a regional power of substance, no more. A century later, Spain was a pre-eminent world power and possessor of a global empire, capable of marshaling and wielding military power on a scale which, at least for the moment, no other state could equal. And yet at the very apogee of Spanish power, Spain was beset by enemies who had begun to take her measure, particularly at sea, and who were to drive her from her position of pre-eminence. It is worth noting that those enemies who were to inflict the most grievous losses on Spain in the centuries ahead, the Dutch and English, had profited from lessons administered by the Spanish in the hard school of war.

Spain's remarkable transformation, or rather series of transformations, commends itself to the military historian, for armed force played a major part in Spain's rise, prolonged eminence and remarkably protracted and graceful decline. This is certainly true of the process of imperial expansion, which proceeded in large measure as a result of feats of arms which are not readily explainable in terms of the normal strategic calculus. To cite the most dramatic examples, the Aztec and Inca empires were overthrown with resources so modest as to strain credulity.[1] Equally impressive, though not so dramatic, was the manner in which Spain maintained her position of eminence for as long as she did, fighting against the Ottomans, Dutch, English and French, frequently all at once. As with the process of expansion, there was a marked imbalance between resources available and success achieved. That success cannot be adequately explained or fully appreciated without understanding its logistical dimension. Spain maintained her position in large measure by means of a remarkable ability to mobilize and deploy the limited resources available to her. Although we are only beginning to perceive the outlines, it is evident that the feats of Spanish logisticians[2] were every bit as impressive as the tactical exploits of her fighting forces. This was at least as true at sea as on land, and it is there that we shall focus our attention.

The Spanish genius for war on land in late medieval and early modern times is universally acknowledged: we need simply mention the name of Gonsalvo de Cordova, *El Gran Capitán*. The roll of Spanish victories over the armies of Valois France in the Wars of Italy makes the point. So does reflection on the fact that much of the English vocabulary of war entered the language from sixteenth century Spanish: colonel from *cabo de colunela*, head of the column; sergeant major from *sargento major*, the senior non-commissioned officer of a tercio; and point blank from *punto de blanco*, aimed [directly] at the target, that is without elevation. Relevant to the subject at hand is major general, from *sargento major general*, the senior sergeant major of an army, originally a logistician.[3] The importance of Spanish arms on land is unquestioned, for to the political impact of the Wars of Italy we must add that of the overthrow of the Aztec and Inca empires, Spain's contribution to the wars of the Austrian Habsburgs and the Revolt of the Netherlands. But perhaps in part because of the acknowledged importance of Spanish land forces and in part because of the subsequent eclipse of Spain's power at sea by the English and Dutch, historians have slighted the maritime dimension.

This is particularly true of the study of logistics, where we are well served on land, notably by Geoffrey Parker's seminal *The Army of Flanders and the Spanish Road* and William Maltby's superb biography of the Duke of Alba.[4] Studies of the Invincible Armada of 1588 aside—an important exception, though one which threatens to distort our view of the broader whole by sheer weight of scholarly effort—little has been written in English on the logistics of Spanish warfare at sea. Indeed, the first specialized monograph in English devoted to the equipping and provisioning of Spanish naval forces in the pre-modern era appeared only in 1986 with Carla Rahn Phillips' well conceived and neatly executed case study, *Six Galleons for the King of Spain*.[5] The Spanish reader is better served, but Francisco-Felipe Olesa Muñido's encyclopedic *La Organización Naval de Los Estados Mediterraneos y en Especial de España Durante los Siglos XVI y XVII* (*The Naval Organization of the Mediterranean States and in Particular Spain During the 16th and 17th Centuries*)[6] remains untranslated and has not received the attention it deserves. This chapter represents a preliminary step toward redressing the balance.

It is axiomatic—or should be—that logistics cannot be meaningfully addressed in isolation, but must be evaluated as a component of the greater strategic equation. Similarly, strategies cannot be meaningfully assessed outside of the political and economic context within which they were conceived and implemented. In a sense it is thus anachronistic to speak of Spanish strategy in the sixteenth century, for few of the historical actors understood or discussed strategy in terms familiar to us.[7] But an implicit strategy is a strategy nonetheless, and the matter need not detain us. More fundamentally, the degree to which the strategies in question were "Spanish" is open to question. Spain's forces were mobilized and sent to war for reasons of state conceived within the context of a divinely sanctioned monarchy, the national identity of which was a more or less accidental product of a game of dynastic genetic roulette. In practice, however, the monarchs' options were conceived, shaped and evaluated within an intellectual framework and administrative structure provided by a hierarchical network of consultative, executive and advisory bodies of an essentially local character. That structure bore the indelible stamp of seven centuries of struggle between Roman Catholicism and Islam for control of the Iberian Peninsula, and in that sense the emergent strategy was unavoidably Spanish at its core.

It is an oversimplification to assert that the strategy of the Spanish Habsburg monarchy, like that of the *Reyes Católicos* before it, was an extension of the *Reconquista*, if for no other reason because it evolved continuously in response to changing cultural and political circumstances. That assertion, however, is close enough to the truth to serve our purpose. To make the point by example, I see no evidence that Charles I saw any essential tension between the strategic problems which he faced as King of Spain and those which he faced as Charles V, Holy Roman Emperor, save as an expression of the assumption of wider responsibilities in the latter capacity.

The sixteenth century, construed here to encompass the period between Spain's entry into the Wars of Italy in 1495 and her disengagement from the Ottoman Turks in 1577-81, from England with the Treaty of London in 1604, and from the Dutch Protestants with the conclusion of the Twelve Years' Truce in 1609, was one of epochal change in the economic, political and cultural affairs of the world. Much of that change revolved around the abilities of European states to marshal and wield military power and, while there are many dimensions to the problem, it is apparent that their ability to do so by sea was crucial. This was particularly true over the long term, and developments in the theory and practice of warfare in the sixteenth century paved the way for momentous developments in the seventeenth and eighteenth. Again, this was at least as true at sea as on land, and it is suggestive that the locus of advances in the theory and practice of war shifted perceptibly toward the former during the period under consideration.

In all of this, Spain was at the heart of things, leading the way at first, only to be matched and then surpassed by the French, English and Dutch. To refine the point further, it seems to me that the events bracketed by the disembarkation of Gonsalvo de Cordova's army in Calabria in 1495, marking the beginning of Spanish political dominance of Italy and initiating an important phase of the military revolution on land, and the signal defeat of Juan Alvarez de Aviles' fleet in Gibraltar harbor by a Dutch force under Jacob van Heemskerk on 24 April 1607, an important benchmark in the military revolution at sea which marked the beginning of Holland's rise as a trans-oceanic power, delineate a discrete and critical epoch in the development of the means and ends of war. The following analysis focuses on that epoch. Our concern is with Spanish logistics of warfare at sea during that epoch.

The magnitude and importance of the changes in the practice of war which occurred across the period in question are visible in many ways. Historians in recent years have begun to assign increasing importance to growth in the size of European armies during the sixteenth and seventeenth centuries, and it is worth noting in this regard that even after the conclusion of "peace" in 1610, Spain's military establishment, with some 30,000 men and a nominal annual budget of over 2 million ducats, was substantially larger than at any time before 1587.[8] The increase in the size of Spain's military forces, of course, was a reflection of important fiscal and logistical realities. But historians have for the most part focused on land warfare, and war at sea has its own peculiar dynamic, not least of all in the realm of logistics. It is worth noting, too, that while macro-economic trends have much to say, or at least to suggest, about the logistics of war, and while micro-economic logistical data might usefully inform economic history, there has been little exchange between specialists in the two areas. A secondary objective of the following analysis is to point out the benefits of such an exchange: my reference is on the one hand to abundant data relating to the secular increase in the prices of key commodities during the period under investigation, notably wheat, meat and other agricultural products, and a corresponding decline in real wages; and on the other to the mass of archival data giving prices paid at specific times and places for a host of products, many of particular interest to students of macro-economic trends, by Spanish military and naval logisticians.[9]

The differences in the logistics of warfare on land and at sea are many and basic. First, and of fundamental importance, is the relative ease of movement by water. Ships are notoriously more efficient than competing methods of transport in terms of energy required to move a given weight a given distance.[10] That is true today in comparison with railroads, trucks, and aircraft; it was true in early modern times in comparison with carts, wagons, pack animals, and human porterage. Moreover, ships are less bound by size constraints than are land vehicles, and bulky loads are more easily carried by ship than by cart or wagon. The reverse side of the coin is that ships, particularly ocean-going ships, are expensive in terms of capital investment. Next, ships encase men, materiel and ordnance in a mobile, self-contained system which takes on an operational and administrative life of its own. Desertion is infinitely more difficult than on land and mutinies less common, a point of particular interest to the historian of Spanish arms. Records are, on the whole, better and more complete because they have to be: if it is not on board when you leave port, properly stored and inventoried, it will not be available when needed... and, given the inherent hostility of the sea, not available at all. There is no foraging at sea. Even for a squadron of war galleys, in effect designed for the purpose, landing to obtain provisions entails an inherently greater level of risk than does sending out foraging parties on land. The non-availability of potable water, almost by definition readily available in land areas worth campaigning for—or even over—is a major constraint in naval operations.[11]

From an external perspective, Spain's impact on the flow of history during the period with which we are concerned here was immense. From an internal perspective, the sixteenth century as delineated above saw the apogee of Spain's institutional greatness... or so I would argue, for this was clearly the case in the military sphere. From the logistical perspective, changes occurred during that period which materially altered the terms of the equation which Spanish commanders and councils had to solve in order to aggrandize Spain's wealth and power in the first instance and to avoid military disaster in the second. Indeed, one may argue that changes in question altered the essential character of the logistical equation itself. Indicative of the magnitude of the change, and perhaps its velocity as well, is the increase in the size of Spain's military establishment noted above. The development and spread of effective gunpowder weaponry and advances in the design and construction of ocean-going vessels were notable among these changes, though they were hardly the only ones. Long term demographic trends, the price revolution and the enormous growth of maritime commerce lurk in the background as shaping factors which both forced logistical change and made it possible; so, too, does the general increase in prices and decline in real wages in Europe.[12]

Within the context implied by these generalizations, use of the sea by Spain to project her armed might was no trivial matter. It was by sea that Spain became a world empire, and while scholarly interest in the foundation of that empire has concentrated on issues of navigation and trade, Spain's naval affairs beyond European waters had an important military dimension from the start. No sooner had Spain established herself in the Caribbean than she was forced to defend her interests there against European interlopers, first French, then English and Dutch. The subsequent effort to keep open the maritime lifelines which connected Spain and her possessions in the New World, though undramatic because it was an essentially defensive task, constitutes one of the most remarkable success stories in the history of arms.

Closer to home, the struggle for control of the Mediterranean between the Spanish Habsburg and Ottoman empires, one of the truly pivotal conflicts of the post-classical world, was prosecuted largely by sea. That struggle ended with the combatants exhausted but essentially in place, Spain ravaged by inflation and drained by the demands of wars far from home and the Ottoman domains weakened by internal economic and political change prompted in no small measure by the social impact of gunpowder weapons.[13] This seemingly inconclusive outcome, however, need not blind us to the reality, clearly seen by contemporary observers, that things might have turned out very differently.[14] To note that little territory changed hands and that neither side was able to gain and exploit command of the sea to decisive economic effect is to miss the strategic point of the conflict through the application of inappropriate Napoleonic and Mahanian formulations. Contemporary observers were in little doubt that the signal victory of the Spanish-led fleet of the Holy Alliance over the forces of Islam at Lepanto on 9 October 1571 was decisive, and there is good reason to believe that they were right. If nothing else, that victory marked the end of Ottoman expansion in the eastern Mediterranean and the definitive isolation of the Iberian Muslims from their co-religionists' centers of power to the east. Lepanto also ensured the survival of Venice as an independent, prosperous and reasonably powerful polity for the next two centuries.

The complex of strategic problems and opportunities confronting Spain during the sixteenth century are not readily disentangled and reduced to simple formulations. The intertwined Habsburg and Spanish—or, more properly, Austrian, Castillian and Aragonese—responsibilities were economic as well as military and ranged far beyond the European and Mediterranean orbits. With Philip II's acquisition of the Portuguese throne in 1580, they expanded to encompass Brazil and the East Indies. Still, it would be a mistake to treat the components of Spain's far-flung strategic problem as if they operated in isolation, for they did not and were not so perceived at the time. The Austrian Habsburg/Ottoman struggle in Central Europe induced perturbations in the Mediterranean, and vice versa, and the mechanics of interaction could be remarkably direct: a small siege train of French cannon, a gift of King Louis XII, gave Khaireddin Barbarossa his start as the scourge of Spain in the Mediterranean and Spanish infantry fought at Vienna in 1529. The Inca emperor Atahuallpa's ransom financed the capture of Tunis in 1535, and Hernán Cortés, the conqueror of Mexico, was present in the Emperor Charles V's suite during the 1541 Algiers expedition. The Habsburg/Valois struggle for Italy spilled over into the Caribbean, and the Revolt of the Netherlands had truly global repercussions. German *Landsknechts* served aboard Spanish galleys at Lepanto in 1571; indeed, 7,300 of the 27,800 infantry in Spanish service at Lepanto were German, outnumbering the 6,000 Italians.[15] Lepanto had important diplomatic repercussions, of which the acquisition of Ragusa, nominally a dependency of the Porte as a surprisingly strong *de facto* Spanish ally, was not the least. Ragusan ships under hire to the Spanish crown formed the core of the principal Spanish squadron in the West Indies, the *Armada de el Mar Oceano*, during much of the late sixteenth and early seventeenth centuries[16] and made significant contributions to other expeditions, including that of 1588.

But our concern here is with the intersection between strategy, operations and logistics, not with that between policy, strategy and operations. That is to say, our focus is not on what was done and why, though that must be considered, but on how. The matrix suggested by the brief and partial recapitulation above can be reduced to manageable proportions by approaching the problem from an operational perspective, dividing Spain's strategic problems into more or less discrete spheres on functional and geographic grounds. Since my concern is institutional rather than episodic, this approach has the additional advantage of paralleling the Spanish institutional structure, specifically the network of consultative and executive bodies alluded to above.[17] Within that network, those most directly involved in setting strategic goals at the highest levels and reckoning the cost of pursuing them during the period of our concern were the *Consejo de Estado*, the Council of State; the *Consejo de la Guerra*, the Council of War; and the *Consejo de Hacienda*, roughly the Council of Finance.[18] From the beginning of the united Spanish monarchy, these bodies were backed and paralleled by the *Consejo de Castilla* and the *Consejo de Aragón*; derived from the two kingdoms' ancient royal councils, they were concerned with local government, notably finances, taxation and the administration of defense.[19] As Spain's imperial interests expanded, the concilar structure expanded according to a chronology which hints at the strategic priorities of Charles I and Philip II. The *Consejo de las Indias* was functioning by 1529; the *Consejo de Italia*, the Council of Italy, was established in 1522 by imperial order of Charles V, though it did not begin functioning until 1555, the year in which the *Consejo de Flandes*, the Council of Flanders, was established.[20] The *Consejo de Portugal* was established by Philip II in 1582, two years after his assumption of the Portuguese throne.[21]

The execution of strategy in the field by operational means was the province of viceroys, captains general, and at times commanders of lesser grade. They, like their royal and imperial superior, functioned within a conceptual context framed within the concilar structure, but in contrast to the complex, interleaved structure of conciliar bodies and their executive organs, the chain of command from monarch to commander in the field was short, uncomplicated and clear. This presents a seeming paradox, for against the apparent dispersion of focus and effort, which the decentralized structure of consultative and support organs implies, stood the powerful, centralizing tendencies of the Spanish Habsburg monarchy.[22] In all of history few monarchs have held the reins of power more closely than Philip II—or more of them—and he only followed and expanded on the precedent of his imperial father, who in turn followed and expanded on the precedent of Queen Isabella of Castile. The seeming paradox of a powerfully centralized command structure working in harness with a widely dispersed consultative and resource mobilization structure was a central characteristic of Spanish strategic planning and implementation throughout the period of our concern.

The institutional framework outlined above formed the uppermost level of a comprehensive administrative structure which controlled the allocation of resources for Spain's projection of power by sea. It is important to note in this regard that Spain's strategic combinations did not separate cleanly into land and sea categories. Even where the primary commitment of military forces was on land, movement and sustenance by sea played a major role in almost every case. Moreover, Spanish operations in the Mediterranean and local defensive operations in the Caribbean were amphibious in character, revolving around the use of war galleys to transport land forces to their objectives and to support them once there. We will therefore proceed by breaking down the Spanish logistical problem into its basic components, following contemporary practice insofar as possible, and then briefly examine the way in which Spain applied her logistical assets strategically and operationally.

For our purposes we can define logistics as the procurement, marshaling and deployment of resources. Procurement involves determining what resources are needed, locating, laying claim to and paying for them. Marshaling entails processing the raw materials into the stuff of war: training recruits; making saltpeter, charcoal and sulphur into gunpowder; converting grain into bread and biscuit; turning raw timber into pikestaffs, gun carriages and the hulls and spars of ships; processing raw hemp into rope and canvas; converting ore, fuel and labor into bronze cannon and wrought iron ordnance, edged weapons, armor, and ships' fittings; turning labor, earth, timber, brick and stone into fortifications and port facilities. Deployment encompasses the process of transporting the processed human and animal resources and materiel where it is needed. With deployment, we have arrived at the intersection between logistics on the one hand and strategy and operations on the other. From the logistical perspective, strategy determines where manpower and materiel are needed, and operations is the process of getting them there.

Spanish officials and planners in the sixteenth century approached logistics in terms of a hierarchy of functions and events which encompassed the procurement, marshaling and deployment of resources for war, beginning with fiscal concerns and ending with the dispatch of armed and equipped ships and men. I will follow contemporary practice as closely as possible in working my way through that hierarchy. This produces some surprises: ships, for example, were "armed" for war not just with ordnance and provisions but with men as well, and I will consider vessels and their complements together.

Money

Spain's fiscal resources for war came from three primary sources: taxes and imposts, the royal share of treasure from the New World, and borrowing. Taxation was the most important of these in terms of revenue realized and was organized along regional and functional lines in a system which showed clear evidence of decentralized feudal origins on the one hand and piecemeal adjustment to meet the crisis of the moment on the other. Relevant examples were rents on Church properties levied with papal consent, in principle to defray the cost of the war against Islam but in practice thrown into the general coffer; the *fardas*, property taxes levied to pay for local defense[23]; and the *avería*, a tax levied on merchandise going to or from America to defray the cost of defending the convoys in which it traveled.[24] As Spain's strategic commitments expanded during the sixteenth century, her populace became one of the most heavily taxed in Europe, and local resistance in the late 1570s to increases in the rate of the *alcabala*, the sales tax, suggests that by that time the practical limits of taxation were being approached.[25] Over the long run, the burden of taxation was a major factor behind the stagnation of commerce and industry in Spain. Over the short run, however, if a century can be so styled, the heavy burden of taxation served its purpose of keeping ships at sea and men in the field.

A major factor behind Spain's ability to bear increased strategic responsibilities during the sixteenth century was the receipt of quantities of bullion from the New World, of which the king received 20 percent of legal imports. This began with gold from the Caribbean from 1494, increased dramatically, albeit briefly, with the ransom of Moctezuma, supplemented from the 1520s by scattered gold finds in Central America, followed by silver discoveries in Mexico from the 1530s.[26] The gold deposits in the Caribbean had played out by the 1530s, but the ransom of Atahuallpa, captured in 1534, produced another spike in receipts; this was followed by the proceeds of the first of a series of gold strikes in Ecuador in the 1540s.[27] The discovery at Potosí in Peru of massive silver deposits in 1545, a veritable "mountain of silver," expanded the flow to a steady torrent; to the silver of Potosí was added Mexican silver from deposits in Zacatecas, found in 1546, followed by finds in Guanajuato and Pochuca.[28] Finally, significant gold deposits were found in Ecuador in the 1540s.[29]

While treasure seems to have accounted for no more than 12-20 percent of royal revenues on a year in and year out basis,[30] the bullion represented discretionary capital which could be deployed immediately and thus had an impact all out of proportion to its monetary value. The disproportionate importance of New World bullion to Spanish strategic designs suggests a strong parallel with the importance of magazine-provided supplies to European field armies in the late seventeenth and eighteenth centuries. Just as tax revenues represented the bulk of Spanish fiscal resources in gross quantitative terms, fodder and provender gathered by forces in the field were quantitatively the most important element of logistical support for European field armies. Hinting at Spanish priorities in this regard is an accounting of monetary disbursements to defray the expenses of the Galleys of Spain, Spain's principal combatant naval unit in the Mediterranean, from August 1545 through May 1551: the amounts disbursed are given not only in Spanish ducats, as we would expect, but also in *pesos de minas*, American-minted pesos in which several of the disbursements were apparently made directly.[31]

But just as Spain would have been hamstrung strategically without American bullion, European field armies would have been crippled operationally without the bread, munitions, materiel, remounts and replacements supplied from magazines.[32] If one looks ahead, it is suggestive that gold imports from America received in Seville peaked during 1541-60.[33] Impelled by the massive flow of silver from Potosí, which leveled off only during the last quarter of the sixteenth century, the value of precious metals from America received in Seville continued to rise through the end of the century, peaking out about 1590-1600.[34]

Spain's strategic requirements exceeded her fiscal resources throughout the sixteenth century—the government declared itself bankrupt in 1557, 1575 and 1597—and increasingly resorted to borrowing to meet extraordinary expenses. Some of this was from banks in a form familiar to governments today, albeit with considerably higher interest (annual rates of 14 percent or more were common); some was from entrepreneurs who provided goods and services on credit; some was from senior commanders who were expected to defray part of the costs incurred by their forces and who might or might not expect reimbursement. Simple non-payment for goods and services rendered, in effect a forced loan, was an important source of revenue as well.

Once collected, monies had to be spent, and the structure of disbursement was as decentralized as that of taxation, though with an important distinction: Royal control was ensured in principle, and for the most part in fact, by an elaborate parallel accounting hierarchy of *contadores* and *veedores* , paymasters and inspectors. Here we can see evidence of logistical genius, for the Spanish were both master bureaucrats and competent soldiers.[35] From the logistical standpoint, the incredibly complex and, to our sensibilities, unfair and arbitrary system of raising and disbursing funds had one salient characteristic: it worked. This is not to say that it worked smoothly or with uniform efficiency; the record of army mutinies in the Netherlands provides eloquent testimony to the contrary. But in assessing the system of collection and disbursement, we must not fall into the trap of applying the standards of a later day but should evaluate it in terms of the strategic challenges which confronted it. We cannot say so definitively, for the data are sparse and the methodological tools imprecise, but it is surely only a slight exaggeration to say that the system squeezed every possible military advantage out of the fiscal resources available. It is also worth noting that decentralization of collection and disbursement gave the fiscal system a defensive robustness which was of immense value to Spain. The system was not particularly efficient in taking advantage of long lead times to marshal large forces, a point of sharp contrast with the Ottoman logistical system. It was highly effective in responding quickly to local threats and it is in this arena that the value of the seemingly paradoxical dispersal of logistical effort and tightly centralized command structure is most evident.

Commanders

To obtain a senior command appointment—or be forced to accept one, as was the case with the unfortunate Duke of Medina Sidonia in 1588—descent within an accepted noble lineage was the first, indispensable requirement. This was not a political technicality or artificial conceit but represented a deeply felt belief in the importance of *nobleza de sangre* —nobility of the blood—at every level of the social and military hierarchy. The possession of significant estates and holdings was important, for commanders were expected to defray much of the cost of their operations; so was the antiquity and status of the family line. Standing at court and familial and personal alliances could be decisive as well. Competence seems to have been more or less presumed, and a record of demonstrated success was less important than we might expect. That having been said, the presumption of competence was far more often justified than not. Though hardly militarized in the modern sense of the word, Spanish society was imbued from top to bottom with values and virtues relevant to the demands of war, and standards of operational competence were extraordinarily high. If anything, those standards of competence were even higher at intermediate and lower levels of command, for an important inheritance of the *Reconquista* was a broadly based local nobility of military service which carried the burden of what we would call officership. Though the values and virtues in question did not translate into competence in blue water naval service as readily as on land, it is probably accurate to say that Spain could muster more competent company and field grade officers, qualitatively or quantitatively, than any other European state.

Galleys

When the sixteenth century dawned, the Mediterranean war galley was the most prominent example of extreme technological specialization for military purposes at sea, and a remarkably successful one. The means by which galleys and their smaller cousins, galiots, *fragatas*, and *bergantines*, were procured, fitted out, armed, provisioned and operated, represented the refinement of a technology which went back to classical times. The design of oared fighting vessels was well understood and essentially standard except for variations in size, and relatively little technical detail was required in contracts for the construction or hire of war galleys; in contrast with sailing ships, the emphasis was on the size and composition of the crew, particularly the rowing gang, or *chusma*, the size of the vessel being determined by the number of banks of oars and oarsmen per bank. A limited number of galleys, and later galeasses, were constructed in royal *atarazanas*, or arsenals; however, the overwhelming majority of war galleys in Spanish service at any given time were furnished and operated under contract by individual entrepreneurs who might or might not command the vessels and squadrons in question. It was common for a galley squadron to include several galleys provided by the squadron commander under *asiento*, or contract, operated alongside royal galleys and the galleys of other *asientistas*. Spain's allies were called upon to provide galley squadrons in time of need, and these generally served under their native commanders.

As a result of the limited seaworthiness of galleys, a direct consequence of their extreme design to maximize performance under oars which yielded impressive military capabilities under benign sea conditions, Mediterranean galley warfare was intensely seasonal in character. Galley fleets and squadrons generally campaigned only between mid-April and late October; during the balance of the year their crews could perform economically useful functions ashore and, according to the inexorable logic of the subsistence economies in which most of them lived, did so. At the beginning of the sixteenth century the manning of war galleys seems to have been a local enterprise in which coastal communities furnished crews on a seasonal basis, partly for plunder and partly for pay, the members receiving a salary according to their function plus a biscuit ration and a monetary food allowance. These crews were relatively non-specialized with the largest number being free oarsmen who were expected to fight when the occasion demanded; the role of marine infantry for boarding operations and skirmishing ashore was filled by sailor/arquebusiers who could apparently perform either function with equal facility.[36]

Though the exact cause and effect relationships are unclear, a general rise in salaries, probably due mainly to inflation, effectively priced the free oarsman out of business by mid-century. He was replaced by rowing gangs filled by slaves and convicts, though he did not immediately disappear altogether; as late as Lepanto small numbers of free oarsmen were hired to fill the rowing benches in times of crisis. At the same time, or perhaps a bit later, the sailor/arquebusiers began to give way to specialist mariners and regular infantry; this evolution reached a critical turning point in the wake of Spanish defeat at Djerba in 1560, where losses of *oficiales* and sailor/arquebusiers forced the use of embarked infantry as a matter of course.[37] These changes had important logistical implications, as outlined below.[38]

The war galley's logistical heart was biscuit, a hard-baked brown bread similar to hard tack; its soul was water. These two commodities were as important to the logistics of galley warfare as were fodder and bread to war on land, where as a rule the availability of water could be more or less taken for granted. Water requirements varied with heat, humidity, cloud cover, how hard the rowing gang was worked and a host of other factors, but a rough average of half a gallon per man per day is a conservative estimate.[39] The mass and bulk of water casks combined with the severely limited stowage space in the long, slender hull of a galley to make water the principal logistical constraining factor in galley operations. This imposed an iron limit of about two weeks, or a one week radius of action, within which a war galley had to replenish its water supply.[40] The dimensions of the problem can be grasped by considering the size of an ordinary galley's crew: some 144-150 oarsmen and 80-120 *gente de cabo*,[41] all crammed into a hull measuring some 136 feet in length and 16-20 feet across, early in the sixteenth century. By 1560 the figures had increased to 164 oarsmen and 80-90 *gente de cabo*;[42] by the time of Lepanto, the figure had increased to 174 oarsmen and 80-90 *gente de cabo*.[43] For *galeras de lanterna*, lantern galleys, more heavily armed and frequently larger than ordinary galleys, the growth in size was larger still. Moreover, additional manpower was habitually taken on board for relief expeditions and major engagements, and the addition could be substantial: no less than 300 infantrymen were crammed onto each of the galleys of the "Big Relief" at the siege of Malta in 1565, and ordinary Spanish galleys were armed with no less than 200 oarsmen and 150 *gente de cabo* at Lepanto.[44]

It goes without saying that the difficulty of obtaining water increased exponentially with larger complements and larger squadrons. That the watering needs of galley fleets were successfully met on a more or less routine basis speaks volumes for high standards of logistic competence. Watering was of such central importance, and was so routinely and competently handled, that it is only alluded to in surviving documents. Nor should this be a surprise: how deep would one have to dig into primary documentation of the Battle of Britain, for instance, to find a clinical description of the way in which the Spitfires and Hurricanes which turned back the *Luftwaffe* were refueled and rearmed? We can, however, reasonably speculate: We know that beaching to send watering parties ashore was a constant feature of galley warfare, analogous to foraging for fodder on land but of even more central importance. We know, too, that sailing ships, warships and logistical support vessels alike accompanied galley fleets on major expeditions. It is reasonable to suppose that, at least on exceptional occasions, they carried water casks to be dispensed to the galleys.[45]

Next to water in importance came biscuit, rich in the carbohydrates needed for rowing endurance, issued on the basis of 26 ounces per man per day, with officers receiving extra rations. This daily allowance was at times supplemented by fresh bread, particularly for the oarsmen when the need for an extraordinary effort was anticipated.[46] After biscuit, in rough order of importance as reflected in the order of listing in provisioning documents, came oil, vinegar, wine, beef (apparently fresh), bacon, cheese, salt and fresh fish, garbanzos and beans. The balance among these, and to whom they were issued in what proportions, changed according to changing economic, social and strategic circumstances. At the beginning of the century, Spanish galleys were rowed by free, salaried men who received the same meat allowance as the *gente de cabo*, an eight ounce ration three times a week; by the 1580s, oarsmen were almost entirely slaves and *forzados* who—in theory—received an eight ounce meat ration on a handful of religious feast days per year and received almost all of their slender protein allowance from a daily cup of garbanzos.⁴⁷ By contrast, the *gente de cabo* received, in addition to the eight ounce ration of beef three times a week, weekly six ounce rations of cheese, fish and bacon, plus a generous daily ration of as much as a quart of wine.

By and large, war galleys seem to have gone forth in search of their provisions rather than having had their provisions dispatched to them, no doubt an echo of patterns of naval commerce and warfare going back to Homer's time and beyond. We know, for example, that in the winter of 1566 two of the Galleys of Spain were sent from their wintering base to collect prisoners from the Seville gaol to be impressed as oarsmen, and that the squadron received monetary compensation for the expense of so doing.⁴⁸

Beyond potable and edible provisions, consumed on a daily basis, war galleys required replacement spars, oars, sails and tackle, clothing for servile oarsmen who lacked a salary with which to purchase their own, naval stores and grease to protect the hull from marine growth. Gunpowder ordnance, cannon and small arms alike, occupied an increasingly pivotal role in galley warfare from the mid-fifteenth century on, and the impact on galley warfare was enormous. As the numbers of available cannon increased, their use aboard galleys became more common. The resultant increase in weight demanded an increase in motive power if the all-important tactical advantage of speed under oars was not to be lost, and the resultant increase in the number of oars and oarsmen further increased the logistical demands of operating a galley. The net result was logistically induced strategic stasis by the century's end.⁴⁹

Last but not least, a war galley consumed not only provisions, munitions, naval stores and replacement parts, sails and tackle, but money in the form of salaries and disbursements for the local purchase of supplies and provisions. The balance between direct provisioning from magazines and arsenals and local purchase will be addressed below, but a word on salaries is in order. Spanish payrolls afloat were apparently met with greater alacrity than on land, for mutinies seem to have been singularly uncommon aboard galleys and sailing warships. We can only speculate as to the reasons: perhaps the crown was protecting its capital investment in hulls and ordnance.

Sailing Ships

In the sixteenth century, deep water sailing warships were at the cutting edge of military technology—or any other kind of technology—in size, power, efficient use of structural materials and sophistication of design. At the same time, the specialized sailing warship was a new technology, and the dividing line between armed merchantman and warship was indistinct. Warships represented a major outlay of capital, and it is safe to say that Spain constructed no more than the absolute minimum demanded by the perceived strategic imperatives of her situation. The logistical wherewithal of war at sea tends not to be readily transferable to other spheres of military or economic activity and to require a commensurately greater degree of technical and organizational specialization. The kinds of wood needed for ship construction were not always readily available close to home, and even when they were, particular care had to be taken to control the size, shape and quality of timbers. Until the mid-nineteenth century, the wooden structures of ships represented the apex of excellence in the art of mechanical design and construction, of pushing materials to as close to their limits as possible as a matter of economic and military necessity.[50] Nor was the extreme nature of the technological and therefore logistical demands of warfare at sea confined to wood. By the sixteenth century, the larger ocean-going warships required iron fittings, specifically, rudder gudgeons and anchors, of a size and strength demanded by no other technology.

The logistical demands of deep water activity entailed a similar degree of specialization, and the structure of government-owned arsenals and shipyards which had evolved in response to conflict in the Mediterranean does not seem to have been suited for the construction of sailing warships. In consequence, the hard core of Spain's deep sea squadrons consisted of vessels constructed by private entrepreneurs under government contract, an arrangement which shifted the burden of initial capital investment from government to contractor. Major items of expense in the construction of sailing vessels included timber, much of which had to be imported from the Baltic, and hemp for canvas, which seems to have been imported for the most part as well. In contrast to galleys, there was considerable variation in the size, design and handling characteristics of sailing warships. Official notions as to what was operationally desirable and most cost-effective varied with time and consequently construction contracts were quite detailed and specific in their provisions. Individual warships, and even squadrons, were hired under contract to supplement the royal standing squadrons, and in time of need, ships of friendly polities were impressed into Spanish service.[51] When this occurred, the captains were generally replaced by royal appointees and the vessel was armed, manned and provisioned under the direction of royal officials.

The manpower requirements of Spain's deep sea squadrons of warships and sailing vessels on the Atlantic run were apparently a matter of more than routine concern to royal officials and merchants alike, and the crews of these vessels seem to have been long term salaried professionals almost from the beginning. In addition, government-supported schools were established for navigators and gunners. Provisioning requirements for sailing vessels were met by the port structure outlined below, and on the whole the sailor's diet seems to have been more than adequate in total caloric content and for the most part in nutritional terms. There was particular official concern for the safety of vessels trading with the Indies, and the *Casa de Contratación*, charged with licensing and supervision, published an elaborate series of rules prescribing minimum standards of armament based on tonnage.

In contrast to galleys and galley squadrons, sailing warships seem to have been provisioned almost entirely in kind from royal stocks, stored in magazines and issued to the ships' masters at the dock. As with galleys, water and biscuit were the most important consumables, with vinegar, olive oil, beef, bacon and cheese, garbanzos and fish placing prominently in provisioning documents. But there the similarity stops. There were two grades of biscuit, *vizcocho comun* or *vizcocho baso*, presumably the same as that issued to galleys, and *vizcocho blanco*, "white" biscuit of better quality issued in smaller amounts.[52] The beef was almost entirely salted and stored in casks rather than fresh; the fish was not only fresh and salted but preserved in casks as well; although the vocabulary is sometimes obscure, the precise manner of storage and preservation is recorded: oil, wine and vinegar in barrels of specific kinds and capacities; cheeses of specific sizes; quantities of beef by total weight and numbers of quarters. Other edibles appear which are not seen in equivalent galley listings, though they do not displace biscuit, oil, vinegar, wine, beef and bacon in importance as judged by quantity and the order of listing: raisins, almonds, rice and garlic.[53] As with galleys, water seems never to have been included in provisioning documents, perhaps because water was so central to survival that responsibility for its collection, storage and dispensation was never delegated beyond the ship. Certainly, the water casks themselves clearly belonged to the ship and thus do not enter provisioning records.

Sailing vessels were routinely impressed to provide logistical support for major expeditions and, though there is little direct evidence of the methods employed, were used to support the logistical requirements of galley fleets and squadrons. We know, for example, that in March of 1566 the magazine at Malaga contracted with the master of a *chalupa*, a small sailing vessel, to deliver biscuit and other supplies to the Galleys of Spain wintering at Puerto de Santa Maria.[54] There is no reason to suppose that this kind of arrangement was exceptional; indeed, during the same period the Malaga magazine went so far as to subcontract not only the delivery of provisions but oversight and legal documentation of their receipt.[55]

Ports and Permanent Facilities

From antiquity, war at sea revolved around a symbiotic relationship between ships, squadrons and fleets and the port cities which created them and gave them sustenance. By the sixteenth century tacit understanding of that relationship had developed to a high degree of sophistication, particularly in the Mediterranean. The procurement and marshaling of resources for warfare at sea rested on an elaborate structure of ports and seaside fortifications, dockyards and arsenals, magazines and replenishing facilities. Particularly important were the major port cities, where physical, human and fiscal resources came together to form fleets and squadrons: for Spain, these included Barcelona, the linchpin of Aragon's old Mediterranean empire and the site of a major royal shipyard and arsenal; Valencia and Cartagena, important focal points for provisioning and local defense; Malaga, of less importance than Barcelona as a port but the location of a major magazine and an important site of artillery manufacture; Genoa, an important fiscal center and the head of its own maritime empire; Naples and Messina, home ports for major galley squadrons and logistical cornucopias through which the resources of their respective kingdoms flowed out into the empire; Seville, eastern anchor of Spain's trans-Atlantic lifeline and commercial heart of the Indies trade; Cadiz, an important provisioning center and strategically located transit port; Lisbon, hub of the Portuguese empire and, once within the Habsburg orbit, Castile's main maritime window to the North Atlantic; Bilbao, an important trading and shipbuilding center; Santa Cruz, Mexico, and Havana, western anchors of Spain's trans-Atlantic lifeline and the Indies trade; Vera Cruz, an important local provisioning center and transshipment point for Peruvian and Mexican silver. Though their military involvement was peripheral until after the Twelve Years' Truce, Lima and Panama City were vital as transshipment points for Peruvian bullion. Each of these cities combined port facilities with arsenals, cannon foundries, powder mills, biscuit ovens and magazines for the collection and storage of expendable supplies. To a large extent, the strategic rhythms of warfare at sea revolved around them.

The major port cities were supported by a network of lesser ports and coastal fortifications which served as points of replenishment, refuge and departure for ships and squadrons. As with finance, the structure of permanent facilities was complex and decentralized, unsurprisingly since it emerged from the local requirements of Spain's component kingdoms and provinces during the *Reconquista*; indeed, the major arsenals were originally founded under Arab rule,[56] suggesting an overarching geographic logic behind their locations.[57] In general terms, ports, dockyard facilities and magazines were the responsibility of the local polity, with an inspector general function residing in the Captain General of the Sea, while major arsenals were maintained and financed wholly or in part by the crown.[58]

A network of magazines where materiel and supplies were collected and stored formed the link between marshaling and deployment, and examination of the way in which they were stocked provides important insights. A document reflecting the disbursements of the magazine at Malaga to the Galleys of Spain, the chief Spanish galley squadron in the Mediterranean, from 1562 to 1568 is of particular interest in this regard as a detailed and apparently comprehensive accounting of provisions, money and supplies furnished a key unit by a major magazine at a critical time.[59] The account suggests that royal arsenals and magazines supplied galley squadrons more by exception than as a matter of routine, and that the burden of day to day provisioning was arranged by squadron commanders and their representatives on the spot. In crude terms, the document suggests that the magazine supplied the Galleys of Spain more often by the dispatch of specie for the local purchase of provisions than by direct supply of the provisions themselves. Significantly, the direct dispatch of provisions was mostly to support the Galleys of Spain when wintering nearby, and even that would appear to have represented only a portion of the squadron's wintering requirements.

Ordnance

Heavy ordnance suitable for arming ships and defending or assailing fortresses was a vital requirement of warfare at sea, particularly with respect to cannon of cast bronze, the premier ordnance of the day. Spanish bronze cannon were considered good, though inferior to the best Venetian, Flemish or German pieces, but local manufacture was never sufficient. The problem became worse when the English learned to cast serviceable cannon of iron after 1543, for cast iron cannon, though heavier, bulkier and less safe than equivalent pieces of bronze, cost only a third as much. Spanish gunners were well acquainted with the strengths and weaknesses of ordnance produced within various national traditions: bronze cannon cast by Spanish founders were considered good, if heavier and more unwieldy than those cast by Venetian or German founders; Genoese ordnance was considered poorly cast and suspect.[60] Spain was forced to procure much of her heavy ordnance abroad, and an important indirect effect of the Revolt of the Netherlands was to cut off an important source of good ordnance. That as a general proposition Spanish naval units do not seem to have suffered from a crippling insufficiency of artillery is therefore a tribute to the efficient distribution of a scarce resource. In this context, the malformed pieces recovered from Armada wrecks suggest just how close to the line those responsible for the procurement of naval ordnance must have been forced to tread.

Soldiers

The remarkable cohesion, tactical effectiveness, fortitude and adaptability of Spanish soldiery was a major source of Habsburg military power and strategic resilience, on sea as on land, but with the advantage of over four centuries of hindsight one is entitled to wonder if Spain was not afflicted with too much of a good thing. From the logistical standpoint, Spanish soldiery represented at one and the same time a vitally important tactical and operational strength and a strategic weakness. On the average, Spanish infantry was the best in the world. The Italian and German units in Spanish service weren't far behind, but they imposed heavy fiscal and logistical demands; they took time to train and their numbers were accordingly small. This combination meshed well—perhaps too well—with the strategic scenario which confronted Spain, particularly in the Mediterranean. Since the initiative lay with the Muslims, particularly prior to the cessation of active Ottoman-Habsburg hostilities, Spain had to be able to respond quickly to unexpected thrusts. For this, companies of salaried regular infantry were ideal, particularly in defensive and counter-offensive operations where skill and fortitude could compensate for a lack of numbers. They could be moved quickly over long distances and served with equal facility in field operations, in sieges or on the decks of war galleys. But the qualities of Spanish infantry were the critical integers in a self-fulfilling strategic prophetic equation. Spain, on the strategic defensive, had no choice but to maintain high standards of readiness. That could only be done with salaried, full-time regulars which for fiscal reasons meant small numbers, and those small numbers locked Spain into a defensive posture. Spain's failure to expand into the eastern Mediterranean in the wake of Lepanto can be better understood in this light. The conquest of Tunis in 1535 was financed with Atahuallpa's ransom, but there were few such ransoms to be had, and as Spain's strategic commitments increased in size and geographic extent, American bullion had to be spent immediately for defensive schemes rather than saved for offensive ones.

The local militias of coastal provinces subject to raids from the sea were the other major component of the Spanish posture on land. Working in conjunction with galley squadrons and aided by systems of watchtowers and fortified villages, these could be reasonably effective. Like so much else in the Spanish system, the militia system was decentralized and localized, in this case trading fiscal efficiency for operational effectiveness.

Overview of Procurement and Marshaling

Before we leave procurement and marshaling, a general summation is in order. As a general proposition, the logistics of warfare on land cannot be cleanly separated from those of warfare at sea until the late seventeenth century at the earliest, particularly in the Mediterranean. In consequence, the two overlapped in Spanish practice, particularly in the critical area of provisioning and supply. At the intersection between marshaling and deployment, the differences in principle were more of degree than of kind but differed enormously in practice. First, the logistics of warfare at sea were far more developed than were those of land warfare. It would be safe to say that the symbiotic relationship between naval forces and their logistical support apparatus, not least of all port cities and fortified ports, was as sophisticated and well developed in the sixteenth century as that between magazine and army came to be in the eighteenth. To cite a salient example, the use of fortified ports to support the raiding activities of galley squadrons in the sixteenth century strongly resembles the use of frontier fortifications in the eighteenth as bases for offensive raiding on land.[61] Second is the importance of water as a driving factor in logistic planning and operational execution; this was not a quantitative difference but a qualitative one. Third is the importance of biscuit, the dry, hard-baked wheaten bread which was the staple of warfare and commerce at sea. Highly nutritious, if not always particularly palatable, biscuit was the essential fuel of galley warfare and less important to warfare under sail only by comparison. Biscuit could not provide the oarsman, sailor or soldier with all of his nutritional requirements, a fact of which sixteenth century Spanish naval logisticians had a surprisingly sophisticated grasp, but it could and did provide him with the bulk of his calories.[62] It did so, moreover, in a form which was relatively economical, and it could be stored almost indefinitely. The operational importance of biscuit was matched by its fiscal importance, particularly in the Mediterranean, for the cost of biscuit was the largest single item in the expense of operating a war galley. It should be no surprise that increases in the cost of wheat during the sixteenth century, and hence biscuit, were reflected in a reduced scale of galley operations.

If the limiting strategic logistical factor in land operations was almost always fodder, biscuit was that of warfare at sea, water being the limiting factor tactically. But there was an important difference: naval tacticians seem to have been more successful in obtaining water and naval logisticians more successful in making biscuit available when and where it was needed than were their land counterparts in securing fodder. This observation is no calumny of soldiers, for their problem was far less tractable to predictable solution; ships, after all, were far more efficient bulk carriers than pack animals or wagons, and each ship was, in effect, its own magazine. Even highly specialized oared fighting ships with severely restricted cargo capacities and enormous crews routinely carried several weeks' supply of biscuit; indeed, biscuit was so compact and light that a relative abundance could be carried, the main limitation for sailing vessels being spoilage on protracted voyages.

As with finances, the process of obtaining and stockpiling biscuit was highly decentralized (though, curiously, the manufacture of gunpowder was apparently a royal monopoly).[63] In Spanish practice, biscuit appears to have been baked by local entrepreneurs[64] and purchased directly by commanders of ships and squadrons, who might be royal officials, private entrepreneurs or both, and on a local basis by royal officials to stock magazines. By contrast, in both the Ottoman and Venetian naval bureaucracies the production and procurement of biscuit was coordinated by a single high-level official.[65]

Deployment

Having outlined procurement and marshaling, we turn briefly to deployment, the link between logistics and strategy. In deployment, as with operations, geography exercises a decisive influence, and the diverse and wide ranging nature of Spain's strategic commitments exercised a preemptive influence on naval logistics in particular. The most venerable of these commitments, and one which left its mark on the institutions described above, was the struggle against Muslim sea *ghazis*.[66] Next in antiquity was the struggle against armed raiders in northern waters.[67] Next chronologically were the wars against Valois France triggered by Charles VIII's invasion of Italy in 1494 and waged intermittently until the Treaty of Cateau Cambresis in 1559; though these wars were predominantly a land struggle, they had an important naval dimension as well.[68] Most important of all was the struggle against the Ottoman Turks, which merged with that against the North African *ghazi* states in the 1520s.[69] That struggle, with its vital land dimension on the Austrian frontier, probably absorbed a greater proportion of Spanish resources than any other until displaced by the Revolt of the Netherlands. Maintenance of the convoy system between Seville and the New World ranks well down the list in terms of resources committed but was arguably Spain's first strategic priority at sea and forced the development of a sophisticated logistical infrastructure which extended from Seville through the Caribbean to Peru. Although containment of the *guerre de course* against Spanish shipping and possessions in the Caribbean absorbed far fewer resources than Habsburg ventures in the Mediterranean and Flanders, the effort was strategically vital and required striking adjustments in terms of organization and technology. Finally, efforts to suppress Dutch Protestantism and resistance to Spanish rule from 1567 on absorbed the bulk of Spanish silver and the lion's share of Spanish manpower, and preemptively so after the Habsburg-Ottoman truce of 1580.[70] Although the political center of gravity of the Eighty Years' War was on land, the economic center of gravity was arguably at sea, and the conflict had a pivotal maritime dimension from beginning to end.

Conclusion

Considered against the backdrop of Spain's strategic commitments, what lessons can we draw from our exercise? How, in the broadest terms, does our analysis of Spain's procurement, marshaling and deployment of resources for the exercise of armed power at sea inform our understanding of logistics?

First, it is apparent that Spain's military successes in the sixteenth century were not attributable to pure tactical grit and operational brilliance. If we view these successes from the logistical perspective, it is apparent that the rational mobilization and allocation of resources played a major role. Crudely put, Spanish operational and strategic success was as much attributable to brains as brawn. To cite one example among many, Lepanto was a brilliant and hard fought battle, but the marshaling and deployment of the fleet which fought it was a minor miracle of applied logistics. Much of the credit goes to Venice to be sure, but Spain was the senior partner in the enterprise and deserves an appropriate share of the credit.

Second, Spain's strategic position during the period under investigation was profoundly affected by the logistical impact of macro-economic trends, and this appears to have been particularly true at sea. Though it is difficult to connect effects to specific events, the net impact of the forces at work is clear. In part because of inflation, itself an important secondary consequence of the import by Spain of large quantities of precious metals from America, the cost of naval operations increased enormously during the period under discussion, and more so in Spain than elsewhere. The price of biscuit provided to Spanish naval forces quadrupled between 1529 and 1587 and was still climbing at century's end,[71] in large measure a reflection of the secular rise in wheat prices already mentioned. Perhaps most obviously, the sharp rise in meat prices in Andalusia from the first decades of the sixteenth century is mirrored by meat's disappearance from the diet of oarsmen aboard Spanish galleys.[72] Though real wages declined, the salaries of the officers, mariners and soldiers aboard Spanish warships increased during the period with which we are concerned. The important exception to this generalization, of course, was the replacement of free oarsmen with slaves and convicts, almost entirely after 1550, but even with this important economy—and contemporary documents make it clear that it was viewed as such—the cost of operating a galley increased by a factor of about four during the sixteenth century.[73] Though the data are scattered, the cost of sailing ship construction seems to have undergone a similar rise.[74] It is interesting in this light to note that the cost of cannon powder used on Spanish galleys seems to have increased by only about a third, 1529-1587, and that the price of arquebus powder apparently held constant during the last quarter of the sixteenth century.[75] It may be stretching a point to say that Braudel's data showing a decline in the price of bricks in England and Valencia during the period 1440-1575[76] cast an interesting light on the increasing importance of permanent fortifications during this period, a factor which was to work to Spain's detriment in the Netherlands.

Third and last, much of Spain's strategic success was attributable to the efficient translation of fiscal assets into operational resources. Credit and bullion were more easily transported across long distances than were troops, and Spanish commanders made good use of this fact to good effect again and again. The benefits of sending money instead of manpower were, moreover, explicitly understood; the Duke of Alba expressed just this point to the Emperor Charles V at the beginning of the Schmalkaldic War. Nor was skill in mobilizing and deploying resources from the center the whole story. Spain was also highly successful in mobilizing limited fiscal resources on a local and regional basis and converting them into strategic power, and it was on this basis as much as any other that the Muslim *guerre de course* in the western Mediterranean was contained.

But there is an opposite side to the coin: Spain reached the end of her strategic tether toward the beginning of the seventeenth century largely because of logistic deficiencies: what had worked well early in the sixteenth century no longer worked well toward its end, a reality nowhere more apparent than in Flanders and in naval operations against the Dutch. This was partly because of limitations of resource availability, which the cleverest of logisticians could not have circumvented—one cannot conjure up forests from cut-over mountains—but it was due also in part to the retention of administrative mechanisms which had evolved during times of relative plenty in a time of increasing want. The decentralized Spanish structure of taxation, resource mobilization, manufacture and disbursement was wonderfully efficient at shifting resources swiftly to the point of maximum danger. But it was a poor one for creating them where they did not exist, and when the Potosí silver mines began to dry up so did Spanish flexibility. The amazing thing is that the residual competence within the logistical mechanism facilitated Spain's survival as a major imperial power for another two centuries.

Finally, and perhaps most basic, the mobilization of Spain's fiscal resources and their conversion into military and naval power was not a simple exercise in ruthless gouging in revenue generation, sharp bookkeeping practices and penny pinching disbursement, the kind of exercise that today we would place under the rubric of cost benefit effectiveness. Spain secured her strategic goals to the extent that she did in large measure because her scribes, inspectors, accountants and disbursers understood her soldiers and sailors and their craft.

Notes

1. In Mexico and Peru tiny bands of Spaniards repeatedly prevailed against seemingly overwhelming numerical odds; see John. H. Elliott, "The Spanish Conquest and Settlement of America," *Cambridge History of Latin America*, Vol. I, *Colonial Latin America* (Cambridge: 1984), pp. 175-76, and John F. Guilmartin, Jr., "The Cutting Edge: An Analysis of the Spanish Invasion and Overthrow of the Inca Empire 1532-1539," in *Trans-Atlantic Encounters: Europeans and Andeans in the Sixteenth Century*, Kenneth Andrien and Rolena Adorno, eds. (Berkeley: 1991), pp. 40-69.

2. I use the term logistician as shorthand for those who provided the logistical wherewithal of war, whether as a primary or peripheral function. I do not mean to imply that they were thought of as logisticians in the modern sense, or that logistics was understood as a discrete subset of the art or craft of war.

3. While a major outranks a lieutenant, a major general outranks a lieutenant general since the former was originally a noncommissioned rank.

4. Geoffrey Parker, *The Army of Flanders and the Spanish Road, 1567-1659: The Logistics of Spanish Victory and Defeat in the Low Countries' Wars* (Cambridge: 1972); William

Maltby, *Alba: A Biography of Fernando Alvarez de Toledo, Third Duke of Alba 1507-1582* (Berkeley: 1983).

5. Carla Rahn Phillips, *Six Galleons for the King of Spain: Imperial Defense in the Early Seventeenth Century* (Baltimore: 1986).

6. Francisco-Felipe Olesa Muñido, *La Organización Naval de Los Estados Mediterraneos y en Especial de España Durante los Siglos XVI y XVII*, 2 vols. (Madrid: 1968).

7. Although some did. Whether they were the exception or the rule we cannot say, but some Spanish commanders were capable of rendering strategic military appreciations of a concise thoroughness and sophistication rarely equalled since. See, for example, that of Don Garcia de Toledo, submitted in his capacity as Viceroy of Sicily in anticipation of the pivotal campaign of 1565; *Colección Navarrete*, Vol. XII, document 79, fol 295 ff.

8. I. A. A. Thompson, *War and Government in Habsburg Spain 1560-1620* (London: 1976), p. 37.

9. For a summary of macro-economic trends, see Fernand Braudel, "Prices in Europe from 1450 to 1750," *The Cambridge Economic History of Europe* (henceforth CEH), Vol. IV, *The Economy of Expanding Europe in the Sixteenth and Seventeenth Centuries* (Cambridge: 1967), pp. 374-486; for the richness of Spanish archival sources, see John F. Guilmartin, Jr., *Gunpowder and Galleys: Changing Technology and Mediterranean Warfare at Sea in the Sixteenth Century* (Cambridge: 1974), pp. 221-27.

10. In BTU per ton mile or Joules per metric ton kilometer.

11. The same point holds for land operations across deserts and arid steppes, highlighting the pivotal importance of the logistical competence of the Arab armies of the conquest and their Byzantine opponents, *cf.* Walter Kaegi, Chapter 3, this volume.

12. Braudel, "Prices in Europe", Fig. 33, p. 484, showing the average nominal price of wheat dropping from a temporary peak *circa* 1440-1520 before beginning a general rise which lasted through the 1650s. The same pattern holds for Spain, though wheat prices seem to have been more stable in the fifteenth century, with a particularly sharp rise for Castile beginning *circa* 1520; *ibid.*, Fig. 19, pp. 470-71.

13. For the internal impact of foreign wars on the Ottoman domains during this period, John F. Guilmartin, Jr., "Ideology and Conflict: The Wars of the Ottoman Empire, 1453-1606," *Journal of Interdisciplinary History*, Vol. XVIII, No. 4 (Spring 1988), pp. 721-47, esp. pp. 729-33.

14. *Cf.* Thompson, *War and Government*, p. 26. I agree with Thompson's conclusion that the Habsburg-Ottoman stalemate in the Mediterranean is explainable largely in terms of the changing logistics of galley warfare, based in part on my own work, see p. 26, n. p. 43. I would argue further that the Ottomans possessed the wherewithal to have broken that stalemate until Lepanto. The Osmanli state fed on expansion in ways that the Habsburg empire did not, and had Malta fallen in 1565 or had the fleet of the Holy Alliance been crushingly defeated in 1571—either outcome a real possibility—then instability rather than strategic stasis might have ensued. Thompson makes a convincing case that Spain suffered from serious internal defensive deficiencies during this period, and a resurgent Ottoman naval presence in the western Mediterranean could have made an enormous difference.

15. *Colección Sanz de Barutell (Simancas),* in the collection of the Museo Naval, Madrid, henceforth *Sanz de Barutell (S),* Art. 4, vol. 2, document 325, fol. 432-34.

16. See, for example, *Sanz de Barutell (S)*, Art. 5, document 53, fol. 225-26, "Relación de los doze Galeones dela Esquadra Yllyrica de Pedro Yuella, y Estafano Dollisn [?] de Yuell...," the inventory of a squadron of twelve well armed galleons.

17. Executive in the sense that they exercised administrative powers of appointment and disbursement over the entities that they supervised.

18. See Olesa Muñido, *Organización Naval*, 1:387-413, for a functional breakdown. Three parallel bodies of lesser importance existed within the same structure: the *Consejo de Santo Oficio*, the Council of the Inquisition, dealing in essence with religious intelligence and counter-intelligence; the *Consejo de las Ordenes*, concerned with the affairs of the military orders of Alcántara, Calatrava and Santiago; and the *Consejo de Cruzada*, Council of the Crusade, established in 1509 to orchestrate the marshalling of fiscal resources for the struggle against Islam; *ibid.* pp. 432-27. The importance of these councils is open to question, but their institutional intent, vestigial or not, is plain. Indicative of the labyrinthine complexities of the structure, the Order of Santiago at times maintained and operated a squadron of galleys.

19. Olesa Muñido, *Organización Naval*, 1:413, 417. *Los Reyes Católicos* organized the *Consejo de Castilla* in 1480; Ferdinand established the *Consejo de Aragón* in 1494.

20. Olesa Muñido, *Organización Naval*, 1:420-22; the Council of Flanders was originally the *Consejo de Flandes y Borgoño*.

21. Olesa Muñido, *Organización Naval*, 1:421.

22. I am indebted to William Maltby of the University of Missouri at St. Louis for pointing out to me this seeming paradox in his critique of the initial version of this paper at the Sinews of War Conference, 3-6 October 1990.

23. Thompson, *War and Government*, pp. 67-8, 81-2; the *farda major* was specifically levied on Moriscos.

24. Phillips, *Six Galleons*, p. 9.

25. Thompson, *War and Government*, p. 68.

26. Lyle N. McAlister, *Spain and Portugal in the New World, 1492-1700* (Minneapolis: 1984), pp. 94-5, 138-43. The discovery of silver deposits in Mexico was followed closely by the introduction of lead-silver smelting techniques by Germans, *ibid.*, p. 228.

27. McAlister, *Spain and Portugal in the New World*, p. 143.

28. McAlister, *Spain and Portugal in the New World*, p. 228. See Braudel, "Prices in Europe," pp. 374-486, and Fig. 34, p. 485, for a graphic depiction of the flow, and A. Rupert Hall, "Scientific Method and the Progress of Techniques," CEH, Vol. IV, pp. 96-154, 100, for the application of the mercury amalgamation process, discovered in 1554-55 by one Bartolomé de Medina, a Mexican miner, see McAlister, p. 228.

29. McAlister, *Spain and Portugal in the New World*, p. 143.

30. Based on figures for government receipts by category for the period 1559-1621 given by Thompson, *War and Government*, p. 288, Table A. Cf. Phillips, *Six Galleons*, p. 14.

31. *Archivo General de Indias* (henceforth AGI), *Relación de loque se pagó desde dicho año* [1545] *hasta le de 1551 á D. Bernardino de Mendoza capitan general de las galeras de España para gastos de su Armada* ; Patronato 269, Relación 5, No. 1. The ducat, a gold coin of exchange, was valued at 375 *marevedis*, and the pesos in this document, whether of gold or silver we cannot say though the former seems more likely, at 450. The *marevedi*, a small copper coin which served as the standard Castillian money of account, retained

the same value in grams of fine silver from just before 1500 until just after 1600, Braudel, "Prices in Europe," Fig. 4, p. 458.

32. A point made forcefully by John Lynn.

33. McAlister, *Spain and Portugal in the New World*, p. 229.

34. Braudel, "Prices in Europe", Fig. 33-34, pp. 484-85; McAlister, *Spain and Portugal in the New World*, p. 229.

35. It is clear from internal evidence that sixteenth century Spanish military scribes understood the mechanics of war exceedingly well. To cite a relevant example, the ordnance of war galleys was not inventoried by type, size, weight or value but according to a sophisticated formula which combined tactical importance with physical location; see Guilmartin, "The Early Provisions of Artillery Armament on Mediterranean War Galleys," *The Mariner's Mirror*, Vol. 59, No. 2 (August 1973), pp. 257-80, for analysis of such an inventory of the Galleys of Spain in 1536.

36. See, for example, *Sanz de Barutell (S)*, Art. 5, document 2, fol. 5-14, detailing the operating costs in 1523 of a 25 bank ordinary galley of the Galleys of Spain, armed with 150 oarsmen, the bulk of them free and salaried; 22 *oficiales*, officers and technicians such as the pilot, gunners, the carpenter, cooper and surgeon; and 90 *compañeros sobresalientes*, armed sailor/arquebusiers. It cost $278^1/_2$ ducats per month to operate with a servile rowing gang and $408^1/_2$ with a free rowing gang; in either case the salaries of the *oficiales* and technicians, the *gente de cabo*, accounted for $149^1/_2$ ducats.

37. Guilmartin, *Gunpowder and Galleys*, pp. 131-34.

38. Compare with the 1523 data, n. 34, above, the manning of the Galleys of Naples, 1552-1557, *Sanz de Barutell (S)*, Art. 4, vol. 2, document 31, fol. 382: each ordinary galley had 24 rowing banks and was armed with 144 convict or slave oarsmen, 32 *oficiales* and mariners and 50 soldiers and cost 580 ducats per month to operate, of which 103 went to the *oficiales'* salaries and 100 to the soldiers' salaries.

39. Guilmartin, *Gunpowder and Galleys*, pp. 62-3.

40. John H. Pryor, *Geography, Technology, and War: Studies in the Maritime History of the Mediterranean, 649-1571* (Cambridge: 1988), pp. 76-78; based on his own calculations and an extensive survey of primary materials, Pryor prefers my estimate of 14 days, cited above, to that of 20 days advanced by William L. Rodgers, *Naval Warfare Under Oars, Fourth to Sixteenth Centuries* (Annapolis: 1939), p. 232.

41. *Sanz de Barutell (S)*, Art. 5, document 2, fol. 5-14, cited above for the Galleys of Spain, 1523, and Art. 3, vol. 1, document 17, fol. 71-72 for the Galleys of Sicily, 1529.

42. *Colección Navarrete, Museo Naval* (henceforth *Navarrete*), vol. XII, document 84, fol. 313, for the Galleys of Spain; *Sanz de Barutell (S)*, Art. 4, vol. 2, document 311, fol. 382, for the Galleys of Naples, 1552-1569.

43. *Sanz de Barutell (S)*, Art. 4, Vol. 2, document 323, fol. 424-428, for the Galleys of Spain; Art. 4, vol. 2, document 324, fol. 430-431, for the galleys of the Genoese condottieri Lucian Centurione and Pedro Bautista Lomellin.

44. Guilmartin, *Gunpowder and Galleys*, pp. 152, 243.

45. See Pryor, *Geography, Technology, and War*, p. 80, for a particularly suggestive example: Khaireddin Barbarossa's 1539 expedition against Castelnuovo, for which Haji Khalifeh lists a total number of water barrels for the expedition rather than per vessel averages, implying that the sailing ships kept a reserve for the galleys.

46. *E.g.*, giving the allowances for Spanish galleys in the Lepanto campaign.

47. E.g., Navarrete, Vol. XII, document 100, fol. 371, an ordinary Galley of Spain, 1580.

48. *Relación de los bastimentos y municiones que por librarse del Proveedor gomez verdugo mi en mano y mias sean dato a las galeras del cargo de don albaro bazan...* [from 8 May 1563 to 24 May 1568], AGI, Patronato : legajo 269, no. 1, r. 9, henceforth *Relación de los bastimentos*.

49. Guilmartin, *Gunpowder and Galleys*.

50. The shipwrights' only serious contemporary competitors in the sophisticated and demanding use of materials who come readily to mind are cannon founders and the builders of the last of the great Gothic cathedrals. The technical problems of cannon founding, of course, were part and parcel of warfare at sea, and the largest, and hence the most technically demanding, cannons were used first and most successfully at sea. Without taking anything away from the cathedral builders, I would argue that the shipwrights' task was the more demanding.

51. See, for example, *La Relacion de la artilleria y municiones que llevaron de dos navios Cierbo bolante y Leon colorado que salieron en busca de la armada del general Don Francisco Coloma del puerto de Lagos...* (1593), AGI, Patronato, legajo 254, no. 3, r. 3, n. 1, an account of two Dutch vessels seized and impressed into Spanish service with detailed inventories of ordnance and cargos, accounts of how the vessels were seized and the crews interrogated.

52. E. g. *Relaciones de las entregadas y bastimentos y municiones que se hicieron a los maestres en los galleones S. Pedro, Santiago, y San Telmo en la armada de las Guardas de Yndias* [1575], AGI, Patronato: legajo 269, no. 1., a list of the provisions, supplies and equipment taken aboard the vessels in question prior to sailing.

53. *Ibid*. No less than 200 strings of garlic were shipped aboard each of the three galleons cited above.

54. *Relación de los bastimentos*.

55. For which a salary was paid the subcontracted auditor, *Ibid*.

56. As the Arabic origins of the word, from *dar al-sin'a*, a workshop or house of work, would imply; Olsea, *La Organización Naval*, vol. II, p. 894.

57. For the geo-strategic structure of the Mediterranean, see John Pryor, *Geography, Technology and War: Studies in the Maritime History of the Mediterranean 649-1571* (Cambridge: 1988).

58. Olesa Muñido, *La Organización Naval*, 2:902.

59. *Relación de los bastimentos*.

60. Luis Collado *Platica Manual de Artilleria* (Milan: 1592), *Tractado Segundo, Capitulo II*, fol. 8.

61. See Lynn, "Food, Funds, and Fortresses: Resource Mobilization and Positional Warfare in the Campaigns of Louis XIV", below.

62. See Phillips, *Six Galleons*, pp. 169-74, for a thorough analysis of the seaman's diet. Phillips' findings concerning the adequacy of Spanish dietary provisions on the Atlantic run generally parallel my own, summarized in *Gunpowder and Galleys*, pp. 221-25, derived from analysis of a series of Spanish records, 1523-87, of the cost of operating war galleys.

63. Thompson, *War and Government*, p. 234.

64. Cf. Phillips, *Six Galleons*, p. 99. My own investigations have turned up no evidence to the contrary.

65. Guilmartin, *Gunpowder and Galleys*, pp. 99-100; Olesa, *Organización Naval*, 2:1004-10. The *Provveditore sopra i biscotti* sat as a member of the *Collegio della Milizia da Mar*, the senior Venetian naval planning body, as a co-equal of, among others, the *Provveditori alle Artiglierie*, in charge of artillery production, and the *Pagador 'all Armar*, the chief of military finance. In the Ottoman structure, biscuit production and supply fell under the purview of the *peksimet emini*, the intendant of the biscuit, a third level official of the *Mevkufat Kalemi*, the naval provisioning bureau, with a direct line of authority running upward to the *Kapudan Pasha*, the head admiral of the fleet; I am indebted to Dr. Joel Shinder for this information.

66. The term *ghazi*, derived from an Arabic root word meaning to raid, designates those who participate in raids for the faith undertaken to expand the abode of Islam at the expense of unbelievers; *The Encyclopedia of Islam*, new ed., B. Lewis, C. Pellat and S. Schacht, eds. (London: 1960), p. 1043, *ghazi*.

67. This struggle has thus remained all but invisible to modern scholars, no doubt because most of the resources deployed were private. These, nevertheless, were considerable. See *Colección Vargas Ponce (Museo Naval)*, vol. III, document 14, fol. 40-41, for the armament of ships seized in the ports of northern Spain in 1539 and 1564 with an eye to using them against Muslim forces in the Mediterranean.

68. A struggle which on occasion merged with that against Muslim forces, as in 1543-44 when the Valois-Ottoman alliance brought the Turkish fleet to Toulon.

69. Andrew C. Hess, *The Forgotten Frontier: A History of the Sixteenth-Century Ibero-African Frontier* (Chicago: 1978), pp. 60-65.

70. Hess, *Forgotten Frontier*, p. 99; Braudel, "Prices in Europe," Fig. 10, p. 463.

71. Guilmartin, *Gunpowder and Galleys*, Fig. 12 and 13, pp. 223-25.

72. Braudel, "Prices in Europe", Fig. 24, p. 478; Guilmartin, *Gunpowder and Galleys*, Fig. 12, p. 223.

73. Extrapolating the data from Guilmartin, *Gunpowder and Galleys*, Fig. 14, p. 225, in light of the macro-economic trends shown by Braudel, "Prices in Europe," esp. Fig. 33, p. 484, showing the average nominal price of wheat in Europe, 1440-1760, which suggests that the cost of operating a galley to Spain may have actually declined a bit between the end of the fifteenth century and the second decade of the sixteenth.

74. Phillips, *Six Galleons*, p. 23, quoting an informed contemporary source to the effect that the cost of constructing a sailing warship increased from 4,000 ducats before 1550 to about 15,000 by 1600.

75. Guilmartin, *Gunpowder and Galleys*, Fig. 13, p. 224

76. Braudel, "Prices in Europe," Fig. 27, p. 479.

7
Food, Funds, and Fortresses: Resource Mobilization and Positional Warfare in the Campaigns of Louis XIV

John A. Lynn

That France would remain inviolate, Louis XIV encircled her with fortresses, whose bristling cannon menaced any who would approach. These stone-faced warriors, standing motionless and defiant, played great strategic roles in the drama of war. Yet they did not always act as staunch guardians or embattled heroes; they often performed as gatekeepers, purveyors, and paymasters—more prosaic parts, to be sure, but absolutely essential.

The Sun King at war overstretched even the great resources of France. He needed to tap wealth beyond his borders while repelling interlopers who would rob him of French booty. Fortifications, both in the guise of fortresses and of entrenched lines, served both these ends. They opened access to lands that could feed his troops with foreign wheat and pay their wages with foreign gold. Such citadels provided safe harbor to French raiders who struck out to reap the wealth of hostile domains and place it in the war chest of the Sun King. Lines guarded conquered territory and native soil to deny their riches to the enemy and to guarantee them for French purposes.

Above all, Louis's wars were wars of attrition—contests of will and wealth in which opponents sought victory by shouldering the toll of conflict while hoping to outlast their enemy's resolve to stand the strain himself. The only brief exceptions to this rule were his War of Devolution and the minor war with Spain, 1683-84. This is not to say that Louis began his great wars with the intention that they would become long and exhausting struggles. Quite the contrary; the Dutch War, the Nine Years' War, and the War of the Spanish Succession were all to have been brief wars to achieve his goals at minimal expense. But the fact is that none developed as Louis expected and all evolved into wars of attrition.

By definition, in wars of attrition victory comes only to those who demonstrate the ability to put the necessary men and material in the field and maintain them there over the long haul. The strain upon the French of Louis's wars increased in direct proportion to his expanding army and his longer conflicts. His army mushroomed from 130,000 troops in the 1660's to 400,000 in the 1690s, at least on paper.[1] Each succeeding war consumed greater and greater lengths of time. The War of Devolution, 1667-68, lasted only a year; the Dutch War, 1672-78, went on for six; the Nine Years' War, 1688-97, equalled its name; and the War of the Spanish Succession, 1701-14, endured for fourteen years. With wars dragging on to exhaustion, the French strained to find sufficient food, fodder, and funds for the war effort. In other words, the sine qua non of survival, let alone victory, became effective resource mobilization.

Louis sought to provide his armies with the money and goods they required in four manners. First, and foremost, he paid, equipped, and supplied his forces directly from the state treasury. An increasing burden of taxation upon his subjects, multiplied by an extensive though inefficient use of credit, financed the wars. These funds went to pay and equip Louis's soldiers and to feed them, often through entrepreneurs, or munitionnaires, but try as Louis's ministers might, they could never collect enough money to finance all the costs of his wars. A second source of support was the amount that regimental officers expended for their own units. The state required that colonels and captains foot many of the bills for their units. It was common for colonels to create entire new regiments in wartime largely at their own expense. In addition, the state made use of the credit of its officers, reimbursing them only later, if at all, for authorized outlays. The nature of the expenses imposed on officers was such that it will never be possible to arrive at exact figures for their losses, but they were substantial, contributing to the financial decline of the aristocracy.[2]

The last two forms of support for the armies of the Sun King came not from within, but from without, France. Impositions in kind levied outside her borders provided a third vital source of the sinews of war. Armies in the field levied grain, hay, transport, and labor from the surrounding population. Inside France, peasants had to be compensated for their lost crops or time, so this amounted essentially to a form of purchase and thus was a draw on state funds. However, outside France, such levies came as the spoils of war. Levies in kind extracted from hostile or even neutral populations were recognized in practice and in the "laws of war" as they existed at the time. The most common form of such imposition was the seizing or gathering of forage to feed the army's horses, as we shall see.

The fourth fountainhead was contributions, or payments made by threatened populations to spare themselves from pillage. Early forms of contributions had filled war chests before the Thirty Years' War, but it was that conflict that defined the sort of contributions exacted by the French under Louis XIV.

In the Low Countries, the French developed contributions into a form of war tax administered by intendants for the benefit of the royal war chest. Payments made along the Rhine retained more of the rapacious flavor of the Thirty Years' War, since the French did not manage them for the long haul as they did in Flanders.³ Contributions could not only feed but pay an army, something requisitions in kind could not accomplish.

This essay deals with the last two sources on the list, in other words, that part of resource mobilization that drew in wealth and goods from outside the borders of France. It will touch on state financed supply to a degree as well; however, I will leave the great matters of the state's exploitation of taxation, credit, and the wealth of its aristocracy for other places and other times.

Louis designed French strategy not simply with a desire to defeat or destroy the enemy's forces but with a resolve to maintain his own army in the field.⁴ In a sense he had little choice. Louis became embroiled in a series of long wars in which he was hard put to support higher and higher numbers of troops. To do so he required all the resources he could tap, including those outside his frontiers. The exploitation of wealth beyond his borders required that French armies occupy or control foreign territory. This was a military task, a strategic goal. War was to feed war.

In particular, success in positional warfare was essential if Louis was to benefit from the wealth of enemy lands and to protect French riches. Let me define positional warfare as the design, construction, defense, and attack of fortifications. Such fortifications included not only fortresses and fortified towns but fortified posts and entrenched lines as well. In the struggle for territory in the second half of the seventeenth century, positional warfare held the key. Not surprisingly, sieges obsessed Louis XIV. They may well have appealed to his methodical nature, but more importantly, they were essential to the survival of his armies.

Supply from Depots and Living off the Country

To appreciate the role played by impositions in kind levied on occupied territory, let us look first to the way in which the armies of the period fed their soldiers and met the needs of their horses. As logistical concerns, food and fodder posed two very different sorts of problems. While a certain amount of food could be requisitioned locally, magazines and munitionnaires were essential to supply an army with its basic foodstuff, bread. They prepared and carted bread to encampments in a system too complex to describe here.⁵ But for such horse driven armies, fodder was also essential, and it had to be found locally most of the time. It was simply too bulky and heavy to cart during the majority of a campaign. So armies labored under too contradictory supply imperatives. On the one hand, it was best that they stay close to their magazines and not run too far or too fast lest they outrun their bread supply. On the other hand, since they consumed huge amounts of forage, eventually exhausting local supplies, they had to keep shifting so that their horses did not starve.

Consider first the matter of bread. There is no way to do this without confronting the work of Martin van Creveld, whose *Supplying War* has defined much of the discussion of logistics since its publication.[6] Van Creveld has spearheaded something of a trend towards emphasizing the way in which armies lived off the country during the second half of the seventeenth century. He asserts, "In *no* instance... is there any question of a force on the move being supplied solely by convoys," and "magazines never contained, nor could they contain, more than a fraction of the army's needs"[7] (van Creveld's emphasis). Such phrases stick in the mind, and while they are technically correct, they create a misleading impression.

In fact, the larger field armies of the second half of the seventeenth century required such great quantities of flour and bread that this supply could only come up from the rear, brought by convoy from grain stores maintained by the government or munitionnaires. In the 1640s Turenne could do things with an army of 15,000 that simply could not be done with the greater numbers of the 1690s. An army could not survive for long on what it could requisition locally if it was stationary, and while it was theoretically possible for it to feed itself on the move, that move would have to be extremely well planned and expertly executed to be self-sustaining.

Some calculations help to clarify the problems of supplying food. Assume an army of 60,000 soldiers. That army would require 90,000 rations of bread daily, once the extra rations for officers and non-combatants are considered.[8] The standard ration was 1 1/2 pounds of bread per day. Therefore this hypothetical force would require 135,000 pounds, or 67.5 tons, of bread each day. Carting the grain to and from state stores, milling it, baking it into bread, and transporting the bread to the troops were certainly Herculean labors, but not beyond the means of munitionnaires and state administrators. Indeed, there was no choice but to provide bread from state stores through a complicated system. Perjés's impressive study of logistics demonstrates that a stationary army in the field could not have found sufficient grain from locally available sources for more than a brief time, nor could it have processed it locally, owing to the scarcity of mills, ovens, and bakers.[9]

Stores of food gathered in magazines and shipped forward by convoy were consequently a fixture of late seventeenth-century warfare. A shuttle system of magazines, bakeries and wagons was a recognized necessity of field warfare. Even such an exponent of mobility as Eugene of Savoy wrote in 1705: "Without a [supply] train... I am unable to advance further, especially when the army is going from one region to another, and the magazine located here or there is too far away, and it takes several days to establish a magazine in the new place, and to put the bakeries into operation. And meanwhile the army is in need of bread and if we cannot take bread with us, how should I help myself?"[10] It may have not been the "five-march system," declared to be a myth by van Creveld, but it certainly was a shuttle from magazines and bakeries to the army.[11] No wonder, discussion of the conduct and protection of convoys fills the volumes of French military correspondence preserved in the archives.[12]

Munitionnaires contracted to undertake major supply efforts involving both productions and transport. Supplies could come from great distances. The intendant of Burgundy was ordered to ship 50,000 sacks of wheat to the armies of Italy and Germany in June 1697.[13] This amounted to 9,000,000 rations of bread, or enough to feed an army of 60,000 (figured at 90,000 rations per day) for well over three months. In 1708 one French official agreed to supply 20,000 rations of bread per day for six months to the army in Rousillon. To carry this he was to collect and maintain 400 mules. Marshal Noailles also insisted that a reserve of 30,000 quintals of wheat be stored in a magazine in Agde. Also he directed that 1,000 mules from Languedoc be found to carry 12,000 quintals of flour to Cerdaigne.[14]

It was recognized that men needed meat in addition to bread, and munitionnaires were called upon to supply it as well. De la Fonds reported in April 1689 that Marshal Duras had ordered him "to find an entrepreneur to furnish meat to the troops that composed his army."[15] In 1709 La Bourdonnaye at Bordeaux ordered 1500 cattle to be sent to Spain at a cost of 56,258 livres.[16] However, armies could also rely on raiding parties to bring in meat, which was so marvelously portable that it arrived on its own legs. The intendant St. Pouenge, for example, could report in June 1677 that parties sent out brought back first 170 cows and 80 sheep and later 700 cows and 200 sheep, which were all distributed to cavalry, dragoons, and gendarmes in the camp at Nimoue.[17]

The supply of forage for the army's horses was another matter. True, munitionnaires might also be hired to supply forage, as in 1708 when one contracted to provide 200 rations of fodder per day per squadron of cavalry and 100 per battalion of infantry in Rousillon.[18] However, the great truth of seventeenth-century logistics was that fodder had to be collected in the immediate vicinity of the army by foraging parties. This task involved a great many men. Perjés estimated at 4,000-10,000 the number of men necessary to mow forage for an army of 60,000.[19]

Each day, a horse required 17-24 pounds of dry fodder, or 50 pounds of green forage.[20] An army of 60,000 men would have 20,000 cavalry horses and 20,000 other horses consuming about 400 tons of dried fodder or 1,000 tons of green fodder daily. To cart fodder over long distances for long periods of time was all but impossible. On occasion, armies depended on fodder supplied from the rear. Lighter and more compact dry forage was generally shipped to the army at the very beginning and end of the campaign season, when local grasses were not available in sufficient quantity. However, because of the weight and bulk of forage, particularly green forage, the arithmetic of trying to ship it by horse drawn carts made such supply impossible over the course of an entire campaign. Not only would it have required hundreds of carts, but then their draft animals and drivers would have had to be fed, multiplying the need for food and forage.[21] The problems involved in carting forage explain why it had to be burnt, rather than removed, to deny it to the enemy when the French withdrew from an area. So in pulling back before enemy forces in 1688, Montclar ordered that Peyssonel "consume all the forage he can,... and burn the rest... I shall take measures to have burnt all the forage which shall be on the outskirts of the said city."[22]

For most of the campaign season, the army's horses lived primarily off green forage, and this had to come from local sources. When Louis's armies passed through French territories, the peasants received compensation for the forage cut, but in hostile lands, the army foraged for free. This explains one of the motives for billeting cavalry in foreign territory if at all possible. Because the presence of an army soon exhausted the available forage in an area, field armies changed camps periodically during the campaign season, even if the strategic picture did not require them to shift position. Louis, for example, instructed Villeroi in 1696 to maintain his camp of Malhelem as long as he could until "the lack of forage obliges you to change it."[23]

Forage became an even more acute problem when an army was forced to stay in one place for some time, as during a siege. Thus Mons could not be besieged effectively in 1684 owing to lack of forage in the area, so less desirable targets were chosen because they could support an army's horses.[24] Also, it was difficult to maintain the cavalry during the 1684 siege of Luxembourg because of the lack of grass.[25] Nearly a year before a later siege of Mons in 1691, Louvois ordered intendants to buy secretly 900,000 rations of hay of fifteen pounds each on condition that the fodder would remain with the seller until called for.[26]

To return to van Creveld, he combines food with fodder in his discussion and misleads his readers as a consequence. For example he states, "It is obvious that the need to obtain the ninety per cent of supplies that were not brought up from the rear must have done more to dictate the movement of armies than the ten per cent that were..."[27] The implication might be, why not just forget the ten percent and dispense with supplies brought up from the rear? But the 10 percent minority of supply included the army's bread, and the 90 percent majority was overwhelmingly forage. So by not considering the restraints of the 10 percent your army would starve or dissolve.

In fact the radius of action of French armies was only rarely such that van Creveld's speculations on the mobility of troops living off the land could apply. Puységur argued that smaller armies of the earlier seventeenth century could undertake long expeditions, but that the larger field armies of Louis XIV were tied to magazines. This limited campaigns to what Puységur called "frontier wars," which he argued were "the most difficult and the most scholarly of all."[28]

A glimpse of the map demonstrates that the French army need not have undertaken great marches to go almost anywhere it needed to go.[29]

Of course, there was one outstanding example of a long and rapid march by a large army during the War of the Spanish Succession. This was not a French army but that led by the duke of Marlborough from the Netherlands to the Danube in 1704. But what did this great maneuver prove; did it establish that seventeenth-century armies might easily have escaped the tyranny of magazines? No. Marlborough maintained his soldiers on the march not by living off the land through forage and pillage but by purchasing foodstuffs at carefully arranged markets along the way. This was only possible because his army moved over friendly territory and faced no opposition. His was a triumph of meticulous administration, planning, and the flexibility promised by a strongbox bulging with gold. Thus, Marlborough's advance constituted a special and fortuitous case of the *étapes* system that typified the logistic arrangements for troops on the march in the seventeenth century. It did not illustrate an easily repeated method of breaking with the dictates of supply by simply taking what one needed *en route*. His achievement shone as an extraordinary feat at the time, but it was not duplicated by any other army of the period.

In sum, to argue as van Creveld does about the potential for mobility of late-seventeenth-century armies based on the calculation that the great mass of its supplies had to be found locally anyway is to obscure the point. Despite his adamant arguments, supply from magazines was a practical necessity. But he is correct in insisting that local impositions were equally essential, and thus the state treasury was much relieved when the army stood outside French borders. Foraging for fodder, and the collections of foodstuffs by foraging parties, became an important method of mobilizing resources outside France to power the French war machine.

Contributions

Contributions provided a manner to raise money as well as fodder and food across the French frontier. After 1659 French contributions became an integral part of the state's fiscal base for war. Administered by agents of the central administration, contributions evolved into regular and rational impositions assessed on areas outside the king's domains. Local commanders normally did not set the level and extent of contributions to suit their whims; now they simply enforced and collected contributions established by civil representatives of Louis XIV. Yet for all their administrative propriety, contributions remained extortion, wrested from a population that did not recognize the French king as their legitimate ruler and backed by the threat of immediate violence. In a sense, contributions split the difference between pillage and taxation. They became a thoroughly absolutist institution; the state appropriated a practice that had before been employed by the privileged elite of society for its own profit and transformed it in order to produce revenue in a rational though violent system.

In the Low Countries, French officials usually set the level of contributions in relation to pre-war tax rolls. In the best of circumstances, the process of assessing contributions involved the consent of those burdened with the new payment, through some sort of bargaining with the intendant.[30] Before the 1670s towns would be notified of contributions assessed through particular treaties or letters sent by courier or by the arrival of a party of troops. However, with the more regular methods of negotiation and assessment, the French employed printed forms, with blanks to be filled in, and sent them out by post.[31] Should the town not pay, it would receive a more military and far less welcome visit. "Executions," the burning of villages and towns that failed to pay contributions assigned them, revealed the brutal nature of this extortion. Louis XIV lamented to Marshal Catinat in 1691, "It is terrible to be obliged to burn villages in order to bring people to pay the contribution, but since, neither by menace, nor by sweetness, can one oblige them to pay, it is necessary to continue to use these rigors."[32] The French also took hostages to enforce the payments of contributions.

The levying of contributions performed several functions in war policy, but its primary one was to mobilize the resources of enemy, or neutral, territory to support the war effort of the French monarchy. The king and his ministers were quite frank about using contributions to fill the gap between the needs of the army and what resources could be raised internally within France. The proud Sun King instructed Villars to draw contributions from Germany in 1703 so as to "husband as much as you can my finances which are too burdened by the immense expenses which I am obliged to bear."[33]

Scattered reports from the French war archives and the provinces suggest the levels of charges born by foreign populations that repeatedly financed French wars. The Spanish Low Countries provided the most lucrative source of contributions, since they were a highly populated, intensively exploited, and extensively urbanized area with a robust economy. Spanish Flanders alone paid at least 1,461,000 livres in 1677, and in the last year of the Dutch War the amount approached 4,000,000 livres.[34] During the period 31 April 1689 - 28 February 1694, during the Nine Years' War, Spanish Flanders paid a bit over 13,000,000 livres contributions and other direct levies to the French.[35] Further south, Luxembourg offered to pay 600,000 livres per year during the War of Devolution. In 1677 this province obligated itself to a levy of 251,000 livres, which rose slightly to 277,000 livres the next year.[36]

In the Rhineland, Württemberg supplied substantial harvests of contributions. For 1675 it delivered 1,500,000 livres.[37] During the horrendous campaigns of 1688 and 1689, representatives of Württemberg agreed to pay the French 300,000 livres per year, however this does not count the many hundreds of livres also collected in money and kind from villages and towns within Württemberg. In 1693 Württemberg owed the French 1,200,000 livres, including arrears which this area had agreed to pay. In 1707 Villars reported that he had fleeced Württemberg for 2,200,000 livres. He took considerable pride in this accomplishment, suggesting to the king that "through these contributions I do myself as great an honor as would be mine by the gain of a battle."[38]

Looking at contributions from the perspective of the treasurers of the primary military account, the *extraordinaires des guerres*, provides a different view of the income. The records and the Archives Nationales usually present surprisingly low figures for contributions, relegating them to a very minor role. An état comparing the size and cost of French troops, 1679-1699, presented total receipts for 1692 of 112,523,000 livres, with only 4,500,000 from contributions, confiscations, and passports (4 percent).[39] I am inclined to believe that an attempt to track contributions from the point of view of the treasurers general is bound to come up short. It would seem that contributions did not make their way into the hands of the treasurers in Paris but stayed with the armies and intendants that raised them. Ample references make it clear that contributions were meant to be used on the spot, not shipped to Paris.[40]

This is not to say that we totally lack evidence from the treasurers of a much more substantial level of contributions, only that this information is rare. The most significant document in this regard qualifies as unique. A magnificently detailed and informative document lists 178 sources of "receptes extraordinaires" paid during the last year of the Dutch War and into 1679.[41] Normally such revenues did not show up on central accounts. The reason these sources appear there is something of a mystery. Perhaps they remained outstanding at the end of the war and were shifted to Paris with the disbanding of the field armies as now unemployed army treasurers and military intendants turned in their accounts—but this is only surmise. In any case, this document gives the most complete survey of contribution payments that I have ever seen. Still, even it is incomplete, since the items on it are numbered only from 107 to 284. This implies that a separate list, now lost, must have dealt with the first 106 amounts. As it stands, the account shows 13,384,000 livres in receipts, of which 12,453,000 qualify as contributions and related impositions on foreign territories. Since the total military expenses posted for 1678 hit 67,901,000 livres, the contributions shown in this key document amount to a hefty 18 percent of the total.[42] With the remaining, but now lost, 106 items, this percentage would probably stand considerably higher.

One provocative, and far more questionable, piece of information comes from the pen of the diarist Dangeau. His entry for 23 August 1691 asserts that shortly after the death of Louvois, the two treasurers of the *extraordinaires des guerres* held 18,000,000 livres in money amassed from "contributions from Flanders and economies."[43] This was at a time when the *extraordinaires des guerres* amounted to 70,918,000 livres and the total budget for the army ran to 99,571,000, so the alleged cache of contributions equaled 25 percent of the *extraordinaires* or 18 percent of the total.[44]

Contributions take on an even more impressive form if viewed from the perspective of armies in the field rather than from that of central bureaucrats in Paris. Villars's 1703 campaign provides the best documented case of reliance upon contributions. The intendant Baudouin reported to the War Ministry that the treasurer of Villars's army brought with him only 450,000 livres and that since his arrival another 350,000 livres had come in letters of exchange; to this sum, contributions had added 460,000 livres, while hostages promised an 128,000 livres.[45] Therefore, cash impositions made by the army accounted for 42 percent of the army's funds. This was at a time when Villars estimated the rock bottom cost of pay and bread for his army at 531,000 livres per month.[46] Knowing this, Louis had only promised Villars 300,000 livres per month, urging Villars to "act in such a way that this sum and that which you shall draw from the contributions may abundantly furnish the needs of my army."[47] These figures reveal that Louis expected Villars to supply at least 43 percent of his financial needs through contributions. Figures from the Army of Italy, 1701-4 suggest even a higher dependence on contributions.[48]

The soundings above forbid any authoritative statement concerning the precise weight of contributions in French military finance. Yet it would probably be taking a coward's way out to shirk any attempt at a rough estimate. To relegate contributions to something as low as 10 percent of the material resources expended in war would be to underestimate. To ascribe half of war finance to contributions seems far too generous, although particular field armies at particular times probably relied on contributions for half or more of their operating funds. Therefore, I will be so bold as to suggest that at the height of a war effort, contributions may have accounted for something in the neighborhood of 25 percent of the cost of land warfare over the long run.

Fortresses

Contributions and other demands upon foreign lands depended on the control of territory, and fortifications held the key to this control. Therefore, fortresses and fortified lines were not just mighty instruments of combat but vital parts of the mechanisms of resource mobilization, making it possible to levy impositions upon foreign populations while protecting French subjects from such burdens.

By the mid-seventeenth century, fortifications played a wider variety of roles in war than might at first be apparent. Most fundamentally, and most obviously, fortifications defended territory. Siting and constructing fortifications was a science of denial. The massive walls, deep ditches, and brooding artillery of modern fortifications, all marshaled in rational and deadly order, defied attackers, threatening them with brutal repulse. While determined foes could overcome a fortress, they triumphed only by great investment of manpower, materiel, and time. Even a victorious attacker emerged beaten and bloody. It might be tempting to try to avoid the great cost of a formal siege by marching around a fortress that blocked an army's path. However, it was unwise for an invader to bypass a fortress, since its garrison could cause mischief entirely out of proportion to its numbers. The garrison could sweep out of the fortress and strike at the attacker's lines of communication and fight with the his foraging parties and raiders, greatly limiting his ability to requisition forage, food, and funds. So dangerous would this threat be that an advancing enemy would have to at least mask the fortress and its garrison, and this would take far more troops than the garrison itself maintained, thus sapping the attacker's troop strength. The defensive potential of a fortress grew from its garrison as well as its geometry. This is why a string of fortresses, even though not physically linked to one another, could render Louis's kingdom, in the words of Vauban, "impenetrable to the enemy."[49] When an enemy could not advance into French-controlled territory, he could not exploit its resources for the maintenance of his army, and as a result that area was reserved as an exclusive preserve for French exploitation.

Implied in a fortress's ability to bar a path to the enemy was its promise to open that path to friendly forces. Vauban linked the two in an essay on the value of fortifications in which he listed as the first value of fortresses, "to close the entries of our country to the enemy and to open for us those into his country."[50] This offensive potential multiplied the value of fortifications, which in many cases were literally bridgeheads across such river barriers as the Rhine. One concerned German observer fretted over the French seizure of Strasbourg in 1681: "everyone says that it is one wheel of the chariot on which [the French] can enter the Empire, and that the gate to Alsace is now closed [to German attackers]."[51]

By dominating major routes, fortresses made communications and supply easier for friends and more difficult for foes. As demonstrated earlier in this essay, supply lines were indeed necessary for a late-seventeenth-century army. Rivers were highly advantageous for moving food and equipment, and fortresses were particularly well designed to dominate rivers and river crossings. Turgot, intendant in Lorraine, described one role literally flowing out of the other: "[Fortresses] occupy almost all the passages and posts advantageous for blocking access and hold... the rivers, in such a way that to enter enemy territory we have only to go down river, and this with much less effort than is required of the enemy since they must go up river."[52] Thus the French tried to hold the Rhine bridges and to control the water courses that penetrated France along its eastern and northern frontiers.

This offensive potential of fortifications bore particularly rich fruit in the question of supply, because the passage of Louis's troops beyond French borders greatly eased the logistical burden on the government. Forces on foreign soil could both raise impositions in kind and exact contributions. Louis XIV expected his commanders to pass through his fortified gates in order to supply themselves off enemy territory and thus spare his treasury. He complained to de Lorge during the Nine Years' War, "I am upset to see my army where it is... you should cross the Rhine to use up the supplies and forage of Germany and to save Alsace."[53] No wonder that in 1702 Chamlay lamented the loss of fortresses on the far side of the Rhine "which enabled [the King's] armies to cross to the other bank and subsist on German territory."[54] Occupation of enemy land became particularly vital as the campaign season drew to an end and troops sought suitable winter quarters. In 1688, La Grange reported to Louvois that by moving the winter quarters of only four cavalry regiments from Alsace to Württemberg and Baden, he expected to save 120,000-140,000 livres.[55] The historian Hubert van Houtte provides even more surprising evidence of the value of foreign fodder. He lists 10,351,400 livres of financial impositions paid to the French by Spanish Flanders during this period, while showing that as much as 12,227,600 livres in fodder were taken or destroyed by the French in the same province.[56]

Fortresses not only guarded the routes of supply, they served as the storehouses for those supplies. Louis XIV's fortresses sheltered his magazines, which gave the French considerable advantage in the conduct of warfare, at least through 1691. The amounts of food and fodder stored in magazines could be impressive. In 1672 Turenne listed 251,000 septiers of wheat stored in Kaiserwerth, Dorstein, Liège, Charleroi, Mezière, and Ath, an amount he estimated as enough for 100,000 rations per day for about a year, or 200,000 rations for the six month campaign season.[57] At the same time, the French had six months' worth of grain stored in the front line magazines at Pignerolo, Briesach, Metz, Nancy, Thionville, Rocroi, Dunkirk, La Bassée, Courtrai, Lille, and Le Quesnoy.[58] In 1675, the entire army of 80,000 men was to be supported for two months solely by food grain stored in Maestricht and Liège.[59] For the 1691 siege of Mons, the French squirreled away 220,000 red-skinned cheeses in the citadel of Tournai.[60] Fortresses also provided a safe place to store arms; in 1697 Metz held 500 pieces of artillery plus small arms for 20,000 men.[61]

Fortresses also served as bases from which to exploit the wealth of occupied territories through the levying of contributions or the launching of raids, known as *courses*. Fortresses each exerted control over the area surrounding them. In these zones, the garrison could exact contributions for its support. Fortresses also provided bases for raiding parties that constantly plundered regions in search of food and forage. At one time or another, Heilbron, Mannheim, and Mons, to name only a few, served as central fortresses from which French troops carried out the brutal business

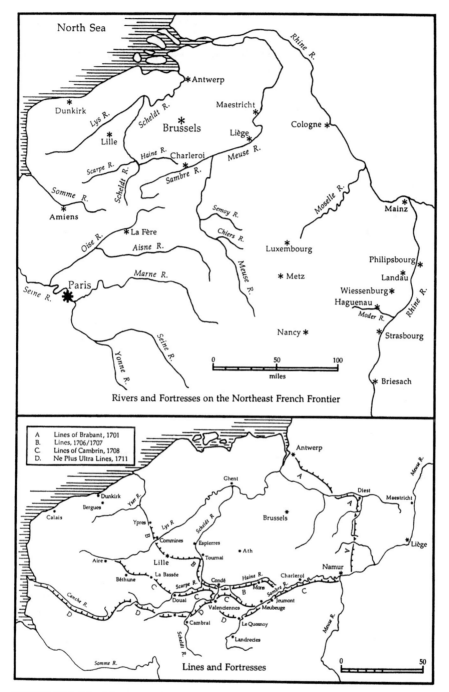

FIGURE 7.1 The Northeast Frontier of France in the Seventeenth Century. *Source*: Lines and Fortresses map based on the map in Christopher Duffy, *The Fortress in the Age of Vauban and Ferderick the Great, 1660-1789* (London: 1985), p. 34.

of assessing and collecting contributions. During the War of the Spanish Succession, Louis regarded Landau as so essential to controlling Lower Alsace for contributions that his armies battled over its possession through four sieges. Smaller posts, often fortified, were also chosen for their use in launching contribution raids.

Of course, enemy fortresses threatened to impose contributions or dispatch raids against French-held territory. In 1687 Louvois feared that because of enemy forces in Philippsbourg, "Lower Alsace remains their pray, and they can always... entirely exhaust [*manger*] that country."[62] Similarly, Vauban pleaded for a French attack on the enemy stronghold of Charleroi in 1693, since it served as a safe harbor for bands of land-pirates who struck at French territory: "This single fortress... obliges us to maintain guards at eighteen or twenty small fortresses... It causes the ruin of a territory equivalent to a good province... and obliges the King... to maintain in his fortresses 15,000 or 16,000 more men who will be lost annually in convoys and escorts."[63]

On the other side of the coin, permanent fortresses were designed to shield areas from enemy raids. In 1672, Vauban argued for maintaining the fortress of La Fére precisely to limit the possibility of *courses*, even though by other criteria La Fére should have been razed.[64] A Vauban memoir of 1689 argued for holding Ypres and a companion fortress in the southern Netherlands, since "these two places if they are ours bar enemy contributions from the sea to the Lys and limit the penetration of their *courses*."[65]

Fortified Lines

Strings of redoubts and entrenched lines provided even better protection from raiders than did great permanent fortifications. This is a category of defensive works which has not received its due from military historians. Lines were essential to the maintenance of the war effort, barring marauders from friendly territories and thus reserving their people and resources for the support of the French war effort.

The French made use of strings of outposts before the personal reign of Louis XIV. In 1643 Mazarin decided to construct 38 redoubts at fords on the Meuse river in order to protect the population along the river from Spanish contributions and *courses*.[66] The practice of setting up outposts did not need to involve the construction of new fortifications. Rivers almost invariably constituted primary elements in outpost lines; therefore, merely cutting bridges could be useful. Still, strings of outposts could be extensive. One fascinating report of 1697 gives a detailed accounting for a double line of outposts, including seventy detachments in posts along the Semoy, from its junction with the Meuse to Arlon, and twenty-four posts along the Chiers and Crusnes rivers from Volmerange to Torgny.[67] Posts were garrisoned either by local peasants paid for their duty or by small detachments of troops.

Food, Funds, and Fortresses   151

River lines could be reinforced with outposts to advantage. The frontier enclosed in the Sambre and Meuse rivers seemed to have been a perpetual worry, and the French sought security in posts. In November 1702, Louis XIV ordered "that the redoubts which had been constructed along the Sambre and Meuse during the last war be reestablished... to prevent enemy parties from passing."[68] While most of the emphasis was on continuous lines during the War of the Spanish Succession, allied victories renewed the interest in outpost lines by 1710. Again, protecting the line of the Semoy concerned government officials.[69] Officials also lavished a great deal of attention on the gap between the Somme and Oise, another potential highway for enemy *courses*. At first, the government promised little help, arguing that the peasants of the area "are almost all people used to war [*agueris*]" and so could be organized to repel raiders.[70] Later, the king judged it better "to establish posts between the Oise and the Somme than to make a line between the two rivers which would cost considerable sums and would not have been of a great utility."[71]

Continuous lines can be said to have descended from outposts. Yet, French planners may also have been influenced by discussions of ancient lines in the works of classical military treatises, but that link would be hard to establish. In any case, strategists had more modern precedents, including similar lines built by the Dutch in 1605.[72]

Louis XIV first relied upon actual continuous defensive lines in the Dutch War. Such defensive works became more prevalent during the Nine Years' War and rose to paramount importance in the War of the Spanish Succession.[73] Such lines used river and canals as wet-ditch barriers whenever possible, buttressing these barriers with redoubts and where necessary running between water courses with entrenchments representing a high state of military engineering. In a sense, then, the lines simply evolved one step beyond the strings of outposts along rivers that had been employed as early as the 1640s. Yet this evolution brought with it a basic change in the method of staffing defensive works. Locally hired guards or unpaid peasants often held outposts.[74] However, lines seem always to have been garrisoned by regular troops. When entrenched lines ran between water barriers, they could be elaborate, judging from plans.[75]

Lines were established quickly in the Dutch War; the Dutch dug a 26 mile long line along the Issel in 1672.[76] The French followed suit later that year, laying out entrenchments from the sea to the Lys.[77] The first, or eastern, section ran from the sea to Commines, incorporating the fortresses of La Kenocque and Ypres, as well as several canals. In 1678 Vauban, under direction by Louvois, proposed entrenchments between Ypres and Commines after Ypres fell to the French in March of that year. He expressed great confidence: "It is almost impossible that the enemy parties could carry out their designs beyond these entrenchments."[78]

In 1683, with the brief war between Spain and France, Louvois ordered lines reestablished between the Lys and Ypres, now a French fortress, to fend off Spanish *courses*. The correspondence first mentions lines to cover the country between Bergues and the Lys; later Louvois stated that lines stretched from Ypres to Tournai, further than they had during the Dutch War.[79] With the coming of the Nine Years' War, Louis ordered the lines protecting Flanders reestablished.[80] These were the old lines of 1678 and 1683, running from the sea to Commines and then from there to Espierres on the Scheldt, following the old paths with only minor modifications.[81] With the French seizure of Mons, new lines linked it with Jeumont on the Sambre by following the stream La Trouille.[82]

Testimony from the 1690s substantiates that these lines proved their value. Vauban thought well of lines late in his career. Recognizing that it was hard to hold them against a large army, since the attacker could choose his time and place, Vauban still believed that "in all other cases, one maintains lines easily with ordinary guards, with good order, against all sorts of [raiding] parties."[83] In 1696 he argued that lines guaranteed the lands they sheltered: "[When] these lines [are] guarded by only a very small corps, no party, large or small, would dare to pass them; it would take an army to do so." However, he objected to "the negligence or rather the feebleness with which one guards them when the army is on campaign."[84] The intendant's memoir for Flemish Flanders, drawn up by the engineer Caligny, 1697-98, credits lines between the Lys and the sea as so effective that "the inhabitants have not been bothered at all by enemy *courses* during the war."[85] It also describes these lines in some detail as connecting fortresses and fighting off enemy parties with small forces from the forts' garrisons.[86]

For the French, the defensive ruled supreme during the War of the Spanish Succession, so it is little wonder that entrenched lines played such a great role in this conflict. The French and Spanish, now allied, constructed the lines of Brabant, beginning at Antwerp and stretching for 130 miles past Diest to the Meuse, just below Namur.[87] This was an unprecedented project. The intention of the first lines of the War of the Spanish Succession was to continue the tradition of halting enemy raids. Documents concerning the siting and construction of these lines make it clear that they were meant to bar *courses*, not enemy armies.[88] Boufflers praised the lines of Brabant to Louis in a letter of April 1701, "The whole of the people of the countryside, as well as the local officials, look upon these lines as their salvation."[89]

While lines provided the most complete coverage in the southern Netherlands, the fashion for entrenchments spread much further. Villeroi dug the lines of Moder in 1704, running from the Rhine to the Vosges and based on Haguenau.[90] A memoir discussing these lines listed as a primary rational "to conserve Alsace from the payment of contributions."[91] Villeroi in 1706 built the lines of Wissembourg on the site of the lines of Stollhoffen, created by Louis of

Badden in 1701.[92] Meanwhile, as the allies forced the French back in the Spanish Netherlands, the French relied on three more lines. In 1706-7 the lines ran from Ypres to Lille to Condé and then along the Haine to the Sambre; however, the loss of Lille in 1708 compromised this position. The French next dug in from Aire to Douai to Valenciennes to Maubeuge in 1708; such were the lines of Cambrin. Yet the losses of Douai, Béthune, Saint-Venant, and Aire in 1710 eviscerated this line too. The French built their last great line in 1711, christening it defiantly the Ne Plus Ultra Lines. By this point lines were meant to do more than stymie raiding parties. The fortifications were intended to resist entire armies.[93] Yet whatever the intention, these lines failed to contain Marlborough, who crossed them at Arleux in a magnificent maneuver in 1711.

But the attempt to stop invasion must not obscure the primary use of lines during Louis's last three wars; they were designed to control the mobilization of resources for war. The evolution of lines in the Low Countries makes this particularly clear. Before the Nine Years' War, Louis tried to deter his foes from raiding French preserves primarily by ordering retaliations against enemy villages. But unfortunately, the enemy reciprocated. Conflicts over contributions and reprisals against those who did not pay clearly got out of hand, so by the close of the Dutch War, Louis tried to make a treaty with the Spanish at Deynze to limit the amount of contributions demanded of local populations.[94] But the negotiations broke down. Deterrence and negotiation having failed, prudence demanded the construction of lines as the main method of forestalling enemy raids, although reprisals remained part of French practice after 1678.

The construction of such lines was determined by the value of the territory they shielded, wealth that could be exploited to supply French armed forces.[95] Discussions of when and where to build defensive lines included analysis of how they would stop parties and the value in tax revenue and contributions of the area they would shelter.[96] One typical piece that proposed moving a 1701 line forward stressed the value of the lines by calculating the amount that the new area to be sheltered had "paid for contributions, forage, cattle, and other impositions" from April 1689 to October 1697.[97]

Conclusion

When Louis XIV issued instructions to Villars for his 1703 thrust across the Rhine, the Sun King urged his marshal to consider"... the immense expenses with which I am burdened. I hope that by your efforts they shall be considerably lightened for this winter, that you shall find ways to maintain my cavalry at the expense of the enemy and draw from him enough money in contributions... to pay part of my troops."[98] In Louis's wars of attrition, questions of resource mobilization were bound to rank high. At times his campaigns were directed solely at attrition as a weapon, as in the Palatinate both in 1674 and 1688-89, or when in 1683 he resolved "to assemble a considerable army on the

Scheldt and to enter with it onto the lands of... the king of Spain [*sa majesté catholique*] in order to cause those lands to support the army until the governor of the... Low Countries resolves himself to come to reason."[99] But even in those campaigns without such an overtly logistical goal, questions of resource mobilization greatly concerned Louis and his generals.

This essay has attempted to indicate that positional warfare played an essential role, both in defending French resource areas and in exploiting those of their enemies. Decisions as to the construction and placement of fortresses and lines hinged on such matters. Campaigns such as those fought by Villars in Württemberg were fought and sieges such as those of Charleroi and Landau were undertaken in order to maximize the wealth that the French could muster in support of their armies. The need for resources helps explain why states fought over places they knew that they must abandon in a later peace settlement. Territory meant supply, so even if land was only held temporarily during a conflict, that conquest was worth the effort, since it lessened the strain of the war of attrition.

Martin van Creveld maintains that the logistics of the late seventeenth century were determined by a sterile emphasis on positional warfare. I reply that he has made a cause out of an effect. On the contrary, the emphasis on positional warfare was a product of the need to mobilize resources for the maintenance of armies in the political and strategic environment that ruled in the age of Louis XIV.

Notes

1. In 1668 the French army hit a theoretical high of 134,000 based on *états* preserved in the "Tiroirs de Louis XIV" at the library of the Service Historique de l'Armée de Terre (SHAT) in Vincennes. A theoretical high of roughly 400,000 in 1696 is sustained by several sources, most noteably by "État des troupes que le Roy a eu sur pied," 1696, Archives Nationales (AN), G⁷1774, #52. This latter figure can be discounted to 335,000 as an estimate of actual forces present under arms. See John A. Lynn, "Recalculating French Army Growth During the *Grand siècle*, 1610-1715", *French Historical Studies*, forthcoming.

2. Regarding the cost to officers of exercising command in the French army, the classic work is Louis Tuetey, *Les officiers sous l'ancien régime* (Paris: 1908). For the period of the 1630s see David Parrott, "The Administration of the French Army During the Ministry of Cardinal Richelieu," (Ph.D. diss., Oxford: 1985). For a short treatment of the subject see John A. Lynn, "The Costs of Command," *MHQ, Quarterly Journal of Military History*, forthcoming.

3. Concerning the French practice of contributions in the seventeenth century see John A. Lynn, "How War Fed War: The Tax of Violence and Contributions During the *Grand Siècle*," *Journal of Modern History*, 65, no. 2 (June 1993). The best discussion of the evolution of contributions in the Spanish Netherlands during the period 1667-1748 is in Hubert van Houtte, *Les occupations étrangères en Belgique sous l'Ancien régime*, 2 vols.,

Université de Gand, Recueil de travaux publiés par la faculté de philosophie et lettres, 62-63 fascicule (Gand: 1930). Van Houtte, 1:167, dates the origin of contribution *traités*, or formal treaties between the French and localities, with the War of Devolution. Geoffrey Parker, *The Army of Flanders and the Spanish Road, 1567-1659* (Cambridge: 1972), pp. 142-43, describes an earlier regularization of contributions in the late sixteenth century, but this was not French practice and did not involve *traités*. The only extensive treatment of French contributions in Germany is Ronald Thomas Ferguson, "Blood and Fire: Contribution Policy of the French Armies in Germany (1668-1715)," (Ph.D. diss., University of Minnesota: 1970).

4. The clearest example of this is in his desire to push his forces onto enemy territory for campaigns or to seize favorable winter quarters. See the directives from the king to Villars for his 1703 and 1707 campaigns, e.g., SHAT, Vincennes, Archives de Guerre (AG), A^{1}1676, #41, 27 April 1703, Louis to Villars in Ferguson, diss., pp. 11, 180, and 190 and AG, A^{1}2015, #26, 28 May 1707, Louis to Villars. Also see Louis's 1691 complaint to Lorge in the letter cited in John B. Wolf, *Louis XIV* (New York: 1968), pp. 466-67.

5. For descriptions of the French supply system, including the basic ration, the stockpiling of grain, the baking of bread, and its preparation transportation to the army see the extremely detailed handbook François Nodot, *Le munitionnaire des armées de France* (Paris: 1697).

6. Martin van Creveld, *Supplying War: Logistics from Wallenstein to Patton* (Cambridge: 1977).

7. *Ibid.*, pp. 25 and 39.

8. The army included non-combatant tradesmen, for example, plus officers received extra rations—a general getting as many as 100 rations. Puységur, the great authority of the day estimated that an army of 120,000 soldiers consumed 180,000 bread rations daily. Jacques-François de Chastenet de Puységur, *Art de la guerre par principes et par règles*, vols. 1 and 2 (Paris: 1749), 2:62 in G. Perjés, "Army Provisioning, Logistics and Strategy in the Second Half of the 17th Century," *Acta Historica Academiae Scientiarum Hungaricae* 16, nr. 1-2 (1970), p. 5.

9. Perjés, "Army Provisioning," pp. 7-11.

10. Prince Eugene of Savoy, *Feldzüge des Prinzen Eugen von Savoyen*, 13 vols. (Vienna: 1876-86), vol. 8, supplement H, 305 in Perjés, "Army Provisioning," p. 29.

11. Van Creveld, *Supplying War*, p. 29. See Perjés, "Army Provisioning," pp. 26-29, for a much more sympathetic and convincing discussion of the "five-days" or "five-march" system, pages 26-29, during which he buttresses his points with appeals to Prince Eugene and Montecuccoli, and Zrinyi.

12. See, for examples: AG, A^{1}209, #38, 18 June 1667, letter from Carlier; A^{1}210, #237, 30 December 1667; A^{1}433, numerous letters concerning the French campaign of May 1675; A^{1}539, #285, 3 July 1677, from Créqui; and A^{1}539, #324, 7 July 1677, from Luxembourg.

13. Archives departementales, Côte d'Or (Côte d'Or), C 3676, June 1697. Calculations are based on a sack weighing 200 pounds. Nodot, *Le munitionnaire*, pp. 4-5, stated that a standard grain sack held 200 pounds and would supply 180 rations. Nodot is an extremely valuable source for all the details of supplying an army with bread. Perjés, "Army Provisioning," p. 7, figures a sack at 165 pounds.

14. AN, G^{7}1093, vivres de Rousillon, 5 May 1708.

15. AG, A^{1}875, 29 April 1689, de la Fonds from Strasbourg.

16. AN, G⁷1094, 11 June 1709.
17. AG, A¹538, #446, 5 June 1677, and A¹539, #37, 18 June 1677, letters from St. Pouenge.
18. AN, G⁷1093, vivres de Rousillon, 5 May 1708.
19. Facts and figures on foraging come from Perjés, "Army Provisioning," pp. 14-19, unless otherwise stated.
20. Perjés, "Army Provisioning," pp. 16-17, states that green fodder should be calculated at 25 kg, or 55 pounds, per horse per day. He also figures a ration of dry forage at anything between 8 and 11 kg but estimates a reasonable ration at 10 kg, or 22 pounds. Van Creveld, *Supplying War*, p. 24, allows a dry ration of 20 pounds and green forage at twice that weight. Just to have a nice round number I have calculated green fodder at 50 pounds per day per horse, since this weight had to be very approximate in any case. Numerous French documents back up Perjés's estimates for dry forage; see, for example, the 1651 instruction for winter quarters in Louise André, *Michel Le Tellier* (Paris: 1906), p. 672, and Nord, C 2230, November 1678.
21. For local foraging alone, Perjés calculates the number of carts required at 400-1000 and the number of men required for mowing the fodder at 4,000-10,000. Perjés, "Army Provisioning," p. 17. This explains why cavalry was constantly on foraging expeditions and the importance of little war.
22. AG, A¹829, 20 December 1688, Montclar to Louvois.
23. AG, A¹888, #68, 22 July 1696, Louis to Villeroi.
24. Louvois to Chamlay, 12 June 1684, in Jacques Hardré, ed. *Letters of Louvois*, University of North Carolina Studies in the Romance Languages and Literatures, no. 10 (Chapel Hill: 1949), pp. 366-67.
25. See siege instructions to Créqui, 1 April 1684, in Hardré, *Letters of Louvois*, pp. 408-14; see also page 425.
26. AG, A¹1043, 13 May 1790, Louvois to Bagnols and Chauvelin in Camille Rousset, *Histoire de Louvois*, 4 vols. (Paris: 1862-64), 4:459.
27. Van Creveld, *Supplying War*, p. 24.
28. Puységur, 2:152-53 in Perjés, "Army Provisioning," p. 38.
29. For example, an eight-day march of 100 miles from its magazines in Lille, Valenciennes, or Philippeville would have allowed the French army to cross at any point along the southern border of the Dutch Netherlands. A hundred mile march was within the parameters of the "five-days system."
30. Douglas Baxter, *Servants of the Sword* (Urbana: 1976), pp. 183-86, gives a good account of intendant Robert's negotiations with the area around Dunkirk.
31. For examples see Nord, C 2333-34, printed orders for 1670s through 1690s. For a draft of a "mandement" sent out by Terruel in the Low Countries in 1667 see AG, A¹209, #301, 15 October 1667. Other drafts of the form letters employed by La Goupillière in Germany during 1688 are contained in AG, A¹829, 30 December 1688. Some historians have found this more than a trifle bizarre; see Myron P. Gutman, *War and Rural Life in the Early Modern Low Countries* (Princeton: 1980), p. 44.
32. AG, A¹1041, #303, 21 July 1691, Louis to Catinat.
33. AG, A¹1676, #41, 27 April 1703, Louis to Villars in Ferguson, diss., pp. 11, 180, and 190.
34. Nord, C 2325, état for 1677; and AN, G⁷1774, #68, "Receptes extraordinaires deçà 1679." In this essay, a Flemish florin is figured at 1.25 livres, and an écu at 3 livres.

According to AN, G^{7}890, "Recepte générale de finances de Flandre, 1689," and 1 florine equaled 1.25 livres.

35. See the tables in van Houtte, *Occupations étrangères*, 2:428-442. The exact figure is 10,437,871 florins.

36. AG, A^{1}209, 9 November 1667, letter from intendant Carlier; and Nord, C 2325, état for 1677.

37. AG, A^{1}1213, #107, 19 March 1693, La Goupillière. In this letter he boasted of his previous accomplishments levying contributions.

38. AG, A^{1}2027, #112, 5 June 1707, Villars. For figures see AG, A^{1}826, #30 and 83, 19 and 26 October 1688, letters from La Goupillière; AG, A^{1}829, 31 December 1688, "Estat de recouvrement des sommes imposées sur les pays d'au dela du Rhin que doiven contribuer à Haïlbron;" and AG, A^{1}2027, #112, 5 June 1707, Villars.

39. AN, G^{7}1774, #52, "Etat des troupes que le Roy a eu sur pied, et leur dépense y compris celle des places." Items on this document correspond to yearly levies established by documents from other archives and from tables in van Houtte, *Occupations étrangères*.

40. When Louis XIV instructed Villars in 1703 to take enough "in contributions to be used to pay part of my troops," the king clearly did not expect Villars's booty to reach the hands of the treasurers general. AG, A^{1}1675, #85, 24 February 1703, Louis to Villars in Ferguson, diss., p. 190.

41. AN, G^{7}1774, #68, "Receptes extraordinaires, déça 1679."

42. This figure of 67,901,118 livres comes from adding together items from Jean Roland de Mallet, *Comptes rendus de l'administration des finances du royaume de France* (London: 1789). If reference is made to AN, KK 355, "Etat par abrégé des recettes et dépenses, 1662-1700," total expenses come out 90,000 livres lower, apparently because of the transposition of two numbers, because otherwise the two sources accord completely.

43. Dangeau, *Journal du marquis de Dangeau*, vol. 3 (Paris: 1854), pp. 387-88. He credits Turmenie with a cache of 15,000,000 and La Touanne with 3,000,000.

44. 70,917,694 livres for the extraordinaires and 99,571,095 for the total. AN, KK 355.

45. AG, A^{1}1676, #183, 20 August 1703, Baudouin.

46. AG, A^{1}1675, #143, 22 March 1703, "Dépense pour un mois de trente jours," memoir by Villars.

47. AG, A^{1}1676, #41, 27 April 1703, Louis to Villars in Ferguson, diss., pp. 11, 180, and 190.

48. AN, G^{7}1775, #54, 1701, "Estat de la dépense qui doit estre fait pour les trouppes qui sont en Italie pendant chacun des mois de Novembre, Decembre, Janvier, Fevrier, et Mars;" AN, G^{7}1775, #322, "Etat par estimation de la dépense de l'armée d'Italie pendant les cinq mois du quartier d'hiver de 1702-1703;" and AN, G^{7}1776, #466, "Estat general des dépenses de l'extraordinaire des guerres des six derniers mois de l'année 1704."

49. Vauban concerning the fortifications of Provence, in Reginald Blomfield, *Sébastien le Prestre de Vauban, 1633-1707* (New York: 1971), p. 127.

50. AG, Bibl. Génie, 11, fol., Vauban, "Mémoire sur l'utilité des places fortes," dated 1689.

51. Letter written from Wurtzbourg on 14 October 1681 to Baron de Montclar, in Rousset, *Louvois*, 3:50.

52. BN, ffr 22210, fol. 107, Turgot's report, in André Corvisier, ed., *Les Français et l'armée sous Louis XIV d'après les mémoires des intendants, 1697-1698* (Vincennes: 1975), p. 115.

53. Louis to Marshal de Lorge, in Wolf, *Louis XIV*, pp. 466-67.

54. Jean Jacques Pelet and François Vault, eds. *Mémoires militaires relatifs à la succession d'Espagne*, 11 vols. (Paris: 1835-62), 3:756.

55. AG, A^{1}827, #78, 12 November 1688, La Grange from Mannheim to Louvois.

56. These figures are arrived at by subtracting the 2,156,740 florins for "grains, forage, and straw" from van Houtte's table of contributions, *Occupations étrangères*, 2:442, and then adding it to "forage and camping" and "forage and straw" from his table of damages, 2:454. The totals probably overstate the value of animal forage alone, but almost certainly by less than 25%. In any case, they give a vivid impression of just how much of a burden forage requisitions could be.

57. Louis XIV, *Oeuvres*, eds. Grimoard and Grouvelle, 6 vols. (Paris: 1806), 3:116-117, "Premier état du maréchal de Turenne, vivres et munitions pour la Meuse et le Rhin."

58. André Corvisier, *Louvois* (Paris: 1983), p. 191.

59. AG, A^{1}433, 5 April and 14 May 1675, letters from Louvois to Estrades and Moreau. I thank my graduate student George Satterfield for pointing the way to this material in a paper he wrote on the campaign of 1675.

60. Christopher Duffy, *The Fortress in the Age of Vauban and Frederick the Great, 1660-1789, Siege Warfare*, vol. 2 (London: 1985), p. 29.

61. BN, ffr 22210, fol. 117-18, Turgot's report, in Corvisier, *Les Français*, p. 219.

62. Letter from Louvois to Vauban, 25 August 1687, in Rochas d'Aiglun, *Vauban, sa famille et ses écrits*, 2 vols. (Paris: 1910), 2:280.

63. Letter of 29 June 1693, from Vauban to Le Peletier, in Rochas d'Aiglun, *Vauban*, 2:390. In 1678 he had urged taking Luxembourg for very much the same reasons, see 1678 memoir in Rochas d'Aiglun, *Vauban*, 1:190-91.

64. AG, A^{1}340, #287, 22 December 1673.

65. AG, Bibl. Génie, 11 fol., Vauban, "Mémoire sur l'utilité des places fortes," dated 1689.

66. AN, KK 1069, fol. 88, letter from Rasle, February 1644; and Gaston Zeller, *L'organization défensive des frontières du nord et de l'est au XVIIe siècle* (Paris: 1928), pp. 43-44.

67. AG, MR 1047, piece 3, "Etat des postes et redoutes sur la rivière Semoy," 28 March 1697.

68. Nord, C 8645, 3 November 1702, affiche issued by Charles Maignart, the intendant in the area.

69. AG, A^{1}2266, #336 & #348, 16 February & 23 March 1710.

70. AG, A^{1}2266, #189, Voysin to Ormesson, 23 June 1710.

71. AG, A^{1}2266, #299, Voysin to Ormesson, 3 December 1710. See as well #263, 266, 272, 318-21, and 324 for further details on the line.

72. See the "The Great Wall of the Dutch Republic" in Geoffrey Parker, *The Military Revolution* (Cambridge: 1988), p. 39.

73. For a good short discussion of lines see Zeller, *Organization défensive*, pp. 107-117.

74. In 1703, for example, major Davignan received 1250 livres to pay for guards in outposts along the Sambre. Nord, C 8645, 8 March 1703, contract for guards.

75. Nord, C 2238, plans accompanying report on 27 June 1703 attack on lines around Hesdin.

76. Stephen Baxter, *William III and the Defense of European Liberty, 1650-1702* (New York: 1966), p. 64.

77. There seems to be some confusion as to when the French built their lines during the Dutch War; P. Lazard, *Vauban, 1633-1707* (Paris: 1934), p. 282, credits the first construction in 1672, while Zeller argues "the first lines worth of the name" came only at the end of the war; in any case, they were not extensive and covered only a space between the Lys and the sea. Zeller, *Organization défensive*, p. 109.

78. AG, A^{1}616, #21, 5 April 1678, letter from Vauban to Louvois.

79. See Louvois letters dated, 24 October 1683, 4 November 1683, 13 November 1683, and 11 May 1684 in Hardré, pp. 286, 296, 302, and 352.

80. Zeller, *Organization défensive*, p. 111.

81. Duffy, *Fortress*, p. 35, argues that the 1694 "Lines of Clare" from the sea to the Scheldt were the first continuous trench lines. This was not the case, as some of these date back no later than 1678.

82. Zeller, *Organization défensive*, p. 112.

83. Vauban letter of 21 July 1693 in Lazard, *Vauban*, p. 28.

84. Vauban to Le Peletier, 27 May 1696, in Rochas d'Aiglun, *Vauban*, 2:443-44.

85. BN, ffr 22220, fol. 53.

86. *Ibid.*

87. Duffy, *Fortress*, p. 35.

88. AG, MR 1047, pieces 9-11 discuss aspects of this first line of the War of the Spanish Succession.

89. Boufflers to Louis XIV, 27 April 1701 in Pelet and Vault, *Mémoires militaires*, 1:66, in Duffy, *Fortress*, p. 36.

90. Zeller, *Organization défensive*, p. 113.

91. AG, MR 1066, #14.

92. *Ibid.*

93. Therefore, Duffy, *Fortress*, p. 36, draws a parallel between the Ne Plus Ultra Lines and the trenches of World War I.

94. See Hubert van Houtte, "Les conferences franço-espangnoles de Deynze," *Revue d'histoire moderne*, Vol. 2 (1927), pp. 191-215. Documents on this peace conference can also be found in van Houtte, *Occupations étrangères*, and Nord, C 2333.

95. See discussion of lines to cover Alsace in AG, MR 1066, nos. 13-16, and lines to cover north of Spanish Netherlands in AG, MR 1047, pieces 9 and 10.

96. See AG, A^{1}616, #21, 5 April 1678; Nord, C 2242, undated but ca. 1700, discussion of lines of Waeste.

97. AG, MR 1047, #9, "Projet du'une ligne...," 6 April 1701.

98. AG, A^{1}1639, #42, 24 February 1703, Louis to Villars in Ferguson, diss., p. 180. I take the translation from Ferguson, although I have changed his punctuation to clarify the sentence.

99. Louvois letter of 18 August 1683 in Hardré, *Letters of Louvois*, p. 234.

8

Logistical Crisis and the American Revolution: A Hypothesis

John Shy

The study of logistics has long been the neglected offspring of military history, itself a stepchild in the historiographical family.[1] The written history of logistics is too often tediously technical, with much emphasis on organization, inefficiency, and corruption. We all know that crucial changes and events in the history of war are rooted in the complex interplay of economics and technology that defines the logistical dimension of warfare: the French Revolution breakthrough in land warfare, the ability of the United States to deploy and sustain mass armies in its war with the Confederate States, and the remarkably quick recovery and victory of the United States in its Pacific war with Japan—all were primarily logistical in nature. And yet Samuel Eliot Morison could not find space in fourteen volumes for any systematic account of how his beloved U.S. Navy engineered something like a logistical miracle, 1942-1945, overturning accepted theory and doctrine about the relationship of bases to naval strategy. Martin van Creveld gets credit for bringing new life to this aspect of military history by questioning traditional views with his own provocative, plausible, but not always persuasive answers.[2]

The eight-year war for American independence may not seem the most promising place to carry on the revival of logistical study stimulated by van Creveld. The impressive British effort to project unprecedented levels of land and sea power across the North Atlantic has been fairly well studied by Edward Curtis, Piers Mackesy, Arthur Bowler, Norman Baker, and David Syrett, among others.[3] The American side of the war, by contrast, seems messy and unattractive. Everything appears to be improvised, nothing seems to function as intended, Congress dithers, state governments fail, ordinary people hoard and cheat, merchants gouge, frustrated soldiers become brutal, and even the putative logistical heroes of the American Revolutionary War, Robert Morris

161

and Nathanael Greene, are seen to be looking out for personal profit as much as for the army and its "glorious cause."

In 1984, Wayne Carp published *To Starve the Army at Pleasure: Continental Army Administration and American Political Culture, 1775-1783*. His extensive research and careful analysis not only gave unprecedented depth to a familiar story, but he located that story in the context of a critical few years in the formation of an independent American polity. Carp was able to build his work on the valuable organizational study by Erna Risch, and on the remarkably original exploration of the wartime psyche by Charles Royster.[4] But the dominant picture of the American side of this war, a picture unshaken by this recent published research, remained one of bloody footprints in the snow at Valley Forge left by shoeless, shivering, sick and undernourished American soldiers. The wonder is how the British managed to lose the war given the magnitude of logistical breakdown on the other side.

Our traditional picture needs some correction. The revision here offered of the standard view is that logistical breakdown in the American Revolutionary War was primarily a result of structural factors, and not of human failure at any level, and that this breakdown had profoundly important consequences after the war for the uniquely American pattern of federal government that soon emerged. Because relatively little intensive research has been done on this unattractive subject, a revisionist argument can only be termed an hypothesis about both the operational nature and the deeper impact of an unusual premodern popular war. The hypothesis originates in my own research on the general character of the American Revolutionary War; evidence is offered more by way of illustration than as any strict test. And because this volume is devoted to military history, I concentrate on the operational aspect of the hypothesis, only sketching lightly the political side of the argument.

The British-American colonies united in armed rebellion in 1775 were often depicted by European travellers and other observers as a land of milk and honey where ordinary white settlers lived far more comfortably than their counterparts in Europe. Overwhelmingly agricultural, the colonial American population had grown at a phenomenal rate during the previous century. Many of the 2 1/2 million American colonists in 1775 were recent immigrants from Ireland, Germany, and, of course, Africa, but most of the rapid population growth is explained by natural increase abetted by good nutrition and low infant mortality. Only in southern New England had this growing population begun to press against the availability of arable land, and high rates of internal migration even before 1775 kept a healthy balance between people and resources. By European standards, population density was low, and labor scarce, with the demand for labor fluctuating seasonally.[5]

Although the commercial sector of the American economy had grown more rapidly than had the population, towns remained small, and perhaps nine of ten people lived off the land, their lives enriched by selling surplus production in the market. But even in the southern colonies, where African slave labor and plantations had carried commercial agriculture furthest, the economy was virtually self-sufficient.

The American economy and society in 1775 appear almost ideally prepared to wage a protracted war of national liberation: a young population with thousands of potential soldiers, backed by a strong, growing economy with no vital center vulnerable to military action. There was no shortage in 1775, nor would there be during the war, of the two key ingredients of premodern warfare: manpower and foodstuffs. Other vital items were also available; domestic weaving, knitting, and shoemaking could supply much of the wartime clothing need, and the widespread ownership of firearms, plus a vibrant commercial sector experienced in illegal trade, could easily make up any shortages in clothing, tentage, and munitions. The papers of George Washington, his generals, and the Continental Congress contain an eight-year litany of shortages—of manpower, of weapons, of food and clothing; but there was in fact no actual shortage of any of these items during the American war for national independence. Resources of all kinds seem adequate to wage war indefinitely. A general sense of the basic richness of the emergent United States lies behind much of the judgment that only human frailty and greed could explain the near-failure of the American military effort.

But there was in fact a single, crucial shortage, an item absolutely inadequate to meet the demand generated by eight years of desultory warfare. What the American rebels absolutely lacked—and it was a crippling deficiency militarily and economically—was adequate means of distribution—the animals, the wagons, the available roads and waterways, and the quantities of skilled manpower needed to operate a wartime logistical network under premodern conditions. Paper money and the reluctance to impose taxes are often blamed for the literal bankruptcy of the American effort by the fifth year of the war, but paper money had worked well in financing colonial wars fought under somewhat different circumstances. It was the absolute shortage of horses, oxen, wagons, teamsters, blacksmiths, and wheelwrights, more than anything else, that drove prices and wages to uncontrollable, destructive levels, dragging the rest of wartime costs with them. Why this should have happened seems, in retrospect, so clear as to be predictable, although contemporary observers, overwhelmed by fiscal disaster on every front, seldom saw the root cause of the problem.

The problem began with the fact that premodern transportation was far more difficult, and more costly, by land than by water. The thriving commercial sector of the late colonial American economy depended on maritime trade across the Atlantic, into the Caribbean, and increasingly between colonies by coastal shipping. Americans had proved so adept at shipping and shipbuilding that on the eve of the Revolutionary War as much as a third of the entire British merchant marine was, in some sense, American. The network of

American roads, fairly primitive tracks by modern (or Roman) standards, had developed in response to this maritime commercial pattern. The best American roads carried farm produce to the coastal port towns and followed, more or less, the easy lines of natural drainage. A few other good roads carried travellers and mail between these coastal towns but were broken frequently by watercourses crossed only by ferry.

The revolution imposed its operational demands on this unsuitable road network. British naval supremacy not only destroyed most of the intercoastal trade but effectively denied American use, except at high cost and risk, of the best coastal roads. Wrongly sited for the logistical needs of a war moving chiefly along a north-south axis, the best interior roads, running to and from the coast, were of limited usefulness, and the American army was driven to rely on secondary and tertiary roads—safely distant from the dangerous coast, but difficult, slow, and expensive.[6] The Swedish traveller Peter Kalm had observed about 1750 that American "roads are good or bad according to the condition of the ground. In a sandy soil the roads are dry and good; but in a clayey one they are bad."[7] Roads on sandier soil were, in general, those near the coast, where British and Loyalists forces were strong, so the American army was using the interior roads, described by Kalm as "bad."

Certain distinctions are vital to understanding the problem: British seapower could never cut off the rebels from the relatively small quantities of munitions, salt, canvas, and hard cash needed to keep the rebellion alive, but British amphibious mobility forced the Americans to use cheaper, faster water-borne transportation only in an irregular, guerrilla fashion, unsuited to the regular movement of the high-bulk supplies required for conventional land warfare. Early in the war, rebel leaders decided, with no explicit attention to consequences or alternatives, that military resistance to British authority should be conducted as much as possible along the lines of contemporary European warfare, and not by local forces, logistically supported by their own localities. Regarded in the broadest political framework, that strategic decision to centralize the war was almost certainly correct, but it meant the imposition on the American environment of organized armies, each the size of a large colonial town, in effect mobile markets moving and consuming in unprecedented patterns.[8]

The severe limitations of these militarily available interior roads, inadequate as they were both in quality and layout, might presumably have been overcome by the application of massive amounts of human and animal energy. After all, a predominantly agricultural society was full of draft horses and cattle and of the willing farmboys needed to tend and drive them.[9] What actually happened, however, was that the farm boys volunteered for the army or were compelled to serve in the militia. From 1775 onward, military service drew manpower away from vital work as teamsters, drovers, hostlers, harnessmakers, farriers, wheelwrights, and wagonsmiths; these vital occupations were not valued as

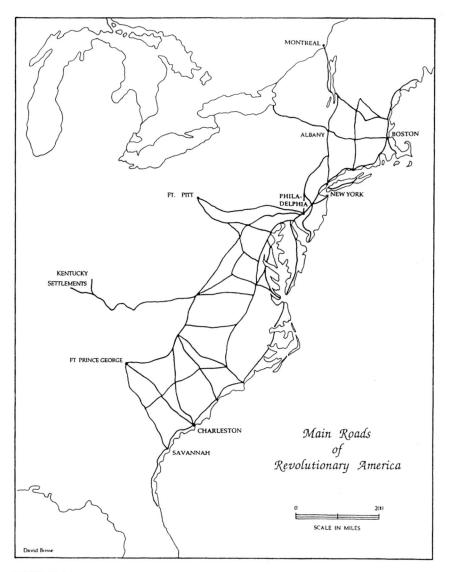

FIGURE 8.1

highly as service in the line and were in fact regarded as havens for cowards and draft-dodgers. The rapid rise of wages for these scarce skills reinforced the general propensity not to count this work as military service. Decades after the war, under a liberal federal law granting service pensions to revolutionary veterans with as little as six months of active duty in the militia, bureaucrats in Washington were still rejecting applications from those who served—often at greater risk of life and limb—only or mainly as army teamsters, in effect perpetuating the cultural perception that had been an important part of the wartime problem.[10]

At the same time, the American supply of farm animals and wagons roughly matched the needs of the prewar American economy and could not be quickly expanded to meet the new, greater demands imposed by the strategic geography of the war.[11] And even that supply of animals—adequate for peace, but too small for war—dwindled alarmingly as inexperienced soldiers, drafted from the line for logistical duty, abused and mismanaged the horses and cattle under their care. Farmers were soon hiding and hoarding their scarce and precious livestock, and for some of them the British market for horses and ox-teams, paying hard cash in a paper-money world, proved an irresistible temptation.

A simple table illustrates the degree to which the absolute shortage and uncontrollable costs of transportation were the root problems of both American strategy and wartime economic policy:

TABLE 8.1 Wartime Costs and Inflation, 1777-1779 (1777=100)

Item	1777	1778	1779	% of 1779 total
Army pay	100	153	164	11%
Provisions	100	365	917	35%
Military stores	100	197	1189	2%
Clothing	100	355	732	5%
Hospital	100	238	310	1%
Barrackmaster	100	300	3092	—
Miscellaneous	100	131	190	8%
Transportation (Quartermaster)	100	568	1808	38%

Source: E. Wayne Carp, *To Starve the Army at Pleasure: Contental Army Administration and American Political Culture, 1775-1783* (Chapel Hill: 1984), P. 69.

If costs are indexed against congressional expenditures for 1777 (the first full year of all-out military effort), only the outlay for military stores and barrack costs rose more rapidly in the next two years than the cost of transportation. But total barrack costs were negligible, while military stores were a very small proportion of the costs of war; the steep rise for both items suggests that the early, "cheap" phase of the war was—in current jargon—fought from inventory. But by 1779 transportation costs were consuming almost two-fifths of total congressional expenditures, and their rapid three-year rise almost doubled that of the next most expensive item, "provisions"—food for the troops. Table 8.1 also illustrates the currency inflation that led to national bankruptcy in 1780, but by scanning the two right-hand columns we can readily see the war-wrecking effects of the single item of transportation.

A critical point in this larger problem of inadequate overland transportation, a point that often constituted a dilemma for all strategists before the advent of mechanical power—a catch-22 of premodern warfare—was the unavoidable need for forage. Men can survive better than horses and cattle on inadequate feeding, but soldiers could not last long without properly fed animals delivering their rations. Hay, oats, and other forage in sufficient quantity were absolutely vital if draft animals were to keep the troops fed and otherwise supplied. The daily forage needs of a number of working teams over any given distance can be calculated with some precision.[12] To skimp on forage was to invite the predictable breakdown and probable loss of draft animals in the American war, animals that became increasingly difficult to replace given the rising demand and ever-shrinking supply.

Localized scarcity of forage added to the upward pressure of wartime prices. Farmers naturally wanted adequate compensation for allowing a cavalry unit or a wagon brigade to pasture on their land, but the meaning of "adequate compensation" in an environment of rapidly rising prices was disputed. Cavalry units might be able to move to an area where pasture and forage were more abundant, as American cavalry regiments were dispersed to winter in New Jersey in 1777 or as Pulaski's Legion was moved to Delaware in the winter of 1779, to feed the horses.[13] But the teams that pulled the wagons that supplied the army were tied to the location of the army and could not readily move to greener, cheaper pastures. In some cases, the main army itself was virtually immobilized by the lack of forage to feed its logistical tail. An early instance came with the American attack on Canada: during the dry summer of 1775, General Philip Schuyler, who had considerable logistical experience during the previous colonial war, found that his available teams were unable to move enough forage northward even to feed themselves as they tried to supply a small army assembling at Ticonderoga for the invasion of Canada.[14] Not until late summer rains nourished the grass that fed his animals could Schuyler gather enough supplies to move an adequate force down Lakes George and Champlain. His late start may have sealed the fate of the campaign; after early successes, winter closed in, blocking vital economic and political support that might have averted what became a military catastrophe.[15] Inadequate forage in June and July was not the only reason for the failure of the Canadian campaign, but it surely was one of them.

The most detailed study of the logistical problems of the Revolutionary War is, not surprisingly, of the winter at Valley Forge, Pennsylvania, 1777-1778, when the main American army under Washington was virtually destroyed, not by British attack or freezing weather but by supply breakdown. Wayne Bodle and Jacqueline Thibaut, co-authors of this study, demonstrate exactly how the breakdown occurred.[16] First, the army had maneuvered strenuously through the late summer and early autumn of 1777, from the hills of northern New Jersey and the mid-Hudson valley to the head of Chesapeake Bay, responding to the frequent and puzzling movements of the main British army, and fighting two major battles as well as several smaller skirmishes. By December, when the British army had occupied Philadelphia and the exhausted American army was moving into its campsite some twenty miles to the northwest at Valley Forge, a site chosen less for its logistical advantages than because it gave some protection to the rich, populous, and politically sensitive region of southeastern Pennsylvania, both the wagons and the teams that hauled the baggage and stores of the army were in wretched condition. During an active campaign there had been little time for the repair of wagons or the shoeing of horses, and more than once army orders had forbidden teamsters to let their animals graze at night on nearby farmland, where they trampled the crops of owners whose support for American independence was already tenuous.

Once in camp, in the midst of a major food-producing region, the army saw its supply situation fluctuate alarmingly, then disintegrate almost completely in early February. Winter always meant that animal fodder was not abundant, so available stocks at or near Valley Forge were soon exhausted. Foraging expeditions into the surrounding countryside required wagons and teams—working animals whose caloric demands could not be safely slighted. As the army consumed nearby sources, it had to push further outward along the network of rough, frozen, and muddy roads, with consequent increases in energy expenditure and demand. Still further beyond Valley Forge, attempts to bring both food and forage to the army from the more remote, militarily untroubled farmlands around York, Lancaster, Reading, and Easton foundered as distance sharply increased the total number of wagons and teams required and there was a lack of winter fodder to keep so many animals working. The army needed a daily minimum of one hundred barrels of flour from the York-Lancaster area, but it proved impossible to find and support the estimated total of a hundred wagons and four hundred draft horses needed to keep that much flour moving steadily over some sixty miles of winter roads.

In its desperate, costly, and futile efforts to defend Philadelphia against the British offensive of 1777, the American army had moved away from its main source of meat, in southern New England, where beef cattle and hogs were abundant. Normally, the onset of winter saw the slaughter of these animals and the salt-packing of their meat for market; but the extraordinary number of wagons and teams, and the fodder to feed them, required to move salted beef and pork from Connecticut to Valley Forge under winter conditions ruled out this type of supply. An alternative was the cattle drive, gathering at Danbury, Connecticut, pushing along the more difficult track to the Fishkill-New Windsor

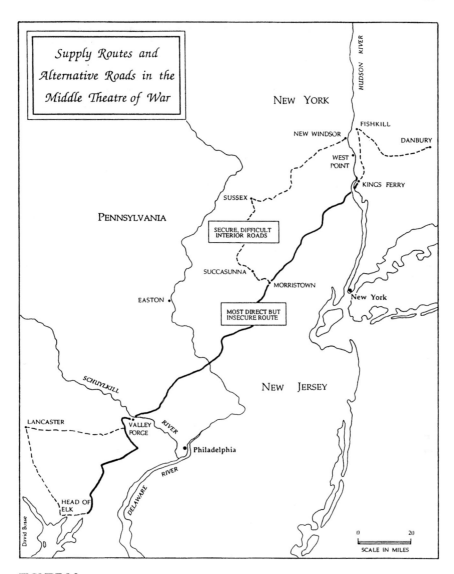

FIGURE 8.2

crossing of the Hudson rather than the easier but more dangerous crossing at Kings Ferry near Peekskill, then down through the Jersey hills and across the Delaware above Trenton to the hungry army. But without grasslands along the route or full stores of fodder well located, the few New England cattle that eventually reached Valley Forge were emaciated, most of their meat burned up by the long wintry trek. Bodle and Thibaut make clear beyond any doubt that supply breakdown at Valley Forge was not wholly a matter of ecological arithmetic, of basic geography and caloric intake. The people responsible for the procurement and movement of supplies also failed badly both to anticipate the problem and to grasp it once the crisis was suddenly upon them. General Washington had remained preoccupied with operational matters, trusting his supply service to run itself until the logistical situation had deteriorated beyond human agency. But no matter how serious the breakdown at the organizational and human levels—and this was a period when the army had no Quartermaster General, who had overall responsibility for transport services—the core problem would have remained an iron trap of distance, road location and condition, weather, wagons, drivers, teams, and fodder. The only variable was army strength, and that inevitably dwindled as sick and hungry soldiers died and deserted. The arrival at Valley Forge of reinforcements from the northern army under General Gates, whose capture of the British invading force from Canada had been the bright spot of 1777, simply exacerbated the supply crisis. No one will ever know whether some logistical wizard might have freed the army from its trap; in any event, the American army at Valley Forge came as close to death as it ever would during the war.

After the ordeal of Valley Forge, Washington's army moved northeastward, trailing the British army as it withdrew from Philadelphia to New York. Intense summer heat in 1778 took its toll on both men and animals. When Washington ordered his army across the Hudson, he led his soldiers and their wagon teams into a crisis of grain supply that was the worst of the war. Demand generated by five separate armies far outstripped the never abundant supply of forage in New England—a French fleet carrying an expeditionary force resupplying at Boston; the British army of General Burgoyne captured at Saratoga plus its American militia guards in eastern Massachusetts; a second American army facing the British garrison of Newport, Rhode Island; and (unknown to Washington) the main British army at New York caught in a provisioning crisis of its own. All competed with Washington's army for corn, flour, wagons, teams, and anything livestock could eat.[17] The French paid in hard money and seldom haggled over price; when local farmers made their way with cattle or provisions through British lines, they also were paid in cash. Both easily outbid their American competition, driving prices further upward. Although Washington's horses and cattle were able to fatten in the pastures of Westchester County, his quartermaster general knew that the grass would soon be gone and once again the animals would be starving.[18] The best British strategy, some thought, would have been to make the long-rumored attack on Boston, drawing Washington further eastward, more deeply into the forage-desert of New England. Instead, redeploying most of his army west of the Hudson, where they could draw during the winter on the better grain supply of New Jersey and Pennsylvania, Washington eased his problem but did not solve it.

A year after the horrors of Valley Forge, the springtime rebuilding of Washington's army, and the grain crisis in New England of 1778, the seemingly simple problem of forage for working animals continued to plague American operations. A single well-recorded case, during the redeployment west of the Hudson 1778-1779, chosen from among dozens, illustrates both the quotidian difficulties of finding the essential daily ration for army horses and cattle and the deeper political ramifications of that quest.

Washington had decided to shift his headquarters and much of his army from east of the Hudson River to the middle Raritan valley of New Jersey. The move involved marching, once the Americans had crossed the Hudson at Fishkill, down through the hilly interior of northern New Jersey, staying out of reach of the main British army based on Manhattan. When a detachment of Maryland troops commanded by Colonel Peter Adams reached the village of Succasunna, New Jersey, after a twenty-mile march in mid-December 1778, it found no forage for its horses, the preceding brigade having consumed the locally available supply. Acting on a tip, Colonel Adams sent a young quartermaster-lieutenant to the mill of Jonathan Dickerson. Dickerson claimed that he had only enough Indian corn, rye, and buckwheat for the needs of his own family, but the lieutenant pushed past him into the mill and took the half-dozen bushels of forage needed by the Maryland horses, tendering a receipt to Dickerson for the requisition. Dickerson rejected the receipt, and instead sought a warrant for the lieutenant's arrest under a New Jersey law prescribing that all military impressment must involve a civil magistrate. Himself a magistrate, Dickerson presumably believed that his status and the state law ought to have secured his property against military seizure. But when Dickerson, assisted by a county constable, tried to arrest the offending officer, he was met by a party of soldiers with bayonets fixed and was held prisoner until the Maryland detachment had marched out of town. General Washington and Governor Livingston of New Jersey were of course bombarded by conflicting versions of this mundane encounter, and by spring 1779 both men confessed their inability to ascertain exactly what had happened and who was at fault. Both knew, however, that six bushels of corn, rye, and buckwheat at Succasunna were symptomatic of a much bigger problem.[19]

Anyone who today, shunning superhighways, drives north on U.S. Route 206 from Princeton, New Jersey, to Somerville, in the upper Raritan valley, then through the hills and lakes of Morris and Sussex Counties, through Netcong and Newton to State 565 and on to Sussex courthouse, and then follows State

284 on to Middletown, New York, where a wall of mountain stands between the town and the Hudson River and its crossing point at Fishkill, still twenty miles further east, will gain a sharp sense of the effect of pushing American logistics inland, on to the secondary roads and bare tracks of the eighteenth-century landscape. These modern back roads follow roughly one line of march for American troops moving from southern New England and the Hudson valley into the middle theater; the village of Succasunna lies just east of U.S. 206, northwest of and on the road to Morristown.[20] An on-site inspection of Succasunna—today a bedroom community of shopping centers next to a superhighway, but still a valley enclosed in the foothills of the Allegheny Mountains—will suggest why the valley's limited supply of forage was exhausted when Colonel Adams and his Marylanders arrived there late in the winter of 1778.

British cruisers in Chesapeake Bay disrupted shipments of supplies northward from Virginia, a prime source of forage, and for a year (1777-78) British forces had controlled the lower Delaware valley, pushing the north-south American supply line well to the west, out of harm's way. Supplies coming from the southern states made it through the blockade by landing near Elkton, Maryland, at the head of the bay. A former member of the quartermaster's staff at Elkton recalled: "Great caution was necessary on account of the occupation of Philadelphia by the enemy. The course pursued was a circuitous one by Cochran's Tavern to the Lancaster Road." He added that there had been "great difficulty and vexation with the wagoners."[21] And moving forage northward from Maryland, Pennsylvania, and southern New Jersey was equally arduous and dangerous, because armed bands of American Loyalists were active throughout the area. Even before the American rebels had lost their foothold in the New York port area at the end of 1776, some teamsters had learned the perils of straying too near the coastal districts. Ambushed by a Tory gang close to Somerset Courthouse, just up the Raritan from New Brunswick, John Wright and his comrades had lost their wagons, horses, and clothes; nothing but a venal jailer had allowed them to get away with their lives.[22] Major supply centers along the logistical arc from Danbury, through Fishkill, Peekskill, Easton, Trenton, Lancaster, and on to Elkton, as well as smaller, intermediate points, were vulnerable to British and Tory raids.[23] Less mobile parts of the system, like the arsenals at Springfield, Massachusetts, and Carlisle, Pennsylvania, were sited more safely behind the arc, but they were also less accessible by road. And the whole network had to service the army at distant strategic locations like Morristown and Valley Forge, as well as at operationally important little points like Succasunna, New Jersey.[24]

Unlike the shortages of wagons, draft animals, skilled teamsters, and operationally suitable roads, there was no absolute shortage of forage in the Revolutionary War. Although quartermaster agents complained at times of steep price increases, our fragmentary data on actual prices for corn, oats, rye, and other forage grains do not indicate that overall demand for these commodities actually drove inflation as the steep rise of teamster wages, wagon-hire, and horse prices surely did. But the peculiar immobility of forage, having it always where and when it was needed, plus the costs—themselves reckoned partly in terms of forage itself—of moving this high-bulk, low-value item to the point of military consumption, made the forage problem an especially acute part of the larger logistical problem of overland transport.

As with the war itself, the American logistical effort was marked by a series of improvisations, all of which failed to solve the basic problem, and some of which made it perceptibly worse. A separate, militarized wagon corps under the Quartermaster General did not work. Attempts to create various market incentives and military-service exemptions to attract the needed animal power and skilled manpower also did not work. Centralizing efforts could never overcome competition for the same scarce, shrinking resources from state and local authorities or even eliminate competition within the army itself, all of which had the effect of bidding prices and wages up to their fantastic levels of 1779. With the failure of every attempt to regulate prices and wages, and the acknowledged national bankruptcy of 1780, logistical responsibilities fell, almost by sheer necessity, from Congress and army headquarters onto state and local authorities. Under the unworkable "system of specific supplies," adopted by Congress in that year, states were supposed to take care of their own troops, and any locality where Continental forces happened to be stationed was expected to provide the rest. This new, decentralized system, which Congress hoped would be both more effective and more economical, proved perhaps the worst of all. Supplies rotted in state depositories for lack of means to move them to the army. In South Carolina, where mobile warfare continued through 1780-81, there are in the state archives thousands of scraps of paper, many covered with semi-literate scrawl, testifying to how the system actually operated: army quartermasters, backed by soldiers, simply took corn and cattle directly from southern farmers, giving them a rough receipt. If supplies could not be moved to the army, then the army would move to the supplies. But no army could hope to sustain itself for long in any part of the thinly settled American countryside, and the direct seizure of supplies simply encouraged hiding and hoarding while raising the incentive to sell to the nearby British.

In the decisive campaign of the war, at Yorktown in 1781, the French expeditionary force in Rhode Island—like the British, paying cash for what it wanted—was able to find the transport needed to move quickly to Virginia. Washington's army, deployed north of New York City, was able to move southward to Chesapeake Bay after a rapid march across New Jersey. It was a heroic, one-time effort, engineered by the new superintendent of American finances, Robert Morris. But the basic logistical problem of insufficient land transport to support a conventional war of sustained maneuver was never solved, even during the brief Yorktown campaign, and under the circumstances could not have been solved.

The American rebels finally won their war for independence despite their unsolvable logistical problem, so the question naturally arises as to the problem's broader significance, aside from its effect on specific military operations. A first answer to this question is directed at traditional historiography of the American Revolution: if the problem was, as I believe it was, inevitable and unsolvable given the nature of the war, then virtually nothing could have been done about it, and indeed its effects were no one's fault—not the fault of Congress, the states, the merchants, or the people. None of them were to blame for the problem, and none of them could do anything effective to solve it. So it is idle, and mistaken, to indulge in the judgmental pastime of deploring the role of Congress or the states or the American people in allowing the army to suffer from undelivered supplies.

This is not to say that there was nothing defective about the organization of the American logistical effort, or that the frequent, angry criticism of various members of that organization for inept, even venal performance in office was ill founded. As in every war, there were ample, well-documented mistakes on the logistical side of this one. But the very obviousness of glaring faults, both in organization and in individual behavior, has obscured the main point: better organization and better people might have ameliorated but could not have solved the underlying structural problem of inadequate overland transport.[25]

A second answer to the question of significance follows from the first and takes us deeper into the political and ideological aspects of the Revolution. The logistical problem, if the argument just presented is correct, was both critical and intractable. But leaders of revolution cannot readily admit that they can do little or nothing about a problem critical to the outcome of their revolutionary struggle. Instead, delegates to the Continental Congress and Continental army officers naturally believed that human ingenuity, energy, and commitment should, if properly mobilized, solve their logistical problem, and when the problem resisted solution, they sought an explanation in human and institutional failure—faulty organization, individual incompetence, and—above all—greed and corruption. Although no one, in retrospect, may be fairly blamed for failing to move supplies in adequate quantity to revolutionary armies in the field, desperate efforts to do so actually tolerated, even encouraged, forms of behavior that were antithetical to revolutionary zeal and self-sacrifice, what Americans of the time called "virtue." Experienced in the context of a revolutionary idealism so eloquently expressed in the Declaration of Independence, the eight years of the Revolutionary War were profoundly disillusioning. Minor incidents of hoarding, price-gouging, bid-rigging, overcharging, and wildly inflated wage demands occurred by the hundreds in the latter years of the war, and these incidents accumulated to depressing effect in the public consciousness. Again, to take a single example: a prominent Pennsylvanian who had jeopardized his good standing as a Quaker by supporting the Revolution, was sickened in 1780 by the sight of quartermaster staff officers running a high-stakes horse race with animals but recently seized from local farmers.[26] The incident can readily be multiplied, but to the same general effect. Even General Washington was moved to bitter complaint in 1782 when Robert Morris used his small stock of cash, recently acquired on loan from Europe, to pay the interest due to bond-holding creditors rather than use this money to pay or supply Washington's ragged army.[27]

A final answer to the question of how the irremediable shortage of land transport during the Revolutionary War left its mark on the postwar republic lies in the peculiar federal structure of the United States. For all their expressed commitment to equality and popular sovereignty, few revolutionary leaders had shown much interest in the specific relationship between central and state government. During the war, the crippling effects of the recently drafted Articles of Confederation on central authority had become apparent. Critical observers like Colonel Alexander Hamilton blamed the Continental Congress for not simply seizing the powers to tax and to direct that the states had refused to relinquish. By extension, many blamed (mistakenly, I argue) this constitutional flaw for perpetuating the logistical problem, which was the root cause of the more general economic crisis. In fact, at the beginning of the war, Congress had exerted considerable power at the grass roots through a system of popular local committees initially organized to enforce the trade boycott voted in 1774 and gradually converted into broader committees of safety. At first directly responsive to directives from the Congress in Philadelphia, these local committees gradually came under state control as their functions expanded to include surveillance and mobilization, particularly in the area of logistics. With the financial collapse of 1779-1780, the process was completed, Congress ceding almost all of its responsibility for the acquisition and movement of supplies to the states. With this cession of responsibility from Congress to the states went power and credibility, at least to the extent that any governmental body could claim credibility at the end of a long, exhausting war. But nothing did more than this logistically impelled process to create the conditions out of which would come the new Federal Constitution of 1789: state governments with more effective power than they could constructively wield during a severe postwar national economic depression and a national Congress so weakened that it could be safely brushed aside and a radically new structure put in its place.

Federalism, in its unique American form, was less a product of theoretical debate among the Founding Fathers of the United States than of their search for ideas to account for more homely, mundane factors—too few horses and wagons, too few skilled teamsters, and too few passable roads running in the right directions. But perhaps (and here I leave the realm of the hypothetical for the conjectural) the key factor was the war-induced disillusionment with human nature. Historians have long noted that beneath the surface of the debate over the drafting and public acceptance of the Federal Constitution there was a deep sobriety, a salutary pessimism about what might be expected from average Americans.[28] In concluding, I do not think it is exaggeration to suggest that the recent, often shocking spectacle of an emergent nation floundering to solve an unsolvable logistical problem had played a major part in transforming the American euphoria of 1775 into the American sobriety of 1787, creating the reduced expectations that underlay public acquiescence in what almost everyone, supporters and critics alike, regarded as an imperfect, improvised set of constitutional arrangements.

Notes

1. I am grateful to friends and colleagues who have helped in formulating, clarifying, and testing the argument presented in this essay: David Bien and Peter Paret (in an early, condensed version), David Bosse, Tom Collier, John Dann, Doron Lamm, Ken Lockridge, Jonathan Marwil, and Jack Price, as well as members of the Military Studies Group at the University of Michigan. The maps were drawn by David Bosse of the William L. Clements Library.

2. Martin van Creveld, *Supplying War: Logistics from Wallenstein to Patton* (Cambridge: 1977).

3. Edward E. Curtis, *The Organization of the British Army in the American Revolution* (New York: 1926); Piers Mackesy, *The War for America, 1775-1783* (London: 1964); R. Arthur Bowler, *Logistics and the Failure of the British Army in America, 1775-1783* (Princeton: 1975); Norman Baker, *Government and Contractors: The British Treasury and War Supplies, 1775-83* (London: 1971); David Syrett, *Shipping and the American War, 1775-83* (London: 1970).

4. E. Wayne Carp, *To Starve the Army at Pleasure: Continental Army Administration and American Political Culture, 1775-1783* (Chapel Hill: 1984); Erna Risch, *Supplying Washington's Army*, in the Special Studies series of the U.S. Army Center of Military History (Washington: 1981); Charles Royster, *A Revolutionary People at War: The Continental Army and American Character* (Chapel Hill: 1979). Richard Buel, Jr., *Dear Liberty: Connecticut's Mobilization for the Revolutionary War* (Middletown, CT: 1980), is an especially detailed study of a single important state. Older, but still useful, are Charles K. Bolton, *The Private Soldier under Washington* (New York: 1902), Louis C. Hatch, *The Administration of the American Revolutionary Army* (New York: 1904), and Victor L. Johnson, *The Administration of the American Commissariat During the Revolutionary War* (Philadelphia: 1941).

5. The best brief picture of colonial America and its 18th-century development is James A. Henretta and Gregory H. Nobles, *Evolution and Revolution: American Society, 1600-1820* (Lexington, MA: 1987). More detailed, and an excellent work, is John J. McCusker and Russell R. Menard, *The Economy of British America, 1607-1789* (Chapel Hill: 1985).

6. The danger of relying on supply points within reach of British seapower was learned early in the war. Washington told Nathanael Greene, White Plains, 7

November 1776: "We find great risque and Inconvenience arising from having Stores near Navigation...," *The Papers of General Nathanael Greene*, eds. R.K. Showman et al. (Chapel Hill: 1979-), 1:339.

7. *Travels in North America*, ed. A.B. Benson, 2 vols. (New York: 1937), 1:222. He also noted that Americans were very careless about repair, not building bridges if streams were normally fordable, and leaving fallen trees in place if travellers could go around them.

8. The best picture of American revolutionary army strength and location through the war is Charles H. Lesser (ed.), *The Sinews of Independence* (Chicago: 1976).

9. Contemporary observers often noted that colonial American farmers were slovenly in their treatment of livestock. McCusker and Menard, *Economy of British America*, p. 305.

10. Numerous indications of the disdain felt by the line army and its officers for those in the wagon and quartermaster corps are in "The Orderly Book of General John Peter Gabriel Muhlenberg, March 26-December 20, 1777," *Pennsylvania Magazine of History and Biography*, XXXIII-XXXV (1909-1911), passim.

11. Before the war, some mainland livestock was exported to the West Indies. For example, Benedict Arnold, sailing out of New London, Connecticut, carried horses from Quebec to the Caribbean. But the total amount was relatively small, and the risks in carrying large live animals on a sea voyage restricted the size of the trade. See Jacques Mathieu, *Le commerce entre la Nouvelle-France et les Antilles au XVIIIe siècle* (Montreal: 1981), pp. 174-75. For other evidence on the existence before 1775 of the horse trade and its difficulties, see the letters published on the commerce of Rhode Island in *Massachusetts Historical Society Collections*, ser. 7, vol. 10 (Boston: 1914), pp. 183-84, 211, 216, 271-72, 320, and 431. McCusker and Menard, *Economy of British America*, p. 199, lump livestock with packed beef and pork in a single category whose value is small. The question here is whether there had been a large prewar surplus of draft animals, generated through natural increase, on the American mainland; while statistical evidence is lacking, other evidence suggests that the surplus was not large enough to have a significant effect on wartime logistics.

On the shortage of wagons for military needs, General Greene blamed the loss of American army stores and baggage when the British captured Ft. Lee, New Jersey, in late November, 1776, on the scarcity of transport; to Gov. Nicholas Cooke, Trenton, 4 December 1776, *Papers of General Nathanael Greene*, 1:362.

12. I have profited greatly from a remarkable book on the logistics of another, very different war reliant on animal power: Donald W. Engels, *Alexander the Great and the Logistics of the Macedonian Army* (Berkeley: 1978), which includes careful calculations of the forage needs of draft animals.

13. QM Benjamin Thompson to Henry Lutterloh, Trenton, 6 February 1777, Papers of the Continental Congress, National Archives microfilm M247, reel 199, 209; Nathanael Greene to Clement Biddle, Philadelphia, 20 January 1779, *Papers of General Nathanael Greene*, 3:172.

14. Schuyler to Gov. Trumbull of Conn., Ticonderoga, 21 July 1775, and to Washington, 31 July, *American Archives*, ed. Peter Force (Washington: 1837-53), 4th ser., 2:1704, 1762.

15. See the Report to Congress of the Committee of Secret Correspondence, on or before 14 February 1776; *The Papers of Benjamin Franklin*, eds. William B. Willcox et al., vol. 22 (New Haven and London: 1982), pp. 350-53.

16. *Valley Forge Historical Research Report*, 3 vols. (U.S. Dept. of the Interior, Valley Forge, PA: 1980). Volume 2 by Bodle is devoted to logistical problems.

17. Richard Buel, "Time: Friend or Foe of the Revolution?" *Reconsiderations on the Revolutionary War*, ed. Don Higginbotham (Westport, CT: 1978), p. 135; Mackesy, *War for America*, pp. 222-24.

18. A graphic description of diminishing grasslands, bad roads, and the debilitating effects on horses and cattle of "innumerable Swarms of Flies created and collected by the Filth of the camp," is Charles Pettit to Greene, Fredericksburg, New York, 1 October 1778, *Papers of General Nathanael Greene*, 2:531.

19. Deposition of Jonathan Dickerson, 31 December 1778, Washington papers microfilm (Library of Congress), 4th ser., reel 55, and Lt. Col. Adams to Washington, 25 May 1779, reel 59; Livingston to Washington, Raritan, 12 April 1779, *The Papers of William Livingston*, eds. Carl E. Prince et al. (Trenton: 1979-), 3:54-57; Washington to Livingston, Middlebrook, same date, *The Writings of George Washington*, ed. J.C. Fitzpatrick (Washington: 1931-1944), 14:370.

20. The modern retracing of the old route outlined in the text probably simplifies but does not exaggerate the contemporary difficulties of moving from Fishkill to Morristown and Bound Brook. The best single source for this question is the collection of manuscript maps by Robert Erskine, Washington's skillful cartographer, in the New York Historical Society. The six strip maps numbered by Erskine 117 and 118 and catalogued as numbers 151-156 clarify the role of Succasunna village in making the secure, westward-swinging loop from the Hudson to the Raritan. I have used the photostatic copies from this collection, in the William L. Clements Library at the University of Michigan. A more direct, less secure route through more rugged country led north from Succasunna to Green Pond and on to State route 94, thence through Warwick, New York, to New Windsor.

21. Pension affadavit of James Johnston, in John C. Dann (ed.), *The Revolution Remembered* (Chicago: 1980), pp. 404-5. Christopher Marshall, who rode out the British occupation of Philadelphia near Lancaster, frequently noted in his diary the movement of troops and supplies from Virginia through that town. Microfilm from the Historical Society of Pennsylvania. On the continuing blockade of Chesapeake Bay, see Nathanael Greene to Clement Biddle, Middle Brook, 26 February 1779, *Papers of General Nathanael Greene*, 3:307 also 280.

22. Pension affadavit of John Wright of Pennsylvania, U.S. National Archives Microfilm Publication No. 805, reel 892, frames 92-95. In light of the incident described previously, it is interesting to see that Wright later hauled corn and hay from "Suckasunny plains" to the army encampment at Morristown. I owe this reference, and others in the unpublished pension files, to John C. Dann.

23. Destructive British raids on Peekskill and Danbury in the spring of 1777 were classic cases.

24. [Clement Biddle], Proposals for the Forage Department with the Army, 25 January 1778, Continental Congress papers microfilm M247, reel 199, 373ff., describes the network in detail.

25. The argument here presented takes issue with, and rejects, those historians who see organization as the crucial weakness. Typical is the judgment of R. Arthur Bowler, in his valuable essay, "Logistics and Operations in the American Revolution," *Recon-*

siderations on the Revolutionary War, p. 56: "... without question, the most persistent and deadly problem of army logistical support was organization and administration."

26. The diary of Christopher Marshall, 1774-1781 (microfilm copy from the Historical Society of Pennsylvania), entries for 24-25 July 1780.

27. Washington to Morris, 17-[25] May 1782, *Writings of Washington*, 24:287-91. And see Chapter 5, "Corruption," in Carp, *To Starve the Army*, pp. 99-135.

28. This deep shift in American attitudes is clearest in Gordon S. Wood, *Creation of the American Republic, 1776-1787* (Chapel Hill: 1969), and its relation to the war itself best traced by Royster, *A Revolutionary People at War*.

PART FOUR

Modern Logistics, 1815-1991

Modern Introduction

During the modern era, rapid technological change brought by the Industrial Revolution altered the form of warfare. The basic facts of logistics changed dramatically, both in terms of the faster speed of transportation and the greater need for war matériel. First the steam engine and later the internal combustion engine promised a mobility to armed forces that they had never known before, although it would take a century for the potential to be achieved. For armies, the final step would depend most upon the common truck, which allowed supplies to move rapidly enough to keep up with troops advancing on mechanized steeds. Improved means of transportation increased the demands on logistics, particularly for fuel to drive engines on sea and land. But in addition, the new ships, naval guns, rifles, machine guns, artillery, tanks, and aircraft manufactured by the Industrial Revolution had a voracious appetite for ammunition and fuel. Mars grew ever hungrier. The transformation of both the means of movement and the items consumed has redefined modern logistics and has gone a long way towards defining modern war itself.

New Means of Transportation: Steamships and Railroads

The carrying capacity of new methods of transportation eventually made supply of all essentials from rear staging areas both possible and necessary. Steam power provided the first mechanical means of transportation. The steam engine, pioneered in the eighteenth century and perfected as a means of transport in the nineteenth, gained its ascendence for long distance cargo-hauling by 1860. Steam power advanced at a remarkably similar pace on land and at sea in the early 1800s. Fulton's *Clermont* plied the Hudson as early as 1807, and the first vessel equipped with auxiliary steam power crossed the Atlantic before 1820; however, regular steam service had to await the 1840s. The period from 1854 through 1866 witnessed the first major use of steam powered war vessels and troop transports in Europe, America, and the Levant. Yet even as the merchant fleets and navies of the world converted to steam, the economy of sail power meant that this ancient method of locomotion remained competitive, at least for some cargo, into the twentieth century.

For river transportation steam promised even greater advantages than it did at sea. The twisting and turning of rivers meant that winds could not possibly blow from the right quarter for long, since each bend changed a ship's angle to the wind. And a river's narrow confines greatly limited the ability to tack. Steam overcame these obstacles. The ready availability of wood or coal along the bank avoided the problems of fuel storage faced by ocean-going vessels. No wonder that major river transport depended on steam paddle wheelers during the American Civil War, while deep water transports and warships still carried full rigging even when they possessed engines.

On land, steam powered railroads debuted in the 1820s and expanded rapidly over the next two decades. Railroads overcame many of the limitations that plagued other forms of wheeled transportation. This was not only because of steam but because the prepared roadways limited friction, escaped the plague of mud, and capped the force of gravity by limiting grades to gentle slopes. Railways purchased these benefits, however, at a great cost. Railroads proved relatively fragile, vulnerable even to small parties of raiders. Moreover, while horse drawn wagons rolled over a ubiquitous network of paved and dirt roads and traveled cross country if need be, railroads were restricted to expensive and rare tracks. The fact that railroads could not duplicate the versatility of horse drawn wagons confined the mode of transportation to a narrower set of operational roles. Railroads might speed mobilization and facilitate the concentration of men and supplies at railheads, but they could not support an advancing army unless that army moved along existing rail lines.

New Means of Transportation: Trucks and Airplanes

Land transportation required a technology which could replace the horse and wagon as the link between railhead and army unit. Enter the truck powered by the internal combustion engine. Certainly trucks had a limited carrying capacity compared to railroads, and they consumed more fuel and required more spare parts, but their value on campaign justified the costs. Trucks could take advantage of the road network and off-road possibilities in a way the railroad could not. Their flexibility was essential to mobile warfare. Only trucks and their well-armed companions, tanks, could liberate warfare from the slow pace of walking man and plodding horse. And only trucks could keep the tanks rolling. Far more than the railroad, the truck ushered in a new age of mobility for field armies.

The adoption of trucks proved to be a great expense, however. To motorize an entire army and its supplies demanded a huge number of vehicles. European Continental states could not produce enough of them to mount their entire armies on the new motorized transport by 1939. At the outset of World War II, the Germans still depended on horse drawn wagons to support the standard infantry division, which had 1,200 wagons but only 942 trucks.[1] The French and Russian armies also remained heavily dependent on horses. Only the British and, later, the U.S. forces were fully motorized, and the German and Russian armies evolved towards this goal in the last years of the war.

Eventually the airplane also carried cargo; however it did not become a major factor in the shipment of war material until after World War II. In that war, it engaged in only a few limited, extremely expensive but highly publicized supply efforts such as flying over the "hump" into China. When the Germans tried to supply their troops in Stalingrad by air, they failed. Probably the first successful use of military airplanes to haul masses of cargo in lieu of overland transport was the Berlin airlift of 1948. Ships continued and continue to this day to carry most of the materiel consumed in war. Aircraft have proven highly valuable in transporting men, as they did in Vietnam and the Gulf War. In addition, the massive cargo aircraft developed after World War II can be employed to airlift a limited amount of equipment, food, ammunition, and fuel for rapid deployment. Tactically, this airborne transport duty can be passed on to helicopters. However, the physics of air transport are so inferior to those of water and land shipment that heavy equipment and the bulk of cargo still need to travel by ship at a ship's pace.

Industrial Logistic Needs: Ammunition and Fuel

Up to this point the discussion of new parameters for logistics has been limited to means of transportation, but at the same time the modern period tremendously increased demands for supplies. The most basic factor on the demand side was the appearance of mass armies composed of mobilized reserves in the late nineteenth century. Armies still remained within Napoleonic proportions as late as the Franco-Prussian War. The French mobilized only about 570,000 troops for that struggle, roughly the same number of French soldiers that Napoleon I had mustered at the height of his campaigns. But for the opening campaigns of World Wars I and II, the Third Republic called up 3-4,000,000 men. Such expansion, a consequence of the reserve system and population growth, obviously put military supply under pressures never before encountered.[2]

At the same time, the Industrial Revolution radically altered the character and compositon of the war matériel that had to be supplied. The rate of ammunition consumed climbed sharply in the late nineteenth and twentieth centuries. Magazine fed rifles, machine guns, and rapid fire artillery increased rates of fire and consumed mountains of ammunition in World War I. Eventually rockets, aerial bombs, and other new destructive packages would be added to the list. Ammunition now rivaled food as an item of resupply.

Fuel provides an even more impressive contrast between the character of supplies consumed in the twentieth century and those required in earlier eras. But here the change centers on the nature and source of supply rather than on simple matters of weight and percentages. If figured as a percentage of total supply, fuel actually amounted to less weight per man per day for a motorized army than did fodder for a horse drawn force.[3] The great difference between fodder and fuel was not in their relative importance in the profile of supplies but in the fact that petroleum-based fuels were industrial products which had to be manufactured in refineries remote from the field of battle, stockpiled, and then shipped to the front. Fodder could be gathered in the field.

Navies became dependent on industrial fuels long before armies did. Navies that had freed themselves of the vagaries of the wind bound themselves to logistic support from coaling stations around the globe. These were laboriously stocked with coal shipped from Europe or America. Gone were the days when cruises were limited only by the ship's capacity to store food and fresh water. As twentieth-century oil-fired power plants replaced nineteenth-century coal-fired boilers, this facilitated refueling at sea and, therefore, somewhat lessened the dependence on pre-established bases. Still, the fuel had to come up from the rear.

The Harnessing of Technology: Research and Production

With the coming of the Industrial Revolution, rapid improvements in technology have continually altered armed struggle, both on the battlefield and behind the lines. The pace of change in the weapons of war has forced those who supply fighting forces to deal with a different sort of conflict, that between the long run benefits of research and development, on the one hand, and the short term need for production and distribution, on the other. War intensifies this conflict, since lives are on the line. It is no surprise to read of a clash between these two alternatives in World War II or during the decades of the Cold War, but in fact they go back at least to the middle of the nineteenth century.

Robert V. Bruce explores this struggle during the American Civil War. Then, political and military leaders tried to mobilize science in the service of Mars but soon had to balance the potential to improve the tools of war against the need to supply those tools in adequate numbers. Should production pause while better weapons were developed and factories retooled to manufacture them, or should tried and true but potentially obsolete weapons already under production be made in greater numbers to ensure their speedy arrival with the troops? At the center of this controversy stood the chief of the U.S. Army Ordnance Department, James Ripley, who did what he could to sidetrack the adoption of new breech-loading and repeating rifles and to safeguard the production of the muzzle-loading Springfield, which he deemed a proven item. In this and in other matters of advanced technology, the assumption that the war would soon be over torpedoed research and development.

While Bruce explores the failed attempt at research and development during the American Civil War, Jon Tetsuro Sumida examines the reverse of the coin, the need to produce existing weapons and ammunition in adequate quantities in the context of twentieth-century warfare. Sumida lays out the factors, the processes, and the decisions that determined war production to satisfy the Royal Navy's appetite in World War I. Pre-war production, largely cornered by the Royal Navy, had to supply the growing needs of the army, particularly for ammunition, once the first shots were fired. However, by virtue of its prewar connections with British heavy industry, the navy could maintain its own supply to the detriment of the army. One of the great accomplishments of the British in World War I was not only to work out a compromise which ensured a logistic base for both army and navy but to institutionalize this compromise in such a manner that it intelligently guided war production and supply in the future. Sumida reminds us that in the modern age, logistics is founded on industrial production.

Daniel R. Beaver also studies the problems of procurement and logistics in the twentieth century, but he changes the focus from war at sea to war on land. He examines the difficulties, debates, and decisions involved in supplying the U.S. Army in World War II with that most essential of modern logistic tools, the truck. World War I experience convinced army planners that they needed standardized, high-quality trucks in large quantities to support a modern force on land. Postwar lack of urgency frustrated their plans, but in the process of studying the challenge, they made key decisions. With the coming of war in Europe, the apparatus swung into high gear, and U.S. industry produced the finest transport equipment employed by any army, most notably the immortal "deuce and a half," the $2^1/2$-ton truck. Tanks and artillery may have caught the public eye, but without the wheeled transport developed and purchased by the army, its European campaigns would have stalled, for supply could not have kept up with the troops.

Creating a Logistic Base for Modern War

The supply of modern armed forces requires not just the production of materiel and the availability of adequate transport. A logistic organization must be structured and plans drafted. In addition, the concentration of massive and technologically advanced armies and navies in new locales demands the construction of entire infrastructures: barracks, warehouses, port facilities, road networks, and airfields. This explains the fact that construction materials became a major item in modern military supply.

For each major twentieth-century war the U.S. fashioned a logistic system tailored to the particular threat; no previous response could simply be dusted off and put back in place. World War I, World War II, and the Korean War all presented unprecedented situations. The decision to increase the U.S. commitment in Vietnam, 1964-65, demanded similar creation and improvisation.

Joel D. Meyerson discusses the difficult task of creating and staffing a supply organization and the problems of trying to construct the physical logistic base in Vietnam before the influx of American ground troops. Americans were well aware of the limitations of Vietnamese docks, airfields, and highways, and of how these could inhibit a rapid deployment of men and supplies. To overcome these problems the Americans would have to build a new infrastructure using civilian contractors and military engineer units. Myerson describes the work of Frank Omanski, who had urged massive construction in Vietnam as early as 1962. Omanski now struggled to create an army logistic command, a military unit comparable to a combat division as an organization with a specifically defined mission. Such commands dated back to 1949. By February 1965 Osmanski's modified plan for a logistic command had been approved with the addition of more engineer units, and the task was now to put the plan into operation. Actual logistic units deployed in the spring of 1965.

Conclusion

The logistic feats of military and naval forces in the Industrial Age are so impressive as to be shocking. In terms of amounts shipped, they reached their peak in the U.S. effort in World War II. In terms of the rapidity of shipment, the U.S. buildup in Vietnam surpassed any previous accomplishment, and the multi-national deployment to the Persian Gulf in 1991 was even more dramatic. These great demonstrations of production, shipment, and distribution came at the price of wedding military success to the uninterrupted flow of industrial bounty. Armies and navies became more powerful, but also more vulnerable, since they could not afford any break in their essential lifelines of supply. Logistics moved ever more to the center of strategy. Perhaps one of the flaws of the U.S. effort in Vietnam is that logistics had become so central, and success in this aspect of war was so great, that it blinded leaders to the fact that victory could not be guaranteed simply by a logistic triumph. Mars must be fed and armed, but he must also fight.

Notes

1. Martin van Creveld, *Supplying War* (Cambridge: 1977), p. 144.
2. John A. Lynn, "The Pattern of Army Growth, 1445-1945," in John A. Lynn, ed. *Tools of War* (Urbana, IL: 1990), pp. 4-6.
3. The highly mechanized U.S. army in Europe in World War II may have required as much as 11.4 pounds of petroleum fuel per man per day, but the armies of Louis XIV needed 33.3 pounds of horse fuel per man per day. The figures for fuel supply to U.S. Army forces in Europe come from Appendix A-5, "Maintenance Requirements, European and Pacific Areas, World War II," in Robert W. Coakley and Richard M. Leighton, *Global Logistics and Strategy, 1943-1945*, vol. 2 (Washington, DC: 1968), p. 825.

Fuel and lubricants for the ground forces added up to 11.4 pounds per man per day, with another 13.4 pounds for army air force needs. The figure for the French under Louis XIV is based on an army of 60,000 containing 40,000 horses which each consume 50 pounds of green fodder per day. Thus (40,000 x 50) ÷ 60,000 = 33.3.

9
The Misfire of Civil War R&D
Robert V. Bruce

I

Three months after the end of World War II, the MIT alumni journal *Technology Review* published "Science and the Civil War" by I. Bernard Cohen. The article concluded with a flourish: "At the close of the third great war in which our scientists have given conspicuous service to the nation, we may look with equal pride on the splendid activities of our present scientific effort and the first large-scale, coordinated scientific war effort, that of the Civil War." This essay is decidedly at odds with that view. Professor Cohen himself, since risen to eminence as a historian of science, would probably not now defend so extravagant a claim. Indeed, the body of his article itself offers little support for it. Still, he might plead as excuses his youthful exuberance and the fact that his audience doubtless expected to hear some such peroration. And there are certain intellectual extenuations as well.[1]

For one, Cohen's article appeared in the immediate afterglow of two spectacular triumphs of military research and development (R&D): long-range rocketry and the atomic bomb. Those two developments dictated the course and nature of what would come to be called the Cold War, a confrontation that would have been utterly different without them, if it world have arisen at all. The Cold War was already looming when Cohen wrote, and for nearly half a century it would dominate the world. Unlike the hot wars of the past, it defined success in terms of potential rather than actual devastation. Weapons were destroyed not by the enemy but by obsolescence, the basic strategy. And so the greatest urgency was in R&D rather than supply, especially since the "war's" long duration was assumed from the start. The conflict was in fact not a "war" in the literal sense but a great technological chess game. Nevertheless the label of "Cold War" may have tended, at least subconsciously, to engraft the assumption of R&D prominence onto historical perceptions of earlier real wars, including the Civil War.

Cohen's assumption, moreover, at first glance seems consistent with the standard view of the Civil War, which has been called the first great modern war largely on the strength of its technological innovations. Railroads; telegraphy; breech-loading and repeating rifles; machine guns; rifled, breech-loading, and steel cannon; land and sea mines; wire entanglements; and ironclad warships were all used effectively for the first time in a major conflict. But none of them were products of a "large-scale, co-ordinated scientific war effort." They were innovations, to be sure, but all of them had been developed *before* the war.

The focus of this essay is not on the mere adoption of existing technology, however novel, but on wartime research and development, on why some called for such a program during the Civil War, why their hopes were largely unrealized, and what difference, if any, that miscarriage may have made.

II

In jumping to his conclusion, it should also be said, Cohen was by no means guilty of anachronism. What he envisioned could well have come to pass in that time and place. There was both precedent and pressure for it. Technology had been transforming warfare since the first rock was heaved in anger. Archimedes' triumphs of R&D in the very thick of battle have been famed for millennia. By the end of the eighteenth century. governments were actively enlisting scientific and technological R&D in the service of war. In revolutionary France, for example, the government offered a prize in 1795 for a method of preserving army rations, thus inspiring Nicolas Appert to develop the technique of canning.[2]

In the United States the recruiting of science and technology for war began at the end of the eighteenth century. Friction with France culminating in the so-called "Quasi-War" of 1797-1801 led Congress to establish national arsenals, and weapons production begat weapons development. Soon after, in 1802, Congress created the United States Military Academy at West Point, which likewise drew the federal government into the support of technology. West Point became what amounted to the nation's first college of engineering, civil as well as military. As a precedent, a model, and a source of faculty, it hastened the rise of higher education in civilian technology during the years before the Civil War. Meanwhile the national armories and army contract specifications generated and spread the principles of the American system of manufactures—mass production of standardized, interchangeable parts by specialized machine tools. And during the 1850s the War Department pleaded for a national foundry that could, among other things, "serve as a great laboratory."[3]

Congress declined that invitation. But whereas small arms development could still get by on the strength of mechanical ingenuity, heavier weapons by the 1840s more and more required a quantitative, experimental approach in metallurgy, ballistics, design, and propellants. West Pointers in the Army Ordnance Corps were ready for that approach in the forties and fifties. Major Alfred Mordecai, as much a scientist as a military man, took the lead among them. In the forties he made the earliest precise measurements by Americans of projectile velocities and the first large-scale, controlled American gunpowder experiments. In 1839 he and his West Point comrade Benjamin Huger became the guiding spirits of a newly established ordnance board, which institutionalized the testing and evaluation of small arms, as well as systematizing and setting standards for military weapons generally. In the fifties Captain Thomas J. Rodman began using calculus in the study of gun endurance. He devised a pressure gauge that became standard for interior ballistics. He extended the range of artillery significantly with his concept of cooling gun castings from within to leave inner layers under compression and with his perforated-cake powder, which increased in surface area as it burned, thus increasing acceleration through the length of the barrel. In 1847 Commander John A. Dahlgren took over the Washington Navy Yard and turned it from shipbuilding to ordnance research and development, with elaborate experiments. He himself designed a cannon that became the navy's principal weapon until well after the Civil War.[4]

The army and navy experimentalists acted in the spirit of the age. The fifties opened with a chorus of articles and sermons celebrating the half-century's progress in science and technology, and in 1851 what Lewis Mumford has called the machine age's "cock-crow of triumph," the Crystal Palace Exhibition in London, exemplified and dramatized the power of technological research and development. Dedicated to international peace, the exhibition purposely limited military items. Nevertheless the public was now thoroughly impressed with the relatively new idea of R&D as a consciously generalized system, the "invention of invention" as it has been called. And it was as obvious to the public as to the specialists that the system was applicable to war materiel per se as well as to the increasingly vital industrial and agricultural underpinnings of war.[5]

Some were more alarmed than exhilarated by the power of technology. Fears that mankind's knowledge might outrun its wisdom went back to the stories of Eve's apple, Pandora's box, and the tower of Babel. In modern literature they surfaced in *Faust, Frankenstein*, and other tales widely read in the antebellum years. The social and economic costs of industrialization were beginning to be felt. And suffering, destruction, and death were the deliberate and primary objects of military technology, not just unfortunate by-products.[6]

In earlier ages that fact had given pause to seekers after knowledge. According to Plutarch, Archimedes had scorned to record his fabled achievements in military technology, and at the beginning of the seventeenth century Sir Walter Raleigh wrote approvingly that to "teach the art of murdering men...was beside [Archimedes'] purpose." Raleigh's contemporary, the scientist and inventor John Napier, likewise reportedly withheld the details of his weapons experiments on the grounds that "for the ruin and overthrow of man, there were too many devices already framed." In the nineteenth century a few still entertained that scruple. It was implied in a reference by the president of Brown University in 1835 to "science and the arts [i.e. technology] furnishing means of destruction before unknown and capable of gratifying to the full the widest love of slaughter." Midway through the Civil War young Henry Adams wrote prophetically, "Man has mounted science, and is now run away with....Some day science may have the existence of mankind in its power, and the human race commit suicide by blowing up the world." But by then such dissidents were voices crying in the jungle.[7]

Technology's dazzling achievements had won it absolution by the vast majority. Even in the field of weaponry, comforting rationalizations were possible, such as Benjamin Franklin's hope of 1784 that invasion by the newfangled balloons would make a future war unthinkable—a line of argument regularly advanced between wars ever since. There was also the proposition that some wars are just and necessary, and improved weaponry therefore all to the good. So said a nineteenth-century English scientist who credited science with saving Christendom from the infidels by coming up with Greek fire. When in the twentieth century some success was at last achieved in limiting certain types of weapons, it was not from compassion or morality but from fear of retaliation. Even then the restraints were not so much on R&D as on the deployment and use of the products.[8]

So philosophical and humanitarian misgivings, popular or governmental, offered little resistance to military R&D programs even in time of peace, let alone in time of war when considerations of national security overrode all others.

In antebellum America, however, there were practical impediments. The outbreak of war with Mexico in the spring of 1846 led Benjamin Huger to offer an improved fuse for artillery shells and "a project for a rocket troop." "If you will promise a reasonably long war," he wrote Mordecai, "I will get some of my notions into use." Fortunately for all concerned except R&D, serious fighting ended in a year and a half. And meanwhile Mordecai was too busy with production and distribution of arms to spend any time on experiments. A dispute with Great Britain over claims to Oregon ended at about the same time. A confrontation between slave and free states began immediately over the status of slavery in the vast territory newly acquired from Mexico, and apprehensions of war between the states, which had arisen occasionally since the Revolution, were now stronger and more frequent. But most of the public and politicians could not bring themselves to believe in the threat. The War Department, headed by southerners anyway, made no military preparations for it. Nor would such preparations have been politically possible or (given secessionist seizures of federal arms) militarily significant. No other armed conflicts were in prospect. So Congress opted for military economy and efficiency at the expense of modernizing arms.[9]

The Army Ordnance Bureau accepted those constraints philosophically, even cheerfully. The individual efforts of Mordecai, Huger, Rodman, and Dahlgren seemed good enough R&D for that peaceful time. Private parties and foreign governments in any case kept bringing out new weapons faster that the bureau could keep up with them, though in April 1855 Secretary of War Jefferson Davis sent Mordecai and two other officers (one of them George McClellan) on a year-long study of European military technology. This led to the adoption of the versatile French fieldpiece known as the Napoleon gun. Making a virtue of necessity, the Chief of Ordnance in 1845 gave priority to standardization. In this, he wrote, the bureau "followed in the steps of the great powers of Europe, deciding that a diversity of arms was productive of evil, and adopting those of ordinary construction which are the simplest managed by the common soldier." This declaration, often reaffirmed, became an article of faith in the department and the bureau through the Civil War. It contributed neatly to both fiscal economy and logistical efficiency.[10]

As Huger had implied in 1846, however, fiscal economy counted for nothing in the exigency of war. Even logistical efficiency might have to yield something to demands for quicker action and greater firepower. Public enthusiasm for technology and pride in Yankee ingenuity gave added force to such demands. "Take our word for it," declared the *Philadelphia Enquirer* soon after the Civil War began, "these geniuses will yet produce some patent Secession-Excavator, some Traitor-Annihilator, some Rebel-Thrasher, some Confederate States Milling Machine, which will grind through, shell out, or slice up this war." That overblown whimsicality may be laid to technological naiveté, but no less distinguished an expert than John Ericsson echoed it seriously in an 1862 appeal to President Lincoln:

> The time has come, Mr. President, when our cause will have to be sustained, not by numbers, but by superior weapons. By a proper application of mechanical devises alone will you be able with absolute certainty to destroy the enemies of the Union. Such is the inferiority of the Southern States in a mechanical point of view, that...if you apply our mechanical resources to the fullest extent, you can destroy the enemy without enlisting another man.[11]

Scientists also held out high hopes. Their spokesman Joseph Henry, head of the Smithsonian Institution and the nation's leading scientist, made their case in his 1863 report. "The art of destroying life, as well as that of preserving it," he wrote, "calls for the application of scientific principles, and the institution of scientific experiments on a scale of magnitude which would never be attempted in time of peace." As possible fields of research he suggested "the strength of materials, the laws of projectiles, the resistance of fluids, the applications of electricity, light, heat, and chemical action, as well as of aerostation [ballooning]." Henry himself had set an example in 1843 by introducing the electrical method of determining projectile velocity. An able chemist, Charles Wetherill, speculated in 1861 that by taking up "the chemistry of warfare I might possibly be of some little use to our country in its present trial."[12]

Granting the sincerity of scientists' patriotism, there were often additional motives behind their appeals. Ericsson wanted the challenge, celebrity, and profit of a major project. "The patentees of articles used in camps and by the army are reaping a rich harvest," claimed their chief organ, the *Scientific American* (which did a thriving business handling patent claims). It spoke not from fact but from wishful and, as it turned out, erroneous assumption. One chemist wrote another in the spring of 1861, "Can't you make use of some of your abundant technical knowledge now for Government & so get some of the flood of money which this war pours out?" Even Joseph Henry, no money-grubber, sought to advance the standing of American science generally.[13]

Such was the call. Such were the hopes. How were they answered, by the North, by the South, by the military and naval establishments, by the civilian authorities, by private initiative, by agriculture, by industry?

III

To understand the Civil War policies and workings of the Army Ordnance Department (as it was now called), we must first consider its chief, Brigadier General James W. Ripley. When he became chief in April 1861, Ripley at sixty-six could look back on forty-seven years of army service. He had distinguished himself in readying Fort Moultrie at Charleston during the nullification crisis in 1832, but he probably took most satisfaction in his record as commander of the Springfield (Mass.) Armory from 1841 to 1854. In the teeth of dogged and often turbulent resistance he had imposed military discipline and order on the work force. From the establishment thus whipped into shape (as Ripley might have put it) came the 1855 Springfield rifle musket. Rifles were to be the basic arms of the Civil War, revolutionizing infantry tactics and the balance between offense and defense. Ripley considered the 1855 and 1861 Springfields the best guns ever put in the hands of infantry, and until breechloaders came along his assessment was on the mark. As his Springfield experience demonstrated, he was a stickler for order, system, and the letter of the rulebook. Age had further stiffened his inflexibility.[14]

The situation that confronted Ripley when he assumed his new post would have daunted a far more resourceful, adaptable, and adroit man. Through no fault of his, he had to make do with a grossly overburdened department that was also grossly understaffed. At the end of 1860 it had fifty-nine officers and about 450 enlisted men. War promised the officers neither glory nor promotion, though line officers rose like rockets. Responsibilities grew out of all proportion to rank. Though the government's only small arms manufactory became the world's largest, its brilliant commander remained a captain. So a number of able and ambitious officers, such as Oliver O. Howard and Jesse Reno, wangled field commands, while some others of southern proclivities joined the rebels. Ripley began with only forty-one officers, and his frantic and repeated pleas could not move either the War Department or Congress to authorize an increase to more than forty-five until late in 1863, when the number was increased to sixty-four. Of the authorized strength, thirteen had been attached to field commands under pressure from the generals, leaving only thirty-two under Ripley's direct command during the crucial years of 1862 and 1863. Meanwhile the enlisted complement had risen to only 600. Though expanded more generously, the civilian clerical staff remained inadequate. Paperwork fell far behind, taking on the character more of history than reportage. Ripley was a year late in filing his monthly return for April 1861.[15]

Confusion was compounded by other circumstances beyond Ripley's control. Field duties often fell to untrained, slipshod line officers not directly accountable to the Ordnance Department. Information about supplies on hand or needed in the field was therefore often inadequate, inexact, or downright inscrutable. Not until the spring of 1864 was the department given more authority over such feckless deputies, whereupon matters were much improved. Ripley's control of procurement and distribution was nibbled away by an assortment of meddlers. The Secretary of War often ordered the issue of arms without asking what was available. Ordnance funds were often appropriated by field commanders to buy arms as they saw fit. Armories and arsenals were virtually autonomous. So in planning operations, Ripley's harried department was never sure what arms or funds would be available. For lack of personnel, inspection of arms was likely to be hasty, sketchy, and random. Yet somehow, at least after the first few chaotic months, the Union army was amply supplied with arms of good quality.[16]

The desperation of those first months, however, hardened and seemed to vindicate Ripley's long standing abhorrence of such time-consuming frills as R&D. Initially, as Lincoln recalled in his second inaugural address, "neither party expected for the war, the magnitude, or the duration, which it has already attained." In June 1861 Ripley assumed that the war would call for 250,000 men, and a month later Secretary of War Simon Cameron wrote, "We have already an army composed of more than 300,000 men, a number greater than we need for the actual crisis." There were only 35,000 converted rifle muskets and new Springfield rifles on hand, but enough smoothbores and old .69 caliber rifles to make up the deficiency, at least until the Springfield Armory could expand its production—or so it was thought. But the older stock was scattered from Maine to California. Congestion and interruption of the railroads made concentration and distribution difficult. After First Bull Run in July complacency changed to dismay and presently to panic. By early September the Ordnance Department was seeking arms "by any means, in any way."[17]

Ways and means were limited at the outset. The destruction of the federal armory at Harper's Ferry, Virginia, in April left the Springfield Armory as the only government small-arms manufactory, and its capacity was only 1200 a month. Private establishments were small, unstandardized, and unprepared for rapid expansion. Moreover they were short of skilled labor, machine tools, and the special imported iron needed for gun barrels. At the start of the war Ripley had urged Secretary Cameron to buy a hundred thousand arms in Europe, but Cameron, a loyal son of industrial Pennsylvania, had vetoed the idea as unnecessary. After three months had slipped by, while Confederate agents had been busily buying up European arms, Cameron changed his tune. Bypassing the Ordnance Department, state governors and the War Department started buying frantically, indiscriminately, and in competition with one another. After much waste and chicanery, panic subsided in January 1862, and by the time serious fighting began in April sizable shipments of good arms were arriving. About three-quarters of a million were purchased by the end of June, and they armed more than half the troops engaged in the major battles of that year.[18]

In May 1861 Ripley set an ambitious goal of 100,000 rifles a year for his pride, the Springfield Armory. Thanks to the energy, efficiency, and managerial skill of its new commander, Captain Alexander B. Dyer, it raised production to 10,000 in the month of January 1862 and to 20,000 a month by October. By the end of the war it had turned out 800,000 rifles.[19]

Ripley's faith in the Springfield Armory, however, along with his expectation of a short, limited war and his commitment to standardization, contributed to his slowness in pressing private manufacturers to expand. When First Bull Run finally jolted him into offering large contracts, he made a significant long-term contribution to American industrial development by insisting on interchangeability of parts, but perhaps at the expense of short-term speed. He was enraged, moreover, by frequent failures to deliver on time, or at all in some cases, and by the multiplicity of makes, calibers, and types of ammunition complicating distribution to the troops. Domestic manufacturers had produced only about 30,000 arms by June 1862. But they were making large deliveries by the end of the year. By then the supply of arms for the first time ran ahead of demand. Most production problems were solved in both public and private arms establishments during 1863, and by the time of Gettysburg foreign arms were being rapidly traded in for American makes. All told, American private arms companies produced more than a million rifles and carbines during the war.[20]

Given the limited number of Ordnance Department officers and the burdens placed on those few, they can scarcely be blamed for having abandoned even such sporadic R&D efforts as had been made before the war. Major Mordecai, torn between his southern origins and his army loyalty, resigned and sat out the war as a civilian. Major Rodman had his hands full in commanding an arsenal.

A congressional committee asked him in 1864 if he and his brother officers had worked at improving weapons since the war began. "No," he answered, "not to any great or practical extent. Their duties have been so much increased." Ripley cannot be held responsible for the shortage of officers, against which he remonstrated strenuously. But even if Congress or the War Department had authorized more, there is reason to doubt that Ripley would have encouraged or even tolerated development of new or improved weapons.[21]

On June 11, 1861, when complacency still reigned, Ripley drew up a memorandum setting forth views that he implemented doggedly and resourcefully through his tenure as Chief of Ordnance to September 1863. "A great evil now specially prevalent in regard to arms for the military service," he wrote, "is the vast variety of the new inventions." Backers of these, he complained, had "already introduced into the service many kinds and calibers of arms,...producing confusion in the manufacture, the issue, and the use of ammunition... This evil can only be stopped by positively refusing to answer any requisitions for or propositions to sell new and untried arms and steadily adhering to the rule of uniformity of arms for all troops of the same kind, such as cavalry, artillery, infantry."

Thus far Ripley's manifesto echoed the standardization policy laid down in 1845, but it added a further consideration raised by the war: "All who seek these contracts want orders for large quantities of arms, which I consider it certain they will not be able to deliver under many years' time, not probably until the present demand for them is over. The Government, however, will be bound to take and pay for all these arms."[22]

The desperation of the early months forced Ripley to deal with a hodgepodge of arms acquired by states, generals, and individual units on their own. The consequent experience of battle fully justified Ripley's concern for standardization. At Malvern Hill one regiment had to leave the fight because no more Sharps cartridges were available. At Second Bull Run eleven kinds and calibers of small-arms ammunition were requisitioned. A requisition for field artillery ammunition was apt to be an exercise in permutations and combinations. Fieldpieces might be rifled or smoothbore, of eight or ten different designs using nine common calibers, firing solid shot, grape shot, canister, case, and seven principal types of shells. By 1863 more than six hundred varieties of ammunition might be called for. But once weapons were in good supply, the introduction of a new one might have been balanced by the withdrawal of one or more old ones, if that meant a significant gain in battle effectiveness. That Ripley's resistance to change went deeper was evidenced by the battle over breech-loading rifles.[23]

The most telling fact about that prolonged tug of war was that research and development were not at issue. The advantages of breech-loading rifles over muzzleloaders being both manifold and manifest, private R&D had long been under way. The breech-loading rifle was used to good effect at Brandywine in

1777. John Hall's improved breechloader was put into federal production and used by various army units for a score of years to the high satisfaction of the enlisted men until production was halted by the stubborn prejudice of officers and bureaucrats, explainable only by a reflexive hostility to change, if we rule out a humane impulse to minimize enemy casualties. Single shot breechloaders could be fired three or four times as fast as muzzleloaders, with greater range and accuracy and without the user needing to rise up from the prone position, thus much reducing the risk of shattered head or arms. A muzzleloader could be disabled for the remainder of a battle if the user, in the stress of combat, happened to insert the bullet before the powder or leave the ramrod in and shoot it off or let the barrel get too fouled or load the cartridge without breaking open the paper. A breechloader was immune to all such mishaps.[24]

As manufacturing techniques improved in the forties and fifties, the Sharps and other prewar models answered earlier, somewhat exaggerated complaints about the escape of gas from the beech. Ripley's antebellum predecessor reversed his opposition and in 1859 urged replacement of muzzleloaders with breechloaders. Ease of loading was especially urgent for cavalry, and breech-loading carbines began to be ordered for that arm. But peacetime lacked urgency, and for infantry the excellent new Springfield muzzleloader seemed entirely adequate.[25]

That last consideration strongly appealed to Ripley's pride in the Springfield. One of Ripley's assistants reinforced the appeal in writing from the Springfield Armory in August 1861: "The gun we are now making is an excellent one...do not, I beg, permit the least variation, it may make a difference of 1000 guns per month." In his holy war against "the least variation" Ripley fired off other arguments. Breechloaders cost too much. They complicated ammunition supply (though at least one proposed breechloader, the Marsh gun, used the same paper cartridges as the Springfield). They were fragile (though both testing and combat experience proved otherwise). They led to careless aiming (though, as soldiers pointed out, less frantic haste in loading meant less desperate haste in aiming). They encouraged waste of ammunition (though battle reports showed otherwise). As the last objection implied, Ripley, and indeed most commanders, underestimated the effectiveness of increased firepower. A logical extension of Ripley's view would have eliminated ammunition and left the rifle as a bayonet shaft.[26]

The validity of Ripley's arguments counted for much less than his mastery of bureaucratic obstructionism. At the start he simply refused to order breechloaders, even carbines. Though sheer exigency later forced him to act, his initial foot-dragging discouraged private manufacturers from tooling up and cost the Union months of breechloader production, a deficit that has been estimated at a hundred thousand arms. The cavalry claimed most of what was produced. Early in 1862 Ripley's projection of needs included no breech-loading rifles at all, despite pleas from the field. Besides giving priority to carbines Ripley fended off breech-loading rifles by refusing to make contracts unless flatly ordered to, setting difficult conditions of delivery and canceling contracts when not met to the letter, refusing or deliberately delaying field requisitions, and derogating favorable reports. As for the carbine crunch, the Chief of Navy Ordnance believed in May 1861 that European firms could be found to produce breechloaders of proven design. At any rate, once Ripley had been forced to give ground, American makers expanded rapidly, turning out nearly half a million breechloaders before the war ended, though most were carbines. In the later opinion of the able Confederate general E. P. Alexander, who had encountered Yankee breech-loading rifles in battle, if his opponents had been thus armed at the start the war would have ended within a year. It was not until October 1864, a year after General Ripley was finally replaced, that the War Department decided to make breech-loading rifles standard, and it was not until after the war that the resolve was carried through.[27]

IV

The Navy Ordnance Bureau also had its problems at first. Commander John Dahlgren, who as commander of the Washington Navy Yard had charge of the only federal cannon foundry, recalled a year later that the shortage of heavy ordnance "had nearly been productive of disaster." The navy's stock was still insufficient, he claimed. But pressure on the navy's bureau did not approach that on the army's, and though Dahlgren did not become chief of the bureau until July 1862, his R&D background helped make it more receptive to technological improvements from the beginning of the war. Dahlgren himself considered and tested the offerings of inventors far more willingly and open-mindedly than did Ripley.[28]

The French and British having built armored warships in the mid-fifties, Secretary of the Navy Gideon Welles in July 1861 rather diffidently asked Congress for an appropriation to that end. Congress came through; and in spite of bureaucratic dawdling, John Ericsson's ironclad *Monitor* in the nick of time rescued the federal fleet from destruction by a Confederate ironclad. Secretary Welles thereupon asked Congress for $100,000 to be used in experiments and in trials of proposed inventions. Though he did not get the money, at least he made the gesture. But as Welles pointed out, the navy's ordnance officers, like the army's, were too busy with supply to undertake serious R&D work. A navy engineer, Benjamin Isherwood, published two massive volumes of *Experimental Researches in Steam Engineering* in 1863 and 1865, a notable contribution to engineering science, but they were sequels to two equally distinguished volumes on the subject he had published just before the war rather than a war-inspired project.[29]

V

As breechloaders and ironclads demonstrated, military R&D did not depend wholly on government. The North teemed with independent inventors in all gradations of sanity. At midcentury the number of patents, mostly mechanical and almost all from the North, had begun to rise in an exponential curve that did not peak until the next century. In those days inventors could get by with little capital or formal training if they had imagination, mechanical ingenuity, and a few tools. R&D went on in tool sheds, barns, and cellars. The number of patents dropped sharply in the first year and a half of the war, perhaps because of the business downturn in those months along with the distraction of military service, but a rebound began by the end of 1862.[30]

Because the navy's ordnance was too massive for individual inventors to experiment with in their backyards, most weapons inventors targeted the army. From the beginning, proposals for new weapons inundated the Army Ordnance Department and were routinely rejected. "Has it been the custom," the chief clerk was asked at a court of inquiry, "to enter into scientific and theoretical discussions with inventors when they presented their inventions...?" "Oh, no!" replied the astonished witness. The *Scientific American* charged General Ripley with "rudeness and circumlocution of the rankest kind." Frustrated inventors consequently appealed to politicians and field commanders. Major General Benjamin F. Butler was the first or an early champion of most new devices used in the war, including balloon reconnaissance, wire entanglements, machine guns, flame throwers, and even a submarine. A still more active intermediary between inventors and the military was President Abraham Lincoln.[31]

Lincoln's aim in seeking better weapons was, of course, to end the war as quickly as possible. He happened also to find the effort congenial. He had a clear, precise, keenly analytical mind. He had been a surveyor and a lawyer in patent cases and had even taken out a patent himself. Hard work with simple tools had made him prize laborsaving devices. Lincoln consequently took a genuine interest in the inventors' letters that poured into his office, and his secretaries were encouraged to be lenient in screening them. They were a welcome change from political and military problems. The inventors themselves had easy access to him, sometimes with their weapons, usually with the stimulus of their ingenuity or the comic relief of their quirks and crotchets. The outdoor trials he often attended were a recreation to him. Some functionaries called them "champagne experiments" in mockery, but in a sense the term was apt.[32]

Lincoln took Ripley's measure early. In weighing proposals he consulted several experts, but most often Captain Dahlgren of the navy and Major George D. Ramsay, commander of the Washington Arsenal. Lincoln did not presume to order the adoption of any new weapon as a standard arm. The formal records show, however, that he often ordered tests, usually over Ripley's objections, and there is evidence that at his request Ramsay and others ran informal tests not recorded in the department's files. On some occasions he took it upon himself to order especially promising arms in quantities sufficient for trial in the field.[33]

Lincoln sponsored or promoted a number of forward-looking novelties such as Thaddeus Lowe's observational balloons, which did useful service in the field until brought down by lack of an organizational niche. Lincoln encouraged Ericsson's *Monitor* and an unsuccessful submarine. He attended a rocket trial that endangered his life when the device exploded in its stand. He ordered and watched trials of breech-loading artillery and made a small purchase of one type, the only federal purchase of breech-loading cannon during the war. Lincoln also made the world's first government purchase of modern machine guns, which he dubbed "coffee mill guns" and which proved effective in combat, though Ripley managed to block further orders. Lincoln promoted incendiary shells, used against Vicksburg and Charleston. Most significant was his key role in promoting and at last peremptorily ordering breech-loading and repeating rifles. In the ensuing struggle Ripley succeeded in blocking or canceling large contracts, but those put through by Lincoln made such arms, especially the Spencer seven-shot repeaters, the most prized and acclaimed infantry arms of the war and hastened their postwar adoption as a standard throughout the world.[34]

The war's closest approach to a modern wartime R&D project, authorized and funded by government but independent of procurement and supply agencies, was set up by Lincoln's direction and on his responsibility. Strained relations with Great Britain threatened the supply of Indian niter, an essential ingredient of gunpowder. When an old Illinois friend, acting as agent for a German chemist, offered a promising formula for chlorate-based powder, Lincoln agreed to finance a secret project to experiment with it, work out a production process, and conduct trials. The chemist of the new Agriculture Department, with three helpers, set to work secretly in a ramshackle building on Timber Creek in New Jersey and by June 1863 had twenty-five hundred pounds ready for testing. The powder proved successful, but the chemist ran into trouble graining it for safe storage and transport. By then the British threat had passed, a two-year supply of niter had been stockpiled, and techniques had been worked out for converting plentiful Chilean sodium nitrate to usable niter. So Lincoln dropped the project.[35]

By September 1863, when Lincoln finally found a willing and competent replacement for Ripley, he himself seems to have thought peace too near for useful development of new weapons. Though Lincoln's efforts had pointed to the future, Ripley's resistance had gone far to nullify them. In any case, the informal and intermittent attention of one man, even Abraham Lincoln, could not have served the purpose of an organized and sustained research and development program. Nor could the Ordnance Department, even without Ripley, so long as its first concern was wartime production and supply.[36]

The logical solution would have been to divorce the conflicting functions: to leave procurement to the ordnance bureaus, and to assign R&D to a separate agency. The idea was put forward by the *Scientific American* as early as May 1861 and at intervals thereafter. Ordnance officers, including Major Rodman, were all for it. Even Ripley professed to think it "very desirable." But, he added, missing the point, he could not spare enough ordnance officers for it.[37]

In the fall of 1862 someone, name unknown, urged Lincoln to set up a council of engineers and naval contractors to advise him on weapons development. As a preliminary, Brigadier General Herman Haupt, chief of military railroads, sent out an elaborate questionnaire to various engineers and contractors. No more is known of the affair. Three leading government scientists, hoping to make a place for science in the war effort, got the Navy Department to appoint them in February 1863 as a "Permanent Commission" to advise it on scientific and technological matters. Unpaid and unfunded, the commission merely evaluated such outside proposals as were referred to it, without significant results. The same trio and two others, having long yearned for an American equivalent of the French Academy of Sciences, also seized the wartime opportunity to wangle a congressional charter for a National Academy of Sciences on the grounds that it could dispense such counsel to the government generally. Being likewise unfunded and also weakened by an uproar over the naming of members, the new academy was ignored by the government, though it became prestigious and influential in the next century. The Permanent Commission and the National Academy had what Lincoln's efforts did not: an official identity, a formally defined mission, and a collective organization. But they lacked what Lincoln had: authority to allocate funds and personnel.[38]

In our day, universities funded by and closely allied with government have come to conduct long-term and large-scale R&D. The Confederacy took a feeble step in that direction in the summer of 1861, when Matthew Maury got the University of Virginia to establish a laboratory for weapons development staffed by faculty but under government authority. But the arrangement was too little productive and too soon forgotten to be called a precedent. The institutions called universities in those years seldom encouraged faculty research and certainly not mission-oriented programs. A few college faculty members made efforts to apply their expertise to weaponry, but they did so as individuals and for personal rather than institutional honor and reward. As for private foundations, only the Smithsonian Institution had the standing to attempt military research. But despite the appeals of its secretary, Joseph Henry, ill-timed investments, wartime inflation, and Henry's long standing repugnance toward government funding deprived it of the necessary resources. Private industry, however, had such resources, and though in-house research was still rare, it was not unknown. How, then, did industry respond to the technological demands and opportunities of wartime?[39]

VI

As with military technology, though to a lesser extent, the war did stimulate some technological innovation in agriculture and industry. In the small-arms industry, existing machine tools were more fully utilized and were diffused among firms that had switched from other lines to making arms, or parts for them. Ripley's insistence on interchangeability similarly diffused higher standards of precision and uniformity. In papermaking, the rising cost of rag paper spurred use of a prewar wood-based patent. War demand and labor shortage turned the shoe industry to the Blake stitcher, also a prewar invention. For similar reasons the clothing industry embraced machine stitching, a prewar development.[40]

Above all in agriculture, so vital to the war effort, the war brought technological innovation at the level of individual farms. Buying a new machine for the coming season did not interrupt output and required a relatively modest investment, since hot competition between makers kept prices down. Crop prices, however, soared with army demand and foreign crop failures. And a high proportion of farm workers enlisted. Though no major invention in the field appeared during the war, existing machines were therefore heavily in demand, some types for the first time in wide use.[41]

But as in the case of military technology, almost all of those innovations, industrial and agricultural, were conceived and developed before the war. And in some ways the war discouraged even innovation. Expecting a short war or at least uncertain of its length, entrepreneurs went for immediate profit as against investment in new machinery for the long term. High prices and cost-plus government contracts conditioned on prompt delivery seemed too good to pass up. And Ripley's policies probably discouraged R&D in the private arms industry.

In Ohio, it has been found, most weapons patents went to men not in the weapons business. Though five inches of solid naval armor plate was known to outdo an equal thickness built up by lamination, Northern rolling mills did not bother to develop or acquire the technology of making thick plates, there being no peacetime market for them. Pressure for production did not require technological solutions, since the depression of 1861-62 reduced demand for civilian goods, and in the subsequent boom government largesse supported many small firms using conventional or outmoded technology.[42]

The Cold War tipped the balance away from production and toward R&D not only because of its expected long duration and its avoidance of physical destruction but also because each side feared the other would excel over it technologically. No such fear spurred the North in the Civil War. As Ericsson had remarked in his 1862 appeal to Lincoln, the "inferiority of the Southern States in a mechanical point of view" offered an opportunity, but not a threat. The Confederacy lagged far behind the Union not only in technological know-how but also in its industrial base. "In this country," wrote one of its ordnance officers, "we have not such facilities as those which enable our enemies to give form to their conceptions and multiply their means of offence." Furthermore, as another wrote, the Confederate Army Ordnance Department had to cope with "constantly increasing pressure for immediate results." Yet that very urgency, together with fresh beginnings and some strokes of luck, made up in part for the Confederacy's deficiencies. At stake for the Union was part of its territory. At stake for the Confederacy was its very existence as a nation. So the Confederates were desperately ready to try new techniques. In building their military and naval bureaucracy from scratch, even those who had come over from bureaucracy left behind or moderated the old rigidities and jealousies. New men of ability could rise more freely. And luck brought the Confederate army and navy ordnance bureaus half a dozen men of extraordinary ability.[43]

One of them, the Virginia-born James H. Burton, had behind him ten years at the Harpers Ferry Armory (six of them as master armorer) and five years in England as chief engineer of the Enfield Armory, where he installed machinery made under his supervision and raised production to 100,000 rifles a year. Enfield rifles would be prized above all other foreign arms by both sides in the Civil War. Burton's modification of the Minié rifle ball, giving it a hollow rather than an iron-filled base, superseded the original design throughout the world. In 1860 Burton played a leading part in getting invaluable drawings of machinery from the Harpers Ferry Armory for the Virginia State Armory. The Confederacy profited further from Burton's ability and expertise by making him Superintendent of Armories.[44]

The chief of the Confederate Army Ordnance Department was Josiah Gorgas, a veteran of twenty years' duty in the U.S. Army Ordnance Corps. Lacking an industrial base for munitions, Gorgas created one. Throughout the war he faced a desperate shortage of skilled workers; many of them headed north at the outset, and still others followed as the war wore on. Even more crippling was the shortage of strategic materials such as iron, copper, lead, and coal. that often kept plants from operating at full capacity. Yet Gorgas and his department somehow managed to crate large arsenals in eight cities and smaller ones in three others, reluctantly scattering them for strategic reasons. A gigantic powder mill complex soon stretched for two miles at Augusta, Georgia. A lead-smelting works, a foundry for heavy guns, one for shot and shell, bronze foundries, a large shop for leather work, factories for carbines, rifles, and pistols, and other establishments were in production before the war ended. "I have succeeded beyond my utmost expectations," Gorgas wrote with good warrant in April 1864.[45]

While keeping firm overall control of this far-flung industrial empire, Gorgas delegated much on-the-spot responsibility to officers in charge of the various establishments. It was Gorgas who had found men fit for those jobs, and he continued to find and allocate the money, labor, materials, and transportation they needed. He obviously had the ability to organize and manage a significant R&D effort. He had subordinates with ample talent and experience for the work. Having always been interested in new weapons, he might have been expected to have the will. But Gorgas failed to organize such a program. Since he did not explain the omission, we can only surmise the reasons. One was probably the aforementioned "constantly increasing pressure for immediate results." Another was probably the general assumption on both sides throughout the four years of war that its end was at hand. So research and development were carried on ad hoc on the independent initiative of certain subordinates.[46]

One such was the North Carolinian George W. Rains, who had led his West Point class in scientific studies. As a colonel in the CSA Ordnance Department, Rains took charge of gunpowder production, set up the Nitre and Mining Bureau, developed one of the major arsenals, and, most notably, planned, constructed, and ran the great powder complex at Augusta. While keeping the Confederate armies well supplied with powder despite their heavy and sometimes profligate use of it, Rains occasionally found time for experiment. He designed new machines for powdering sulfur, purifying saltpeter, mixing powder, and combining drying, dusting, and glazing into one operation. He developed a fireproofing process that permitted the use of cotton cloth instead of woolen for artillery cartridges. He measured pressures and velocities in powder experiments and discovered independently what the French had already learned, that an air space behind the artillery cartridge reduced the danger of bursting the gun, thus permitting heavier charges and longer ranges. Those sporadic and harried yet fruitful researches suggest what Rains might have achieved in a sustained and intense program.[47]

The Irish-born Lieutenant John W. Mallet, having earned a Ph.D. in chemistry under the celebrated Friedrich Wöhler at Göttingen and having married an Alabama girl, joined the Confederate army in 1861. In the following spring Gorgas assigned him to create a "Central Ordnance Laboratory" and to supervise the production of ammunition and certain needed chemicals. For the proposed laboratory Mallet built a large complex outside Macon, Georgia, but the labor shortage and his other duties kept him from completing it. He had little time to do more than improvise a modest research laboratory at Macon. He designed a shell with a polygonal cavity to make its fragments more uniform and an improved guncotton time fuse, but little more of note. He made little use of his scientific training. A percussion fuse considered "one of the best pieces of ordnance equipment developed during the war" was the work of his assistant, who was not a scientist at all.[48]

The Confederate government undertook no formal *scientific* research programs other than the aforementioned brief and unproductive University of Virginia arrangement. In the years before the war the South had lagged far behind the North in science, and what little it produced was predominantly descriptive natural history, which had little to offer the military. The Confederacy enlisted a dozen or so professional scientists in its Nitre and Mining Bureau. The chemists looked for and worked deposits of niter for gunpowder, mostly in caves and on farms, and produced some in artificial beds. A few geologists in the bureau searched out sources of iron, copper, lead, and coal. But none of this required original research. Others untrained in science did the same work for the bureau just as well.[49]

Far more readily than the U.S. Army Ordnance Department, that of the Confederacy considered outside ideas from both soldiers and civilians, whether scientists or not. Mallet adopted an army captain's patent fuse igniter that proved highly successful. Captain D. R. Williams invented a small breech-loading cannon (not a true machine gun as some have claimed) of which a score were marginally useful in service. The Confederate army successfully used several types of shell designed by an Alabama physician. But invention was alien to Southern culture. The Confederate Patent Office issued less than three hundred patents during the entire war, as against more than sixteen thousand granted by the Union. Notwithstanding ordnance department receptivity, few individuals came up with useful novelties.[50]

Neither did private arms makers, who were less consequential in the Confederacy than in the Union. On the contrary, the Tredegar works in Richmond, the only important private company making cannon and heavy machinery, stubbornly resisted Rodman's cannon-casting technique, a contrariness that cost the Confederacy dearly. As the war went on and prospects of victory receded, makers of small arms employed their ingenuity mainly in scheming to sell out to the government. So Confederate military innovations tended to be not the sort mass-produced with specialized machinery, such as small arms, but those fashioned individually and conventionally, such as naval guns and ironclads, or crafted with common materials and simple techniques, such as land mines and hot-air balloons. In this the Confederates dodged the dilemma of choosing between production and innovation.[51]

VII

That technical bias may have been one reason why the Confederate navy had more successes than the army in developing effective new weapons. There were other possible factors. Its encounters with the enemy were not so relentlessly forced upon it as the army's, and so it could find more time for contriving and testing weapons. And since a smaller proportion of naval than of army officers deserted the Union in 1861, the Confederate navy had an even lighter burden of custom and habit than the Confederate army.

Of the relatively few naval officers who forsook the Union in 1861, the one best known to the public was Commander Matthew F. Maury, superintendent of the U.S. Naval Observatory. Asked how the rivers of Virginia might be defended, he thought at once of "torpedoes," as mines were then called.

Underwater mines, both contact and electrical, were far from new, but Maury experimented busily with improved models and meanwhile spread the torpedo gospel by correspondence with Confederate commanders along the Mississippi. The mines proved effective against not only the ships but also the morale of the enemy, despite Farragut's famous defiance at Mobile Bay. In September 1862 Maury was sent to buy ships in England, where he remained to set up an experimental torpedo laboratory and also to pump British experts in behalf of the cause.[52]

In October 1862 the Confederate Congress established the Submarine Battery Service of the navy and the Torpedo Bureau of the army, both charged with developing and using mines. This step not only regularized and centralized those operations but also certified them as legitimate in warfare. Such a bureaucratic base was a crucial aid to weapons development. Laboratories of the new units turned out increasingly ingenious mines, used more and more widely. By 1864 their dramatic successes had impressed not only the public, North and South, but also the navies of Europe. These mines took their greatest toll late in the war, in part because Union vessels were pressing into shallower and smoother waters, where mines were most effective. Being a defensive measure, such weapons benefited the Confederates far more than the advancing Union forces. All told, they sank more Union vessels than did all Confederate surface warships. But their ingenuity did not involve the development of new technological principles.[53]

The navy was less hospitable to the device proposed by one of its officers, a semi-submersible craft with a long, torpedo-armed spar on its bow for ramming the enemy. Built at last by a private company and christened *David*, it put the Union's largest ironclad out of action for a year. Though other *"Davids"* were built for the army, they brought down no more Goliaths. Private funds also built the Confederacy's famous submarine, the *Hunley*, which drowned two volunteer crews in trial runs and a third in sinking a single Union corvette. But the most memorable of Confederate naval innovations, the ironclad warship, was a navy project from the outset.[54]

Having acquired only one U.S. naval vessel, an old sidewheeler, at the start, the Confederate navy had no stake in established modes and good reason to try anything that seemed promising. Taking note of the French and British ironclads, navy lieutenant John M. Brooke urged the idea on the secretary of the navy, who asked him to draw up plans. Brooke ran systematic tests on armor plate to determine proper slope and thickness. Raised for the purpose, the sunken U.S. steam frigate *Merrimack* steamed forth in March 1862, rechristened *Virginia*. Though checkmated by Ericsson's *Monitor*, the *Virginia*'s easy dispatch of wooden warships opened the new age of naval armor throughout the world. Yet the Confederacy itself had trouble living up to that change. Several of its ironclads were left unfinished for want of iron. Skilled workers were scarce and grew scarcer. So did the South's few construction facilities as Union forces advanced. Some unfinished ironclads had to be destroyed to avoid capture. Nevertheless, the twenty-two put into service did well, mostly in defending rivers and harbors.[55]

Lieutenant Brooke became the naval counterpart of Gorgas. Though not an ordnance expert at the start, Brooke was schooled in science and skilled in technology. In the summer of 1861 he designed not only the *Virginia* but also a seven-inch rifled muzzleloader for her that, while not fundamentally original, became widely known as the most powerful and accurate Confederate cannon. By the fall of 1861 Brooke had become an unofficial clearinghouse for new ideas in naval ordnance, whereupon the navy secretary formally assigned him to evaluate all proposed improvements in ordnance and hydrography. Brooke recruited agents to gather technical literature in Europe and others to pick up what they could about Northern developments. Besides testing such things as an underwater gun, a magnetic floating mine, and an incendiary liquid to burn out ironclads, Brooke himself devised fuses, projectiles, and gunsights. Even as defeat manifestly drew near he persisted in experiment and innovation. But he did not organize a formal R&D effort. And in 1863, when he became chief of navy ordnance, his energies were largely diverted to production, with emphasis on standardization and quality control. In this he faced the problems that beset Gorgas. Considering those problems, it is not surprising that the Confederacy fell short of mounting a full-scale R&D program. It is more surprising that it went as far in that direction as it did.[56]

VIII

Since the North, as we have seen, might have done more in the way of R&D than it did, the question arises of who, if anyone, was to blame for the misfire. General Ripley, of course, whatever the exculpation of circumstance, worked tirelessly to suppress or frustrate R&D. Lincoln tried to counterbalance him, but perhaps not as assertively as he should have. Ad hoc interventions were no equivalent for an ongoing, wide ranging, well funded, organized program. In Timber Creek, perhaps, was the germ of Oak Ridge, but it failed to sprout. Secretary of War Edwin Stanton, despite having been the leading counsel in a notable patent case, took no interest in military technology, leaving oversight of ordnance to Assistant Secretary Peter H. Watson, acclaimed by some as the foremost patent lawyer in the nation. But Watson's health deteriorated during the war, and he did not presume to push for major policy changes. It is tempting to speculate about what might have happened if instead of Stanton, Lincoln had appointed another wily, hard-driving Democratic lawyer-politician, Benjamin F. Butler, who in fact became the most gadget-minded of all Civil War generals. But we should remember that hindsight needs no glasses. What we now see so clearly, including the unanticipated length of the war, was far from clear at the time, even to Abraham Lincoln.[57]

The further question presents itself of what was lost by the R&D misfire. Ripley's obstruction of breech-loading and repeating rifles was a glaring and costly blunder. But R&D was not a factor, since the Sharps, the Spencer, and other highly effective models were patented before the war began. The pioneering "coffee mill gun" sidetracked by Ripley proved workable in its brief chance at combat, and it could have been improved further in time for significant use. Dr. Richard Gatling's famous follow-up was conceived in 1862 and developed, without government support, in time to serve successfully in Civil War battle. In May 1862 a New York schoolteacher named John W. Doughty wrote Lincoln to urge the use of chlorine gas in shells. Moral qualms aside, such shells would have saved thousands of lives squandered in the months of trench warfare outside Petersburg in 1864 and 1865. But Ripley intercepted and pigeonholed Doughty's letter. Perhaps incremental improvements in other weapons might have been effected in time to be useful.[58]

Notwithstanding Joseph Henry's suggestions in 1863, the natural sciences at that stage were not up to generating timely breakthroughs in weaponry. Still, chemists might have somewhat improved the effectiveness of propellants, rockets, and incendiary shells. And it is suggestive that a British chemist came close to smokeless powder in 1865.[59]

IX

The realization of such potentials came too long after the Civil War to point any morals in retrospect. No lessons were drawn from the Civil War experience. In any case, the absence of a credible military threat from 1865 to the early twentieth century, as in the antebellum period, imposed a severe contraction on the army and its funding. The rule seemed to be: in war, no time; in peace, no rush. The European arms race in the early twentieth century, which might be called Cold War I, and the outbreak of the First World War sounded an alert in American military circles. Even before American entry, the National Research Council and the National Advisory Committee for Aeronautics (eventually evolving into NASA) were established. But this time American participation in the war was indeed too brief for R&D to play a part in the victory.

World War II offered a parallel to the Civil War experience. The initial German victories persuaded the Germans that the war would be short, and their adversaries that it would be long. Only a year after the war, James Phinney Baxter wrote:

> The fixed belief in a short war had serious effects over the whole field of German industrial production. In war research it cost Germany the lead acquired in peacetime. Industry in America had long since learned that to subordinate the research staff to the production department is the shortest road to failure. Germany made this faulty conception the basis of her system.[60]

Though Baxter did not have the Civil War in mind, his comment fits it with striking precision. It was fortunate for humanity that in drawing lessons from the American Civil War, the German military experts had overlooked the misfire of its R&D.

Notes

1. I. Bernard Cohen, "Science and the Civil War," *Technology Review* 48 (January 1946), p. 167ff..
2. David S. Landes, *The Unbound Prometheus* (Cambridge: 1969), p. 135; Melvin Kranzberg and Carroll W. Pursell, Jr., eds., *Technology in Western Civilization*, 2 vols. (New York: 1967), 1:472, 491.
3. Alex Roland, "Science and War," in Sally Gregory Kohlstedt and Margaret W. Rossiter, eds., *Historical Writing on American Science* (Baltimore: 1986), pp. 251-52; Robert V. Bruce, *The Launching of Modern American Science, 1846-1876* (New York: 1987), p. 309.
4. Bruce, *Launching*, pp. 157-58; Robert V. Bruce, *Lincoln and the Tools of War* (Indianapolis: 1956), pp. 5-6.
5. Bruce, *Launching*, pp. 132-33.
6. *Ibid.*, pp. 129-30.
7. John U. Nef, *War and Human Progress* (Cambridge, Mass.: 1950), pp. 121-23; Bruce, *Launching*, p. 131; Bruce, *Lincoln*, pp. 59-60.
8. Bruce, *Launching*, p. 132.
9. B. Huger to A. Mordecai, May 29, 1846, South Carolina Historical Society, Misc. MSS; Stanley L. Falk, "Soldier-Technologist: Major Alfred Mordecai and the Beginnings of Science in the United States Army," (Ph.D. dissertation, Georgetown University, 1959), p. 365; Robert V. Bruce, *The Shadow of a Coming War* (Fortenbaugh Memorial Lecture, Gettysburg College, 1989), pp. 7, 18, 21; Carl L. Davis, *Arming the Union* (Port Washington, N.Y.: 1973), pp. 8-9.
10. Falk, "Mordecai," 490-91; Davis, *Arming*, p. 9.
11. Bruce, *Lincoln*, p. 68.
12. Bruce, *Launching*, pp. 131, 306, 308.
13. Bruce, *Lincoln*, pp. 68-69; Bruce, *Launching*, p. 308.
14. Bruce, *Lincoln*, pp. 25-26.
15. *Ibid.*, 32; Davis, *Arming*, pp. 14-18, 21, 23-24, 26, 71.
16. Davis, *Arming*, pp. 21-22, 31-33.
17. *Official Records of the Union and Confederate Armies in the War of the Rebellion* (cited as "O.R.") 130 vols. (Washington, D.C.: 1880-1901), series 1, 3:245, 260, 322, 361, 525; Davis, *Arming*, p. 63; Donald A. MacDougall, "The Federal Ordnance Bureau, 1861-1865" (Ph.D. dissertation, University of California at Berkeley, 1951), p. 30; Kenneth P. Williams, *Lincoln Finds a General*, 5 vols. (New York: 1949-59), 1:64.
18. Bruce, *Lincoln*, pp. 42-43, 49-50; Davis, *Arming*, p. iii; Daniel M. Roche, "The Acquisition and Use of Foreign Shoulder-Arms in the Union Army, 1861-1865" (Ph.D. dissertation, University of Colorado, 1949), pp. 34, 70, 157; O.R., series 3, 2:855.
19. J. Ripley to G. Dwight, May 1, 1861, transcript in Springfield #670+U58w, Springfield Collection, Springfield (Mass.) City Library; Davis, *Arming*, pp. 70-71, 173; *Scientific American*, Mar. 15, 1862, 6, p. 98; *Boston Transcript*, Nov. 15, 1862.

20. Davis, *Arming*, pp. iii-viii, 47, 73-75, 79, 84; *Washington Star*, Jan. 1, 1863; MacDougall, "Federal Ordnance Bureau, " p. 177.

21. U.S. Congress, Senate, Committee on the Conduct of the War, *Report on Heavy Ordnance*, Senate Report No. 121, 38th Congress, 2d session, Feb. 13, 1865, p. 107.

22. O.R., series 3, 1:264.

23. Bruce, *Lincoln*, pp. 105-6, 124.

24. *Ibid.*, 100-1; Davis, *Arming*, pp. 110-14.

25. Davis, *Arming*, pp. 117-18, 121-22.

26. G. Balch to J. Ripley, Aug. 16, 1861, Record Group 156, OCO-Doc. File, Box 183, Doc. No. 530, National Archives; Bruce, *Lincoln*, pp. 104-6, 284-87; Davis, *Arming*, pp. 123, 129-32.

27. Davis, *Arming*, 79-80, 84, 95, 118, 124-25, 128-29; Bruce, *Lincoln*, pp. 106-8, 116, 252-53, 261-62, 264, 288; Edward P. Alexander, *Military Memoirs of a Confederate* (New York: 1907), p. 53.

28. J. Dahlgren to J. Hale, June 3, 1862, John A. Dahlgren MSS, Library of Congress; Bruce, *Lincoln*, p. 71.

29. Robert U. Johnson and Clarence C. Buel, eds., *Battles and Leaders of the Civil War*, 4 vols. (New York: 1888), 1:616-17; Bruce, *Lincoln*, p. 71; Bruce, *Launching*, p. 157.

30. Bruce, *Lincoln*, pp. 64-67.

31. *Ibid.*, pp. 70-73.

32. *Ibid.*, pp. 11-14, 62, 75-76, 81-82, 89.

33. *Ibid.*, pp. 82-84, 88-90, 93-97.

34. *Ibid.*, passim.

35. Bruce, *Launching*, pp. 311-12.

36. *Ibid.*, p. 307.

37. Bruce, *Lincoln*, pp. 223-24.

38. *Ibid.*, pp. 215-17; Bruce, *Launching*, pp. 301-5, 307-8.

39. Bruce, *Launching*, pp. 300, 308.

40. Felicia J. Deyrup, *Arms Making in the Connecticut Valley* (York, Pa.: 1970), pp. 193-94, 196, 201; Saul Engelbourg, "The Economic Impact of the Civil War on Manufacturing Enterprise," *Business History*, XXI (1979), pp. 150-57.

41. Wayne D. Rasmussen, "The Impact of Technological Change on American Agriculture, 1862-1962." *Journal of Economic History*, XXII (1962), pp. 579, 581-82; Paul W. Gates, *Agriculture and the Civil War* (New York: 1965), pp. 224-29, 238; Alan L. Olmsted, "The Civil War as a Catalyst of Technological Change in Agriculture," in Paul Uselding, ed., *Business and Economic History. Papers Presented at the Business History Conference, 12-13 March 1976* (Urbana, Ill.: 1976), pp. 44-46; William T. Hutchinson, *Cyrus Hall McCormick: Harvest, 1856-1884* (New York: 1935), pp. 92, 96, 395-96; Emerson D. Fite, *Social and Industrial Conditions During the Civil War* (New York: 1963, reprint of 1910 edition), pp. 6-7; Donald P. Greene, "Prairie Agricultural Technology, 1860-1900" (Ph.D. dissertation, Indiana University, 1957), pp. 133, 227-28, 232, 262; Allan G. Bogue, *From Prairie to Corn Belt* (Chicago: 1963), p. 165; Charles W. Marsh, *Recollections 1837-1910* (Chicago: 1910), 86-88, 131.

42. Carl M. Becker, "Entrepreneurial Invention and Innovation in the Miami Valley During the Civil War," *Bulletin of the Cincinnati Historical Society*, January 1964, pp. 7, 19-20,; Victor S. Clark, *History of Manufacturing in the United States*, 3 vols. (New York: 1929), 2:18-19; Raymond H. Robinson, "The Boston Economy During the Civil War"

(Ph.D. dissertation, Harvard University, 1958), pp. 229-30; W. Paul Strassmann, *Risk and Technological Innovation* (Ithaca, N.Y.: 1959), pp. 88-97.

43. J. Brooke to J. Whitworth, Sept. 13, 1862, q. in George M. Brooke, Jr., "John Mercer Brooke, Naval Scientist" (Ph.D. dissertation, University of North Carolina, 1956), p. 860; J. W. Mallet and O. E. Hunt, "The Ordnance of the Confederacy," in Francis T. Miller, ed., *The Photographic History of the Civil War*. 10 vols. (New York: 1911), 5:166; Frank E. Vandiver, *Ploughshares into Swords: Josiah Gorgas and Confederate Ordnance* (Austin, Tex.: 1952), pp. 105-6.

44. Merritt Roe Smith, *Harpers Ferry Armory and the New Technology* (Ithaca, N.Y.; 1977), pp. 310-13; Charles B. Dew, *Ironmaker to the Confederacy* (New Haven, Conn.: 1966), pp. 64-65; unidentified clipping, Jan. 29, 1875, Burton diary entries, July 17, Nov. 17-Dec. 8, 1860, Feb. 1, 2, 1861, James H. Burton MSS, Yale University; Davis, A*rming*, p. 149, 172; Vandiver, *Ploughshares*, pp. 45, 79.

45. Vandiver, *Ploughshares*, p. 161; Emory M. Thomas, *The Confederate Nation: 1861-1865* (New York: 1979), pp. 210-11.

46. Vandiver, *Ploushshares*, pp. 144-45.

47. Allen Johnson and Dumas Malone, eds., *Dictionary of American Biography*, 22 vols. (New York: 1928-1958), 15:329 ("Rains"); Maurice K. Melton, "Major Military Industries of the Confederate Government" (Ph.D. dissertation, Emory University, 1978), pp. 99-104, 108-110, 496-98, 500; Vandiver, *Ploughshares*, p. 154.

48. Melton, "Military Industries," pp. 125, 299-303, 443-45, 507-518; Vandiver, *Ploughshares*, pp. 114, 183, 192.

49. Ralph W. Donnelly, "Scientists of the Confederate Nitre and Mining Bureau," *Civil War History*, II (1956), pp. 69-92; John S. Lupold, "From Physician to Physicist: The Scientific Career of John LeConte, 1818-1891" (Ph.D. dissertation, University of South Carolina, 1970), pp. 170-78.

50. Lupold, "LeConte," pp. 145-46; Melton, "Military Industries," 379-80, 466-68; Milton F. Perry, *Infernal Machines* (Baton Rouge, La.: 1965), p. 58; Warren Ripley, *Artillery and Ammunition of the Civil War* (New York: 1970), pp. 176, 290, 304-312; B. Huger to J. Read, June 18, 1861, Miscellaneous MSS, South Carolina Historical Society; George M. Chinn, *The Machine Gun* (Washington, D.C.: 1951), p. 42,; William B. Edwards, *Civil War Guns* (Harrisburg, Pa.: 1962), p. 232; Bruce, *Lincoln*, p. 68.

51. Dew, *Ironmaker*, pp. 44-50; Vandiver, *Ploughshares*, pp. 59, 231.

52. Frances Leigh Williams, *Matthew Fontaine Maury: Scientist of the Sea* (New Brunswick, N.J.: 1963), pp. 377-81, 383, 391-94, 397, 411-12, 415-17; Perry, *Infernal Machines*, p. 14.

53. Perry, *Infernal Machines*, pp. 4, 30-31, 38, 43-44, 164-65, 178-79, 196-97, 199-201; Joseph T. Durkin, *Stephen R. Mallory* (Chapel Hill, N.C.: 1954), p. 261.

54. Perry, *Infernal Machines*, pp. 63-70, 81-86, 94-107, 122-28.

55. William N. Still, *Iron Afloat: The Story of the Confederate Armorclads* (Nashville, Tenn.: 1971), pp. 7, 10, 12, 15, 97, 227-29, 231.

56. George M. Brooke, Jr., *John M. Brooke* (Lexington, Va.: 1979), pp. 145, 226, 238, 243, 261-63, 265-69, 271-74, 277-81; Melton, "Military Industries," p. 132; Dew, *Ironmaker*, pp. 118-20; Brooke, "Brooke," p. 852.

57. Bruce, *Lincoln*, pp. 169, 275-76.

58. *Ibid.*, pp. 247-48.

59. Bruce, *Launching*, p. 308.

60. James Phinney Baxter III, *Scientists Against Time* (Boston: 1946), p. 8; see also Mark Walker, *German National Socialism and the Quest for Nuclear Power, 1939-1949* (New York: 1989), passim.

10

Forging the Trident: British Naval Industrial Logistics, 1914-1918

Jon Tetsuro Sumida

In August 1914, the British Expeditionary Force (B.E.F.) was equipped with 476 field guns. The Grand Fleet, however, was armed with 1,560 pieces of artillery, of which the 330 big-guns that composed the main batteries of the capital ships and armored cruisers were far more powerful than anything possessed by the army. Tanks had yet to be invented (and by the navy at that), while the Grand Fleet's battleships and cruisers were all protected with thousands of tons of armor. At the start of the war, the B.E.F. possessed 950 trucks and 250 cars, whose combined engine output could not have exceeded 50,000 horsepower, the bulk of the troops travelling by foot or on horse. All of the Grand Fleet's men, guns, and armor were moved by mechanical energy, the propulsion plant capacity of the capital ships, cruisers and destroyers coming to some three million horsepower. Britain began the First World War, in other words, with an essentially unmechanized army and a highly mechanized navy.[1]

Before the war, the relationships of the two forces to Britain's industrial economy were entirely different. The army, which was diminutive by Continental standards, required little more than artillery and small arms, and these not in large quantity—equipping such a force, Lord Kitchener remarked in 1914, "was not much more difficult than buying a straw hat at Harrods."[2] The navy, which was the world's largest, in contrast depended upon an extensive complex of steel works, engineering workshops, ordnance foundries, and dockyards for the manufacture, repair, and maintenance of its ships and associated equipment. Over the course of the war, the army's appetite for industrial production was magnified by its manifold growth, the enormous increase in the numbers and use of artillery, the expansion of the motor pool and air force, and the adoption of tanks. At the same time, the navy was greatly enlarged by new warship construction programs; the intensive use of more warships resulted in a far heavier maintenance and repair schedule, while the anti-submarine campaign and the discovery of defects in capital ship projectiles demanded the large scale manufacture of mines, depth charges, and improved heavy caliber ammunition.

From 1915, the Ministry of Munitions, a new authority separate from the War Office, became responsible for the supply of army equipment and by the end of the war directed the operation of much of Britain's industrial economy. The Admiralty retained, however, in the words of Winston Churchill, a

> separate and privileged position. They had their own great supply departments, their own factories, their own programmes, and their own allegiances. In a period when a general view and a just proportion were the master-keys, they vigorously asserted their claim to be a realm within a realm—efficient, colossal, indispensable, well-disposed, but independent.[3]

No substantial separate official account of naval production was ever written, and although the 12 volume official history of the Ministry of Munitions contains much of value on the navy,[4] its main concern was production for the army. Of the balance of related works on the First World War, the official and Carnegie Endowment monographs devoted to British civil and economic affairs give incomplete coverage to naval procurement and administration,[5] recent scholarly studies of Britain's industrial effort have paid little attention to the naval aspect of their subject,[6] and the standard histories of the Royal Navy operations and policy practically ignore economic matters.

The present study of British naval industrial logistics between 1914 and 1918 will deal with three subjects: the relationship of industrial production for the navy and that for the army; the relationship of industrial production for the navy and that for the merchant marine; and the development of wartime naval industrial administration. Four major questions will be addressed: What was the magnitude of Royal Navy consumption of industrial resources during the First World War? What impact did the satisfaction of Royal Navy industrial requirements have on Britain's overall war effort? What were the means by which the Admiralty maintained its access to British industrial production? And more generally, what were the strategic implications for Britain of naval industrial economics during the first half of the 20th century? It should be stated at the outset that the amount of British industrial capacity devoted to war production has been accepted as a given, and no attempt has been made to deal with the significant but separate question of whether civilian consumption could have been further reduced in favor of increased munitions output.

Statistical data on Royal Navy consumption of industrial resources between 1914 and 1918 have been gathered from scattered sources, many of which are not readily available. This material has, therefore, been placed in an annotated appendix. Graphs based on data in the appendix, however, have been placed in the text, and text references given to both the figure and the appendix table.

Naval Industrial Logistics

During the First World War, the fighting on land involved the use of artillery on a massive scale. The formation of the Ministry of Munitions in June 1915 was provoked by widespread public concern over reports of army artillery ammunition shortages, and the ministry's ultimate success in vastly increasing the production of projectiles became the foundation of its high reputation. At sea, major encounters were few and the limitations of naval fire control such that shooting by capital ships was for the most part slow and deliberate. The operational expenditure of ammunition by the navy was, therefore, a tiny fraction of that by the army, and although the production of projectiles for naval artillery was relatively small, shell supply was ample and even bountiful.[7] The major problems of naval industrial logistics were not determined by expenditures in battle, of which there was little, but by the requirements of expanding and maintaining the world's largest mechanized armed force.

On the outbreak of hostilities, the Admiralty, with long experience in dealing with the private manufacturing sector and with a relatively high proportion of its war complement of ships and men in hand, was able to place production contracts swiftly, in many instances preempting the War Office,[8] which prior to the war had depended almost exclusively upon the output of government arsenals and which was preoccupied with the overwhelming task of managing the expansion of the army. The Admiralty also moved quickly to prevent losses of industrial labor from firms engaged in naval work to the army, in December 1914 obtaining cabinet approval for the institution of a system of work badges, which was meant to discourage the recruitment of selected workers. This protection was further strengthened in the spring by the formal prohibition of enlisting men from certain trades.[9] By July of 1915, of the total of 480,000 male workers reserved from military service on account of their occupations, 400,000, or more than 80 percent, were those engaged in production for the Admiralty,[10] which covered nearly three fourths of Britain's maritime industrial labor force (see Statistical Appendix, Table 10.1).

The Admiralty continued to hold more than its own even after formation of the Ministry of Munitions in June 1915. Early efforts by the new body to coordinate steel supply failed, and it was not until January 1916 that the ministry was able to obtain an agreement giving it priority for steel earmarked for projectile production, with the navy guaranteed first call on whatever remained. This did not amount to much in practice. In the first place, shell manufacture was estimated to require only one-third of Britain's steel output, which meant that the field left to the navy was considerable (see Statistical Appendix, Table 10.2). The agreement, moreover, covered only steel for shells, while the Ministry of Munitions required steel for such purposes as artillery production and the extension of steelworks. The official history of the Ministry of Munitions thus noted that through most of 1916 the priority granted to the Admiralty for all its requirements, without consideration of their relative importance, resulted in a shortage for necessary War Office and munitions work, and steel could only be obtained in doles granted by the Admiralty.[11]

From the fall of 1916 to the fall of 1917, the problems of steel allocation were handled by an interdepartmental consultative committee with little success. In September 1917, however, shortages in steel for merchant shipbuilding—an activity which by this date was under the control of the Admiralty—prompted the formation of a new body, the Central Steel Committee, which was made up of representatives from the Ministry of Munitions, Admiralty, and steel industry. The naval members came from the Admiralty's Materials and Priority Department, which Admiral Sir John Jellicoe, the First Sea Lord, later recalled "controlled the distribution of steel for all services" to the great advantage of the navy.[12] The official history of the Ministry of Munitions simply stated that the deliberations of the Central Steel Committee "resulted in a considerable easing of the steel situation."[13] In any case, Admiralty access to steel production in 1918 was drastically increased, the amount allocated to warship and merchant shipbuilding exceeding that for shell production for the first time during the war (see Statistical Appendix, Table 10.2).[14]

The Ministry of Munitions enjoyed no more success when it came to the coordination of labor supply. In January 1916, increasingly bitter competition for workers, which was exacerbated by large scale army recruitment, prompted the formation of the Labour Priority Committee, which was made responsible for coordinating the industrial labor requirements of the army and navy. In practice, however, the new committee was "incapable of determining the relative urgency of the Admiralty's programme as compared with the programme of the Ministry," which meant that serious disagreements had to be decided by the War Council.[15] The War Priorities Committee of the Cabinet, formed in September 1917, also failed to resolve conflicts between the Ministry of Munitions and Admiralty over priority access to labor, as well as machining capacity and contractors.[16]

In response to the general shortage of manpower, the Ministry of Munitions resorted to the large scale employment of women, the female proportion of its workforce rising from 12 percent in July 1915 to over a third by July 1918. Such "dilution" was facilitated by virtue of the fact that much of the work of producing army munitions was simple, repetitive, and did not involve heavy lifting, making it suitable for execution by unskilled workers, many of whom were women. The Admiralty, however, was opposed to the dilution of its industrial workforce, arguing—with good reason—that shipbuilding required skilled and physically strong labor and that high labor standards were essential in the manufacture of naval engines and ordnance in order to avoid critical and possibly even disastrous equipment failures. This position was strongly backed by the unions in the maritime industries, whose bargaining power would have been weakened by the widespread introduction of unskilled labor into areas that had formerly been the preserve of skilled workers. The workforce involved in production for both the navy and merchant marine, which was close to all male in July 1915, thus remained almost 90 percent male in July 1918 (see Figure 10.1; Statistical Appendix, Table 10.2).[17]

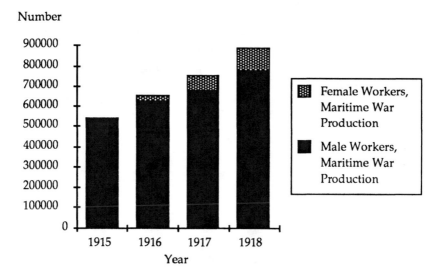

FIGURE 10.1 Maritime Production Labor Force by Gender, July 1915-July 1918.

In 1917, the need for additional soldiers for service in France was such that nearly 70,000 men were transferred from industrial work supervised by the Ministry of Munitions to the army; in 1918, the dangerous German advance in the spring provoked manpower reallocation on an even greater scale, the Ministry of Munitions surrendering no fewer than 130,000 men.[18] The total loss for 1917 and 1918 equalled nearly 10 percent of the number of male workers employed by the munitions industry in July 1917.[19] In 1917 and 1918, moreover, the large scale production of tanks, motorized transport, and aircraft greatly increased Ministry of Munitions requirements for labor in general and skilled—that is, male—labor in particular. The amount of additional skilled industrial labor requested for tank production in 1918 was relatively modest; but that for aircraft production equalled that demanded by the Admiralty, while the requirement for more unskilled workers was even larger.[20] But in spite of these circumstances, the size of the navy's industrial workforce was not only maintained but increased.

The replacement of badging by the protected occupations scheme in the spring of 1917 did not significantly reduce the size of the maritime industrial work force immune to army enlistment,[21] and Admiralty releases of male industrial workers for service in the army were negligible.[22] In July 1917, industrial workers engaged in naval and mercantile production, both of which were under Admiralty control as of May, numbered some 750,000. By July 1918, the Admiralty's labor force had grown to 887,000—an increase of some 18 percent, of which most were male. This growth contrasts with the relatively static size of the male work force of the Ministry of Munitions and War Office during this period, which because of the losses to the army just described remained practically constant, and even including women workers rose by little more than 5 percent. The effect of the "absolute labor priority" enjoyed by the Admiralty from the spring of 1917,[23] therefore, was considerable (see Figure 10.2; Statistical Appendix, Table 10.3).

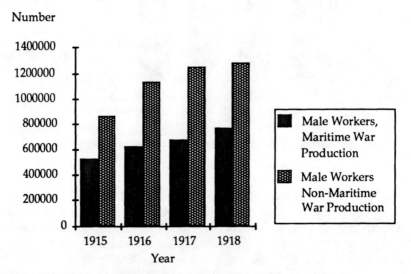

FIGURE 10.2 British Munitions Labor, July 1915-July 1918

In the fall of 1915, the Admiralty had argued that four-ninths (45 percent) of Britain's skilled industrial labor (almost exclusively male) should be reserved to meet the requirements of the navy "if they needed so much."[24] This was clearly intended as a maximum, and yet navy consumption of male labor was already approaching this figure. In July 1915, nearly 40 percent of the male munitions workers were employed in maritime industrial work (see Statistical Appendix, Table 10.3), the overwhelming majority of whom, as will be explained shortly, must have been engaged by the navy. And in spite of the enormous expansion of munitions production for the war on land, the great differences in the application of dilution meant that the proportion of male workers engaged in naval and mercantile work remained largely unchanged over the course of the war (see Statistical Appendix, Table 10.3). The growth of Britain's shipbuilding labor force in terms of absolute numbers was also substantial, the figure for July 1918 being some 72 percent greater than that for July 1914 (see Statistical Appendix, Table 10.2).

Within the domain of maritime industry, the Admiralty enjoyed not mere priority but virtually unlimited ascendancy. From the outset the navy's task of gaining access to manufacturing capacity was far easier than that of the army because shipbuilding, unlike the production of munitions for the land fighting, was a large and established industry that was already well suited for war work. The navy commandeered select private shipbuilding resources on an emergency basis at the opening of the war, and with the passage of the Munitions of War Act in 1915 acquired even broader powers of compulsion over civilian establishments;[25] exercised a large measure of control over the bulk of Britain's maritime industrial labor force by mid 1915 through the introduction of badging previously described; gained authority over steel supplies for merchant ship construction intended for war service from the Board of Trade in early 1916;[26] and in May 1917 was granted formal complete control of Britain's maritime industrial resources by the War Cabinet. Such power was sufficient not simply to limit or reduce merchant shipbuilding but to bring it to the verge of extinction.

Before the outbreak of war in 1914, almost all repair and maintenance work, and one third of warship construction including over half the capital ships, were carried out in the Royal Dockyards. Administrative reforms introduced between 1904 and 1906 had reduced the naval establishments to the bare minimum required to service the peace-time force,[27] there being no spare capacity to deal with the mobilization of second-line units, increased warship construction, and the harder working of all warships in the event of hostilities. Britain's private shipyards, however, possessed enormous repair, maintenance, and building resources, in 1914 supplying no less than 64 percent of the world's annual output of merchant tonnage, one quarter of which went to foreign shipping companies.[28] Army requirements for soldiers and munitions, however, limited the expandability of the private shipbuilding sector, and heavy navy utilization of private facilities beyond that which had been engaged in work for non-British firms thus was bound to result in large reductions in the maintenance of and new construction for the merchant marine.

From 1914 to 1916, the Royal Dockyards were largely preoccupied with warship construction and as a consequence the bulk of the repair and refitting of the Royal Navy was carried out by private yards.[29] The number of naval vessels undergoing maintenance by 1916 was over 10 times that of peacetime, the bulk of the increase being attributable to work on flotilla vessels and auxiliaries (see Statistical Appendix, Tables 10.4 and 10.5). Naval vessels had priority over merchant vessels for repair and refitting, while labor for maintenance work was in short supply; and thus although there were eight times as many merchant steamers than warships and naval auxiliaries combined,[30] many more naval than merchant vessels were docked for servicing.[31] Mercantile craft, not surprisingly, suffered severely from inadequate maintenance,[32] and this, combined with the damage caused by submarines in 1917, resulted in 3,000,000 tons of British merchant shipping requiring major overhaul in 1918.[33]

The making up for years of deferred maintenance on merchant vessels had a significant impact on labour utilization in 1917 and 1918. Less labor, and much less steel, were required to repair a ship than to build a new one,[34] and thus from the summer of 1917 the allotment of labor to merchant ship repair work was increased in order to maximize the number of ships available at the least cost in work personnel and materials.[35] Between July 1917 and April 1918, the number of men occupied in the repair of merchant shipping doubled from about 33,000 to 65,000.[36] Through this effort, the monthly tonnage of merchant vessels returned to service was substantially increased and maintenance arrears nearly caught up by the spring of 1918 (see Statistical Appendix, Table 10.6).[37] The large allocation of workers to repairs, however, must have consumed much if not all the private shipyard capacity released by the reassumption of the Royal Dockyards of responsibility for most naval maintenance from 1916 onwards,[38] while repair work required a much higher proportion of skilled labor than did new ship construction.[39]

The problems posed by warship maintenance, however, were dwarfed by those generated by the Royal Navy's requirements for new warships and auxiliaries. On the outbreak of war, the ten battleships of the 1912-13 and 1913-14 programs were still under construction, the five units of the latter having just been laid down. Between October 1914 and the end of the war, the Admiralty ordered an additional nine battle cruisers, thirty-eight monitors, five trade route cruisers, thirty-one light cruisers, over three hundred destroyers, and more than a thousand other warships and naval auxiliaries.[40] Between August 1914 and November 1918, 842 warships amounting to over 1.6 million tons displacement were added to the fleet, to which must be added 571 naval auxiliaries that came to nearly 800,000 tons, for a grand total of almost two-and-one-half million tons of construction, or more than that carried out during the quarter century that preceded the war.[41]

The industrial resources needed to support such a program were enormous. Between 1914 and 1918, the Royal Navy's steel consumption as a proportion of total output was more than double what it had been during the five year period prior to the outbreak of war, even though the wartime steel total output was a third higher than it had been between 1910 and 1913 (see Statistical Appendix, Table 10.7). Increased warship construction also resulted in an overall increase in the demand for cast and forged marine machinery parts, which were, however, scarce because a large proportion of the supply during peace had come from Germany.[42] And warship construction required far more labor per ton of displacement than did merchant ship building.[43]

To meet the Royal Navy's massive requirements for new warships and auxiliaries required the appropriation of shipbuilding labor and plants that had in peace time been utilized for merchant ship construction, compounding the effect of the shift of repair and maintenance work from the Royal Dockyards to the private shipbuilding sector. In 1914, naval units had accounted for a quarter of the gross tonnage output of British yards. In 1915 the proportion had more than doubled, and in 1916 had nearly trebled to 74 percent, while the building of mercantile vessels during this period fell to a third the level of 1913 (see Figure 10.3, Statistical Appendix, Table 10.8). The combined annual increase in warship gross tonnage from 1914 through 1916 over the level of 1913 was equal to 62 percent of the deficit in merchant ship new construction over the same three years (see Statistical Appendix, Table 10.8).[44]

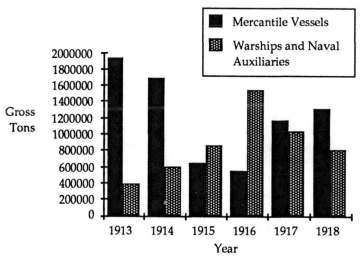

FIGURE 10.3 British Warships, Auxiliaries, and Mercantile Vessels Completed, 1913-1918

Royal Navy utilization of maritime industrial resources in 1915 and 1916 was undoubtedly much greater than that indicated by the record of tonnage completions, high as they were. In the first year of the war, maintenance would have included the work of commissioning large numbers of reserve vessels, many of which had not been kept in good repair, and the fitting out of merchant vessels as armed auxiliaries. Work on five battle cruisers ordered in early 1915 was expedited by the use of more labor, the first two units being built in a third less time than that required normally by a battleship, and similar practices resulted in the rapid construction of 35 monitors.[45] The fulfillment of Royal Navy shipbuilding and maintenance requirements prompted Sir Joseph Maclay, the shipping controller to recall that "very early in the war practically the whole shipbuilding facilities of the United Kingdom were required for Naval purposes...."[46] In April 1916, the Board of Trade reported that "the shipyards have been so actively engaged in building all classes of vessels for the Fleet that merchant shipbuilding has been brought very largely to a standstill."[47]

Britain attempted to make up for the fall in domestic construction by ordering abroad, but for a variety of reasons foreign output was incapable of meeting the demand.[48] In the spring of 1917, heavy losses from German submarine attacks made a great increase in new merchant ship construction imperative.[49] Efforts by the Board of Trade and Ministry of Shipping to obtain the steel and labor required, however, had been largely unsuccessful in the face of the competing demands of both the Ministry of Munitions and the Admiralty.[50] In recognition that dire circumstances warranted drastic action and in the apparent belief that only the navy had the power and organization to obtain the industrial resources necessary, the War Cabinet transferred responsibility for merchant shipbuilding from the Ministry of Shipping to the Admiralty in May 1917. Direction of both naval and merchant vessel construction was placed in the hands of a former railway executive, Sir Eric Geddes, who was appointed to the newly created post of navy controller.[51]

The Admiralty had good reason to welcome the change. Three-quarters of the navy's battle cruiser program was suspended in March on the grounds that such units consumed resources required for merchant shipbuilding.[52] This must have raised serious fears that further reductions in warship construction would follow unless steps were taken to strengthen the navy's claims to steel and labor. Indeed, it would not be unreasonable to surmise that the Admiralty's willingness to assume responsibility for the merchant shipbuilding effort stemmed mainly from its belief that a mandate to garner increased resources for merchant ship construction would improve its capacity to maintain its warship program in the face of the demands of both the War Office and Ministry of Munitions.[53] It is in any case noteworthy that within weeks of the transfer of authority, the Admiralty approached the War Cabinet with proposals to add considerably to the warship program already approved.[54]

In early July, Geddes set the goal of completing 4,600,000 tons of ships per annum, of which 3,100,000 tons, or almost three quarters, were to be merchant vessels, a figure that was nearly six times the amount of mercantile building completed in 1916. The 1.5 million ton warship construction goal stated by Geddes would have kept naval output nearly at the peak level of the previous year (see Statistical Appendix, Table 10.8), which is a strong indication that increased merchant ship construction was from the start meant not to interfere with building for the navy. The merchant shipbuilding target was to be reached gradually over the course of some 18 months, anticipated output for 1917 being 1,566,000 tons, that for 1918 coming to 2,300,000 tons. To achieve this required the more than doubling of the existing amount of steel used for naval and mercantile shipbuilding and maintenance, and the allocation of 80,000 workers to the shipyards over and above the 400,000 thought to be already engaged.[55]

By mid 1917, the accumulation of shell steel and finished projectiles had become so great that the Ministry of Munitions was able to reduce the army's steel allocation substantially through 1918 without compromising the provision of army ammunition at the front.[56] Serious shortages of engines for new merchant ships that were caused by the priority given to outfitting naval vessels appear to have been overcome by increased production by engineering firms.[57] Strikes, holidays, and lack of ore during the summer of 1917 (June-August), however, resulted in much lower steel production than had been anticipated, causing shortfalls in steel deliveries to the shipyards, which in turn restricted the building of merchant ships.[58] And even though greater quantities of steel were delivered to the shipyards beginning in September 1917, this only exposed the inadequate quantity of shipyard labor.[59]

In late 1917, only 16 percent of private shipyard labor was committed to the construction of merchant vessels.[60] By the spring of 1918, of the additional 80,000 shipyard workers called for by Geddes in his memorandum of July 1917, 32,000 had been supplied, but the same number had been withdrawn from shipbuilding in order to carry out repairs on mercantile vessels.[61] Of the 28,000 men added to the shipyard labor force during the first nine months of 1918, only 8,000 were assigned to building merchant vessels, the balance being required for warship and merchant ship repairs, and new warship construction.[62] Large transfers of labor from naval to mercantile construction did not begin until October 1918,[63] which was too late to have significant effect before the end of the war in November.

The labor distribution within the shipbuilding industry was a reflection of the continued priority of naval over mercantile ship construction,[64] and although the naval tonnage completed in 1917 and 1918 was half the 1.5 million tons per annum projected, it remained well above peak peace-time figures (see Figure 10.3). The labor requirements of warship construction, moreover, did not fall in proportion to the decline in tonnage output because the naval programs of 1917 and 1918 contained large numbers of anti-submarine small craft, which required more labor per ton than the larger units that had accounted for much of the tonnage of the first three years of the war.[65] Thus although new warship tonnage declined substantially in 1917 and again in 1918, the labor employed in private yards on warship construction was higher in June 1918 than it had been in January 1917.[66] In September 1918, a third of the shipyards allocated to the exclusive construction of merchant shipping were still engaged in building warships.[67]

Substantial increases in merchant ship production in 1917 and 1918 were achieved through the completion of hulls that had been on the stocks for several years, the simplification and standardization of hull design, and improved coordination of labor and materials.[68] But in the absence of the additional labor requested, new merchant ship construction in 1917 turned out to be 25 percent less than that projected and in 1918 was some 67 percent below what had been anticipated,[69] the latter a remarkable figure even in light of the greater shortfall in warship tonnage output and allowing for unrealistic expectations at the outset.[70] The 1918 production figure, indeed, was 16 percent below the minimum level called for by the navy controller in 1917, which was to have required no expansion of building plants and the addition of only 5,000 new workers.[71] The inadequacy of merchant shipbuilding under the Admiralty only strengthened its position with respect to the War Office over the use of manpower, the War Cabinet in January and June 1918 refusing the army's demand for the call-up of shipyard workers on the grounds that mercantile construction was lagging.[72]

The navy's appropriation of labor for warship construction and maintenance at the expense of merchant shipbuilding through 1918 did not pass without comment. In comparing the use of labor by the Admiralty and the Ministry of Munitions, Churchill observed in April 1918 that while the former had "failed to produce ships" the latter had "not failed to produce munitions."[73] "It is not for me to criticize the policy of the Government in regard to construction for the Navy," observed Sir James Lithgow, the deputy controller of merchant shipbuilding, in the fall of 1918,

> but I am entitled to draw attention to the fact that although the Naval authorities had for three years the entire run of the shipbuilding resources of the country they have still considered it necessary to augment the manpower so engaged throughout the whole of the fourth year of the war.[74]

The appropriation of private shipbuilding facilities to refit and repair warships and naval auxiliaries was unavoidable given pre-war economies in the Royal Dockyards and was essential to the operation of the fleet upon which Britain's exercise of sea control depended. Two wartime First Lords, however, were convinced that a substantial proportion of the Royal Navy's new construction was not strictly required. The light battle cruisers and monitors ordered in 1914 and 1915, whose combined gross tonnage was more than half that of mercantile construction completed in 1916, were considered by Arthur J. Balfour to be "naval luxuries" that contributed "nothing to secure the command of the sea."[75] The War Cabinet during the last two years of the war, Churchill observed,

> riveted by the U-boat attack and rightly determined to give the Navy all it wanted for the purpose of meeting it, was not found capable of drawing the

necessary distinction between this and less imperious services. In consequence the Grand Fleet absorbed in the final phases of the war a larger share of our resources than was its due...[76]

While neither Balfour nor Churchill were disinterested parties, their views on the excesses of Royal Navy industrial consumption cannot be dismissed. The early war building of battle cruisers, which were intended to fulfill Admiral Sir John Fisher's fanciful vision of a battle cruiser revolution in capital ship design, was carried out on the mistaken presumption that British manufacturing resources were great enough to cover any eventuality.[77] During the last two years of the war, work on fleet units not required for the anti-submarine campaign, which accounted for 45 percent of the naval tonnage laid down and launched in 1917 and 1918 (see Statistical Appendix, Table 10.9),[78] were justified as necessary to meet German new construction, estimates of which were, however, wildly inflated.[79] Some allowance may be made for faulty intelligence and, in the case of Admiralty demands for substantial battle cruiser construction, loss of confidence in existing vessels as a consequence of the heavy casualties at Jutland,[80] but other factors were probably involved.

There can be little doubt that British naval officers were alarmed by American and Japanese declarations in 1916 of intentions to expand their fleets. While the War Cabinet wanted to defer a building response to maintain Britain's naval supremacy until after the war was won,[81] the Admiralty leadership, with memories of the sharp contraction in naval construction that had taken place before the war in hard financial times[82] and looking forward to the prospect of even more straightened financial circumstances after the war, may have tried to obtain large amounts of high value warship construction through appeals to wartime exigency, in the knowledge that little was likely to be forthcoming later. Battle fleet expansion was, in addition, at least to a degree a reflexive response, as much an attitude as the product of rational consideration of the relationship between ends and means. "We can deal with the submarine menace," Fisher advised Jellicoe in early 1917, "but a disaster to the Grand Fleet would be irreparable, irretrievable, eternal."[83] The wartime Admiralty, Churchill wrote, believed that "the Navy came first not only in essentials, but in refinements, not only in minima but in precautionary margins..."[84]

Turning from motives to effects, it is clear that for all the complaints of the War Office,[85] the navy's unwillingness to release manufacturing manpower for military service probably did not have a critical impact on army strength. The maintenance of the maritime industrial labor force at its pre-war level through the summer of 1916, which would have reduced its actual size by a third, could have provided no more than 200,000 men or less than 6 percent of the number that actually enlisted during the first two and one half years of war (see Statistical Appendix Tables 10.1, 10.3).[86] The dilution of the Admiralty's work force to the extent of that of the Ministry of Munitions could have produced 174,000 men for the army in 1917 and over 200,000 in 1918 (see Statistical Appendix, Table 10.3), which by raising enlistments by 20 and 40 percent respectively could have increased the number of British fighting troops in France by almost 20 percent.[87] In neither of these hypothetical and in fact extreme to the point of unrealistic cases, however, would the amounts have been sufficient to turn stalemate into victory.

Royal Navy consumption of steel and skilled labor had substantial negative effects on the output of the Ministry of Munitions. Scarcity of both materials and workers delayed the output of guns and ammunition, degraded their quality in 1915 and 1916, and retarded tank and aircraft engine production in 1917 and 1918. Faulty ammunition and poor artillery resulted in serious operational miscarriages in 1916, while the shortfalls in tank and aircraft engine output in 1918, which were half that expected, shattered Churchill's hope of creating a mechanized army.[88] The transfer of substantial Admiralty steel and labor resources to the Ministry of Munitions, however, would most likely not have transformed either of the British offensives of 1916 and 1917 into decisive victories. Churchill's vision of machine war, moreover, was not shared by the army command,[89] steel and labor shortages were not the only major impediments to tank production,[90] and in the end victory was achieved with conventional land forces. Navy appropriation of industrial resources, if unquestionably disproportionate and disruptive, cannot be said to have had a pivotal effect on the course of the fighting on the Continent.

There can, however, be little doubt that high navy consumption of industrial resources had a near war-losing impact on the merchant shipbuilding industry. In 1917, losses to German submarines came close to reducing the amount of allied shipping below the level needed to carry on the war. The crisis was caused not only by poor shipping administration and defective anti-submarine policy but also by shortfalls in British merchant ship construction and the inadequacy of merchant ship maintenance during the preceding two and one half years, which had resulted in the non-building or deactivation of tonnage almost equal to the amount of British shipping sunk by German submarines in 1917.[91] During the last two years of war, moreover, increases in merchant shipbuilding fell well short of anticipation, and the circumstances of grave danger thereby prolonged through the spring of 1918.[92]

In the event, the absolute necessity of attaining the maximum merchant shipbuilding level projected in 1917 was obviated by the adoption of convoy, which reduced shipping losses sharply; administrative changes, which improved the efficiency of shipping utilization; and the late but massive expansion of the American shipbuilding industry, whose capacity by the end of the war exceeded that of Britain.[93] But the margin between survival and disaster had been perilously small.

The disruption of merchant ship construction and maintenance was not caused by the contraction of the shipbuilding industry, which in fact grew rapidly throughout the war, or by the demands of the army,[94] which took second place to those of the navy, but by navy utilization of the great bulk of Britain's maritime labor, steel, and manufacturing plants. The Admiralty's need for new warships and increased maintenance, priority over the Ministry of Munitions for steel and labor, and capacity to render a large and ever growing number of male workers exempt from the army, ensured that Britain's maritime industrial sector would expand in spite of the requirements of the land war. Having fostered the growth of and having gained almost complete control over Britain's maritime industrial production, the Admiralty possessed powers of allocation that enabled it to defy even the express wishes of the War Cabinet. With power, however, comes responsibility. The very superiority of the Admiralty's authority over competing supply departments and its near immunity to direction from supreme political authority meant that it alone was accountable for what can be called—given the extent of frivolous or superfluous warship construction—the misappropriation of the considerable economic assets in its charge.[95]

Churchill attributed the "unchallenged power" of the Admiralty on the outbreak of the war to "the august authority of naval tradition" and its possession of "the fullest authority available."[96] The intense competition for scarce industrial resources from 1916 onwards, however, compelled the Admiralty to buttress its initially strong position by drastic increases in the size of its administrative staff. The bureaucratic growth of the Admiralty departments concerned with logistical matters during the first two years of war was relatively small—on the whole little more than 20 percent, (see Figure 10.4; Statistical Appendix, Table 10.10) because a great deal of procurement could be done without paperwork. In the belief that the war would be short and that material resources were superabundant, the principal aim of orders for goods and services was rapidity of delivery, with the requirements of control, coordination, or audit in many cases ignored.[97] The fitting of main battery directors to most of the battleships and battle cruisers of the Grand Fleet, for example—which involved a substantial manufacturing and complicated installation effort, and large expenditure—was initiated in the fall of 1914 "without any letter writing."[98]

From 1916 onwards, however, the operations of the Ministry of Munitions began to threaten seriously the Admiralty's access to industrial resources. Ministry of Munitions control over the war economy was extended through the establishment of a system of procurement based on formal contracting at all levels of material supply and production, a process that generated an enormous quantity of paperwork that in turn required a commensurate expansion of the bureaucracy. In the first quarter of 1916, the Ministry of Munitions headquarters staff was nearly 5,000, or probably quadruple the number at the Admiralty. By the end of the war, this figure had grown to over 25,000.[99] Most were clerical personnel, who were needed to administer communications with firms engaged in war work. To maintain the navy's relations with industrial suppliers, the Admiralty probably had little choice but to develop a comparable instrument of direction. The number of Admiralty clerks, in any case, more than tripled over the course of 1916 (see Figure 10.4; Statistical Appendix, Table 10.10), well before the major changes in Admiralty administrative structure and the addition of responsibility for merchant ship construction, which did not take place until the spring of 1917.[100]

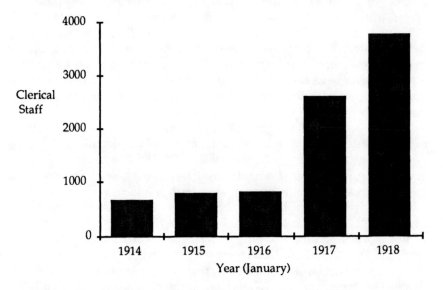

FIGURE 10.4 Clerical Staff, Logistics Departments of the Admiralty, 1914-1918

In the spring of 1916, Admiral Sir John Fisher, who had served as First Sea Lord during the winter of 1914-15, argued that strong personal leadership was capable of producing the required increases in production.[101] Admiral Sir Percy Scott, another wartime administrator, in his memoirs insisted that the enlarged wartime bureaucracy and accompanying paperwork were no more than impediments to action.[102] But while there can be little doubt that Fisher's hustling when First Sea Lord had achieved a degree of compliance on the part of industrial producers, informal methods of commanding resources had also been the cause of inefficiency, poor workmanship, and greater expense. It was useless, Arthur J. Balfour, the First Lord, thus argued in March 1916 in reply to Fisher, to bring contractors up to the Admiralty and proceed to threaten or cajole them. Such a procedure does not...make the impossible possible. What it does do is to produce a plentiful crop of broken promises and a certain amount of bad work.[103]

And while the proliferation of paperwork later in the war undoubtedly resulted in delays, from 1916 onwards, with demand for industrial output outreaching supply, the necessity of setting priorities and otherwise coordinating Britain's manufacturing effort meant that there was no practical alternative to the bureaucratization of procurement.[104]

The lesson was not lost on either the army, whose mechanized development had been much accelerated by the war, or the air force, a new service whose mechanized requirements on a per capita basis were greater than those of the Admiralty. When the admittedly half-hearted attempt to create a centralized Ministry of Supply based on the wartime model of the Ministry of Munitions failed not long after the war, both the non-naval services developed independent relations with industrial suppliers along Admiralty lines, posing the prospect in a future conflict of a bitter three-way competition for limited manufacturing capacity that would disrupt vital war production. This was averted by the creation in the 1920s of the Principle Supply Officers Committee, a coordinating authority whose work laid the foundations for the rapid and effective mobilization of Britain's industrial resources so critical to her survival during the desperate years of 1940 and 1941. This story has been well told by G. A. H. Gordon in his important study of British naval procurement during the interwar period, and for which the present brief survey may be considered a prologue.[105]

Conclusion

Churchill maintained that "there were two Ministries of Munitions"—one by that name and the other called the Admiralty.[106] The latter enjoyed higher priority for both labor and steel and exercised a control over the private shipbuilding industry that much exceeded that of the Ministry of Munitions over its share of the war economy. The proportion of navy requirements fulfilled was as a consequence much higher than that of the army, although the navy's consumption of industrial resources was substantially smaller, which meant that it was navy procurement that limited the army rather than the other way around. The navy, moreover, was able to appropriate virtually the whole of Britain's expanding maritime manufacturing output to the satisfaction of its needs at the expense of new merchant ship construction, which was to have near disastrous results with the advent of unrestricted submarine warfare. The industrial logistics of the Royal Navy, therefore, were comparable in importance to army munitions supply, and the neglect of these industrial logistics was a major obstacle to the proper understanding of British economics and strategy during the First World War.

During the first eighteen months of the war, the Admiralty's almost complete command of private shipbuilding was executed by an administrative force that was not much larger than had existed in peace. Over the course of 1916, however, the number of clerks serving in the Admiralty's logistical departments more than tripled, apparently in response to the transformation of industrial procurement by the Ministry of Munitions, whose massive clerical expansion made access to manufacturing resources a function of the capacity to process paperwork. The proliferation of the navy's office workers thus arguably had less to do with increases in the scale and complexity of materiel acquisition *per se*, or the inherent tendency of organizations to expand, than to the rise of bitter interdepartmental competition for industrial assets.[107] The hostile change in the administrative environment, which prompted the Admiralty to respond with what may be called an act of "defensive bureaucratization," had a lasting effect on military bureaucracy in the 20th century, whose subsequent expansion at a rate in excess of that of fighting forces and beyond what might be expected as necessary to deal with technical change has, in the absence of serious historical analysis, largely defied satisfactory explanation.

In March 1919, the Admiralty declared that the control of naval supply was "an essential part of naval strategy."[108] During the first two-and-one-half years of war, the navy's leadership was if anything more concerned with procurement than with the direction of operations, in effect paying greater attention to conflicts with the War Office and Ministry of Munitions over the allocation of industrial resources than to dealing with the actual war at sea. As a consequence, the navy's command in London failed to give important operational problems the consideration that was their due, particularly in regard to the development of an effective response to the submarine threat. This situation was rectified by the Admiralty reorganization of 1917, which separated responsibility for operational control from administration,[109] but not before the navy's victory in the competition for labor and materiel had disrupted merchant shipbuilding to such an extent that Britain was rendered critically vulnerable to submarine attacks on her overseas lines of supply, and not before the inattention of the naval staff had vitiated the anti-submarine effort. In winning the domestic conflict over access to industrial capacity, the Admiralty, it would seem, came close to losing the war against Germany.

Between 1919 and 1939, Britain responded to the obvious danger posed by uncontrolled interservice competition for manufacturing capacity by devising a remarkably effective interdepartmental system of industrial resource allocation. Britain's continued dependence on maritime lines of supply, however, required her to maintain Europe's strongest navy, whose attendant industrial logistical obligations imposed restrictions on the kind of army and air force that could be supported in the event of war and thus shaped the development of force structure, operational planning, and strategic expectations. Germany, however, with minimal naval forces to mobilize and maintain, was able to develop highly mechanized land and powerful tactical air forces, and new doctrine and innovatory strategy for their use, which in 1940 brought Britain even closer to the brink of defeat than she had been in 1917. The negative influence of naval industrial logistics on Britain's military fortunes in the Second World War may thus be seen to have been no less important, though different in form, than in the First, her finding of a solution to the problem of economic coordination notwithstanding.

Navies, until recently, were mechanized to a far higher degree than armies and thus in the event of war consumed a disproportionately large share of industrial output. Britain's navy, in particular, because of its great size, used up manufacturing resources on such a scale as to have major economic effects. The Royal Navy for this reason was not only an instrument of power but an economic entity whose industrial logistical requirements had a strategic significance that was no less important than its fighting role. Naval strategy, it thus could be argued, must address those questions of technology, economics, and administration that concern the relation of navy procurement to that of the other military services and the merchant marine in addition to matters related to the proper deployment of navies and the extent to which economic and geopolitical factors might limit the development or efficacy of naval supremacy. Or put another way, the interrelationship of essential civilian and land, sea, and air power industrial procurement constitutes a new subject, as yet without a name but nonetheless of central importance to the consideration of the great wars of the 20th century.

Notes

1. Brigadier-General Sir James E. Edmonds and Lieut.-Colonel R. Maxwell-Hyslop, *Military Operations, France and Belgium*, 14 vols. (London: Macmillan/HMSO, 1922-49), 1:7; F. J. Dittmar and J. J. Colledge, *British Warships 1914-1919* (London: Ian Allan, 1972); and John Sutton and John Walker, *From Horse to Helicopter* (London: Leo Cooper, 1990), p. 82.

2. Quoted by Chris Wrigley in "The Ministry of Munitions: an Innovatory Department," in Kathleen Burk, *War and the State: The Transformation of British Government, 1914-1919* (London: George Allen & Unwin, 1982), p. 35.

3. Winston S. Churchill, *The World Crisis*, 5 vols. in 6 (New York: Charles Scribner's Sons, 1923-31), 4:3.

4. *History of the Ministry of Munitions*, 12 vols., subdivided into parts (Hassocks, Sussex: Harvester, 1976), microfiche at the Library of Congress, Washington, D.C. (henceforward cited as *Ministry of Munitions*).

5. C. Ernest Fayle, *Seaborne Trade*, 3 vols. (New York: Longmans, Green, 1924); N. B. Dearle, *An Economic Chronicle of the Great War for Great Britain & Ireland 1914-1919* (London: Humphrey Milford, 1929); C. Ernest Fayle, *The War and the Shipping Industry*

(London: Humphrey Milford, 1927); J. A. Salter, *Allied Shipping Control: An Experiment in International Administration* (Oxford: Clarendon Press, 1921); W. R. Scott and J. Cunnison, *The Industries of the Clyde Valley During the War* (Oxford: Clarendon Press, 1924); and Humbert Wolfe, *Labour Supply and Regulation* (Oxford: Clarendon Press, 1923).

6. For example, see Gerd Hardach, *The First World War, 1914-1918* (Berkeley and Los Angeles: University of California Press, 1981; first published 1977), pp. 44-6, 77-86, and David French, *British Economic and Strategic Planning, 1905-1915* (London: George Allen & Unwin, 1982).

7. Winston S. Churchill to Lord Curzon, 26 July 1917, in Churchill, *World Crisis*, 4:286. Production of naval artillery projectiles of all calibers must have been less than one percent of ammunition output for the army, for which see the statistics in Great Britain, Admiralty, Director of Statistics, "General Review of the Work of Production of Material for the Navy" (29 March 1918), Crease Papers, Box 4, Naval Library, Ministry of Defence, London (henceforward cited as "General Review"); Great Britain, Admiralty, Technical History Section, *Ammunition for Naval Guns*, TH 29 (May 1920), p. 15, Naval Library, Ministry of Defence, London; and Adams, *Arms and the Wizard: Lloyd George at the Ministry of Munitions, 1915-1916* (College Station: University of Texas Press, 1978), p. 244. For the difficulty, however, of obtaining fuzes, primers, and adapters of the required high standard in sufficient quantities for the navy, see Eric Geddes, "Report on the Output of Materiel. Half-year ended 30th June 1918" (26 August 1918), G.T. 5510, Cab. 24/62, Public Record Office, Kew (henceforward cited as "Report on the Output of Materiel").

8. Scott and Cunnison, *Industries of the Clyde Valley*, p. 93.

9. *Ministry of Munitions*, IV/iii: 8-17, and Adams, *Arms and the Wizard*, pp. 76-7. Board of Trade statistics covering the early months of the war indicate that losses of labor to the army in shipbuilding trades were lower than in British industry as a whole and that the inflow of labor from other sectors resulted in an increase in the numbers employed in shipbuilding, for which see Great Britain, Parliament, *Parliamentary Papers* (Commons), 1914-16, vol. 21 (*Reports*, vol. 17), "Report of the Board of Trade on the State of Employment in the United Kingdom," October 1914, December 1914, February 1915, Cd. 7703, 7755, 7850.

10. Wolfe, *Labour Supply and Regulation*, p. 27.

11. *Ministry of Munitions*, VII/ii:15.

12. Viscount Jellicoe of Scapa, *The Crisis of the Naval War* (London: Cassell and Company, 1920), p. 246.

13. *Ministry of Munitions*, VII/ii:16-7.

14. See also Churchill, *World Crisis*, 4:26.

15. *Ministry of Munitions*, IV/iv:5-10.

16. *Ministry of Munitions*, II/i:81-84. For the failure to reach agreement on the question of joint projectile manufacture, see *Ministry of Munitions*, III/ii:144-46.

17. *Ministry of Munitions*, VI.

18. Great Britain, Parliament, *Parliamentary Papers* (Commons), 1919, Vol. 30 (*Reports*, Vol. 23), Cd. 325, "War Cabinet. Report for the Year 1918," pp. 122-4.

19. Director-General, National Labour Supply, "Report on Existing and Prospective Labour Demand and Suggested Methods for Meeting the Demand" (17 December

1917), p. 14, G. 181, Cab. 24/4, Public Record Office, Kew (henceforward cited as "Report on Existing and Prospective Labour Demand").
 20. "Report on Existing and Prospective Labour Demand," p. 10.
 21. *Ministry of Munitions*, VI/iv:52-3, Tables XVI and XVII.
 22. Between March and November 1917, the Ministry of Munitions released 53,000 workers, while the Admiralty produced 700, for which see *Ministry of Munitions*, VII/ii:82.
 23. *Ministry of Munitions*, II/i:82.
 24. *Ministry of Munitions*, IV/iv:6.
 25. Hugh B. Peebles, *Warshipbuilding on the Clyde: Naval Orders and the Prosperity of the Clyde Shipbuilding Industry, 1889-1939* (Edinburgh: John Donald, 1987), p. 89. For the Admiralty's control over all Britain's dockyards by 1917, see Great Britain, Parliament, *Parliamentary Papers* (Commons), 1918, Vol. 14 (*Reports*, Vol. 10), Cd. 9005, "War Cabinet. Report for the Year 1917," p. 37.
 26. "Memorandum by President of Board of Trade. Mercantile Shipping" (24 October 1916), p. 5, G. 88, Cab. 24/2 (also Cab. 37/158/10), Public Record Office, Kew (henceforward cited as "Board of Trade. Mercantile Shipping"), and *Ministry of Munitions*, VII/ii:13-4.
 27. Great Britain, Admiralty, "Report of a Committee of the Board of Admiralty formed to inquire into and report to the Board upon the question of Docking Accommodation on the East Coast" (April 1913), p. 9, FISR 8/32, F.P. 4893, Fisher Papers, Churchill College, Cambridge.
 28. "War Cabinet. Report for the Year 1918," p. 182, and Sidney Pollard and Paul Robertson, *British Shipbuilding Industry: 1870-1914* (Cambridge, Massachusetts: Harvard University Press, 1979), p. 45.
 29. 31,470 warship and auxiliary dockings had taken place by the end of 1917, and roughly 1,000 per month occurred in 1918, for which see "War Cabinet. Report for the Year 1917," p. 37, and Charles N. Robinson, "The British Navy: Construction in War Time," in Earl Brassey and John Leyland, eds., *The Naval Annual 1919* (London: William Clowes, 1919), p. 158 (henceforward cited as "Construction in War Time").
 30. In 1918, there were 1,354 warships of all types plus 800 naval auxiliaries, as opposed to 18,191 merchant steamers, for which see Corbett and Newbolt, *Naval Operations*, 5:430, and Dearle, *An Economic Chronicle of the Great War*, p. 240.
 31. In 1918 (January-November), by which time labor allocations to mercantile repairs had higher priority than that for new construction, 11,416 naval units were refitted or repaired, as compared with 8,539 merchant vessels, for which see Statistical Appendix, Table 10.4 and "War Cabinet. Report for the Year 1918," p. 184.
 32. Great Britain, Parliament, *Parliamentary Papers* (Commons), 1918, vol. 13 (*Reports*, vol. 9), Cd. 9092, "Reports of the Departmental Committee Appointed by the Board of Trade to Consider the Position of the Shipping & Shipbuilding Industries after the War," p. 59 (henceforward cited as "Position of the Shipping & Shipbuilding Industries") and Fayle, *Seaborne Trade*, 3:78.
 33. Salter, *Allied Shipping Control*, p. 82. On 31 January 1917, shipping totalling 131,000 gross tons was undergoing repair, which by 28 February had risen to 330,000 tons, for which see Fayle, *Seaborne Trade*, 3:78. See also Scott and Cunnison, *Industries of the Clyde Valley*, pp. 78-9.

34. For the small quantity of steel required by repair work, see "Position of the Shipping & Shipbuilding Industries," p. 41.

35. Fayle, *Seaborne Trade*, 3:79.

36. "Shipyard Labour, Supply and Regulation. Memorandum by Lord Pirrie (Controller General of Merchant Shipbuilding) and Sir Alan Anderson" (30 April 1918), G. T. 4460, Cab. 24/50, Public Record Office, Kew (henceforward cited as "Shipyard Labour, Supply and Regulation").

37. "Report on the Output of Materiel," p. 4.

38. The joint requirements of merchant ship and warship repair in 1918 consumed labor equal to no less than 60 percent of the numbers of workers engaged in the building of new merchant vessels, for which see Robinson, "Construction in War Time," *Naval Annual 1919*, p. 159. In August 1918, merchant ship repair work absorbed roughly 50 percent more labor than warship repair, for which see Eric Geddes, "Naval Effort— Great Britain & United States of America. Admiralty Memorandum to the War Cabinet" (2 August 1918), G.T. 5307, Cab. 24/60, Public Record Office, Kew. For the switch in the Royal Dockyards from warship construction to maintenance, see D. K. Brown, *A Century of Naval Construction: The History of the Royal Corps of Naval Constructors, 1883-1983* (London: Conway Maritime Press, 1983), p. 278; Philip MacDougall, *Royal Dockyards* (Newton Abbot: David & Charles, 1982), p. 178; and Keith Grieves, *The Politics of Manpower, 1914-18* (New York: St. Martin's Press, 1988), p. 171. For the rationing of warship maintenance in 1918, which had some effect, see "Report on the Output of Materiel," p. 2.

39. "Report on the Output of Materiel," p. 4.

40. Robert Gardiner and Randal Gray, *Conway's All the World's Fighting Ships 1906-1921* (Annapolis: Naval Institute Press, 1985).

41. Brown, *Century of Naval Construction*, pp. 121-23.

42. "Position of the Shipping & Shipbuilding Industries," pp. 41-2.

43. In 1913, warships cost 55 percent more per ton of displacement to build than did merchant vessels, most of this cost being labor, for which see the statistics in Pollard and Robertson, *British Shipbuilding Industry*, p. 32 (and remarks on pp. 216 and 238) and Peebles, *Warshipbuilding on the Clyde*, pp. 166-7.

44. For the complexity of the tonnage measurement problem, see Pollard and Robertson, *British Shipbuilding Industry*, pp. 237-8. There is good reason, however, to believe that the tonnage conversion coefficient used in the present work (see Statistical Appendix, Table 10.8) underestimates rather than overestimates the degree to which warship construction reduced merchant shipbuilding, for which see Lord Pirrie's view of 1918 that the completion of two battle cruisers whose combined displacement was some 90,000 tons would cost 450,000 tons of merchant shipbuilding, in Marder, *Dreadnought to Scapa Flow*, 5:140.

45. R. A. Burt, *British Battleships of World War One* (Annapolis: Naval Institute Press, 1986), p. 291, and Ian Buxton, *Big Gun Monitors: The History of the Design, Construction and Operation of the Royal Navy's Monitors* (Annapolis: Naval Institute Press, 1978), pp. 12-3, 23.

46. "Statement by the Shipping Controller on the Mercantile Marine and the Shipping Programme" (22 March 1917), G.T. 284, Cab. 24/8, Public Record Office, Kew. For corroborative assessments of the effect of the fulfillment of naval require-

ments on the merchant shipbuilding industry, see Fayle, *Seaborne Trade*, 2:168-69; Scott and Cunnison, *Industries of the Clyde Valley*, pp. 76-8, 87-8; and Peebles, *Warshipbuilding on the Clyde*, pp. 88-94. For the relatively weak shipbuilding capacity of the United States and Japan, which prevented foreign purchases from making up the shortfall in British output during the first two years of the war, see Fayle, *Seaborne Trade*, 3:80, and Salter, *Allied Shipping Control*, pp. 82-4.

47. "British Merchant Shipping" (5 April 1916), p. 5, Cab. 37/145/9, Public Record Office, Kew (henceforward cited as "British Merchant Shipping"). See also "Board of Trade. Mercantile Shipping," p. 5, and "Shortage of Merchant Shipping" (19 April 1916), Cab. 37/146/10, Public Record Office, Kew.

48. William J. Williams, *The Wilson Administration and the Shipbuilding Crisis of 1917: Steel Ships and Wooden Steamers* (Lewiston: Edwin Mellen, 1992), p. 23.

49. As late as in December 1915, the Board of Trade's main concern about the reduction in merchant shipbuilding was in regard to how this would affect Britain's shipping position after the war, for which see "Extracts from a Report of the Committee on Merchant Shipbuilding" (20 December 1915), Cab. 37/139/43.

50. "Merchant Shipping" (24 October 1916), Cab. 42/22/6; "Board of Trade. Mercantile Shipping," p. 5; "Statement by the Shipping Controller on the Mercantile Marine and the Shipping Programme" (22 March 1917), G.T. 284, Cab. 24/8; "Memorandum by the Shipping Controller on the Labour Employed in Shipbuilding, Ship Repairing, Marine Engineering Works, and Ports" (24 March 1917), G.T. 275, Cab. 24/8; and untitled memorandum by John Anderson, Secretary to the Ministry of Shipping (14 April 1917), G.T. 457, Cab. 24/10; all in Public Record Office, Kew. The Board of Trade believed that the prime cause of low merchant shipbuilding, however, was the use of shipbuilding facilities and resources generally by the Admiralty for the purposes of warship construction, with labor and steel shortages *per se* being secondary factors, for which see "British Merchant Shipping," p. 5.

51. For the creation of the positions shipping controller in 1916 and navy controller in 1917, see Fayle, *Seaborne Trade*, 3:6-9, 108, 204-5, and Jellicoe, *Crisis of the Naval War*, pp. 231-6. For the shipping controller's complaints in the spring of 1917 about the disruption of merchant ship construction by the navy's 1918 program, see "Memorandum by the Shipping Controller on the Labour Employed in Shipbuilding, Ship Repairing, Marine Engineering Works, and Ports" (24 March 1917), G.T. 275, Cab. 24/8, Public Record Office, Kew.

52. "Cessation of Work on Battle-Cruisers in Relation to Merchant Shipbuilding" (14 March 1917), G. T. 165, Cab. 24/7, Public Record Office, Kew.

53. For the Admiralty's earlier suggestion that it assume responsibility for merchant ship building, see notes on meeting held 11 February 1916, "Arrears in Naval and Mercantile Ship Construction," in "Memorandum on Merchant Shipping" (3 March 1916), p. 5, G. 61, Cab. 24/2, Public Record Office, Kew.

54. "War Cabinet. Memorandum of New Programme" (22 June 1917), G. T. 1133, Cab. 24/17, Public Record Office, Kew.

55. Sir Eric Geddes, "The War Cabinet. Through the First Lord. Copy to the Controller of Shipping" (1 July 1917), Adm. 1/8491/148, and "War Cabinet. Report on the Shipbuilding Situation" (5 July 1917), G.T. 1312, Cab. 24/19, Public Record Office, Kew; "War Cabinet. Report for the Year 1917," p. 69; and Fayle, *Seaborne Trade*, 3: 205-9.

56. By mid 1917, enormous reserve stocks of shell steel and finished projectiles had been built up, allowing a substantial reduction in steel production for the army, whose ammunition supply remained secure through 1918, for which see Scott and Cunnison, *Industries of the Clyde Valley*, pp. 60-1, and Edmonds and Maxwell-Hyslop, *Military Operations France and Belgium*, 5:601. For the extent of the decline in ammunition production in 1918, see Hardach, *The First World War*, p. 87.

57. On 1 June 1917, 467,690 gross tons of merchant shipping could not be completed for want of engines because of the priority of Admiralty orders at the engine shops, for which see Sir Eric Geddes, "The War Cabinet Through the First Lord," Appendix E. Geddes noted in the body of his report, however, that the output of engines was generally above that of hulls and that the shops were capable of increasing output if additional steel were forthcoming and labor increased through the hiring of women.

58. A. G. Anderson, "Report of the Controller of the Admiralty on the present position of Merchant Shipbuilding Both as Regards Labour and Material—with an Estimate of the Amount of Shipbuilding During the Next Year" (19 November 1917), G.T. 2712, Cab. 24/33, Public Record Office, Kew.

59. *Ibid.* For the inability of shipbuilding yards engaged in the construction of merchant vessels to consume their allocations of steel in 1918, see Churchill, *World Crisis*, 4:21-22, 26. For material that somewhat qualifies Churchill's *World Crisis* account, see Winston Churchill, "January Shipbuilding Output" (8 February 1918), G.T. 3597, Cab. 24/41, and A. G. Anderson, "Industrial Situation and Merchant Shipping Output" (15 February 1918), G.T. 3642, Cab. 24/42, Public Record Office, Kew.

60. Grieves, *Politics of Manpower*, p. 171. Grieves' numbers differ substantially from those given in the Appendix, Table 2, the latter probably being more accurate, but the proportion seems correct.

61. "Shipyard Labour, Supply and Regulation." The problem of labor shortages, moreover, was not insignificantly aggravated by labor relations difficulties, for which see R. E. Wemyss, "The Industrial Situation and Merchant Shipping Output" (5 February 1918), G.T. 3540, Cab. 24/41; "The Labour Situation on the Clyde in Relation to the Reduced Out-Put of Merchant Tonnage. Memorandum from the Minister of Labour" (15 February 1918), G.T. 3639, Cab. 24/42; and "The Labour Situation. Report from the Ministry of Labour for the Week Ending the 13th March, 1918" (March 1918), G.T. 3910, Cab. 24/45, Public Record Office, Kew.

62. Fayle, *Seaborne Trade*, 3:409.

63. "War Cabinet. Report for the Year 1918," p. 184.

64. Scott and Cunnison, *Industries of the Clyde Valley*, p. 84. For the substantial additions to the projected 1918 warship program of major units for fleet work during the summer of 1917, see "War Cabinet. Memorandum of New Programme" (22 June 1917), G.T. 1133, Cab. 24/17, Public Record Office, Kew.

65. "Report on the Output of Materiel," p. 1.

66. "Report on the Output of Materiel," p. 1.

67. Fayle, *Seaborne Trade*, 3:409. For the Admiralty's consideration of the need to transfer labor from warship construction to merchant shipbuilding, see Eric Geddes, "The Battlecruiser Position and the Shipbuilding Programme" (31 August 1918), G.T. 5575, Cab. 24/62, Public Record Office, Kew.

68. "War Cabinet. Report for the Year 1918," p. 185

69. "War Cabinet. Report for the Year 1918," p. 182 (mercantile output for 1917 and all 12 months of 1918, the latter calculated by multiplying a monthly average derived from the figure in Statistical Appendix, Table 10.8, by 12), and Fayle, *Seaborne Trade*, 3:205.

70. For the belief by some Admiralty officials that the goals set by Geddes were unrealistic, see Jellicoe, *Crisis of the Naval War*, p. 242.

71. "The War Cabinet. Through the First Lord. Copy to the Controller of Shipping," p. 6 (as before, the mercantile output of 1918 considered in terms of a 12 month year).

72. Grieves, *Politics of Manpower*, pp. 197-8.

73. "Shipyard Labour" (April 1918), p. 2, G. T. 4373, Cab. 24/49, Public Record Office, Kew.

74. Draft letter from Lithgow to Lord Pirrie, September 1918, quoted in Peebles, *Warshipbuilding on the Clyde*, p. 90.

75. Arthur J. Balfour, "Growth of Our Fleets in Home Waters, August 4, 1914, to March 31, 1916" (31 March 1916), p. 5, G. 69, Cab. 24/2, Public Record Office, Kew.

76. Churchill, *World Crisis*, 4:4.

77. For Fisher's intended battle cruiser revolution during World War I, see Jon Tetsuro Sumida, *In Defence of Naval Supremacy: Finance, Technology and British Naval Policy, 1889-1914* (Boston: Unwin Hyman, 1988), pp. 289-95. For the overly optimistic views on the availability of productive capacity at the opening of the war, see Churchill, *World Crisis*, 4:2.

78. The three suspended battle cruisers continued to impede merchant ship building by taking up building slips, while the remaining battle cruiser (Hood) and the three large trade route cruisers consumed both slips and their low priority notwithstanding not insubstantial quantities of labor, for which see "Battle Cruiser Programme" (13 March 1919), G. T. 6979, Cab. 24/76, Public Record Office, Kew (not given complete in Simpson, pp. 595-6, cited below); Maurice Northcott, *Hood: Design and Construction* (London: Bivouac, 1975), pp. 5-6, 10-11, 14, and Alan Raven and John Roberts, *British Battleships of World War Two: The Development and Technical History of the Royal Navy's Battleships and Battlecruisers from 1911 to 1946* (London: Arms and Armour Press, 1976), p. 75.

79. For the battle cruiser situation, see Jellicoe to Geddes, 21 July 1917, in A. Temple Patterson, ed. *The Jellicoe Papers: Selections from the Private and Official Correspondence of Admiral of the Fleet Earl Jellicoe*, 2 vols. (London: Navy Records Society, 1966-8), 2:185-87, and "Battle Cruiser Position and Ship-Building Programme" (31 August 1918), G. T. 5575, Cab. 24/62, Public Record Office, Kew.

80. Jellicoe to Geddes, 21 July 1917, in Patterson, ed., *The Jellicoe Papers*, 2:185-87.

81. David Trask, *Captains and Cabinets: Anglo-American Naval Relations, 1917-1918* (Columbia: University of Missouri Press, 1972), p. 191.

82. Sumida, *In Defence of Naval Supremacy*, pp. 186-87.

83. Fisher to Jellicoe, 26 January 1917, in *Jellicoe Papers*, 2:140.

84. Churchill, *World Crisis*, 4:3.

85. Grieves, *Politics of Manpower*, pp. 23-4, 30-2, 35-6, 157.

86. For the number of army enlistments, see Grieves, *Politics of Manpower*, p. 217.

87. Ibid., and Edmonds and Maxwell-Hyslop, *Military Operations France and Belgium*, 5:592.

88. For the impact of the shortages of steel and skilled labor on the Ministry of Munitions in 1915 and 1916, see Edmonds and Maxwell-Hyslop, *Military Operations France and Belgium*, 5:601, Adams, *Arms and the Wizard*, p. 179, Grieves, *Politics of Manpower*, p. 47. For the shortfalls in tank and aircraft engine production and Churchill's vision of mechanized war, see Tim Travers, "The Evolution of British Strategy and Tactics on the Western Front in 1918: GHQ, Manpower, and Technology," *Journal of Military History*, 54 (April 1990) (p. 198n for tank and aircraft engine production in particular).

89. Travers, "Evolution of British Strategy and Tactics," pp. 173-200.

90. For the various negative factors affecting British tank production in 1917 and 1918, see "War Cabinet. Output of Tanks" (21 March 1917), G. 239, Cab. 24/8, and "Minutes of a Conference Held at 10, Downing Street, S.W., on Thursday, August 8, 1918, at 10.30 A.M., to Consider the Question of Tanks," G. 220 (August 1918), Cab. 24/5, Public Record Office, Kew; and *Ministry of Munitions*, XII/iii:48-50, 65-6, 75-8.

91. In 1917, Britain lost 3,729,785 gross tons of merchant shipping and by February of that year had some 330,000 tons of merchant shipping under repair, for which see Fayle, *Seaborne Trade*, 3:78 and 465. For the extent to which the submarine crisis was created by the shortfall in merchant shipbuilding, see Fayle, *Seaborne Trade*, 3:205-6, and Vice Admiral Sir Arthur Hezlet, *The Submarine and Sea Power* (New York: Stein and Day, 1967), p. 105.

92. Fayle, *Seaborne Trade*, 3:255.

93. For the American surpassing of British mercantile output in 1918, see "Draft. Naval Effort—Great Britain & United States of America. Admiralty Memorandum to the War Cabinet" (n.d. but August 1918), Crease Papers, Box 4, Admiralty Library, Ministry of Defence, London. By 1919, the tonnage of the American merchant marine, which in 1914 was one quarter that of Britain, had risen to nearly three quarters that of the latter, for which see Alexander Richardson and Archibald Hurd, *Brassey's Naval and Shipping Annual, 1921-2* (London: William Clowes and Sons, 1921), pp. 432-33.

94. For the blaming of the shortfall in merchant ship construction during the first two-and-one-half years of war on the satisfaction of army requirements, see Fayle, *Seaborne Trade*, 3:206, and David French, *British Strategy and War Aims, 1914-1916* (London: Allen & Unwin, 1986), p. 224.

95. For the independence of the Admiralty during the First World War, see N. A. M. Rodger, *The Admiralty* (Lavenham: Terence Dalton, 1979), pp. 139-40. For the weaknesses in the supervisory powers of the War Cabinet, see John Turner, "Cabinets, Committees and Secretariats: The Higher Direction of War," in Burk, ed., *War and the State*, pp. 57-83.

96. Churchill, *World Crisis*, 1:257.

97. Churchill, *World Crisis*, 4:2.

98. Admiral Sir Percy Scott, *Fifty Years in the Royal Navy* (New York: George H. Doran, 1919), p. 278. For the production difficulties related to the manufacture of directors, particularly with regard to skilled labor, and considerable financial cost, see Great Britain, Admiralty, Technical History Section, *Fire Control in H.M. Ships* (December 1919), pp. 10-16, TH 23, Naval Library of the Ministry of Defence, London. For Fisher's procurement of labor outside of normal bureaucratic channels for the construction of his battle cruisers, see Arthur J. Marder, ed., *Fear God and Dread Nought: The*

Correspondence of Admiral of the Fleet Lord Fisher of Kilverstone, 3 vols. (London: Jonathan Cape, 1952-9), 3:325.

99. Wrigley, "The Ministry of Munitions," pp. 42, 46-7, 54.

100. For the changes in Admiralty organization, see "War Cabinet, Report for the Year 1918," pp. 179-80; John Leyland, "Administration and Personnel," *Naval Annual 1919*, pp. 200-12 (henceforward cited as "Administration and Personnel"); and Jellicoe, *Crisis of the Naval War*, pp. 232-36.

101. Admiral Sir John Fisher to H. H. Asquith, 15 March 1916, in Marder, ed., *Fear God and Dread Nought*, 3:324-31, printed for the C.I.D., for which see FISR 1/22, Fisher Papers, Churchill College, Cambridge. Fisher also presented his views to the War Committee at this time and without much effect, for which see Ruddock F. Mackay, *Fisher of Kilverstone* (Oxford: Clarendon Press, 1973), pp. 510-11.

102. Scott, *Fifty Years in the Royal Navy*, pp. 273, 281.

103. Arthur J. Balfour, "Growth of Our Fleets in Home Waters, August 4, 1914, to March 31, 1916" (31 March 1916), p. 6, G. 69, Cab. 24/2, Public Record Office, Kew.

104. Churchill, *World Crisis*, 4:2-3.

105. G.A.H. Gordon, *British Seapower and Procurement Between the Wars: A Reappraisal of Rearmament* (Annapolis: Naval Institute Press, 1988).

106. *Ministry of Munitions*, II/ii:81.

107. For a consideration of the other factors that contributed to naval bureaucratic expansion during the First World War—none of which, however, account for the timing of the increase—see Jon Sumida, "British Naval Administration and Policy in the Age of Fisher," *Journal of Military History*, 54 (January 1990), pp. 22-25.

108. Board Minutes, 6 March 1919, quoted in Gordon, *British Seapower and Procurement Between the Wars*, p. 19.

109. Leyland, "Administration and Personnel," pp. 201-6, and Marder, *Dreadnought to Scapa Flow*, 4:174-81. The reorganization appears to have had little effect on the efficiency of supply, which was already high, for which see Jellicoe, *Crisis of the Naval War*, pp. 244-46.

Statistical Appendix

TABLE 10.1 Maritime Production Distribution of Labor, 1914-1918 (known data in roman type, extrapolated data in italics)

	July 1914	July 1915	July 1916	July 1917	July 1918
Royal Dockyards	54,310	68,000	74,100	87,700	101,900
Private Shipyards	181,000	194,443	217,512	*247,500*	*279,500*
Marine Engineering	67,000	*87,000*	103,628	*120,000*	*135,515*
Sub-Total	301,655	*349,443*	388,437	*455,200*	*516,915*
Maritime Basic Industries and Naval Munitions	-	*192,557*	*263,563*	*294,800*	*370,085*
Total Maritime Production Workforce (from Table 10.3)	-	*542,000*	*652,000*	*750,000*	*887,000*

Note on Computations: Labor in private shipbuilding in 1916 was one-third the total navy production work force (it was 35 percent in 1915); the 1917 figure was thus produced by multiplying the total known figures by one-third and rounding to the nearest 500. Labor in marine engineering in 1916 was 16 percent of the total navy production work force; the 1915 and 1917 figures were thus produced by multiplying the total known figures by .16 and rounding to the nearest 500. The extrapolated sub-total for July 1917 differs from the rough estimate given by the Navy Controller to the War Cabinet in 1917 by 12 percent (see memorandum of 1 July 1917 in Adm. 1/8491/148). The 1918 extrapolated figures were calculated by adding 32,000 to the 1917 figure for private shipyards and increasing the figure for marine engineering in proportion (see memorandum of 30 April 1918, G.T. 4460, in Cab. 24/50). In effect this gave greater weight to the expansion of maritime basic industries than would have been the case had the proportions of 1917 been applied, which is consistent with the substantial increase in steel allocation and the known substantial increase in the manufacture of naval munitions that took place in 1918.

Sources: Great Britain, Ministry of Munitions, *History of the Ministry of Munitions*—for workforce of the Royal Dockyards, see VI/iv: 61; for the partial statistics for the Private Shipyards and Marine Engineering, see IV/iv: 139; "Shipyard Labour, Supply and Regulation. Memorandum by Lord Pirrie (Controller General of Merchant Shipbuilding) and Sir Alan Anderson" (30 April 1918, T. T. 4460, Cab. 24/50, Public Record Office, Kew.

TABLE 10.2 Estimated Allocation Requirements of Steel Production for the Coming Year, 1916-1918 (in tons)

	January 1916	January 1917*	January 1918
Admiralty	700,000	660,000	2,000,000
Merchant Marine	550,000	620,000	included in above
Sub-total	1,250,000	1,280,000	2,000,000
Shell Production	2,500,000	4,087,200	1,500,000
Other	5,000,000	5,882,800	4,000,000
Total	7,375,000	11,250,000	7,500,000
Admiralty, Merchant Marine % of Total	17.0	11.4	27.0

*Admiralty, Merchant Marine, and Shell figures are based on a half year prediction, the total figure, however, being an annual prediction.

Source: Great Britain, Ministry of Munitions, *History of the Ministry of Munitions*, VII/ii: 19-24.

TABLE 10.3 British Munitions Labor (Numbers Employed in Government Establishments and on Government Work in the Metal and Chemical Trades), 1914-1918

	July 1914	July 1915	July 1916	July 1917	July 1918
Male Workers, Non-Maritime War Production	-	865,000	1,135,000	1,250,000	1,274,000
Female Workers, Non-Maritime War Production	-	126,000	340,000	630,000	710,000
Total Male & Female Workers, Non-Maritime War Production	-	991,000	1,475,000	1,880,000	1,984,000
Male % of Total Male & Female Workers, Non-Maritime War Production	-	87.3%	76.9%	66.5%	64.2%
Male Workers, Maritime War Production	-	532,000	617,000	673,000	772,000
Female Workers, Maritime War Production	-	10,000	35,000	77,000	115,000
Total Male & Female Workers, Maritime War Production	-	542,000	652,000	750,000	887,000
The Male % of Total Maritime Male & Female Workers, War Production	-	98.2%	94.6%	89.7%	87.0%

(*continues*)

TABLE 10.3 (continued)

	July 1914	July 1915	July 1916	July 1917	July 1918
Grand Total Male & Female Workers, War Production	1,514,110	1,533,000	2,127,000	2,630,000	2,871,000
Maritime % of Grand Total	-	35.4%	30.7%	28.5%	30.9%
Grand Total Male Workers, War Production	1,431,521	1,397,000	1,752,000	1,923,000	2,046,000
Maritime Male % of Grand Total Male Workers, War Production	-	38.1%	35.2%	35.0%	37.7%

Sources: Great Britain, Ministry of Munitions, *History of the Ministry of Munitions*, IV/iv: 139-140, and VI/iv: 49-51. The figures for 1914 were computed on a slightly different basis than those for the later years, the discrepancy between the 1916 total computed on the basis of the 1914 number amounting to 3 percent.

TABLE 10.4 British Warship and Auxiliary Vessels, Completed Repairs and Refits, 1916-1918

Ship Category	1916	1917	1918 (11 Months)
Battleships	90	65	56
Battle Cruisers	37	15	11
Cruisers (including Auxiliary Cruisers)	374	422	397
Gunboats, etc.	534	649	663
Destroyers	1,231	1,448	1,341
Torpedo Boats	532	622	361
Submarines	170	262	273
Misc. & Aux.	9,992	8,622	8,314
Total	12,960	12,105	11,416

Source: Great Britain, Admiralty, "The British Naval Effort, 4th August 1914 to 11th November 1918. Statistics" (September 1919), p. 9, Naval Library, Ministry of Defence, London.

TABLE 10.5 British Naval Warships and Auxiliaries, Quarterly Comparison of War- and Peace-Completed Repairs and Refits

Ship Category	4th Quarter 1913	4th Quarter 1916	4th Quarter 1917
Battleships	19	21	20
Battle Cruisers	3	2	7
Cruisers (including Auxiliary Cruisers)	46	88	128
Gunboats, etc.	16	110	221
Destroyers	109	351	452
Torpedo Boats	44	123	209
Submarines	28	56	79
Misc. & Aux.	30	2,733	2,160
Total	295	3,484	3,276

Source: Great Britain, Admiralty, Director of Statistics, "General Review of the Work of Production of Material for the Navy" (29 March 1918), p. 7, Crease Papers, Box 4, Naval Library, Ministry of Defence, London.

TABLE 10.6 Mercantile Major Repairs, October 1917-September 1918

	Number of Ships	Gross Tonnage
4th Quarter, 1917	1,691	4,925,654
1st Quarter, 1918	1,899	5,821,854
2nd Quarter, 1918	2,301	7,323,992
3rd Quarter 1918	1,511	6,762,446

Source: Great Britain, Admiralty, "The British Naval Effort, 4th August 1914 to 11th November 1918. Statistics" (September 1919), p. 9, Naval Library, Ministry of Defence, London.

TABLE 10.7 Crude Steel and New Warship Production, 1909/13 and 1914/18

	Crude Steel Output (Tons)	New Warship Construction Displacement	Wasrship Displacement Tonnage % of Crude Steel Output
1909-1913	33,710,000	832,100	2.5
1914-1918	45,359,000	2,356,201	5.2

Sources: Sidney Pollard and Paul Robertson, *The British Shipbuilding Industry, 1870-1914* (Cambridge, Mass.: Harvard University Press, 1979), p. 217; D. K. Brown, *A Century of Naval Construction: The History of the Royal Corps of Naval Constructors, 1883-1983* (London: Conway Maritime Press, 1983), pp. 121-2; and B. R. Mitchell, *European Historical Statistics, 1750-1970*, abridged edition (New York: Columbia University Press, 1978), pp. 223, 225.

TABLE 10.8 British Warships, Auxiliaries, and Merchant Vessels Completed, 1913-1918

	1913	1914	1915	1916	1917	1918*
Warships & Auxiliaries, displacement	193,800	294,436	425,428	770,819	519,631	402,623
Warships & Auxiliaries in Mercantile Gross Tons**	387,600	588,072	850,856	1,541,638	1,039,262	805,246
Merchant Vessels (Gross Tons)	1,932,153	1,683,553	650,919	541,552	1,163,474	1,415,834
Warships, Auxiliaries, & Merchant Vessels Total (Gross Tons)	2,319,753	2,272,425	1,501,775	2,083,190	2,202,736	2,221,080
Warships & Auxiliaries % of Total	16.7%	25.9%	56.7%	74.0%	47.2%	36.3%
Mercantile Gross Tonnage Deficit Below 1913 Level		248,600 1913 to Date: 248,600	1,281,234 1913 to Date: 1,529,834	1,390,601 1913 to Date: 2,920,435	768,679 1913 to Date:: 3,689,114	516,319 1913 to Date: 4,205,433
Warship & Auxiliary Mercantile Gross Tonnage Above 1913 Level		201,272 1913 to Date: 201,272	463,256 1913 to Date: 664,528	1,154,038 1913 to Date: 1,818,566	651,662 1913 to Date: 2,470,228	417,646 1913 to Date: 2,887,874

*11months (January-11 November 1918)

**Warship and naval auxiliary displacement tonnage multiplied by 2 to approximate mercantile gross tonnage, for which see "General Review of the Work of Production," p. 1, cited below.

Sources: Great Britain, Admiralty, Director of Statistics, "General Review of the Work of Production of Material for the Navy" (29 March 1918), Crease Papers, Box 4, Naval Library, Ministry of Defence, London; Eric Geddes, "Report on the Output of Materiel. Half-year ended 30th June 1918" (26 August 1918), G.T. 5510, Cab. 24/62, Public Record Office, Kew; Great Britain, Admiralty, "The British Naval Effort, 4th August 1914 to 11th November 1918. Statistics" (September 1919), Naval Library, Ministry of Defence, London; and Great Britain, Parliament, *Parliamentary Papers* (Commons), 1919, Vol. 30 (*Reports*, Vol. 23), Cmd. 325, "The War Cabinet. Report for the Year 1918," p. 182.

TABLE 10.9 British Warship Construction, 1917-1918

Warship Type	Warships Laid Down/Launched: 1917-1918	Warship Tonnage Laid Down/Launched: 1917-1918
Battle Cruisers	1	42,670
Large Cruisers	3	29,250
Light Cruisers	25	123,090
Carriers	3	46,980
Fleet Submarines	18	25,080
Large destroyers	90	105,388
Fleet Units Subtotal	140	372,458
Submarines	81	52,050
S Destroyers	62	65,695
Patrol Gunboats	81	72,090
Sloops	50	65,220
Minesweepers	125	93,070
Flotilla Subtotal	399	348,125
Warships Subtotal	539	720,583
Navy Oilers	24	80,247
Total	563	800,830

Sources: *Conway's All the World's Fighting Ships 1906-1921* and Anthony Preston, *'V & W' Class Destroyers 1917-1945* (London: Macdonald, 1971).

TABLE 10.10 Growth in the Clerical Staffs of the Industrial Logistics Departments* of the British Admiralty, 1914-1918

	January 1914	January 1915	January 1916	January 1917	January 1918
Departments in 1914	666	779	805	2,576	3,179
Additional Departments	-	-	-	12	578
TOTAL	666	779	805	2,588	3,757

*Departments in 1914: Naval Equipment, Naval Construction, Engineer in Chief, Dockyards, Dockyard Expense Accounts, Naval Stores, Naval Ordnance, Air, Accountant General, Contract and Purchase. Departments added in 1916 or later: Deputy Controller for Dockyards and Shipbuilding, Warship Production, Deputy Controller for Auxiliary Shipbuilding, Deputy Controller for Armament Production, Airship Production, Shipyard Labour, Priority Section (later Materials and Priority), Finance Division, Costings Investigation Division, and Torpedoes and Mines.

Sources: *Navy List*, January 1914-January 1918.

11

"Deuce and a Half": Selecting U.S. Army Trucks, 1920-1945

Daniel R. Beaver

> *The more I see of war, the more I realize how it all depends on administration and transportation.*
> —Sir Archibald Wavell

> *Damn truckers! Rear echelon bastards!*
> —Anonymous Infantryman

I

This essay is about how the U.S. Army developed a system to select motor trucks. It examines the connections between and among the soldiers who designed and bought the trucks and the soldiers who depended on them for logistical support in the field. Armies have always had such systems. Sometimes they have been corporate, mechanistic, hierarchical and formal—often they have been cooperative, organic, consultative, familial and informal. The essay is also about people in organizations. Since the appearance of ancient divisions of labor brought functional specialization, one characteristic of military organizations has been political conflict between the combat arms who believed they were the only ones entitled to the perquisites of a military calling, and soldier/logisticians, whom "real soldiers" considered unentitled to recognition as co-participants in the military life. The American army has been no exception, and bureaucratic politics—battles between warriors and soldier/logisticians for recognition and among them all for preference and control—has been the stuff of most institutional histories of the American military establishment.[1]

The nineteenth-century American army was a cooperative, organic, familial, informal system, a confederation of self-interested subgroups, and it was difficult to persuade parochial branch lobbies to take an armywide perspective on technological innovation. Relations between soldier/logisticians and combat soldiers were seldom more than officially cordial. The combat arms wanted the best possible equipment, but they wanted it to be abundant and reliable as well as effective. Military inventors and designers wanted to press technology to the edge of its capacity, while soldier-producers demanded standardized designs that could be mass produced. The army depended on a mixed system for supply and logistical support. The Ordnance Bureau and the Quartermaster Bureau managed large public arsenals, armories and depots which produced weapons and clothing on an impressive scale by contemporary standards and, with a small number of favored civilian client producers, formed a small national defense sector in the nineteenth-century American economy.

Before the Great War, with thousands of miles separating the country from any hostile nation and no immediate threat from powerful neighbors, it was possible to select and introduce new equipment in a leisurely manner. But the speed of technological innovation, which had expanded geometrically during the nineteenth century, did require a military/technological bureaucracy to adopt new inventions and to link designers, producers and users. A feedback loop was required to allow soldiers who used the equipment to recommend changes to ensure that they met combat requirements. The bureau, staff and line system that emerged involved discrete yet cooperative relationships among inventors, designers, producers and those who controlled the army. It operated through boards and committees of officers which selected and tested new technology. A school system, founded near the end of the century, permitted line soldiers to experiment with weaponry and incorporate it into doctrine. The real power rested with the bureau technicians who controlled the boards that conducted experimental tests and selected the weapons. Line soldiers ran the schools that learned to use them. The feedback loop was the prolonged field test. With so many interests involved and no identifiable threat to national security, the army was conservative in adopting new technologies. Even after the post-Spanish American War reforms and the creation of a more formal corporate staff system in 1903, the relations between combat soldiers and bureau logisticians were often contentious.[2]

The Quartermaster Bureau, the agency with which this essay is primarily concerned, manufactured some of its own products and purchased much else built to its own specifications from civilian merchants. It transported troops and supplies by land and water on a continental scale. The bureau designed the army's general purpose wagons but bought them from private suppliers like the Studebaker, Espenschied and Murphy wagon companies of South Bend, Indiana, and Saint Louis, Missouri.[3] But it never had exclusive control of wagon procurement. Each of the technical bureaus procured its own special purpose wagons, and for over two decades after the Civil War, the Ordnance Bureau sought control of wagon production for its own publicly owned production plants.[4] All the technical and logistical bureaus were very small and depended on personnel detailed from the combat arms and civilian contractors for operations in the field. Such conditions proved eminently unsatisfactory, and the history of nineteenth-century army logistics involved a drive which culminated successfully in 1912 to create a special corps of logistical troops to militarize the support of the army.[5]

In 1906 when the army began to experiment with motor transport the Quartermaster General was formally charged with the design and development of unarmed and unarmored wheeled vehicles. The bureau decided on the field characteristics and design specifications and then contracted for motor transport with the private sector. But authority was not exclusive. As in the past, every other supply bureau bought vehicles to its own specifications, and five separate War Department agencies contracted with the automobile industry for trucks. In 1913 the Quartermaster Bureau began to develop a working relationship with the growing automobile industry and the new Society of Automotive Engineers (SAE). In mid-1916 a design team selected by the Quartermaster Bureau, the Ordnance Bureau and the automobile industry began work on standardizing all military trucks. But on the eve of the Great War, aside from color—and even that was sometimes an issue—there was still nothing standard about any motor vehicles in the United States Army.

In 1917, after the United States entered the Great War, an attempt was made to put the standard designs into production. Only the Standard B or "Liberty" 3 ton truck ever saw the light of day. It was a 4X2 rear-wheel drive non-commercial design with parts, chassis and unit assemblies built by 164 separate contractors and assembled in 14 separate plants. Following traditional bureau policy, the assemblies and parts were to be as interchangeable as existing technology allowed. Great things were expected, but manufacturers, already loaded with contracts, preferred to build their own models. Parts and sub-units from different manufacturers would not interchange. Inspection was lax at the assembly plants and production was just getting under way at the armistice.

Meanwhile, in France the Americans were chronically short of motor transport. Pershing's logisticians proved insensitive to production problems and equipment changes and modifications faced by the bureau. The feedback loop worked badly and Chaumont consistently cabled requests for new equipment and demanded changes in equipment already ordered that were impossible to achieve. There was no standardization in the field, and the American Expeditionary Force (AEF) used 274,000 vehicles, including 219 makes and models of American, French, British and other allied design during the conflict. A post-war commentator asserted that maintenance was a nightmare. "There were so many parts that no one really knew what was there; there was no way of finding out." During the Meuse-Argonne offensive in the fall of 1918 it was not uncommon on a given day for 50 percent of American transport to be dead-lined. Six months after the armistice, in the spring of 1919, one officer reported from France that there were still just forty-one operational Standard B Liberty trucks in the whole First Army area.[6]

But there were plenty of them in the United States and they were giving everybody headaches. Production contracts had been canceled after the armistice, and no civilian manufacturers were interested in making parts for the Standard B. After the war the Quartermaster Bureau complained that it had not gotten the kind of rugged, reliable truck transports that it needed during the battle. Commercial, off the rack, trucks would not do at all, the Quartermaster General asserted, and responsibility for design, development and procurement of all general purpose motor transport must be lodged in one clearly defined place in the army.[7]

II

Institutional relationships change slowly. After the First World War, old loyalties, antagonisms, habits of mind and routines still played significant roles in army politics. Although in form the National Defense Act of 1920 continued the movement toward a corporate military organization, it retained much of the spirit of the older, organic, military community. It placed command and control of the army under the Chief of Staff, the representative of the line, and industrial matters under the Assistant Secretary of War. Coordination between the line and the logistical and supply bureaus was improved and a section of the legislation formally encouraged the assignment of young officers to universities for advanced study.[8]

For a time during the 1920's it seemed that logisticians had achieved an equal place in the military hierarchy. "Logistics," declared a staff text in 1926, "cannot be separated from tactics and strategy. It is a major factor in the execution of strategic and tactical conceptions, so inextricably interwoven that it is a part of each."[9] But in reality logisticians were still held in low esteem. Combat soldiers gave them only perfunctory recognition and treated them as they might treat expert civilian advisors rather than as fellow soldiers actively engaged in military affairs.[10] In 1930 General Charles P. Summerall, the retiring Chief of Staff, asserted that the failure to consolidate command and control of supply and logistics under the combat arms after the Great War would bring difficulties similar to those encountered in 1917 and 1918.[11] General Summerall could only see one way to achieve his purpose. He insisted on a single hierarchical command system with supply and logistics under an Assistant Chief of Staff, but until the middle thirties, strategic planning, procurement and logistics remained separate. It was not until Malin Craig became Chief of Staff (1935-1939) that any attempt was made to link strategy and resources. The Protective Mobilization Plan of 1937, undertaken at his request, was the first to take into account the industrial capacity of the nation.[12] That was the situation in September 1939 when George C. Marshall succeeded him as Chief of Staff and war again broke out in Europe.

Meanwhile the War Department moved to improve communication between the combat arms and the logisticians. The Harbord Board, which implemented the National Defense Act of 1920, created a complex division of labor between the supply division of the General Staff (G-4) which set requirements; the supply and logistical bureaus, which designed, tested and issued equipment; and the office of the Assistant Secretary of War, which handled the business aspects of military procurement. The Harbord system was cumbersome but a vast improvement over pre-war practices. The problems lay in its implementation within the War Department bureaucracy. Communication with the industrial sector was strengthened through the new Industrial College, which brought top leaders in the army and industry together to familiarize supply officers with procurement and distribution problems, enhanced awareness of common problems and clarified in the minds of soldiers what the civilian economy could and, more important, could not do in an emergency. But return of control over supply and logistics to the bureaus posed unacknowledged problems of scale for the future. Coordination was achieved through a system of inter-branch committees which included members of the issuing agency, all concerned bureau and combat arms and the office of the Chief of Staff. In each case there were provisions to add representatives from the industrial sector when appropriate. A War Department coordinating committee resolved differences that could not be ironed out formally inside the committee structure or informally between the Chief of Staff and the Assistant Secretary of War.

In a significant innovation, designation of types of equipment, priority of development, adoption and issue was placed with the using arms and services, and the feedback loop was modified to meet the long standing complaints of the using arms that they were not adequately consulted in matters of weapons and equipment. The changes formalized and reformed the informal nineteenth-century system and linked consumers, designers and producers far more intimately than they had been before 1917. Although procurement still rested with the individual supply bureaus, the Assistant Secretary's office cleared all purchases. A most innovative approach to problems of research and development was made through the creation of technical committees in each of the supply bureaus which included representatives of the issuing agency, all concerned bureaus, services and combat branches, the Chief of Staff's office and the Assistant Secretary of War's office. Provision was made to add representatives from the industrial sector when appropriate. A War Department technical committee resolved any differences that could not be ironed out in the bureau committees or informally between the Chief of Staff and the Assistant Secretary of War. All requests for new or improved equipment went first to the appropriate bureau technical committee. If the request was considered worth pursuing by the technical committee it was referred to the Chief of Staff for a statement of need. Upon favorable action by the Chief of Staff, the item was placed on the design and development list of the branch of service responsible for its issue to the army. Under the scrutiny of the branch technical committee it moved from design to development to field testing. Representatives from industry were formally consulted regarding the feasibility of production. If the reports were favorable, a recommendation for adoption as standard equipment went forward from the issuing branch to the Secretary of War, who placed it on the War Department procurement priority list pending availability of funds.[13]

Communication with the industrial sector was strengthened through the Army Industrial College. Established in 1923 under the authority of the Assistant Secretary of War, it introduced top business leaders and army officers to the production and procurement problems they might encounter in an emergency. An important organizational intersect which formalized previous informal connections, it was the first institution of its kind in the world and offered "...opportunity for full time study and investigation of the basic industrial, economic, political administrative and other aspects of harnessing national resources in modern war" and symbolized the profound transformation of the American economic landscape since the turn of the century. Indeed, the ability of the United States to support a forward policy and conduct industrialized war at long range continued to improve. Expanded corporate organization and the trade association movement of the twenties brought business leaders to perceive the nation as an economic unit controlled through voluntary cooperation. During the thirties New Dealers experimented with national planning and brought into government people who were comfortable thinking about American society as an organized corporate entity rather than as an association of localities and regions. By 1940 the United States had the logistical infrastructure, the experienced managerial talent and the available industrial potential to undertake an organizationally unprecedented war effort.[14]

III

The new system came into play during the years between the wars in the development of a fleet of standardized trucks by the Quartermaster Bureau. In the National Defense Act of 1920, the Office of the Quartermaster General assumed responsibility for the design and procurement of all army general purpose vehicles and in early 1923 Quartermaster General William H. Hart appointed a Quartermaster Technical Committee to bring together the people responsible for motor transport, representatives of industry and the soldiers who would have to rely on the trucks in the field. The bureau took full advantage of the Industrial College. Among the subjects chosen for study on an annual basis was the production and procurement of motor vehicles. The work there increased the understanding of potential difficulties and brought out the capabilities of the American automobile industry. It was within that institutional framework that the discussion and debates over motor trucks for the army took place.

Most of the army had little love for the draft horse or the mule, but the state of motor-technology and ever present budget problems made the movement toward motorization incremental. The report of the Ordnance Department Calibers Board forwarded to the Secretary of War in 1919 recommended the motorization and mechanization of American field artillery of even the largest calibers. In 1920 the Chief of Field Artillery announced that the day of the horse was passing, and aside from tactical movement beyond the road net, old dobbin would no longer be needed.[15] Truck technology would soon make even that exception unnecessary. During the twenties and early thirties there were great advances in braking systems, suspension systems and high torque engines for commercial vehicles. Multi-speed rear axles, transfer cases and constant velocity joints made it possible to construct a vehicle with good highway speed and satisfactory cross-country performance. The United States was also in the forefront of the internal combustion revolution, and more Americans were employed in manufacturing and servicing motor vehicles and producing spare parts than in any other industry in the country. According to Industrial War College statisticians, the United States built 75 percent of all the motor vehicles in the world. But money was scarce and it was not until after 1935, when large amounts of Civilian Conservation Corps and Works Progress Administration money were channeled into army re-equipment, that the War Department began to replace the remaining animal transport with motor trucks.[16]

But what kind of vehicles would they be? The combat arms insisted on narrowly specialized equipment for their own particular purposes and cared little about production and procurement problems. The automobile industry made it clear that it simply wanted to supply off the rack commercial trucks. As we have seen, the Quartermaster Bureau had views of its own that went back to 1916. Since the end of the war, with no reliable source for spare parts, quartermaster transportation officers at the depot at Holabird, Maryland, had been scavenging spare parts, ordering what new ones they could find and tinkering lovingly with the "Standard B"s left over from the war. They put on pneumatic tires. They replaced four-cylinder engines with six-cylinder engines. They added multi-wheel drive. It was not that they forgot the problems that had come up during the war; it was that they still believed, as they had in 1916, that a special truck assembled from the best commercially available parts to quartermaster specifications would meet the needs of the service better than any commercial model or any special vehicle the using branches might design.[17]

Meanwhile, in 1926 Secretary of War Dwight L. Davis announced a ten year motor vehicle development program for the army. Three years later a clear doctrine of motor vehicle development emerged. Army trucks were divided into administrative and tactical-strategic groups. The latter were to combine "standard road performance with maximum cross country ability." With the exception of very special vehicles they were to be "commercial types...capable of prompt quantity production."[18] It was soon clear that the engineers and policy makers in the Quartermaster Bureau had their own ideas about what "standard" and "commercial" meant and had no intention of surrendering positions they had maintained since the designing of the "Standard B." In fact bureau engineers were already developing their own peculiar motor trucks.

At that point the careers of three officers and Quartermaster Bureau motor vehicle philosophy for a time ran parallel courses. Major General John L. DeWitt, a former infantryman, now Quartermaster General and destined for notoriety as army commander in California when the Japanese-Americans were interned, presided over the program's progress; Colonel Brainerd Taylor, Chief of the Motor Transport Branch, encouraged the affair from its inception; and Colonel Edgar S. Strayer, Commanding Officer of the Holabird Quartermaster Depot, transformed ideas into army trucks. All three officers had served in the AEF during the war. Taylor had been with Pershing in Mexico and had also been in charge of motor transport at Saint-Mihiel, where the American supply trains literally disintegrated. That logistical nightmare made him an evangelist for standardization after the war. DeWitt, who commanded First Army transport after the armistice, remembered its deplorable state because of lack of spare parts and maintenance. Strayer was the idea man. They all wanted something like the "Standard B" truck with procurement and spare parts problems worked out. Strayer labored for almost three years. Commercial trucks were tested with the cooperation of the SAE. Specially designed trucks were constructed. Finally Strayer, adopting methods current in the heavy truck industry, went into the open market, purchased the very best components available and assembled them at the Holabird Depot, where in 1931 the "Standard Quartermaster Fleet" was born. There were five standard dimensions for military trucks. Within each dimension parts and unit assemblies were interchangeable and all possible spare parts for the entire fleet were interchangeable. All parts of the fleet were convertible to either two wheel or multi-wheel drive. Built from the best procurable parts and components and assembled at government plants, the new motor transport system would be rational, symmetrical and procurable. Colonel Taylor was enthusiastic and recommended Strayer for a medal. Colonel Strayer modestly hailed the program as "the most important step in the advancement of military transport that has ever taken place." On October 5, 1931, DeWitt forwarded the recommendations to Secretary of War Patrick J. Hurley.[19]

The plan might have had a chance if it had not been for the Great Depression; as it was its impact was catastrophic. There had already been some apprehension among representatives of the combat arms at the audacity of the Quartermaster Corps (QMC). Infantrymen thought all the trucks were too heavy. The Chief of Ordnance said it was the old "Standard B" business all over again, and regardless of what Strayer claimed, none of the trucks would prove producible in an emergency.[20] The SAE had some misgivings but was not actively hostile. Some parts suppliers were enthusiastic. The major automobile producers, who saw the market for complete vehicles evaporating in the hard times, raised a storm of protest. Under great bureaucratic pressure the Comptroller General's office insisted that contracts must by law go to the lowest bidder and only for complete vehicles. On November 15, 1931, Secretary Hurley rejected the program out of hand. Subsequently Congress made it illegal for the army to buy component parts for independent assembly or even to design and test motor vehicles other than current American commercial designs. During the Great Depression, contracts were spread around to help the automobile industry, and there was little immediate effort to achieve standardization. In 1936 there were 360 different motor vehicle models in the army with nearly a million different spare parts, none of which were interchangeable except within individual models. Conditions were little better in 1939 when it was found that army inventories stocked 960 different models of vehicles, 251 different types which required an average of 1000 different spare parts for each model. General DeWitt, convinced that bureaucratic politics made any attempt to develop a rational policy futile, asserted in exasperation later that year: "We actually constructed a fleet of trucks divided into five groups as to tonnage capacity [and] tested them out. Industry said it could build them. We can get [them] if we want [them]; if we will decide what we want." Another officer wrote cynically, "Vehicle types and models that fully meet military requirements are not practicable of production in time of war nor legally procurable in time of peace."[21]

But the essential outlines of a compromise development and procurement program were already apparent by 1936. Ten years earlier it had been established that the army would be completely motorized and that its trucks were to have "standard road performance with maximum cross country ability." The fleet would have five standard dimensions and maximum interchangeablity of parts and unit assemblies. But DeWitt, Taylor and Strayer's dream of one perfect system would not survive. There would be no rational and systematic implementation of the program. Rather, it would be political, pragmatic and incremental, reflecting the realities of American institutional and political life. The combat arms would influence performance abilities, but there would be few exclusive models. The automobile industry would not pawn off the rack commercial vehicles on the army either. Contrary to DeWitt's understanding, the SAE wanted design and production left to the truck builders. In fact, the industry had already moved forward technologically, and most American light and medium truck builders were operating on the principle of interchangeablity. The rear axles of two popular makes of ton and a half trucks, for example, were made by the same parts supplier, and many units, especially engines, for heavier trucks came from the same companies. If the full cooperation of the industry's engineers could be obtained, commercial vehicles could be modified to army specifications and a motor fleet constructed "which would be the equal of any nation's."[22]

Meanwhile DeWitt's tour as Quartermaster General ended and he was succeeded by officers who were less committed to a fleet of vehicles of special design. Major General Louis H. Bash and his successor, Major General Henry Gibbins, were pragmatists and worked with what they had. In 1934 there was only one producer of multi-wheel drive trucks in the United States. As more money became available the automobile giants vied for the new money. Profit was a marvelous stimulant and by late 1938 there were thirteen truck and automobile companies ready to produce similar military vehicles. In August 1939 the Secretary of War announced that the doctrinal and performance requirements set by the QMC and the combat arms would be retained in the new truck procurement program, but design and production questions would be in the hands of the SAE and the automobile industry. Competitive features insisted upon by Congress and the Comptroller General were retained. The most significant part of the document declared:

> The procurement of motor vehicles [will] be limited to models in commercial production by two or more competing companies.... Minimum deviation from commercial models may be necessary to conform to military characteristics set up by the using arm or service to which the vehicle is allocated. The parts of unit assemblies will be standard in the automobile industry. All military requirements in general purpose vehicles will be met by using five [standard] chassis types.... The standard for all tactical motor transport will be the all wheel drive.... The maximum interchangeablity of major parts and unit assemblies obtainable within the industry and applicable to the standard chassis adopted for army use will be employed.[23]

Later in 1940, in a virtually unprecedented action, representatives of all the using arms and services supported recommendations for systematic implementation of the quartermaster program. The five general purpose chassis were $1/2$ ton, $1\,1/2$ ton, $2\,1/2$ ton, 4 ton, and $7\,1/2$ ton. In 1941 the $1/2$ ton was eliminated and replaced by the famous $1/4$ ton "Jeep" and $3/4$ ton "Weapons Carrier." The fall of France in the spring of 1940 unloosed a torrent of money for motor vehicles. A civilian observer at the Regular Army maneuvers early that spring announced with some astonishment that he saw very few horses and mules but many obviously new multi-wheel drive trucks. Even before the summer crisis of 1940 the motorization of the Regular Army was far advanced, and for the first time they had "enough motor transport to carry their men, weapons, food and ammunition." And everybody was happy. When the lavish contracts came in, the "Big Three" manufacturers all got their share of the motor transportation pie. Even Willys-Overland, which shared the Jeep contract with Ford, got into the action. Dodge got the $^3/_4$ ton weapons carrier, Chevrolet got the 1 $^1/_2$ tonner and GMC got the "deuce and a half".[24]

IV

The basic doctrines and policies developed by the Quartermaster Technical Committee during the thirties with all their Manichean political manifestations shaped the army motor transport program during the Second World War. But there were conflicts and miscalculations involved in truck selection which went back to the connections between and among the using arms and the design, selection and procurement agencies in the army. The issues at the time were not those of right or wrong but ones involving effectiveness of the mix among the various types of equipment procured.

After the Japanese attack on Pearl Harbor, it was clear to General George C. Marshall that a major reorganization of the army along more corporate, industrial lines was necessary to control the massive war effort upon which the nation was about to embark. Only such a crisis could have paved the way for passage of the War Powers Act of 18 December 1941, which in turn made the complete restructuring of American supply and logistics possible. The new organization pushed through by Marshall secured effective executive control over the War Department and the army and rationalized American military structure by creating the Army Ground Forces (AGF), Army Air Forces (AAF) and Army Service Forces (ASF). Strategic decision making was concentrated in Marshall's office in March 1942, which in turn was linked a short time later with the overseas theaters of operations, the Joint and Combined Chiefs of Staff and civilian war agencies.[25] Major General Brehon B. Somervell, a dynamic engineer officer with broad experience with civilians as well as soldiers, became Commanding General of the ASF. Supply and logistics support became Somervell's responsibility.[26]

In July 1942 as part of the Marshall Reforms and in an effort to rationalize and systematize logistical functions, Somervell's office transferred all soft transport development, procurement and maintenance to the Ordnance Department under Lieutenant General Levin H. Campbell, Jr. Thousands of civilians, officers, enlisted men, bases, depots and schools from the Motor Transport Service were transferred to ordnance while the Motor Transport Service, including the Quartermaster Technical Committee and its research and development staff, moved from Washington to the Tank-Automotive Center in Detroit, Michigan. The operation of military trucking in the field went to the newly created Transportation Corps under Major General Charles P. Gross. In addition all army construction work was transferred to the Corps of Engineers under Lieutenant General Eugene Reybold. It was a very complicated undertaking. Personnel for the Transportation Corps came from traditional quartermaster organizations. Supply, maintenance and support was divided between the engineers, who now built and repaired the roads and constructed the pipe lines, the Quartermaster Corps, which still controlled all petroleum, oil and lubricants (POL), and the Ordnance Corps, which handled vehicle maintenance. Most of the Quartermaster Motor Transport Service accepted the decision, but its chief, Brigadier General James L. Frink, refused to leave the Quartermaster Corps.

The reorganization ended for the time being, at least, conflicts over a century old, but it also brought subtle changes in outlooks, attitudes and priorities. The Ordnance Department was interested in tanks, half-tracks and guns rather than such prosaic matters as trucks, and when the first major contracts to motorize the army were executed, ordnance experts had no idea that truck transport would carry the enormous logistical responsibilities that later fell to it. Most logisticians believed that the transportation of supplies and equipment over long distances would be borne by rail and water carriers. General purpose trucks would handle on and off road hauls between railheads, rear and intermediate depots and forward dumps and provide fast, emergency lifts of critical material. In 1941 the only people interested in what were called heavy "strategic vehicles" were the transportation experts on the Quartermaster Technical Committee. And they had no support from the other branch and service representatives. Later that year, in a decision similar to the one made by the AGF to "win the war with the Sherman tank," all the using arms and services except for the Quartermaster Corps recommended that the army rely for general transportation on the 2 1/2 ton light-heavy 6X6 truck rather than on heavy-heavy vehicles capable of meeting all foreseeable logistical crises.

Aside from minor engineering change orders the design of the 2 1/2 ton truck was frozen in 1942. The automobile makers could produce the chassis easily. It had a simple, reliable GMC or Hercules engine, Bendix or Bendix compatible constant velocity joints, and a Spicer, Timken-Detroit or Borg-Warner transmission. It was maneuverable, maintainable, and could be operated by relatively unskilled manpower. It could be packaged and boxed and, in an era of strained shipping, could be made available in the field in great numbers. And everybody knew that the more trucks the army had in the field the less vulnerable it was to being immobilized.[27]

The decision also took the current structure of the American automotive industry into account. The relatively underdeveloped highway and bridge system as well as legal restrictions on the over-all dimensions and load limits of such vehicles had worked against the development of the long distance trucking business. In peace time, production of "heavy-heavy" trucks and tractor-trailers had never reached more than 600 vehicles a year. Diamond T, Mack, International, White, Federal, Corbitt, and Auto-Car were the major suppliers. The first heavy-heavy trucks, wreckers and tank transporters went to the engineers, the Signal Corps and the newly formed armored force. Diamond T built 4 tonners. Auto-Car and Federal built 5 ton truck-tractors. Mack, White, and Corbitt built 6 ton truck-tractors, and Mack built heavy 7 1/2 ton prime-movers. Except for Mack, which made its own engines and drive trains, the heavy-heavy producers were assemblers and secured their components from independent suppliers like the Hercules Motor Company of Canton, Ohio, which supplied power plants for most of the heavy-heavy trucks as well as smaller engines for the Studebaker built 2 1/2's which went to the Russians. Very specialized producers like Four-Wheel-Drive, Marmon-Harrington, Ward-La France, Brockway and the Biederman Truck Company of Cincinnati, Ohio, built heavy wreckers, pontoon carriers, and tank transporters.[28]

Just as in the First World War, the feedback loop posed serious problems. ASF logisticians complained that theater commanders abroad and the AGF at home seldom understood the connections between strategy and logistics. They insisted to no avail that they be involved from the earliest stages of strategic planning.[29] With an understandable though mislocated desire to maximize fighting power, army strategists gave top priority to combat divisions and their equipment at the expense of support organizations and general purpose motor transport. Army combat arms representatives and ordnance procurement officers simply took trucks for granted and, unless seriously pressed, never gave motor transport high priority. Tanks, self-propelled guns and other armored vehicles of all descriptions took precedence.[30]

Yet compared to other armies the Americans lived in the lap of luxury. In the European theater of operations (ETO) with which the remainder of the essay will be concerned, independent Transportation Corps organizations attached to the Communications Zone (COMMZ) and to army and corp in accord with the pooling principle introduced by AGF Chief General Lesley J. McNair gave strategic and operational mobility. For tactical mobility each American infantry and armored division had over 6000 transport and support vehicles. That included everything from jeeps and weapons carriers with the combat regiments to general purpose trucks and heavy-heavy specialized vehicles assigned to divisional quartermaster, artillery, signal, engineers and ordnance units. The truck shortage, at least in the ETO, was as much a matter of tables of organization and equipment, mix, and inefficient utilization as it was of actual scarcity.[31]

The first signs that truck priorities might cause trouble came from another direction. In late 1942 logisticians in the China-Burma-India theater (CBI) who were building a great motor transport base in Calcutta, India, to support the Ledo road across northern Burma into China, persuaded procurement officers in the Ordnance Motor Transportation Service to place modest orders for heavy-heavy trucks and tractor trailers. It was only later in the spring of 1943, during the latter stages of the campaign in Tunisia, that logisticians in Europe became convinced that more heavy-heavies were absolutely essential. By late 1943 requests were pouring in to change production priorities, which if implemented would increase production from 600 to 6000 of the big trucks and tractors a year. Such a program required at least twelve months' lead time, and production facilities in the United States were already swamped with higher priority work.

The ETO transportation crisis of the summer of 1944 was bred by success. The air interdiction of Normandy blasted the railroads and bridges between the beachhead and the Seine River to pieces and opened a logistical gap of seventy-five to a hundred miles, which pre-invasion planners had projected would take several months to repair. According to their calculations Allied forces would advance systematically and arrive at the Seine barrier about three months after D Day, giving sufficient time to restore the French logistical infrastructure. For the first month of the campaign there were few transportation difficulties. The battle moved more slowly than expected, and when "Operation Cobra" began on 25 July 1944, the Anglo-Americans were forty days behind schedule. But a month later Paris had fallen and American troops were approaching the German border. Rebuilding and repair fell far behind. With neither rail and water lines nor intermediate and forward depots immediately available to support the advance, it fell to the truckers to haul everything from the beaches to the battleline.

When the breakout and pursuit began, it wasn't that there were not enough trucks; it was that suddenly there was not enough of the kinds of trucks the theater wanted. All available transport was seized from wherever it could be found, and three new divisions which had arrived at Cherbourg were immobilized and their trucks used to support George S. Patton, Jr.'s Third Army and Courtney H. Hodge's First Army. Frantic calls for big trucks and tractor-trailers could not make up for lost production time. It was pure luck that divisional heavy trucks, transporters and prime-movers as well as heavy-heavies from independent engineer and ordnance field forces were available to add cargo capacity to the "Red Ball Express" and very fortunate indeed that some of the heavy-heavies, especially the 4X4 5 and 6 ton tractor-trailers ordered for the CBI in 1942, arrived in the autumn of 1944 in time to provide support during the last months of the war.[32]

Truck production lagged throughout the war. Only the manufacture of light trucks met procurement goals. Even production of the "deuce and a half" fell behind until late in the war. And in mid-1944 the hurried efforts to pick up the slack in heavy-heavy production upset procurement schedules across the industry. Final production figures revealed both the strengths and the shortcomings of the American automotive industry. Out of 2,382,311 trucks of all types delivered during the war, 2,228,625, or over 90 percent of total deliveries were light $^1/_4$ ton jeeps and $^3/_4$ ton weapons carriers, medium ton and a halfs and light-heavy two and a halfs. Over 800,000 were "deuce and a halfs," the most numerous single type procured,. The remaining 153,686 included heavy-heavy 4 to 7 $^1/_2$ ton prime-movers, truck-tractors, specialized heavy carriers, wreckers and tank transporters.[33]

It has been said that "in war the best is always the enemy of enough." The American wartime truck fleet may not have been the best, but at least it was enough. The vehicle mix could have been more appropriate, but given the pressure from the combat arms and using services to win the war with the "deuce and a half" as well as the contemporary structure of the American automobile industry, its configuration was understandable. After the war ordnance historians simply relegated the debate to "honest differences of opinion," asserting that production and deployment of greater numbers of light and light-heavy trucks had given "little cause for regret."[34]

V

It is appropriate to end this essay with an old logisticians maxim: "Amateurs study tactics; professionals study logistics." On June 22, 1941, German troops in numbers never before committed to one battle crossed the Russian frontier. Organized in three great army groups and spearheaded by thousands of tanks and planes, they raced forward from the Ukraine to the Baltic in "Operation Barbarossa," precipitating the greatest battles of encirclement and annihilation in modern history. The "blitzkrieg myth," based on the quick successes of German arms in Poland and France and embroidered by the self-serving apologias of defeated generals and out-maneuvered politicians, continued for a time, but the German army was not really the mechanical marvel of the era at all. It was the creation of soldiers and politicians who went to war with an inadequate industrial base and who would not or could not face all the realities that entailed. The Germans relied too heavily on the nineteenth-century eastern European railroad system to support a mechanized campaign that outran its logistical support in the first seventy-two hours of battle. Behind the mechanized spearheads slogged the infantry and behind them plodded the horse drawn support of the *Wehrmacht*. The campaign floundered at least in part because the Germans lacked motor transport in sufficient quantities. Three years later Anglo-American soldiers were shocked when they surveyed the carnage in the Falaise Gap—roads choked with the wreckage of wagons and the swollen carcasses of hundreds of horses. The Germans still lacked that most prosaic part of the logistical system of a modern army, the motor truck.[35] But American and British forces were fully motorized and operated on an industrial model of warfare marking the maturation of the industrial revolution, which had begun a hundred years earlier. War certainly was no longer simply a business for soldiers. The demands of the battlefront integrated the total resources of societies, and the Anglo-Americans developed effective systems of production and control and effective feedback loops to improve weapons and equipment. It was fortunate for the Allies that Chancellor Hitler, who preferred the study of tactics to the less exciting examination of logistics, refused to mobilize the German economy for total war until it was too late.[36]

By the end of the Second World War, the ubiquitous "deuce and a half" had became a symbol of modern, corporate internal combustion culture and a microcosm of American military prowess.[37] The motor transport program was pronounced a smashing success by General Somervell, who wrote: "When Hitler put his war on wheels, he drove it right straight down our alley." General Marshall wrote that the greatest advantage in equipment the United States had enjoyed in the fighting on the ground had been its multi-drive motor equipment, principally the Jeep and the 2 1/2 ton truck, which had moved the United States troops in battle while the German army still depended heavily on animal transport. The United States, he concluded, profiting from the mass production achievements of its automotive industry, motorized all its forces and supplied the British and Russian armies as well. But even then American combat soldiers still gave their colleagues engaged in logistics only perfunctory recognition. In 1944 after nearly three years of distinguished work as Director of Material in the ASF, General Lucius D. Clay's plaintive request of General Somervell, "Can I go to war, NOW?" revealed that at least one logistician had not yet completely achieved recognition, even in his own eyes, as a "real soldier."[38]

Notes

1. The author is grateful to the editors of the *Journal of Military History* (formerly *Military Affairs*) for permission to use portions of this essay, which appeared as "Politics and Policy: The War Department Motorization and Standardization Program 1920-1940" in *Military Affairs* (October 1983).

2. Graham A. Cosmas, *An Army for Empire: The United States Army in the Spanish American War* (Columbia, Missouri: 1971); Daniel R. Beaver, "Logistics: Managing and Coordinating American Military Supply in Historical Perspective" in John E. Jessup (ed), *The Encyclopedia of the American Military* (New York, Forthcoming) hereinafter cited as "Logistics."

3. The best discussion of the office of Quartermaster General in the nineteenth century is Erna Risch, *Quartermaster Support of the Army: A History of the Corps 1775-1939* (Washington, DC: 1962).

4. See Major Stephen Vincent Benét to Secretary of War William W. Belnap, May 21, 1973 and Quartermaster General Montgomery C. Meigs to Secretary of War Belnap, May 27, 1973 in *A Collection of Ordnance Reports and Other Important Papers Relating to the Ordnance Department Taken from the Records of the Ordnance Office and Other Sources*, 4 vols (Washington, DC: 1878-1890), 3:72-74, for an example of the correspondence involved in the battle for control of wagon manufacturing after the Civil War.

5. James A. Huston, *The Sinews of War: Army Logistics 1775-1953* (Washington, DC: 1966), p. 296.

6. Maj. William C. Dunckel, "The Procurement and Maintenance of Automotive Vehicles in the Next War," Appendix 4 (Army War College, Fort Humphreys, Washington DC, January 1938) in US Army Military History Collection, Carlisle Barracks, Penn. For a full discussion of maintenance problems during the war see John C. Speedy III, "From Mules to Motors: Development of Doctrine for Motor Vehicle Maintenance by the United States Army" (Ph.D. diss., Duke University, 1977). For the AEF's failure to understand the problems of "production lag" and the difficulties of modifying equipment already on order within limited time requirements see Harvey A. DeWeerd, "Production Lag in the American Ordnance Program 1917-1918" (Ph.D. diss., University of Michigan, 1940).

7. See Norman M. Cary, Jr., "The Use of the Motor Vehicle in the United States Army 1899-1939" (Ph.D. diss., University of Georgia, 1980), for the early years of the military truck program.

8. The War Department was moving along organizational lines which paralleled those being followed by major industrial firms like Dupont, Sears-Roebuck and General Electric. The continuing organization revolution of which it was a part linked corporate America and government in ways far removed from the *laissez-faire* system sentimentalized in the rhetoric of the Harding and Coolidge administrations. It was more in harmony with the "New Era" Progressivism of the Department of Commerce under Herbert Hoover, which was articulated more clearly after the latter became president in 1929. See Alfred D. Chandler, *Strategy and Structure: Chapters in the History of the Industrial Enterprise* (Boston: 1962) and Ellis Hawley, *The Great War and the Search for a Modern Order: A History of the American People and Their Institutions 1917-1933*, new ed. (New York: 1990.) For similar interpretive approaches in military affairs see James E. Hewes, *From Root to McNamara: Army Organization and Administration 1900-1963* (Washington, DC: 1975), and Daniel R. Beaver, "The Problem of Military Supply 1890-1920," in B. Franklin Cooling (ed.) *War, Business and American Society: Historical Perspectives on the Military-Industrial Complex* (Port Washington, NY: 1977), pp. 73-92.

9. Richard M. Leighton and Robert W. Coakley, *The War Department: Global Logistics and Strategy*, 2 vols. (Washington, DC: 1955-1968), 1:10, hereinafter cited as *Global Logistics*.

10. Ray S. Cline, *The War Department: Washington Command Post: The Operations Division* (Washington, DC: 1951), pp. 1-7; 258-61.

11. Leighton and Coakley, *Global Logistics*, 1:26-27.

12. Hewes, *From Root to McNamara*, pp. 54-55.

13. For a full discussion of the decision making process on equipment see Army Industrial College study, "Specifications and Standardization," Problem 16A, Part I, pp. 3-7 (Washington, DC: 1928-1929), in US Army Military History Collection, Carlisle Barracks, Penn., hereinafter cited as "Specifications and Standardization."

14. R. Elberton Smith, *The War Department: The Army and Economic Mobilization* (Washington, DC: 1958), p. 43.

15. *War Department Annual Reports, 1920*, 1:1915; *War Department Annual Reports, 1921*, 1:28-29.

16. Maurice Matloff, *American Military History* (Washington, DC: 1969), p. 416.

17. *War Department Annual Reports, 1921*, 1:150-51.

18. Adjutant General to Quartermaster General, July 15, 1926, as quoted in *Report of Administration of Motor Transport Branch, Office of the Quartermaster General* (June 30, 1932); Adjutant General to Quartermaster General, Feb. 21, 1929, *War Department Annual Reports, 1932*.

19. Biography of Col. Brainerd Taylor, n.p., mss; "War Department Policy on Motor Vehicle Procurement 1939-1940, Minutes of a Conversation with General DeWitt" (Dec. 9, 1939), US Army Military History Collection, Carlisle Barracks, Penn.; Dewitt to Adjutant Gen., Oct. 5, 1931, in *Report of Administration of Motor Transport Branch, Office of the Quartermaster General* (June 30, 1932); Harry C. Thompson and Lyda Mayo, *The Ordnance Department: Procurement and Supply* (Washington, DC: 1960), p. 268; Cary, "Use of Motor Vehicles," p. 216.

20. For example, the infantry insisted that it had to have a 1 1/2 ton truck with an unloaded weight of 950 pounds. It could only be slowly custom produced on a one-by-one basis. See Captain E. W. Ridings, "Motor Vehicle Procurement" (Dec. 9, 1939), US Army Military History Collection, Carlisle Barracks, Penn.

21. Adjutant General to QMG, Nov. 16, 1931; William R. White, "Motor Vehicle Maintenance in a Theater of Operations" (Feb. 15, 1932); Dunckel, "Automotive Vehicles"; A. W. Rogers, "Memo for the Commandant of the Army War College," Dec. 9, 1939, including "Minutes of a Discussion with General DeWitt," US Army Military History Collection, Carlisle Barracks, Penn.; Thompson and Mayo, *Procurement and Supply*, pp. 268-69; Sydney Fine, *The Automobile Industry Under the Blue Eagle: Management and the Automobile Manufacturing Code* (Ann Arbor: 1963); Ellis Hawley, *The New Deal and the Problem of Monopoly* (Princeton: 1965).

22. Dunckel, "Automotive Vehicles," Appendix 8; Ridings, "Motor Vehicle Procurement," Appendix 5; Chief of Infantry to QMG, July 26, 1938; Minutes of the QM Technical Committee, June 26, 1936; AGO file, RG 94, National Archives, Washington, DC; Mark L. Watson, *Chief of Staff: Pre-War Plans and Preparations* (Washington, DC: 1950); Allan Nevins and Frank D. Hill, *Ford: Decline and Rebirth 1933-1962* (New York: 1963).

23. Secretary of War to Quartermaster General, August 12, 1939, US Army Military History Collection, Carlisle Barracks, Penn.

24. Thompson and Mayo, *Procurement and Supply*, p. 271; A. Wade Wells, *Hail to the Jeep* (New York: 1946) and Herbert F. Rifkind, *The Jeep —Its Development and Procurement Under the QMC 1940-1942* (Ordnance Historical File, RG 92, NA, Washington, DC). The original 2 1/2 ton contract went to the Yellow Truck Company which was later absorbed by GMC. Studebaker, International, and Reo also made "deuce and a half"s. The only big loser was the American Bantam Car Company, which had originally conceived of the small general purpose and reconnaissance vehicle. When the "Jeep" contracts were awarded, the small Pennsylvania firm was cut completely out of the action.

25. Forrest C. Pogue, *George C. Marshall: Organizer of Victory* (New York: 1973), pp. 67-102; Hewes, *From Root to McNamara*, pp. 67-102.

26. John D. Millett, *The Army Service Forces: The Organization and Role of the Army Service Forces* (Washington, DC: 1954), pp. 23-42.

27. The QMG recommended freezing designs in 1941. See Memorandum QMG to Under Secretary of War Patterson, "Procurement of Motor Vehicles by Negotiation,"

April 15, 1941; QM 451 M-P, Chief of Ordnance File, 1940-1941, RG 156, Federal Records Center, Suitland, Maryland. Making changes in a vehicle while continuing production uninterrupted was one of the important engineering and managerial breakthroughs of the war. For a brilliant discussion of the problem of major change orders and their impact on production in a much more sophisticated arena see I. B. Holley, *Buying Aircraft: Material Procurement for the Army Air Forces* (Washington, DC: 1964).

28. Specifications and photographs of all vehicles procured during the war can be found in the Ordnance Research and Development Service notebook of March 1945, *A Handbook of Transport Vehicle Engineering* (RG 156, Federal Records Center, Suitland, Maryland). Fred Crismon, *US Military Wheeled Vehicles* (Andover, New Jersey: 1983) is the most complete and easily available book about army trucks, but there are many pictures and some data reproduced from original sources in J. Hoffschmidt and W.H. Tantum (eds.), *U.S. Military Vehicles, World War II* (Boulder, Colorado: 1979).

29. Beaver, "Logistics," pp. 132-34.

30. It would be interesting to speculate about what would have happened if control of soft and general purpose transport had remained in the Quartermaster General's hands or been transferred to the new Transportation Corps. But that is beyond the scope of this essay.

31. Immediately after the war the army in Europe conducted a full study of the use of general purpose motor transport during the war. See William M. Hines, *History of the General Purpose Vehicle: Its Availability and Utilization in the European Theater of Operations*, 6 vols. (Washington, DC: 1945). In *Eisenhower's Lieutenants: The Campaigns of France and Germany 1944-1945* (Bloomington, Indiana: 1981), Russell F. Weigley states that it took six truck companies from corps or army to put the infantry of an American division on wheels. That is not quite right. General McNair never quite got the "lean and mean" divisional organization that he wanted. In a pinch, a division could mount up effectively simply by putting its own organic transport to full use.

32. This section has been synthesized from the accounts found in the American official histories of World War II: Gordon A. Harrison, *European Theater of Operations: Cross Channel Attack* (Washington, DC: 1951); Martin Blumenson, *European Theater of Operations: Breakout and Pursuit* (Washington, DC: 1961); Roland G. Ruppenthal, *European Theater of Operations: Logistical Support of the Armies*, 2 vols. (Washington, DC: 1953-1959); Harry C. Thompson and Lyda Mayo, *Procurement and Supply*; Lyda Mayo, *The Ordnance Department: On Beachhead and Battlefront* (Washington, DC: 1968); Alfred M. Beck, Abe Bortz, Charles W. Lynch, Lida Mayo and Ralph E. Weld, *The Corps of Engineers: The War Against Germany* (Washington, DC: 1985); and William F. Ross and Charles F. Romanus, *The Quartermaster Corps: Operations in the War Against Germany* (Washington, DC: 1965).

33. Smith, *The Army and Economic Mobilization*, pp. 9-10; Thompson and Mayo, *Procurement and Supply*, pp. 290-96. Deliveries of heavy trucks were ahead of schedule in early 1942, but that reflected the small number and low priority of the contracts. What was available in some quantity was a 4/4 Chevrolet truck-tractor built on a modified standard 1 $^1/_2$ ton chassis capable of towing a six ton semi-trailer over improved roads.

34. Constance M. Green, Harry Thompson and Peter C. Roots, *The Ordnance Department: Planning Munitions for War* (Washington, DC: 1955), p. 277. The authors give one paragraph to trucks in a volume of over 500 pages.

35. Max Hastings, *OVERLORD: D Day and the Battle for Normandy* (New York: 1984), p. 311. For a general discussion of the weaknesses of the German army see Basil Liddell-Hart, *History of the Second World War* (London: 1973). For an account of the weaknesses of German logistics on the eastern front and in Normandy see Martin van Creveld, *Supplying War: Logistics from Wallenstein to Patton* (London: 1977), pp. 142-80, 202-30.

36. Ralph W. Baldwin, *The Deadly Fuse* (San Raphael, California: 1980), p. 296.

37. Thompson and Mayo, *Procurement and Supply*, p. 281.

38. Thompson and Mayo, *Procurement and Supply*, p. 281; *Biennial Report of the Chief of Staff of the United States Army*, July 1, 1945, pp. 95-96. For excellent new biographies of two leading American logisticians see John K. Ohl, *General Supply: General Brehon B. Sommervell and the American War Effort* (forthcoming) and Gene E. Smith, *Lucius Clay: An American Life* (New York: 1990).

12

War Plans and Politics: Origins of the American Base of Supply in Vietnam

Joel D. Meyerson

The picture of ground and helicopter assaults pushing rapidly through paddies and jungle obscures the complex preparations that precede and support them. When the United States committed its forces to combat in 1965, it fielded an army whose logistics was emerging with difficulty from a decade of fragmentation and institutional neglect. Years spent sustaining a limited advisory and assistance effort, and planning for conventional war, had only hinted at the inescapable boundaries of action and political circumstance that would attend the development of a supply system while Washington experimented with escalation and reprisals. Long after troops had gone ashore to fight, the American military in Vietnam awaited the most basic policy decisions on such issues as supply organization, support levels, and procurement. This reluctance to address the hard choices on the structure of supply encapsulated the whole nervous ambivalence toward American involvement in the Vietnam War.

The Strategic Prospect

The deployment of logistical units in the spring of 1965 marked the formal beginning of the support base, but the origins of the system went back to the planning for intervention many months earlier. The United States had been anything but eager to enter more forthrightly and at increased cost and risk into a war that had been going badly for the Republic of Vietnam since 1963. The growing aggressiveness of the Communist-led guerrillas, or Viet Cong, and the rampant instability of the government in Saigon had offered little immediate hope for military improvement, with or without American ground forces. Yet even as American officials were publicly reaffirming the existing policy of contributing only equipment and counsel, the United States was tilting toward progressively stronger military measures to achieve its objective of independence for South Vietnam. By the summer of 1964, strategists of political war and limited military assistance had drifted out of the policy making circles at the State and Defense departments in favor of officials who were disposed to applying a greater degree of military force. For the first time in the long involvement, there was serious planning at the interdepartmental level for actions against North Vietnam, including covert operations much more ambitious than those that had been authorized three years earlier, and the identification of targets suitable for American air attack. With the quiet encouragement of President Lyndon B. Johnson, the broad spectrum of official opinion was slowly coalescing around the idea that intervention in some form would be necessary to save South Vietnam. While future operations had still not been fully delineated in terms of objectives and supporting courses of action as 1964 came to a close, the Joint Chiefs of Staff and the army were already well along in their investigations of the logistical requirements and readiness that would be needed for an expanded war.

From one point of view the investigations were merely a continuation of the war games and exercises that had been held intermittently for Southeast Asia since the early 1950s. But in a larger perspective they were a new and critical development. For with this updating and clarifying of support requirements, processed under the pressure of a growing crisis in the conduct of the war, the question of logistics in Vietnam was permanently displaced in official thinking onto a higher and more comprehensive plane of strategic urgency. By late 1964, the issue of Vietnam's military role in Pacific strategy, often touched on but addressed with little consistency during the previous decade, was being infused with entirely fresh meaning and conspicuous importance. Defects of design in the logistical system in the theater that had been more or less tolerated during the desultory combat of the counterinsurgency period now seemed, with the possible approach of a major war, intolerably threatening.

Military planners had no doubt in 1965 about the extent of Vietnam's lagging development as a theater of operations and the acute dangers this posed to the safety of American policy. In the eleven years since the crisis at Dien Bien Phu, when logistics had weighed so heavily in the American decision against intervening to save the French, the only significant logistical improvements recorded, besides a project for a road network in the Central Highlands, had been those efforts financed by America's Military Assistance Program and geared to support the battle against the guerrillas in the countryside. While such projects had provided a certain "bonus effect" in satisfying some of the requirements in the contingency plans for the deployment of American forces to Southeast Asia, Vietnam remained, just as it had always been, a mostly harsh, primitive, agrarian country lacking in skilled labor, vital facilities, and basic supplies. Construction costs for ports, highways, storage and maintenance areas, and communications promised to be enormous in the event of an outbreak of a major war.[1]

The ports offered one of the more formidable obstacles to the first requirement of a successful intervention, which was to feed in troops and materiel at a rate higher than the enemy's. Although Saigon and the secondary ports, according to the latest American surveys, had enough commercial and military wharfage to unload some 21,000 tons of freight a day, which was more than triple the maritime replenishment believed to be needed during a North Vietnamese and Chinese invasion, the amount of military cargo could be cleared from the ports and pushed inland to combat units was estimated at a little over half of discharge capacity. Yet even this figure was suspect, ignoring as it did the obsolescence of much of the handling equipment on the wharves and quays in Saigon and elsewhere—the cargo cranes, fork lifts, and tractors of various kinds—as well as the nonquantifiable problems of security and maintenance on the roads, rail lines, and waterways leading from the seaports. According to a 1964 base development plan prepared at the headquarters of U.S. Army, Pacific, in Honolulu, the three secondary ports at Nha Trang, Qui Nhon, and Da Nang would suffer a 50 percent decline in efficiency if operations had to be sustained at a high level of intensity for more than two weeks. It looked as though port clearance operations would be a major logistical bottleneck if the United States were forced to deploy rapidly into the war zone. To hedge against this possibility, military engineers had begun surveying the scores of beaches on the country's eastern coastal strip for possible sites for "over-the-shore" operations. The beaches, unfortunately, had their own serious drawbacks, the most forbidding being the impossibly high surf conditions during the Northeast monsoon season that extended from October to early April.[2]

If the ports and beaches were troublesome, so also were the country's highways. Apart from small stretches around Saigon and Ban Me Thuot which had been rehabilitated in the late 1950s by South Vietnamese engineers and American contractors, the capacity of the road system was entirely inadequate to sustain more than limited traffic, especially in the rainy season. It was not just the overall condition of the roads and bridges that alarmed American planners looking ahead to heavily laden supply convoys and fifty-ton medium tanks. It was the pattern of limiting sections in the road net as a whole, especially several lengths of highway in the Central Highlands, which threatened to impede the northward movement of cargo from Saigon into what was likely to be heavily contested terrain around Pleiku and Kontum. In one estimate, the critical link on Highway 14 from Ban Me Thuot to Pleiku had a wet season capacity of only 200 tons a day, far below the wet season capacities of the road sections immediately to the south. Given the critical importance of expanding the highways as early as possible after the onset of hostilities, a higher than standard proportion of engineer units, both combat and construction, was planned for inclusion in the first waves of troops going ashore.³

But there was another problem beyond that of ports, beaches, and highways which was central to the issue of readiness and emblematic of Vietnam's disadvantage as a theater of operations and its lack of development. The controlling logistical fact in the Pacific was the sheer expanse of that ocean and the enormous time and distance involved in moving men and supplies. A cargo ship at 15 knots required nineteen days to make the voyage of 6,900 nautical miles from San Francisco to Saigon, while a round trip by air from the west coast took some forty hours, depending on the kind of aircraft flown. Prepositioning troops and equipment in the theater was not the only way to reduce American reaction times over these distances. But it did hold out the promise of creating a more uniform flow of military force onto the battlefield, thereby easing the strain on strategic airlift in the Pacific, which was always in short supply, and reducing the likelihood of saturating the seaports with a pileup of merchant ships. The only difficulty with the idea of prepositioning, from the point of view of the theater's planners, was that the impressive buildup in supplies and forces that had taken place elsewhere in the western Pacific in recent years had not included South Vietnam.

The buildup had started in the Eisenhower administration with the formulation of the 32-59 Operation Plan, "Defense of Mainland Southeast Asia," and the army's decision as a consequence of that blueprint to increase the deployability of its forces in the western Pacific in order to be more competitive with the forward elements of the Marine Corps. By the early 1960s a long chain of forward staging areas and supply bases, anchored by U.S. Army, Ryukyu Islands, on Okinawa (the principal forward element of U.S. Army, Pacific), extended southwestward in a gradual arc from Japan to the hinterlands of Thailand. Large prepositioning complexes containing the equipment for quick reaction forces up to a division in size were now located on Okinawa and at Korat and Udorn in Thailand. The field testing in 1964 of a floating depot at Subic Bay in the Philippines consisting of three obsolete merchant ships stocked with enough equipment and supplies to support a brigade task force for two weeks of combat was the most recent step taken to reduce the army's penalty for long supply lines to Southeast Asia.⁴

These developments had no counterpart in Vietnam. As late as 1964 the 16,000 American advisers and support troops were being supplied from service depots offshore (Okinawa, Japan, and the Philippines respectively for the U.S. Army, Marine Corps, and Air Force). The only reserve stocks available in the country were some twenty days of petroleum product, the bulk of it kept in commercial storage at the port of Saigon, for current use by American support elements, chiefly aviation units.⁵ To logisticians whose goal in planning was having enough lead time to assemble troops and resources in sufficient quantity to influence the course of battle, this lack of a supply base was unendurable.

No one in the theater was more intent on establishing a formal service area on South Vietnamese soil than the Assistant Chief of Staff for Logistics (J-4) at Military Assistance Command, Vietnam, in Saigon, Brig. Gen. Frank A. Osmanski.[6] As early as 1962, just months after arriving for duty with the new unified headquarters for American forces in the country, he had called for a program of "Special Logistic Actions" in Vietnam. It was almost identical to the massive construction project which had just taken hold in Thailand under the same name and which was turning the country into an advance American logistical base—with storage sites, highways, and airfields—for use if it became necessary to send ground forces into Laos under the provisions of 32-59 or the war plans of the Southeast Asia Treaty Organization.[7] His proposal had gotten nowhere, a casualty of the Kennedy administration's commitment to counterinsurgency with its insistence on keeping military action in a minor key, subordinate to the political side of the war. The idea flickered and died within the headquarters.

He had fared no better in 1962 in calling for a logistical command. Once again events in Thailand, notably the experience of the 9th Logistical Command there, had offered him a glimmer of optimism. True, a small element of the 9th had been stationed at Korat for a relatively short period of time, having deployed from Okinawa to support an extended show of force by American combat units during the on-again, off-again civil war in neighboring Laos. But its expert management of the Special Logistic Actions in Thailand had made a deep impression on Osmanski, suggesting the good that a logistical command could do if given a clearly stated mission and support from Washington. Once again he was undone by political considerations outside his fixed orbit of influence, although not before the proposal attracted support up the military chain into the higher tiers of Department of the Army.

On technical grounds the proposal had merit. The unrestrained growth of logistical organizations in Vietnam because of the semiautonomous nature of American support agencies during the advisory period had resulted in rampant duplication, overlapping, and gaps in function. A dozen military and civilian bureaus provided logistical service to the advisory population. Four furnished utility repairs, and each service had its own medical supply organization with separate lines for requisitioning from the Pacific depots or from the United States.[8] Because a four-star Navy admiral at Honolulu, the commander in chief of American forces in the Pacific, exercised logistical responsibility for Southeast Asia, a navy organization had been established in Saigon to support the two joint headquarters in the city—Military Assistance Command and Military Assistance Advisory Group—and to furnish American troops with a number of "common-user" items that were shared across military service lines, such as rations, clothing, and post exchange supplies. But as a navy organization, General Osmanski pointed out, Headquarters Support Activity, Saigon, had neither the authority, the funding, nor the know-how required to support what was primarily a ground war. Each extension of its authority to fill a support need arising from the fighting became a time-consuming process requiring a formal extension of its charter by the Chief of Naval Operations back in Washington, a levy on the army or air force for the manpower to perform the service since the navy was underrepresented in the battle zone, plus a laborious negotiation on funding arrangements because the Navy insisted on being reimbursed for services it provided. More than a year passed before the support activity was able to obtain the various permissions and inter-service support agreements it needed to station military agents in the ports outside Saigon to oversee the transfer of military cargo from ship to aircraft for distribution to American advisers and stations inland. The agreement to start a joint clothing store in the capital with a retail mail order department to serve advisers and units at remote up-country locations took fourteen months to finalize. Yet the Pacific commander, Adm. Harry D. Felt, took serious exception to the efforts by Osmanski to supplement the support activity with an army organization, even though a logistical command, which had access to supply and transportation detachments throughout the active army, was in many ways designed for and uniquely capable of operating in the interstices of a joint environment. Felt believed that the U.S. Navy could do the job.[9]

But there was a larger obstacle to deploying a logistical command than a parochial skirmish between two services. Logistical commands were not among the venerable institutions in the tables of organization and equipment of the United States Army. Conceived in the War Department in 1944 by the chief logistical officer on the General Staff, Maj. Gen. Russell L. Maxwell, and organized and tested over the next several years at the Command and General Staff College at Fort Leavenworth, Kansas, the logistical command had been activated as a formal unit of the U.S. Army as recently as 1949. Two such commands had seen service during the Korean War, one at Pusan to provide replenishment for U.S. Eighth Army, the other near Inchon to sustain the U.S. X Corps. It was the one support unit in the army's hierarchy of organizations that was more or less comparable in organization and functioning to a combat division, a balanced grouping of combined technical and administrative services just as the infantry division was a balanced grouping of combat arms. And its mission was as clearly defined as that of a division. Whereas logistical rear areas, or communications zone sections, had been hastily thrown together during World War II with the confusion, wasted effort, and tendency toward empire building that were bound to occur in the absence of a standardized support system overseas, the logistical command was designed to bring organization to the communications zone before the zone started to function.

It was to provide a permanent structure of supply for combat units at the very beginning of battle. It was to anticipate the logistical demands of America's land wars.[10]

These organizing functions, which were not only outlined in each of the contingency plans for Southeast Asia but also considered crucial to their execution, explain why deploying a logistical command, whatever practical value it might have had, was also deemed an escalation of the conflict by most officials in Washington and thus unthinkable in Vietnam short of the threat of general war. As late as the summer of 1964, Osmanski's proposal was being dismissed by many as the premature and provocative musing of a strategic logistician nostalgic for the heavy support systems of World War II, that of a man who had been unwilling or unable to develop a low-level logistical control plan appropriate to the fragmented nature of guerrilla conflict, and who, in fact, on more than one occasion as J-4, had gone on record as seeing no practical or doctrinal difference between providing logistical support for a counterinsurgency and a conventional war.[11] When the Pacific command in 1964, on instructions from Secretary of Defense Robert S. McNamara, worked up another proposed course of military action, Operation Plan 37-64, to ensure stability in Laos and South Vietnam under conditions of limited conflict, the weight of American intervention was directed almost entirely through Thailand at the Laotian panhandle and points farther north where ground combat forces could be supported in mobile operations by previously deployed elements of the 9th Logistical Command and prepositioned stocks. Vietnam was to remain a holding action, and any American units landing in Saigon to secure the airfield as a mounting out base for future operations along the borders were to be provisioned as usual from Okinawa. There was nothing in the 37 Plan, or in the administration's policies generally, to suggest that a strategic buildup might be desirable in South Vietnam.[12]

Plans for a Logistical Command

This deliberate caution at the highest levels, frustrating for so long to so many planners, slowly and hesitantly began to change in late 1964. Gradually the point of view that had kept logistics decentralized and uneconomical, and that was expressed in a policy of limited assistance to the South Vietnamese, gave way to a growing acceptance of the logic and inevitability of more direct American participation in the Vietnam War. The steady decline in South Vietnamese military strength in the provinces, punctuated in early August by the dramatic naval clash in the Gulf of Tonkin between American and North Vietnamese forces, seemed to offer the United States no practical alternative but to escalate the war or allow the communists to prevail. In this context, the administration's decision to increase American forces in Southeast Asia as part of a controlled program of graduated pressure against the Viet Cong and the North Vietnamese produced new requirements for supply and transport that could only be met by reforming and expanding the logistical effort. Although the initial deployments to the theater represented no shift in national policy but were rather an intensification of the existing advisory effort in a sort of last cleaving to counterinsurgency, it was only a matter of months before the crisis on the South Vietnamese battlefield forced upon the White House a definitive transformation in its strategy of war.

Washington approved the new forces in August, and they constituted a sufficiently large expansion in soldiers and supplies, as well as equipment (a 50 percent increase in troops alone), to send the services scrambling, particularly the army staff, to meet the administration's urgent schedules of activation and deployment. By the end of 1964, the authorized strength of American forces in Vietnam had risen to nearly 23,000. Advisers composed about one-fifth of the total and could now be found in South Vietnamese army battalions as well as at the district level in eight provinces judged to be critical, doubling the number of locations of advisers at the end of the communications and supply lines. To help connect the two hundred fifty American stations scattered about the country and to improve South Vietnamese mobility, the air force deployed a fourth squadron of C-123 transports, the army a third company of CV-2B cargo planes, or Caribous, while seventy-five helicopters, UH-1B light-transport "Hueys" with turbine engines, the latest helicopters in the army's inventory, were taken directly from the production lines at Bell Helicopter in Fort Worth to form two airmobile companies and two airlift platoons. In the words of the commander of American forces in Vietnam, Gen. William C. Westmoreland, the increase in advisers, aircraft, and support units, and the ensuing surge in construction for messes, billets, motor pools, and medical facilities, as well as maintenance hangers and parking areas at nine major airfields from Soc Trang to Da Nang, became "the straw that broke the camel's back" of an already overburdened and diffuse structure of logistical support.[13] As early as August he warned Honolulu and Washington against compressing the scheduled arrival of American forces because of the saturated condition of the airfields and the inadequacy of cantonments in the provinces. He also asked army officials in early October about the availability of sixty-five support units in the United States, how fast they could be organized, equipped, and trained, and which of them could be sent to Vietnam by the end of December. This was the first intimation Department of the Army staff had that Westmoreland's J-4, General Osmanski, was again working up a recommendation for introducing a logistical command. The search for support units had only just begun when the Osmanski proposal reached the Commander-in-Chief, Pacific, at the end of October.[14]

If the mood in the administration in Washington was still one of caution on intervening in force, the new commander in Honolulu, Adm. Ulysses S.G.

Sharp, was already clearing the decks for war. He had succeeded Admiral Felt in late June 1964 as commander of the Pacific theater and barely a week later had suggested to his staff that it was time to free the navy from the anomalous mission of providing for a ground war in South Vietnam. After his destroyer and carrier forces had skirmished and been bloodied in the Gulf of Tonkin, he was one of the few high ranking officials who had unhesitatingly advocated a continuing buildup in the western Pacific, including troops, ships, aircraft, and logistical resources, in order to maintain a credible threat and keep the leadership in Hanoi in doubt as to American intentions.[15] While the administration continued to temporize through early November so as not to jeopardize its chances in the elections, he and his staff had pressed forward with the detailed force tailoring that would be needed to sustain combat in Vietnam under various contingency plans. Convinced that intervention was approaching and that an efficient support base must be introduced well ahead of time, he had no sooner received the Osmanski draft study than he expanded it and sharpened it for the coming war.

Two months later, in December 1964, the finished blueprint for the army logistical command, restructured and reordered by the admiral's staff, was ready to be transmitted to the Joint Chiefs of Staff in Washington. It had not been an easy piece of work to pull together. The danger of asking too much too quickly of an administration still feeling its way forward on the war had placed the document at risk from the beginning and was never fully resolved before completion of the final draft in late December. The most serious threat to the workability of the plan had been a belated inclusion of a construction group of engineers numbering 2,400 men to help alleviate the two-year backlog in projects facing the primary civilian contractor in the theater, Raymond, Morrison-Knudsen, and to prepare for requirements in 1965 when the buildup of American forces was expected to accelerate. No one in Honolulu questioned the need for the engineers, but the construction group more than doubled the number of troops in the proposal to 4,331. It was a figure that left many planners profoundly uneasy.[16]

However, several changes in the initial draft significantly improved its prospects for approval. For example, the Joint Chiefs alerted Sharp to the bilateral agreements being negotiated for the introduction of allied troops into Vietnam, and of the almost certain deployment of South Koreans and Filipinos sometime within the next year. Although the American contribution to the foreign contingents was still being processed in December, massive subsidies could not be ruled out. The need for a logistical system fully adaptable to "third country" requirements figured importantly in the admiral's request for introduction of the logistical command.[17]

The dominant tone of the blueprint, however, not only its reasoned argument and comprehensiveness but also its skillful and compelling picture of the coming year, was the achievement of the staff in Honolulu, notably the planners working for the theater army G-4, Maj. Gen. Andrew J. Adams. It was they who took the terse recommendations of the Osmanski original, which they thought had been too cautiously "addressed to the present military assistance environment," and broadened them to fit the ever growing possibility of large-scale combat in Vietnam involving American ground forces.[18] They made no attempt to minimize the difficult challenges incident to deployment, from the problems of phasing in the logistical units and the likely changes in the relationship among the services to the expected impact of the logistical command on the activities of the offshore bases, U.S. Army, Ryukyu Islands, especially.

But their most significant contribution to the blueprint, reaching farther and anticipating more of the future than their other contibutions, was their refinement, indeed their wholesale overhaul, of the troop list drawn up for the logistical command. For once they stripped down and reconstituted the roster of units and introduced a small number of companies and platoons to establish logistical services in the secondary ports—a full range of services from depot supply, transportation, and maintenance by ordnance and engineer elements to construction and terminal support at the water's edge. The theater, which for years had seemed so shapeless and unsettled to those responsible for sustaining the advisory effort, was never conceived of in quite those terms again. The blueprint did not constitute a complete and unambiguous commitment to a communications zone divided along geographical fault lines into discrete and coherent regions of logistical support, but the implications were unmistakable to military professionals. Months in advance of intervention, the planners were calling for an "area system" of supply and distribution founded on a command headquarters in Saigon and a series of semiautonomous coastal installations or complexes reaching from Da Nang and Qui Nhon in the North through Nha Trang and Vung Tau into the Mekong Delta. It was testimony to the military's confidence in the overwhelming persuasiveness of this area concept and its fit to strategic circumstances that they had already obtained the rights to warehouses on the Da Nang and Saigon waterfronts and were awaiting the authority to rehabilitate them when the blueprint was formally submitted in mid January to the highest levels of the Defense Department, bringing key issues into focus, and becoming entwined in a dramatic escalation of the Vietnam War.[19]

Toward a War Footing

The turn toward force, which McNamara warned the president in late January could be delayed no longer, arrived in sudden and startling fashion two weeks later. On February 7, and again on the 8th and 11th, Johnson ordered reprisal air raids against the North after enemy guerrillas struck American installations at Pleiku and Qui Nhon, killing thirty-one soldiers and wounding more than a hundred. In the next few days, dissatisfied with the strategic implications of his tit-for-tat policy, the president took the next step up the ladder of escalation toward a wider war, authorizing the start of the sustained bombing offensive called Rolling Thunder, which the Joint Chiefs and Pacific command had been planning since November.

It was a watershed in American policy. For the bombers had no sooner started north in a measured program of graduated air attacks than serious discussions began in Washington on dispatching ground troops to the South, both to protect the American air bases supporting the offensive (two battalions of marines would go ashore at Da Nang on March 8) and to improve the readiness of American forces in Southeast Asia to cope with a North Vietnamese or Chinese military riposte. Logistics was only one element in these high level deliberations of February and March as the commitment of combat units hung in the political balance. But once a decision was made on preparing a support base to receive American soldiers, other decisions followed in evolutionary order from the administration, not perhaps with the speed or precision that the Joint Chiefs and theater commanders thought advisable but with just enough cumulative administrative force to begin swinging the theater of operations to a wartime footing.

The logistical command was approved on February 12 "in principle" after the Defense Department sent a team of logistical professionals to Saigon to confirm the deficiencies in the supply system. It was not yet the fully articulated structure of four thousand soldiers, including the engineer construction battalions, that Sharp and Osmanski had requested a month before. The Johnson administration remained determined in February to avoid a major increase in forces in Vietnam as well as new commitments for cantonments and other facilities not already programmed in the current year's defense budget. Nonetheless, the decision to deploy an advance party of seventy-five men, which would include a planning group of thirty-eight for Saigon, and seven detachments of thirty-seven others for the secondary ports to arrive before the end of March, was an event of major importance. It was the first tacit acknowledgment by officials in Washington that any significant future troop deployments would likely so strain the existing logistical base as to reduce the operational effectiveness of combat units. The decision was important from another point of view: almost as soon as it was promulgated in Washington, pressure arose from the military leadership to expand it.[20]

Within days of the start of air attacks, Sharp and Westmoreland began raising storm warnings about the vulnerability of Vietnam's ports, highways, and airfields to Viet Cong interference. The warnings grew measurably more insistent in March as positive evidence developed of strong enemy concentrations in the Central Highlands, including elements of a North Vietnamese division. Westmoreland interpreted these concentrations as the earliest indication of the revival of an old Viet Minh strategy against the French to drive eastward to the coast when the rainy season started, thereby dividing the country and interdicting the north-south supply routes. Convinced that disaster was in the offing and quietly encouraged by the Johnson administration to ask for what he wanted, Westmoreland saw no practical alternative but to commit American battalions for offensive action, at the very least in the strategic highlands but also in the area around Saigon and perhaps Da Nang. The Joint Chiefs, after quickly endorsing the proposal, expanded it to three full divisions (two American and one South Korean) toward the end of March.[21]

By this time, the theater's "limiting logistical factors" had begun to loom large in Washington. Working groups had convened before at the Pentagon to take up the requirements for intervention in Southeast Asia and to offer detailed recommendations, but never in less abstracted, less academic circumstances than the service secretaries and the military staffs found themselves in in March once the troop requests reached the Defense Department. Years of nagging uncertainty about the theater and the hazards of transoceanic supply came to a focus in a few urgent weeks of high-level conferences that defined with greater clarity and precision than before the actions the administration needed to take immediately in order to lay the groundwork for war. The recommendations grappled with fundamental sources of unpreparedness from the need to enlarge the theater's ports and fuel storage capacity and to stockpile construction materiel offshore within a few days sailing time to the importance of deploying the full logistical command to Saigon and obtaining critical holdings of real estate from the South Vietnamese government and even going to Congress if no quick release funds were available in the current budget for a supplemental appropriation on the war.[22]

But another logistical problem was brought into the open by the request for ground troops. It was no secret in planning circles that full implementation of the 32 Plan without a call-up of army reserve units would deplete the logistical base in the United States, making impossible reinforcement of Europe in event of war or full support of the plan for the invasion of Cuba—or for any other major contingency for that matter, such as reconstituting the land line of communications in Western Europe to serve the Atlantic alliance through the rest of the decade. But the 32 Plan, the community of military planners now knew, was itself suspect logistically. According to the latest analysis from Department of the Army, many of the support units in the regular forces earmarked for deployment to Southeast Asia would simply not be available in the first critical months to sustain the ground troops, not only because of the lead time required to bring them up to full strength prior to commitment but also because strategic airlift capability appeared to have been overstated in 1964 and was not now available from the units of the air force's Military Air Transport Service in anything like the quantity required. Barring emergency personnel procedures, and mobilization of the Air Force Reserve and civil air fleet, which would require a presidential declaration of national emergency,

American infantrymen, the Joint Chiefs pointedly warned in March, were going to enter the war in Vietnam with too little support.[23]

These were the paramount concerns of the military planners, what they thought of as self-evident dangers in need of attention, when the White House in mid March took active control of the intervention, imposing its own measured pace upon ground deployments. The ensuing behind-the-scenes decisions made just enough headway to satisfy the military without raising alarms in Congress or among the public. A first decision was made in a meeting with McNamara and the Joint Chiefs on the 15th when the president agreed to recommendations from the army Chief of Staff, Gen. Harold K. Johnson, just back from Saigon, and ordered the dispatch of ten landing ships to theater waters in an effort to reorient supply flow from the north-south coastal axis based on Saigon to the shorter and less vulnerable ocean axis of east to west. It was not in itself a difficult decision in the sense of producing an immediate and highly visible buildup of men and equipment. The LSTs (landing ship, tank) would not arrive in Vietnamese waters for many weeks, nor would dredges, also approved, begin deepening key harbors for merchant ships until a survey of the coast was completed in the spring. But the decision did convey a signal of administration intent to the military leadership, a perception that was bluntly reinforced at the same meeting when President Johnson urged the Joint Chiefs of Staff to propose measures to kill more Viet Cong. Five days later, on March 20, the day the Joint Chiefs first submitted their proposal to commit three divisions to combat, the administration took another step toward a fuller support base along the coast, approving the construction of a new runway at Da Nang air base and a jet airfield farther south at Chu Lai, two projects Pacific headquarters had been pushing as construction priorities since the fall of 1964.[24]

The main priority of the theater's planners, a decision for a complete logistical command and engineer construction group, took place during a meeting of the National Security Council on the 1st of April. After months of anxiety and vacillation, and with his military and civilian advisers obviously at loggerheads over the question of ground troops, the president negotiated a middle course between the extremes of staff opinion, deferring the three-division force for the moment at least but approving what amounted to its logistical train for deployment, plus two more battalions of marines and an enlargement of their mission. If the decision fell short of the military's wishes, it still offered a serious commitment of American ground forces, approving not just the original proposal for a theater logistical command (afterward amended to a contingent of 5,900 soldiers) but also 13,000 more spaces in over a hundred additional support units, among them a second engineer group to speed construction of new bases, depots, ports, and airfields.[25]

In the days that followed, the president's intent in approving the 19,000 would become the focus of acrimonious debate in Washington, various

Defense officials claiming that the increase was designed with existing or previously approved forces in mind, the Joint Chiefs convinced it constituted nothing less than the beginning of the long-awaited supply base in Vietnam and presaged the early introduction of large combat formations. While Defense civilians fought a rear guard action, the uniformed military pressed forward, refining their deployment lists, certain that time was of the essence.[26]

Time was on the minds of many observers as the war moved into April and toward the start of the summer rainy season when the enemy was expected to resume its nationwide offensive. The sense that the logistical troops had been approved at the eleventh hour, with little regard to the logistical facts of life, was never far from the surface of military opinion. This perception began to be reinforced in the most direct and compelling fashion in early April with news from Department of the Army that arrival of the engineer construction element, which was expected to pace the rate of arrival of all other support units, had slipped until sometime in May. Some theater officials, such as American ambassador Maxwell D. Taylor, long irritated by the talk of a combat buildup, took the news of slippage more or less in stride and withheld judgment. They were awaiting the results of Marine Corps operations around Da Nang and Phu Bai, hoping these actions would stiffen the South Vietnamese army.[27] The view from Westmoreland's headquarters was a good deal less hopeful. Already in April there were signs of hastening deterioration in the northern provinces, prompting speculation that American divisions would have to intervene much sooner than expected, much sooner, in other words, than bases would be ready to receive and properly sustain them. The problem remained theoretical for the moment at least, but no one was taking short odds against the possibility—the fact that it was beginning to look increasingly as though combat troops would come ashore with their logistical units, or even ahead of them, the worst of nightmares, and build their support base on the fly.

Notes

1. For the idea of a "bonus effect," see Commander in Chief, Pacific (CINCPAC) Conference Agenda, 15 January 1962, especially Item 10 (CINCPAC Construction Priorities in South Vietnam), Historians Files, U.S. Army Center of Military History (CMH), Washington, D.C.

2. Mary E. Anderson, et al., *Support Capabilities for Limited War Forces in Laos and South Vietnam* (Santa Monica: 1962), pp. 30-38; U.S. Army, Pacific (USARPAC) Base Development Plan No. 1-64, Vol. VI, Southeast Asia, 1 January 1964, Section V (Ports, Harbor Facilities and Beach Landing Areas), Historians Files, CMH.

3. Anderson, et al., *Support Capabilities for Limited War Forces*, pp. 75-79; U.S. Army, Ryukyu Islands, Operation Plan 32-64, 3 August 1964, Appendix 1 (Concept of Logistic Support) to Annex E (Logistics and Personnel), Section III/IV, Historians Files, CMH.

4. CINCPAC Operation Plan No. 32-59, 16 December 1959, especially Annex B (Concept of Operations), Record Group (RG) 334/70A 582, box 2, National Archives

and Records Administration (NARA), Washington, D.C.; CINCPAC Information Book for Joint Chiefs of Staff (JCS) Visit, January 63, Item II-A (Okinawa), RG 338/74 685, box 1, NARA; USARPAC Information Brief, 17 March 1964, sub: Floating Depot Concept, Historians Files, CMH.

5. U.S. Army Prestockage as of 1 February 1964, CINCPAC Command Digest, February 1964, p. 90, RG 334/71A 226, box 3, NARA.

6. A forty-eight year old West Point graduate when he arrived in Saigon in 1962, Osmanski, in addition to serving in the field artillery, had spent almost twenty years in logistical assignments. During World War II he was a strategic logistics planner with the Supreme Allied Command and the Supreme Allied Expeditionary Forces, European theater. He later returned to U.S. Army, Europe, as a supply planner before going on to Harvard Business School in the mid 1950s.

7. Briefing by Brig. Gen. Frank A. Osmanski, (Assistant Chief of Staff J-4, U.S. Military Assistance Command, Vietnam [MACV]), 11 December 1962, sub: Logistics in South Vietnam, p. 9, Historians Files, CMH; Conference, Headquarters CINCPAC, 23 July 1962, Item 8: Status of Special Logistic Actions Thailand, RG 338/74 585, box 1, NARA; CINCPAC Command History 1962, pp. 222-25.

8. Osmanski called the logistical system in Vietnam "the most complicated, most un-military, and in many ways the clumsiest I have ever known." See Memo, J-4 MACV for Deputy Commander U.S. Military Assistance Command, Vietnam (Dep COMUSMACV), 11 February 1964, sub: Logistics of the Counter-Insurgency in RVN, p. 6, Westmoreland History Backup Book 2, CMH.

9. *Ibid.*, pp. 6-8; MACV Command History 1964 (unpublished source), pp. 135-37. For Admiral Felt's position, see Interview with Col. Michael J.L. Greene, Secretary of the Joint Staff, MACV, 1965, p. 21, RG 334/69A 702, box 6, NARA.

10. The beginnings of the logistical command are described in George C. Reinhardt, "The Logistical Command: Its Origin and Place in Modern Warfare," *Military Review* 30 (January 1951), pp. 25-31; and Thomas F. Donahue, "Communications Zone: Asset or Liability?" *ibid.* 35 (January 1956), pp. 3-12. Also Interview with Lt. Gen. Joseph M. Heiser, Jr., Senior Officer Oral History Program (1976), sect. 3:29-31, sect. 4:24-25, U.S. Army Military History Institute, Carlisle Barracks, Pennsylvania.

11. For the characterization of Osmanski, see Interview with Col. Michael J.L. Greene, 1965, p. 17, RG 334/69A 702, box 6, NARA. Osmanski's position on the logistics of the counterinsurgency is described in MACV Command History 1964 (unpublished source), p. 151.

12. USARPAC Operation Plan No. 37-64, 15 April 1964, especially Annex B (Concept of Operations), RG 338/74 685, box 1, NARA.

13. The expansion in forces is described in Memo, Michael Forrestal for McGeorge Bundy, 21 July 1964, sub: Additional Support for RVN, National Security Files, Vietnam, Vol. XIV, Memos to the President, box 6, Lyndon Baines Johnson Library (LBJ Lib), Austin, Texas. Westmoreland is quoted in Message, COMUSMACV MACJ31 6180 to CINCPAC, DAIN 348033, 16 July 1964, sub: Support Requirements for Extension of US Advisory Program, Historians Files, CMH.

14. Msg, COMUSMACV MACJ3 7738 to CINCPAC, 11 August 1964, sub: Additional Support RVN, Historians Files, CMH, warns against compressing deployment schedules. For Westmoreland's query on support forces, see Msg, COMUSMACV MACJ42 10862 to Commander in Chief USARPAC (CINCUSARPAC), 8 October 1964,

sub: Availability of Troop Units, RG 338/69A 5736, box 1, NARA. The Osmanski proposal is MACV, Improvement of US Logistic Systems in RVN, 26 October 1964, RG 338/69A 5736, box 1, NARA.

15. Msg, CINCPAC to JCS, 17 August 1964, sub: Next Course of Action in Southeast Asia, excerpted in *The Pentagon Papers as Published by the New York Times* (New York: 1971), pp. 306-8.

16. The admiral's proposal is CINCPAC, MACV Plan for the Introduction and Employment of a US Army Logistical Command, 21 December 1964, RG 338/69A 5736, box 1, NARA.

17. Msg, JCS 003042 to CINCPAC, DAIN 495402, 18 December 1964, sub: Logistic Support of Third Country Forces; Msg, Commander, U.S. Forces, Korea UK 50915 to CINCPAC, DAIN 496408, 19 December 1964, sub: Increase of Third Country Representation in Vietnam. Both in Historians Files, CMH.

18. The U.S. Army, Pacific, comment on the Osmanski draft is in Msg, CINCUSARPAC ARP 19023 to CINCPAC, 21 November 1964, sub: Improvement of U.S. Logistic System in RVN, RG 338/69A 5736, box 1, NARA.

19. For an early reference to an "area system," see Memo, Lt. Gen. Richard D. Meyer (Director of Logistics, JCS) for Asst. Secretary of Defense (Installations and Logistics), 26 January 1965, sub: Justification for the US Army Logistical Command in the Republic of Vietnam, Historians Files, CMH.

20. Memo for the Record, Brig. Gen. Frank G. White (J-4 CINCPAC), 8 February 1965, sub: Establishment of U.S. Army Log Command in VN, RG 338/69A 5736, box 1, NARA; Memo, Cyrus R. Vance (Deputy Secretary of Defense) for Chairman, JCS, 12 February 1965, sub: COMUSMACV Plan for the Introduction and Employment of a US Army Logistical Command, Historians Files, CMH.

21. Msg, COMUSMACV MACJ41 6125 to CINCPAC, DAIN 565932, 27 February 1965, sub: Southeast Asia Logistic Actions, Historians Files, CMH; General William C. Westmoreland, *A Soldier Reports* (Garden City: 1976), p. 126.

22. Memo, Office Chief of Staff Army, 22 February 1965, sub: VN Discussions; Msg, CINCUSARPAC to CINCPAC, DAIN 584467, 19 March 1965, sub: Contingency Planning for SE Asia/Western Pacific. Both in Historians Files, CMH.

23. Memo, Maj. Gen. Lawrence J. Lincoln (Asst. Deputy Chief of Staff for Logistics) for Deputy Chief of Staff for Military Operations, 18 June 1964, sub: Support of Contingency Plans Southeast Asia; Msg, JCS 005511 to CINCPAC, DAIN 553054, 18 February 1965, sub: Sea and Airlift Requirements vs. Port Capabilities; Msg, JCS 007030 to CINCPAC, DAIN 577484, 13 March 1965, sub: Contingency Planning for Southeast Asia/Western Pacific; Msg, JCS 008371 to CINCPAC, DAIN 599746, 3 April 1965, sub: Transportation Planning Factors. In Historians Files, CMH.

24. For the problem of theater supply flow, see Gen. Harold K. Johnson, Report on Survey of the Military Situation in Vietnam, 14 March 1965, especially pp. 9-10; Msg, JCS 007929 to CINCPAC, DAIN 592999, 26 March 1965, sub: COMUSMACV Requirement for Additional LST Support. Both in Historians Files, CMH. The airfields are discussed in The History of the Joint Chiefs of Staff—The Joint Chiefs of Staff and the War in Vietnam: 1960-1968 (unpublished source), Part II, chapter 20:12-14.

25. The logistical requirements of the three-division force were developed at Pacific command headquarters and reached the Joint Chiefs in a personal message from Admiral Sharp on March 27. See Msg, Adm. Sharp CINCPAC to Gen. Earle G.

Wheeler, Chairman JCS, 27 March 1965, sub: U.S. and ROK Deployments, Westmoreland Message Files, CMH. For the president's decision, see National Security Action Memorandum 328 to Secretary of State, et al., 6 April 1965, RG 330/70A 5127, box 13, NARA.

26. Msg, CINCPAC 93006 to JCS, DAIN 602485, 5 April 1965, sub: Deployment of Logistic Support Forces in SE Asia, Historians Files, CMH.

27. Taylor's position is described in Msg, Saigon 3332 to State, 12 April 1965, National Security Files, Vietnam, National Security History: Deployment of Major U.S. Forces, box 41, LBJ Lib.

Bibliography of Logistics from the Ancient Greeks to the 1980s

George Satterfield

The user will find in the following pages works in military and naval logistics ranging from the supply of Alexander the Great's phalanxes to U.S. Strategic Air Command refuelling operations during the Vietnam War. This bibliography emphasizes works on supply, but in the interest of focus, I have opted to eschew war finance and arms production. Both of these topics have been the subject of a considerable body of work, particularly for the nineteenth and twentieth centuries. Variety has been the goal here. A balance has been attempted between the ancients and the moderns, but as in the case of the great literary debate of the time of Fontenelle and Swift, the moderns come out ahead. Hopefully, something of the rich logistic experience of European and American armies and navies has been captured in the following pages.

General Works

Aboucaya, Claude. *Les Intendants de la marine sous l'ancien régime.* Paris: 1958.

Appler, Bill. "History of the Naval Supply Corps." *Review* (May-June 1968).

Aron, Raymond. *War and Industrial Society.* London: 1958.

Audoin, Xavier. *Histoire de l'administration de la guerre.* 4 vols. Paris: 1811.

Bartlow, Gene S. "Operator-Logistician Disconnect." *Airpower Journal* 2 (Fall 1988), pp. 23-37.

Baumann, Bernhard von. *Studien uber die Verpflegung der Kriegsheere im Felde.* 3 vols. Leipzig: 1867-1880.

Bondil, Général. "Les transports militaires dans l'histoire." *Revue historique de l'armée* 15, no. 1 (1959), pp. 63-80.

Boyer, Lieutenant-Colonel. "Le droit français de réquisitions." *Armée*, no. 65 (1967), pp. 14-29.

Breitenbücher, Otto. "Die Entwicklung des württem-bergischer Militärversorgungwesens nach dem dreissigjährigen Krieg bis zum Jahr 1871." Ph.D. dissertation, Tübingen, 1936.

Bynum, W.F. *Starving Sailors: The Influence of Nutrition upon Naval and Maritime History.* Greenwich: 1981.
Child, W.G. "Field Forges of the British Army, 1700-1900." *Journal of the Society for Army Historical Research* (Summer 1983), pp. 67-76.
Couget, Géneral C.R.G. "L'Armée du Train de l'Empire à nos jours." *Revue historique des Armées* 34, no. 3 (1978), pp. 8-20.
Creveld, Martin van. *Supplying War: Logistics from Wallenstein to Patton.* Cambridge: 1977.
Deese, David A. "Oil, War, and Grand Strategy." *Orbis*, vol. 25, no. 3 (1981), pp. 525-55.
Deruelle, G. "Aperçu historique sur les fabrications d'armement en France." *Revue historique de l'armée*, vol. 12, no. 4 (1956), pp. 89-101.
Fortescue, Sir John W. *The Early History of Transport and Supply.* London: 1928.
Fortescue, Sir John W. *The Royal Army Service Corps: A History of Supply and Transport in the British Army.* 2 vols. Cambridge: 1930-31.
Frémont, Paul-Jean-Michel-Raoul. *Les payeurs d'armées. Historiques du service de la tresorerie et des postes aux armées, 1293-1870.* Paris: 1906.
Gaudin, M. "Historique de la fabrication des armes légères." *Revue historique de l'armée* 12, no. 4 (1956), pp. 115-126.
Halibarton, Arthur, 1st Baron. *Army Administration in Three Centuries.* London: 1901.
Hawthorne, Daniel. *For Want of a Nail: The Influence of Logistics on War.* New York: 1948.
Huston, James A. *Sinews of War: Army Logistics 1775-1953.* Washington, DC: 1966.
Huston, James A. "Army Logistics: Lessons of Experience." *Military Review* 49 (September 1989), pp. 76-88.
Kiesling, Martin. *Geschichte der Organisation und Bekleidung des Trains der kgl. preussischen Armee 1740-1888.* Berlin: 1889.
Kling, C. *Geschichte der Bekleidung, Bewaffnung und Ausrüstung des königlich preussischen Heeres.* 3 vols. Weimar: 1902-12.
Lepère, Capitaine. "Le service des poudres." *Revue historique de l'armée* 14, no. 3 (1958), pp. 109-54.
Meixner, O. *Historischer Rückblick auf die Verpflegung der Armeen im Felde.* Vienna: 1895.
Mentzel, E.O. *Die Remontirung der preussischen Armee in ihrer historischer Entwicklung.* Berlin: 1870.
Milot, Jean. "Du commissaire des guerres à l'intendant militaire." *Revue historique de l'armée*, special number (1968), pp. 39-48.
Milot, Jean. "Du conducteur des gens de guerre à l'intendant militaire." *Forces arméesfrançais*, no. 3 (1972), pp. 52-59.
Milot, Jean. "Evolution du corps des intendants militaires (des origines à 1882)." *Revue du Nord*, 50, no. 168 (1968), pp. 381-84.
Molias, D., et al. "Le corps de l'intendance militaire." *Revue historique de l'armée* 13, no. 4 (1957), pp. 83-124.
Olson, Mancur, Jr. *The Economics of the Wartime Shortage: A History of British Food Supplies in the Napoleonic War and the World Wars I and II.* Durham, NC: 1963.
Peck, Frederic T. "History of the Naval Gun Factory in Washington, D.C." Ph.D. dissertation, Georgetown University, 1950.
Pernot, A. *Aperçu historique sur le service des transports militaires.* Paris and Limoges: 1894.

Raiffaud, Colonel. "Evolution de l'administration et de la logistique au cours des âges." *Armée*, no. 50 (1965), pp. 2-13.
Risch, Erna. *Quartermaster Support of the Army*. Washington, D.C.: 1962.
Sars, Comte R. de. *Le recrutement de l'armée permenante sous l'ancien régime*. Paris: 1920.
Schnackenburg, E. *Das Invaliden-und Versorgungswesen des brandenburgisch-preussischen Heeres bis zum Jahre 1806*. Berlin: 1889.
Shaw, G.C. *Supply in Modern War*. London: 1982.
Slade, Andrew. "When Private Contractors Fed the Army." *Army Quarterly Defence Journal* (April 1985), pp. 160-66.
Souchal, Intendant Général. *L'intendance militaire des troupes de marine. Trois cent-quarante ans d'histoire, 1626-1966*. Paris: 1969.
Thompson, Julian. *The Lifeblood of War: Logistics and Armed Conflict*. London: 1991.
Tylden, Major G. *Horses and Saddlery: An Account of the Animals used by the British and Commonwealth Armies from the Seventeenth Century to the Present Day with a Description of their Equipment*. London: 1965.
Vaultier, Roger. "La fabrication des uniformes sous l'Ancien Régime (de Louis XIV à la Révolution)." *Revue de l'intendance militaire*, no. 51 (1959), pp. 46-55.
Vaultier, Roger. "Le havresac et le sac à travers notre histoire militaire." *Revue de l'intendance militaire*, no. 49 (1959), pp. 109-21.
Westwood, John. *Railways at War*. London: 1980.
Wheldon, J. *Machine Age Armies*. London: 1968.

Ancient and Medieval

Adams, John P. *Logistics of the Roman Imperial Army: Major Campaigns on the Eastern Front in the First Three Centuries A.D*. Ph.D. dissertation, Yale University, 1976.
Anderson, J.G.C. "The Road-System of Eastern Asia Minor with the Evidence of Byzantine Campaigns," *Journal of Hellenic Studies* 17 (1897), pp. 22-44.
Bachrach, Bernard S. "Animals and Warfare in Early Medieval Europe," *Settimane di Studio del Centro Italiano di sull'alto medioevo* (Spoleto, 1985), XXXI: 716-26
Bachrach, Bernard S. *Merovingian Military Organization, 481-751*. Minneapolis: 1972.
Bachrach, Bernard S. "On the Origins of William the Conquerer's Horse Transports." *Technology and Culture* (July 1985), pp. 505-53.
Bachrach, Bernard S. "Some Observations on the Military Administration of the Norman Conquest." *Anglo-Norman Studies*, VIII, ed. R. Allen Brown. Woodbridge, Suffolk: 1986.
Bartusis, Mark Charles. "The Late Byzantine Soldier: A Social and Administrative Study." Ph.D. dissertation, Rutgers University, 1985.
Boussard, Jacques. "Services feodaux, milices et mercenaires dans les armées en France aux Xe et XIe siècles." In *Ordinamenti militari in Occidente, 15a Settimane de Spolete, 1967*. 1 (1968), pp. 131-68, 221-28.
"Ein Brandenburgischer Mobilmachungsplan aus dem Jahre 1477." *Kriegs-geschictliche Einzelschrifften*. III. Berlin: 1884.
Brunt, P.A. *Italian Manpower, 225 B.C.-A.D. 14*. Oxford: 1971.
Byerly, Benjamin F. "Military Administration in Thirteenth Century England: A Study Emphasizing the Contributions of the Wardrobe in the Wars of Henry III and Edward I, 1216-1307." Ph.D. dissertation, University of Illinois, 1965.

Contamine, Philippe. *Guerre, état et sociéte à la fin du moyen âge. Études sur les armées des rois de France 1337-1494.* Paris: 1972.
Critchley, J. "Military Service and Organization in England, 1154-1272." Ph.D. dissertation, University of Nottingham, 1968.
Cruickshank, W.W. "Topography, Movement and Supply in the Warfare of Ancient Greece, South of Thessaly and Epirus." Ph.D. dissertation, University of London,1955.
Engels, Donald W. *Alexander the Great and the Logistics of the Macedonian Army.* Berkeley: 1978.
Fehr, Hans. "Landfolge und Gerichtsfolge im fränkischen Recht." In *Festgabe für R. Sohm.* Munich: 1914.
Gaier, Claude. "Pauvreté et armement individuel en Europe occidentale au moyen âge." In *Sedicesima Settimana di Studio, Istituto Datini.* Prato: 1984.
Hammond, N.G.L. "Army Transport in the Fifth and Fourth Centuries." *Greek, Roman, Byzantine Studies,* no. 1 (1983), pp. 27-31.
Hanson, Victor. "Warfare and Agriculture in Ancient Greece." Ph.D. dissertation, Stanford University, 1980.
Hay, Denys. "Division of the Spoils of War in Fourteenth Century England." *Transactions of the Royal Historical Society,* 5th series, 4 (1954), pp. 91-109.
Hewitt, H.J. *The Organization of War Under Edward III, 1338-62.* Manchester and New York: 1966.
Hollister, C. Waren. *Anglo-Saxon Military Institutions on the Eve of the Norman Conquest.* Oxford: 1962.
Hollister, C. Waren. *The Military Organization of Norman England.* Oxford: 1965.
Hooker, J.R. "Notes on the Organization and Supply of the Tudor Military Under Henry VII." *Huntington Library Quarterly* 23 (1959-60), pp. 19-31.
Jordan, Borimer. "The Administration and Military Organization of the Athenian Navy in the Fifth and Fourth Centuries, B.C." Ph.D. dissertation, University of California, Berkeley, 1968.
Kepler, J.S. "The Effects of the Battle of Sluys upon the Administration of English Naval Impressment, 1340-1343." *Speculum* (January 1973), pp. 70-77.
Luttwak, Edward N. *The Grand Strategy of the Roman Empire from the First Century A.D. to the Third.* Baltimore: 1976.
Macmullen, Ramsay. "The Roman Emperor's Army Costs." *Latomus,* no. 3 (1984), pp. 571-80.
Newhall, Richard Ager. *Muster and Review: A Problem of English Military Administration, 1420-1440.* Cambridge: 1940.
Noyes, A.G. *The Military Obligation in Mediaeval England.* Columbus, Ohio: 1931.
Oppenheim, Michael, ed. *Naval Accounts and Inventories of the Reign of Henry VII, 1485-88 and 1495-97.* London: 1896.
Peaks, Mary B. "The General Civil and Military Administration of Noricum and Raetia." Ph.D. dissertation, University of Chicago, 1905.
Poonder, Robert L. "A Hellenistic Arsenal in Athens." *Hesperia,* no. 3 (1983), pp. 233-56.
Powers, James F. *A Society Organized for War: The Iberian Municipal Militias in the Central Middle Ages, 1000-1284.* Berkeley: 1988.

Powicke, M.R. "The General Obligation to Cavalry Service Under Edward I." *Speculum*, 28, no. 4 (1953), pp. 19-43.
Prestwick, Michael. "Victualling Estimates for English Garrisons in Scotland During the Early Fourteenth Century." *English Historical Review* (July 1967).
Prince, A.E. "The Payment of Army Wages in Edward III's Reign." *Speculum* 19 (1944), pp. 137-60.
Pritchett, W. Kendrick. *The Greek State at War*. 4 vols. Berkeley: 1971-74.
Pryor, John H. *Geography, Technology, and War: Studies in the Maritime History of the Mediterranean, 649-1571*. Cambridge: 1988.
Rabaut, David Ronald. *Logistics and the Roman Army of the Late Republic*. M.A. thesis, University of Illinois, Urbana, 1962.
Ruckley, N.A. "Water Supply of Medieval Castles in the United Kingdom." *Fortress* 7 (November 1990), pp. 14-26.
Sanders, I.J. *Feudal Military Service in England*. Oxford: 1956.
Sitwell, N.H.H. *Roman Roads of Europe*. New York: 1981.
Smail, R.C. *Crusading Warfare, 1097-1193*. Cambridge: 1956.
Solon, Paul D. "Valois Military Administration on the Norman Frontier, 1445-1461: A Study in Medieval Reform." *Speculum* (January 1976), pp. 91-111.
Vaultier, Roger. "Les fournisseurs d'armures au Moyen Age et au XVIe siècle." *Revue de l'intendance militaire*, no. 49 (1959), pp. 109-21.
Walker, Simon. "Profit and Loss in the Hundred Years' War: The Subcontracts of Sir John Strother, 1374." *Bulletin of the Institute of Historical Research* (May 1985), pp. 100-106.
Walsh, Alice G. "The Administration of the Duchy of Spoleto 1303-1334." Ph.D. dissertation, Boston University, 1974.
Weir, Michael. "The Preparation for War in Medieval England, 1199-1307." Ph.D. dissertation, Brown University, 1970.
Yehya, L. "Military and Naval Administration in Athens in the Fourth Century B.C., Including Finance." Ph.D. dissertation, University of London, 1953.
Ziezulewicz, William. "The Fate of Carolingian Military Exactions in a Monastic Fisc: The Case of Saint-Florent-De-Saumur (c. 950-1118)." *Military Affairs*, 51, no. 3 (July 1987), pp. 124-127.

The Sixteenth and Seventeenth Centuries

André, Louis. *Michel Le Tellier et l'organisation de l'armée monarchique*. Paris: 1906.
André, Louis. *Michel Le Tellier et Louvois*. Paris: 1942.
Ashley, Roger. "Getting and Spending: Corruption in the Elizabethan Ordnance." *History Today* 40 (November 1990), pp. 47-53.
Bamford, Paul W. "Slaves for the Galleys of France, 1665-1670." In *Merchants and Scholars*. Minneapolis: 1965, pp. 171-91.
Barbier, Alfred. *Notice biographique sur René de Voyer d'Argenson, intendant d'armée du Poitou, ambassadeur à Venise (1596-1651)*. Poitiers: 1885.
Baxter, Douglas C. *Servants of the Sword: French Intendants of the Army*. Urbana: 1976.
Blair, Claude. "The Armourers' Bill of 1581. The Making of Arms and Armour in Sixteenth-Century London." *Journal of the Arms and Armour Society*, 12, no. 1 (March 1986), pp. 20-53.

Bouyala d'Arnaud, André. "L'arsenal des galères à Marseille au XVIIe et au XVIIIe siècles." *Revue historique de l'armée* 14, no. 4 (1958), pp. 31-46.
Boynton, L.O.J. "English Military Organization, c. 1558-1638." Ph.D. dissertation, Oxford University, 1962.
Breysig, Curt. "Die Organisation der brandenburgischen Kommissariate in Zeit von 1660-1697." *Forschungen zur brandenburgischen und preussischen Geschichte,* V. Berlin: 1892, pp. 136-156.
Caron, Narcisse-Léonard. *Michel Le Tellier, son administration comme intendant d'armée en Piémont (1640-1643).* Paris: 1883.
Clark, Sir George. *War and Society in the Seventeenth Century.* Cambridge: 1958.
Clayton, N. "Naval Administration Under James I." Ph.D. dissertation, University of Leeds, 1935.
Coleman, D.C. "Naval Dockyards Under the Later Stuarts." *Economic History Review,* 1, no. 2 (1953).
Corvisier, André, ed. *Les Français et l'armée sous Louis XIV d'après les mémoires des intendants, 1697-1698.* Vincennes: 1975.
Cruickshank, C.G. *Elizabeth's Army.* 2nd ed. Oxford: 1966.
Cruickshank, C.G. "The Organization and Administration of the Elizabethan Foreign Expeditions, 1585-1603." Ph.D. dissertation, Oxford University, 1940.
Davies, C.S.L. "The Administration of the Royal Navy Under Henry VIII: The Origin of the Navy Board." *English Historical Review* 80 (1965), pp. 268-88.
Davies, C.S.L. "Provisions for Armies, 1509-1560." *Economic History Review* 17 (1964-65), pp. 234-48.
Essen, L. van der. "Kritische studie over de oorlogsvoering van het Spaanse leger in de Nederlanden tijdens de XVIe eeuw." *Mededelingen van de Koninklijke Vlaamse Academie...van Belgie. Klasse der Letteren* 12 (1950), 14 (1954), 15 (1955), 17-22 (1955-1960).
Ferguson, Ronald T. "Blood and Fire: Contribution Policy of the French Armies in Germany (1668-1715)." Ph.D. dissertation, University of Minnesota, 1970.
Finkel, Caroline. *The Administration of Warfare: The Ottoman Military Campaigns in Hungary, 1593-1606.* In *Beihefte zur Wiener Zeitschrift für die Kunde des Morgenlandes,* 14. Vienna: 1988.
Guilmartin, John. *Gunpowder and Galleys: Changing Technology and Mediterranean Warfare at Sea in the Sixteenth Century.* Cambridge: 1974.
Gutman, Myron P. *War and Rural Life in the Early Modern Low Countries.* Princeton: 1980.
Hale, J.R. *War and Society in Renaissance Europe, 1450-1620.* Baltimore: 1985.
Hammond, Wayne N. "The Administration of the English Navy, 1649-1660." Ph.D. dissertation, University of British Columbia, 1974.
Hubert van Houtte, *Les occupations étrangères en Belgique sous l'Ancien règime,* 2 vols., Université de Gand, Recueil de travaux publies par la faculté de philosophie et lettres, 62-63 fascicule. Gand: 1930.
Jung, Jean-Eric. "L'organisation du service des vivres aux armées de 1550 à 1650." *Bibliothèque de l'Ecole de Chartes,* 141 (1983), pp. 269-306.
Jung, Jean-Eric. "Service des vivres et munitionnaires sous l'ancien régime: la fourniture du pain de munition aux troupes de Flandre et d'Allemagne de 1701 à 1710." *Positions Thèses Ecole de Chartes* (1983), pp. 113-22.

Kroener, B. "Die Entwicklung der Truppenstarken in den französischen Armeen zwischen 1635 und 1661." In *Forschungen und Quellen zur Geschichte des dreissigjahrigen Krieges*. Edited by K. Repgen. Munster: 1981.

Kroener, B. *Les Routes et les etapes. Die Versorgung der französischen Armeen in Nordostfrankreich 1635-1661*. 2 vols. Munster: 1980.

Lewis, D.E. "The Parliamentary Board of Ordnance, 1642-49." Ph.D. dissertation, Loughborough, 1976.

Lovett, A.W. "Francisco de Lixalde: A Spanish Paymaster in the Netherlands (1567-77)." *Tijdschrift voor Geschiedenis* (1971), pp. 14-23.

Lynn, John A. "How War Fed War: The Tax of Violence and Contributions During the Grand Siècle," *Journal of Modern History* 65, no. 2 (June 1993).

Mallett, M.E., and Hale, J.R. *The Military Organization of a Renaissance State: Venice c. 1400 to 1617*. Cambridge: 1984.

Michaud, H. "Aux origines du secrétariat d'état à la guerre: les règlements de 1617-1619." *Revue d'Histoire moderne et contemporaine* (1972), pp. 389-413.

Milot, Victor. "Le Richelieu, Route Militaire de la Nouvelle-France." Ph.D. dissertation, Laval University, 1949.

Murphey, Rhoads. "The Functioning of the Ottoman Army Under Murad IV." Ph.D. dissertation, University of Chicago, 1979.

Nodot, François. *Le munitionnaire des armées de France*. Paris: 1697.

Olesa Muñido, Francisco-Felipe, *La Organización Naval de Los Estados Mediterraneos y en Especial de España Durante los Siglos XVI y XVII*, 2 vols. Madrid: 1968.

Oppenheim, Michael. *A History of the Administration of the Royal Navy and of Merchant Shipping in Relation to the Navy: From MDIX to MDCLX with an Introduction Treating of the Preceding Period*. London: 1896.

Parker, Geoffrey. *The Army of Flanders and the Spanish Road, 1567-1659: The Logistics of Spanish Victory and Defeat in the Low Countries Wars*. Cambridge: 1972.

Parker, Geoffrey. *The Military Revolution*. Cambridge: 1988.

Parker, Geoffrey, and Thompson, I. A. A. "The Battle of Lepanto, 1571: The Costs of Victory." *Mariner's Mirror* (February 1978), pp. 13-21.

Parrot, David. "The Administration of the French Army During the Ministry of Cardinal Richelieu." Ph.D. dissertation, Oxford University, 1985.

Parrott, David. "French Military Organization in the 1630's: The Failure of Richelieu's Ministry." *XVIIth Century Studies*, no. 9 (1987), pp. 151-67.

Pearce, Brian. "Elizabethan Food Policy and the Armed Forces." *Economic History Review* 12 (1942), pp. 39-49.

Perjés, G. "Army Provisioning, Logistics and Strategy in the Second Half of the 17th Century." *Acta Historica Academiae Scientarium Hungaricae*, no. 16 (1970), pp. 1-51.

Phillips, Carla Rahn. *Six Galleons for the King of Spain: Imperial Defense in the Early Seventeenth Century*. Baltimore: 1986.

Pollitt, Ronald L. "Elizabethan Navy Board: A Study in Administrative Evolution." Ph.D. dissertation, Northwestern University, 1968.

Redlich, Fritz. "Contributions in the Thirty Years' War." *Economic History Review* 12 (1959-60).

Redlich, Fritz. *The German Military Enterpriser and His Work Force, 13th to 17th Centuries*. 2 vols. Wiesbaden: 1964-5.

Redlich, Fritz. *De Praeda Militari: Looting and Booty, 1500-1815.* Vierteljahrschrift für Sozial und Wirtschaftsgeschichte, no. 39. Wiesbaden: 1956.
Ritter, M. "Das Kontributionsystems Wallensteins." *Historische Zeitschrift* 90: 193-247.
Rousset, Camille. *Histoire de Louvois,* 4 vols. Paris: 1862-64.
Salm, Hubert. *Armeefinanzierung im Dreitzigjahrigen Krieg: Der Niderrheinishc-Westfalische Reichkreis 1635-1650.* Munster: 1990. (Also concerns local resource mobilization.)
Schrötter, F. Frh. von. *Die brandenburgisch-preussische Heeresverfassung unter dem Grossen Kurfürsten.* Leipzig: 1892.
Stearns, S.J. "A Problem of Logistics in the Early 17th Century: The Siege of Ré." *Military Affairs,* 62, no. 3 (October 1973), pp. 121-26.
Stewart, Paul J. "The Army of the Catholic Kings: Spanish Military Organization and Administration in the Reign of Ferdinand and Isabella, 1474-1516." Ph.D. dissertation, University of Illinois, 1961.
Stradling, R.A. "Spain's Military Failure and the Supply of Horses, 1600-1660." *History* (June 1984), pp. 208-21.
Thompson, I.A.A. *War and Government in Habsburg Spain 1560-1620.* London: 1976.
Tóth, Sándor Lásló. "A TörÖk Haditevékenyég Akcoradiusza a 15 Eves Habouruban." *Hadtörténelmi Közlemények,* 32, no. 4 (1985), pp. 761-85. (The action radius as limited by logistics of Ottoman military activities During the Fifteen Years' War, 1593-1606.)
Vaultier, Roger. "La cuisine militaire au XVIIe siècle, d'après des documents du temps." *Revue de l'intendance militaire,* no. 44 (1957), pp. 136-42.
Waddell, Louis M. "The Administration of the English Army in Flanders and Brabant from 1689 to 1697." Ph.D. dissertation, University of North Carolina, 1971.

The Eighteenth Century

Albion, Robert G. *Forests and Sea Power: The Timber Problem of the Royal Navy, 1652-1862.* Cambridge: 1926.
Aldridge, Frederick S. "Organization and Administration of the Militia System of Colonial Virginia." Ph.D.dissertation, American University, 1964.
Aubry, Ch. *Le Ravitaillement des Armées de Frédéric Le Grand et de Napoléon.* Paris: 1894.
Baker, Norman. *Government and Contractors: The British Treasury and War Supplies, 1775-83.* London: 1971.
Bamford, Paul Waldon. *Forests and French Sea Power, 1660-1789.* Toronto: 1956.
Baugh, Daniel A. *British Naval Administration in the Age of Walpole.* Princeton: 1965.
Beskrovnii, L.G. "Proizvodstvo Voruzheniia i Boepripasovna russkikh Zavodakh v pervoi Polovine XVIII v."*Istoricheski Zapiski,* no. 36 (1951), pp. 101-141.
Bourland, Richard Dean, Jr. "Maurepas and His Administration of the French Navy on the Eve of the War of the Austrian Succession (1737-1742)." Ph.D. dissertation, University of Notre Dame, 1978.
Bowler, Arthur. *Logistics and the Failure of the British Army in America, 1775-1783.* Princeton: 1975.
Burnett, Edmund C. "The Continental Congress and Agricultural Supplies." *Agricultural History* 2 (1928), pp. 111-28.

Calhers, Darryl I. "Powder to the People: The Revolutionary Structure Behind the Attacks on Fort William and Mary, 1774." *History of New Hampshire* (Winter 1975), pp. 261-80.

Carp, E. Wayne. *To Starve the Army at Pleasure: Continental Army Administration and American Political Culture, 1775-1783.* Chapel Hill: 1984.

Chennevières, François de. *Détails militaires dont la connaissance est necessaire à tous les officiers et principalement aux commissaires des guerres,* 6 vols. Paris: 1750.

Cilleuls, Jean des. "Un grand intendant d'armée: Moreau de Séchelles (1690-1760)." *Revue de l'intendance militaire,* no. 26 (1953), pp. 39-79.

Cilleuls, Jean des. "Le service de l'intendance à l'armée de Rochambeau." *Revue historique de l'armée,* no. 2 (1957), pp. 43-61.

Cole, David William. "The Organization and Administration of the South Carolina Militia System, 1670-1783." Ph.D. dissertation, University of South Carolina, 1953.

Dalrymple, Campbell. *A Military Essay, Containing Reflections on the Raising, Arming, Clothing and Discipline of the British Infantry and Cavalry.* London: 1761.

De Valinger, Leon. *Colonial Military Organization in Delaware, 1638-1776.* Wilmington, Delaware: 1938.

Dublanchy, Lieutenant Charles-Nicolas. *Une intendance d'armée au XVIIIe siècle. Etude sur les service administratifs à l'armée de Soubise pendant la Guerre de Sept Ans, d'après la correspondance et les papiers inédits de l'intendant François-Marie Gayot.* Paris: 1908.

Dupré d'Aulnay, Louis. *Traité générale des subsistances militaires qui comprend la fourniture du pain de munition, des fourages & de la viande aux armées et auxtroupes de garnisons; ensemble celle des hôpitaux & des équipages des vivres & de l'artillerie, par marché ou résultat du Conseil, à forfait ou par régie.* Paris: 1744.

Durand-Vaugaron, Louis. "Louage de muletiers (à Guérande pour la campagne de 1748)." *Société d'histoire et d'archéologie de Bretagne. Bulletin* (1960).

Duval, Michel. "Les bois de marine et la crise des armements à Brest pendant la guerre de succession d'Autriche (1746-1748)." *Cahiers de l'Iroise,* no. 4 (1959), pp. 200-205.

Foret, Michael J. "The Failure of Administration: The Chickasaw Campaign of 1739-1740." *Louisiana Review* 11 (1982), pp. 49-60.

Fowler, William M., Jr. "The Business of War: Boston as a Navy Base, 1776-1783." *American Neptune* 42 (January 1982), pp. 25-35.

Griffenhagen, George D. "Drug Supplies in the American Revolution." *United States National Museum Bulletin* 225 (1961), pp. 110-33.

Guiaro de Vierna Augel. "Organizacion de la Armada durante el Reinado de Felipe V: Diferencias y Semejanzas con la Britanica." *Revista de Historica Naval,* 5, no. 18(1987), pp. 73-86.

Guy, A. J. "The Standing Army Under George II and the Duke of Cumberland, 1727-63: Command, Regimental Administration and Finance." Ph.D. dissertation, Oxford University, 1983.

Hertz, Allen Z. "Armament and Supply Inventory of Ottoman Ada Kale, 1753." *Archivum Ottomanicum* 4 (1972), pp. 95-172.

Huston, James A. "The Logistics of Arnold's March to Quebec." *Military Affairs,* 32, no. 3 (December 1968), pp. 110-24.

Johnson, Victor L. "The Administration of the American Commissariat During the Revolutionary War." Ph.D. dissertation, University of Pennsylvania, 1938.

Kennett, Lee. *The French Armies in the Seven Years' War: A Study in Military Organization and Administration.* Durham: 1967.
Korn, J.F. *Von den Verpflegungen der Armeen.* Breslau: 1779.
Little, H.M. "Thomas Pownall and Army Supply, 1761-1766." *Journal of the Society for Army Historical Research,* 65, no. 262 (1987), pp. 92-104.
"Logistics of the Yorktown Campaign." *Army Logistician* (September/October 1981), pp. 2-7.
Mahon, Capitaine Patrice. "Une commissaire des guerres sous l'ancien regime. Pierre-Nicolas de Lasalle (père du Général Lasalle)." *Carnet de la sabretache* 8 (1900), pp. 343-353.
Malone, J.J. "The British Naval Stores and Forests Policy in New England, 1691-1775." Ph.D. dissertation, University of London, 1957.
"Marché pour l'habillement du régiment de Brancas, 6 mai 1702." *Carnet et Sabretache,* sér. 5, 5, no. 417 (1958), pp. 517-19.
Merriman, Reginald Dundas, ed. *Queen Anne's Navy: Documents Concerning the Administration of the Navy of Queen Anne, 1702-1714.* London: 1961.
Mevers, Frank Clement III. "Congress and the Navy: The Establishment and Administration of the American Revolutionary Navy by the Continental Congress, 1775-1784." Ph.D. dissertation, University of North Carolina at Chapel Hill, 1973.
Parker, King Lawerence. "Anglo-American Wilderness Campaigning, 1754-1764: Logistical and Tactical Developments." Ph.D. dissertation, Columbia University, 1970.
Pool, Bernard. *Navy Board Contracts: 1660-1832.* London: 1966. (See below for Navy Board contracts after 1832.)
Risch, Erna. *Supplying Washington's Army.* Washington, D.C.: 1981.
Salay, David L. "The Production of Gunpowder in Pennsylvania During the American Revolution." *Pennsylvania Magazine of History and Biography* (October 1975), pp. 422-442.
Schrötter, F. Frh. v. "Die Ergänzung des preussischen Heeres unter dem ersten Könige." *Forschungen zur brandenburgischen und preussischen Geschichte* XXIII (1910), pp. 81-145.
Schwartz, F. *Organisation und Verpflegung der preussischen Landmilizen im Siebenjärhigen Kriege.* Leipzig: 1888.
Scouller, Major R.E. *The Armies of Queen Anne.* Oxford: 1967.
Scouller, Major R.E. "Marlborough's Administration in the Field." *Army Quarterly* 95 (January and April 1968), pp. 196-208.
Stephenson, Orland W. "The Supplies for the American Revolutionary Army." Ph.D. dissertation, Michigan University, 1919.
Stephenson, Orlando W. "The Supplying of Gunpowder in 1776." *American Historical Review* 30 (1925), pp. 271-81.
Stillson, A.C. "The Development and Maintenance of the Naval Establishment." Ph.D. dissertation, Columbia University, 1959.
Sturgill, Claude C. "L'administration des bataillons de la milice en Auvergne, 1726-1730." *Bulletin historique et scientifique de l'Auvergne,* a. 86, no. 645 (1975), pp. 391-414.
Sturgill, Claude C. "Changing Garrisons: The French System of Etapes," *Canadian Journal of History,* 20, no. 2 (August 1985).
Sturgill, Claude C. *Claude Le Blanc: Civil Servant of the King.* Gainesville: 1976.

Sturgill, Claude C. *Les commissaires des guerres et l'administration de l'armée française, 1715-1730* Vincennes: 1985.
Thayer, Theodore. "The Army Contractors for the Niagara Campaign, 1755-1756." *William and Mary Quarterly* 14 (1957), pp. 31-46.
Vaultier, Roger. "Le pain de la troupe au XVIIIe siècle." *Revue de l'intendance militaire*, no. 50 (1959), pp. 49-57.
Watson, Paula. "The Commission for Victualling the Navy, the Commission for Sick and Wounded Seamen and Prisoners of War and the Commission for Transport, 1702-1714." Ph.D. dissertation, University of London, 1965.
West, W.J. "The Supply of Gunpowder to the Ordnance Office in the Mid-Eighteenth Century, with Special Reference to Supply, Distribution, and Legislation During the Seven Years' War." Ph.D. dissertation, University of London, 1986.
Willcox, William B. "Too Many Looks: British Planning before Saratoga." *Journal of British Studies* 2 (November 1962), pp. 56-90.
Williams, Justin. "England's Colonial Naval Stores Policy, 1588-1776." Ph.D. dissertation, University of Iowa, 1933.
Williamson, John. *A Treatise on Military Finance: Containing the Pay, Subsistence, Deductions, and Arrears of the Forces on the British and Irish Establishments...with an Inquiry into the Method of Clothing and Recruiting the Army.* London: 1782.
Young, Henry Ayerst. *The East India Company's Arsenals and Manufactories.* Oxford: 1937.

The French Revolution and the Napoleonic Wars

Anon. "Le commissariat des guerres, son organisation, son évolution, ses attributions." *Revue de l'intendance militaire* 46 (1958), pp. 40-78.
Bertaud, J.P. "Les armées de l'an II: administration militaire et combatants." *Revue historique de l'armée*, no. 2 (1969), pp. 41-49.
Brereton, Greehous. "A Note on Western Logistics in the War of 1812." *Military Affairs*, 34, no. 2 (April 1970), pp. 41-44.
Cadis, J. "Histoire de l'arsenal maritime de Toulon de 1789 à 1815." *Mémorial de l'artillerie française*, 31, fasc. 3 (1957), pp. 693-766.
Carbonneaux, Col. Jean. "Le train des équipages militaires en Russie: une épreuve et un espoir." *Revue historique des armées* 34, no. 3 (1978), pp. 21-38.
Chalmin, P. "Un anniversaire discret: l'escadron du Train des Equipages de la Garde impériale. *Revue du Train*, no. 22 (1955), pp. 33-39.
Chalmin, P. "Les premiers régiments du Train." *Revue du Train*, no. 23 (1955), pp. 45-54.
Colquhoun, P. *Treatise on the Population, Wealth, Power, and Resources of the British Empire.* London: 1814.
Condon, Mary E.A. "The Administration of the Transport Service During the War Against Revolutionary France, 1793-1802." Ph.D. dissertation, University of London, 1968.
Kimball, Jeffrey. "The Fog and Friction of Frontier War: The Role of Logistics in American Offensive Failure During the War of 1812." *Old Northwest* 5 (Winter 1979-80), pp. 323-43.
Lefranc, Pierre. "Histoire de mulets (1808)." *Revue de l'Institut Napoléon* 5 (1970).

Lepotier, Contre-Amiral. "Arsenaux de la marine." *Revue historique des armées* 30, no. 1 (1974), pp. 25-44.
Lucas, Catherine. "Gifts of Clothing to the Troops in 1793-1795." *Journal of the Society of Army Historical Research*, 55, no. 221 (Spring 1977), pp. 2-7.
Muracciole, Capitaine de vaisseau. "Napoléon et les arsenaux de la marine." *Revue historique des armées*, no. 1 (1974), pp. 83-97.
Nanteuil, H. de. *Daru et l'Administration de militaire sous la Révolution et l'Empire*. Paris: 1966.
Perjés, G. "Die Frage der Verpflegung im Feldzuge Napoleons gegen Russland." *Revue Internationale d'Histoire Militaire* (1968), pp. 203-31.
"Die preussischen Kriegsvorbereitungen und Operationspläne von 1805."*Kriegsgeschichtliche Einzelschrifften*. I. Second edition. Berlin: 1883.
Steer, Michael. "The Blockade of Brest and the Victualling of the Western Squadron, 1793-1805." *Mariner's Mirror* 76 (November 1990), pp. 307-16.
Stephenson, Captain George M. "Napoleon—Master Logistician." *Army Logistician* (November/December 1979), pp. 20-23.
Steppler, Glenn A. "Logistics on the Canadian Frontier 1812-1814." *Journal of the Company of Military Historians* (Spring 1979), pp. 8-10.
Stiot, R. "Le commissariat des guerres: les administrateurs militaires des troupes des puissances et des provinces étrangères ou rattachées à l'Empire et de la Grande Armée (1804-1815)." *Bulletin de la Société des Collectionneurs de figurines historiques*, a. 39, no. 6 (1969), pp. 146-50.
Stiot, R. "Le commissariat des guerres, son organisation, son évolution, ses attributions." *Revue de l'intendance militaire*, no. 46 (1958), pp. 40-78.
Stiot, R. "Le commissariat des guerres." *Bulletin de la Société des Collectionneurs de figuines historiques*, no. 4 (1967), pp. 119-24; no. 5 (1967), pp. 153-54.
Tulard, J. "La Depôt de la Guerre et la préparation de la Campagne en Russie." *Revue Historique de l'Armée* (1969).
Ullmann, J. *Studie über die Ausrütung sowie über das Verpfegs- und Nachschubwesen im Feldzug Napoleon I gegen Russland im Jahre 1812*. Vienna: 1891.
Vaultier, Roger. "La cuisine militaire à la Grande Armée." *Revue de l'intendance militaire*, no. 42 (1957), pp. 90-96.
Vaultier, Roger. "La cuisine militaire pendant la Révolution, d'après des documents inédits." *Grandgousier*, nos. 1-2 (1954), pp. 38-42.
Waquet, Jean. "Note sur le fonctionnement des institutions du recrutement militaire dans les départements du Nord français, et belge sous le Consulate et l'Empire." *Revue du Nord* 49, no. 192 (1967), pp. 197-99.
Washburn, Mabel T.R. "The Du Pont Powder Wagon and How It Helped Win Perry's Victory." *Journal of American History* 9 (October 1915), pp. 598-621.
Wetzler, Peter. *War and Subsistence: The Sambre and Meuse Army in 1794*. New York: 1985.
White, Leonard D. *The Jeffersonians: A Study in Administrative History, 1801-1829*. New York: 1951; reprint ed., 1965. (With study of the Navy administration.)
Winton-Clare, C. "A Shipbuilder's War." *Mariners' Mirror* 29 (July 1943), pp. 139-148. (The War of 1812 on the Great Lakes.)

The Nineteenth Century

Anon. *Aperçu historique et observations sur l'administration des subsistances militaires, par un ancien agent de cette administration.* Paris: 1827.

Anon. *De l'Emploi des Chemins de Fer en Temps de Guerre.* Paris: 1869.

Alison, Sir Archibald. *On Army Organization.* London and Edinburgh: 1869.

Baldet, Marcel P. "L'administration dans les armées impériales." *Bulletin de la Société des Collectionneurs de figurines historiques*, no. 1 (1967), pp. 28-30; no. 3 (1967), pp. 93-94; no. 4 (1967), pp. 125-26.

Beaudoin, Frederic J. "Union Victory: Manpower, Management of Resources, or Generalship?" *Naval War College Review* (March-April 1973), pp. 36-40.

Black, Robert C. *The Railroads of the Confederacy.* Chapel Hill: 1952.

Boeger, Palmer H. "Hardtack and Coffee: The Commissary Department, 1861-1865." Ph.D. dissertation, University of Wisconsin, 1954.

Bondick, E. *Geschichte des Ostpreussischen Train-Battalion Nr. 1.* Berlin: 1903.

Brassey, Sir Thomas. *The British Navy: Its Strength, Resources, and Administration.* 5 vols. London: 1882-83.

Briggs, Sir John Henry. *Naval Administrations 1827 to 1892.* London: 1897.

Bruce, Robert V. *Lincoln and the Tools of War.* Indianapolis: 1956.

Budde, H. *Die französischen Eisenbahnen in deutschen Kriegsbetriebe 1870/1.* Berlin: 1904.

Cäncrin. *Über die Militärökonomie im Frieden und Krieg.* St. Petersburg: 1821.

Chronology of Events Connected with Army Administration 1858-1907. London: 1908.

Committee of Inquiry into the Organisation and Administration of the Manufacturing Departments of the Army. London: 1888.

Drake, W.B. "Grant—The Logisitician." *Army Logistician* 90 (May-June 1990), pp. 28-31.

"Die Eisenbahntrasporte für Mobilmachung und Aufmarsch der K. Bayerischen Armee 1870." In *Darstellungen aus der Bayerischen Kriegs- und Heeresgeschichte.* Hrsg. vom K.G. Kriegsarchiv. Munich: 1896.

Eloy, Michel. "Provisions de bord, il y a cent ans." *Escale*, no. 65 (1959), p. 6.

Engelhardt, W. "Rückblicke auf die Verpflegungsverhältnisse im Kriege 1870/71." *Militärwochenblatt*, no. 11 (1901).

Ernouf. *Histoire des chemins de Fer Francais pendant la Guerre Franco-Prussienne.* Paris: 1874.

Faulk, Odie B. *The U.S. Camel Corps.* New York: 1976.

Fay, Cpt. Mary L. "Civil War Signal Logistics." *Army Communications* (Summer 1984), pp. 30-35.

François, H. von. *Feldverpflegung bei der höheren Kommandobehörden.* Berlin: 1913.

"Französische Ansichten über die Militärische Benutzung und Bedeutung der Eisenbahnen, vornehmlich für Frankreich." *Beihften zum Militär-Wochenblatt.* Berlin: July and August, 1845.

Gates, Arnold. "Of Men and Mules: A Modest History of Jackassery." *Civil War Times Illustrated* (November 1984), pp. 40-46.

Gibson, Charles Dana. "Military Transports in the Civil War." *Periodical Journal of the Council on America's Military Past* (16 April 1989), pp. 3-20.

Goff, Richard D. *Confederate Supply.* Durham: 1969.

Goltz, C. von der. "Eine Etappenerinnerung aus dem Deutsch-Französischen Kriege von 1870/71." *Militärwochenblatt* (1896).
Gow, June I. "Military Administration in the Confederacy: The Army of the Tennessee, 1862-1864." Ph.D. dissertation, University of British Columbia, 1970.
Gray, John S. "The Pack Train on George A. Custer's Last Campaign." *Nebraska History* (Spring 1976), pp. 52-68.
Harper, Major Gilbert S. III. "Logistics of the Gettysburg Campaign." *Army Logistician* (July/August 1983), pp. 29-33.
Heeresverpflegung. Studien zur kriegsgeschichte und Taktik. VI. Ed. Gr. Generalstab. Berlin: 1913.
Hold, A. "Requisition und Magazinverpflegung während der Operationen." *Organ der Militär-Wissenschaftlichen Vereine* (1871), pp. 405-87.
Hugo, Conrad. "Carl von Brandenstein, Chef des Feldeisenbahwesens und engster Mitarbeiter Moltkes 1870-71." *Wehrwissenschaftliche Rundschau* (1964), pp. 676-84.
Jacqmin, F. *Les Chemins de fer pendant la guerre de 1870-71.* Paris: 1872.
Johnston, James A. II. "Virginia's Railroads in the Civil War, 1861-1865." Ph.D. dissertation, Northwestern University, 1959.
Kessel, E. "Die Tätigkeit des Grafen Waldersee als Generalquartiermeister und Chef des Generalstabs der Armee." *Welt als Geschichte* XIV (1954), pp. 181-211.
Keuchel, Edward F. "Chemicals and Meat: The Embalmed Beef Scandal of the Spanish-American War." *Bulletin of the History of Medicine* (Summer 1974), pp. 249-264.
Kime, Marlin G. "Sherman's Gordian Knot: Logistical Problems in the Atlanta Campaign." *Georgia Historical Quarterly* 70 (Spring 1986), pp. 102-110.
Lachmann, Manfred. "Probleme der Bewaffnung des kaiserlichen deutschen Heeres." *Zeitschrift für Militärgeschichte* VI (1967), pp. 23-37.
Lash, Jeffrey N. "Joseph E. Johnston and the Virginia Railways, 1861-62." *Civil War History* 35 (March 1989), pp. 5-27.
Lee, Jen-Hwa. "The Organization and Administration of the Army of the Potomac Under General George B. McClellan." Ph.D. dissertation, University of Maryland, 1960.
Lehmann, Gustaf. *Die Mobilmachung von 1870/71.* Berlin: 1905.
Lepère, Capitaine. "Transports d'animaux pour l'armée d'Orient (1854)." *Revue du corps vétérinaire de l'armée,* 12, no. 1 (1957), pp. 14-16.
Lord, Francis A. *Civil War Sutlers and Their Wares.* New York: 1969.
Luard C.E. "Field Railways and Their General Application in War." *Journal of the Royal United Services Institute* (1873), pp. 693-715.
Miller, Darlis A. "Civilians and Military Supply in the Southwest." *Journal of Arizona History* 23 (1982), pp. 115-38.
Moore, Albert B. *Conscription and Conflict in the Confederacy.* New York: 1924.
Murdock, Eugene C. *One Million Men: The Civil War Draft in the North.* Madison: 1971.
Murracciole, Captain. "La guerre de Crimee. Les Transports." *Revue Historique des armées* 43, no. 4 (1987), pp. 3-10.
Niox, M. *De l'Emploi des Chemins de Fer pour les Mouvements Stratégiques.* Paris: 1873.
Olivier, M. "Le train des equipages dans la campagne du Mexique." *Revue du Train,* no. 26 (1956), pp. 39-42.
Olivier, M. "Le train des equipages dans les premières années de la campagne du Maroc (1907-1912)." *Revue du Train,* no. 29 (1956), pp. 24-31.

Pool, Bernard. "Navy Contracts After 1832." *Mariner's Mirror* (August 1968), pp. 209-26.
Pratt, Edwin A. *The Rise of Rail-Power in War and Conquest 1833-1914*. London: 1915.
"Reglement der französischen Armee vom November 1855 über den Transport der Truppen aller Waffengattungen auf Eisenbahnen." *Beihefte zum Militär-Wochenblatt*. Berlin: October-December, 1855.
Rezneck, Samuel. "Horsford's `Marching Ration' for the Civil War Army." *Military Affairs*, 33, no. 1 (April 1969), pp. 249-55.
Rouget, Christoph Marie Michel, Comte. *De l'approvisionement des armées au XIXme siècle*. Paris: 1848.
Schäfer, E. *Der Kriegs-Train des deutschen Heeres*. Berlin: 1883.
Schreiber, Harry N. "The Pay of Confederate Troops and Problems of Demoralization: A Case of Administrative Failure." *Civil War History* (September 1969), pp. 226-36.
Shannon, F.A. *Organization and Administration of the Union Army*. 2 vols. New York: 1965.
Showalter, Dennis E. "The Influence of Railroads on Prussian Planning for the Seven Weeks' War." *Military Affairs* 38 (April 1974).
Showalter, Dennis E. *Railroads and Rifles. Soldiers, Technology and the Unification of Germany*. Hamden, Connecticut: 1975.
Spear, Donald P. "The Sutler in the Union Army." *Civil War History* (June 1970), pp. 121-38.
Swain, Richard M. "The Development of a Logistics System for the British Army, 1856-1896." Ph.D. dissertation, Duke University, 1975.
Sweetman, John. "Military Transport in the Crimean War, 1854-1856." *The English Historical Review* (January 1973), pp. 81-91.
Thomas, Thomas H. "Armies and the Railway Revolution." In *War as a Social Institution*.. Ed. J. D. Clarkson and T. C. Cochran. New York: 1941.
Thompson, S.B. *Confederate Purchasing Operations Abroad*. Chapel Hill: 1935.
"Truppenfahrzeuge, Kolonnen und Trains der I. und der II. Deutschen Armee bis zu den Schlachten westlich Metz." *Kriegsgeschichtliche Enizelschrifften*. XVII. Ed. Gr.Generalstab. Berlin: 1895.
Turner, George E. *Victory Rode the Rails*. Indianapolis: 1953.
U.S. Adjutant General's Office. Military Information Division. *Subsistence and Messing in European Armies*. Washington, D.C.: 1897.
Valabrega, Guido. "Il servizio trasporti e tappe nella Guerra Libica (1911-1912)." *Africa*, 39, no. 3 (1984), pp. 435-52.
Weber, Thomas. *The Northern Railroads in the Civil War*. New York: 1952.
Willisen, K.W. von. *Theorie des grossen Krieges*. 4 vols. Berlin: 1840-68.

World War I and the Interwar Period

Beaver, Daniel R. "Politics and Policy: The War Department Motorization and Standardization Program for Wheeled Transport Vehicles, 1920-1940." *Military Affairs* 47 (October 1983), pp. 101-108.
Cary, Norman M., Jr. "The Use of the Motor Vehicle in the United States Army, 1899-1939." Ph.D. dissertation, University of Georgia, 1980.

Chambers, Frank P. *The War Behind the War, 1914-1918*. London, 1939.
Chapier, Georges. "La contribution du département de la Haute-Savoie au ravitaillement des armées pendant la guerre 1914-1918." *Revue la savoisienne*, a. 95 (1954), pp. 33-38.
Chapier, Georges. "Le ravitaillement de l'armée française d'Orient en 1915-1916. *Revue de l'intendance militaire*, no. 39 (1956), pp. 52-68.
Chapier, Georges. "La ravitaillement d'une division d'infanterie pendant la guerre 1914-1918." *Revue de l'intendance militaire*, no. 52 (1959), pp. 76-83.
Fairlie, John A. *British War Administration*. Oxford, 1919.
Fallows, Thomas. "Politics and the War Effort in Russia: The Union of Zemstvos and the Organization of the Food Supply, 1914-1916." *Slavic Review* (March 1978), pp. 70-90.
Farrar, Marjorie M. "Preclusive purchases: politics and economic warfare in France during the First World War." *Economic History Review*, ser. 2, 26, no. 1 (1973), pp. 117-33.
Goltz, C. von der. *The Nation in Arms*. London: 1913.
Haldenwag, Artur V. "Felderwaltung im Weltkrieg 1914-18." In *Württembergs Heer im Weltkrieg*. Stuttgart: 1925.
Henniker, A.M. *Transportation on the Western Front, 1914-1918*. London: 1937.
Kuhl, H. von, and Bergmann, J. von. *Movements and Supply of the German First Army During August and September 1914*. Fort Leavenworth, Kansas: 1920.
Laux, James M. "Trucks in the West During the First World War." *Journal of Transport History*, vol. 6, no. 2 (1985), pp. 64-70.
Lugand, Lieutenant-Colonel. "Les grands transports automobiles de l'année 1918." *Revue du Train*, a. 23 no. 35 (1958), pp. 52-70.
Maurer, John H. "Fuel and the Battle Fleet: Coal, Oil, and American Naval Strategy, 1898-1925." *Naval War College Review* 34 (November-December 1981), pp. 60-77.
Merand. "Le ravitaillement de la 3e division de cavalerie au début de la guerre, 1914-1918. *Revue de l'intendance militaire*, no. 37 (1956), pp. 112-23.
Millard, George A. "U.S. Army Logistics During the Mexican Punitive Expedition of 1916." *Military Review* 60 (October 1980), pp. 58-68.
Napier, C.S. "Strategic Movement by Rail in 1914." *Journal of the Royal United Services Institute* 80: 69-93 and 361-80.
Napier, C.S. "Strategic Movement over Damaged Railways in 1914." *Journal of the Royal United Services Institute* 81: 315-46.
Playne, Caroline E. *Society at War, 1914-1916*. London: 1931; reprint ed., New York: 1969.
Pratt, Edwin A. *British Railways and the Great War: Organization, Efforts, Difficulties and Achievements*. 2 vols. London: 1921.
Speedy, John C. III. "From Mules to Motors: Development of Maintenance Doctrine for Motor Vehicles by the U.S. Army, 1896-1918." Ph.D. dissertation, Duke University, 1977.
Sumida, Jon. "British Naval Administration and Policy in the Age of Fisher." *The Journal of Military History*, 4, no. 1 (January 1990), pp. 1-26.
Treeger, Karen. "No Supplies, No Benefits, but Earned Respect: The Dietitians of World War I." *Minerva*, 4, no. 4 (Winter 1986), pp. 93-104.
Villate, R. "L'Etat matériel des armées allemandes en Aôut et Septembre 1914." *Revue d'Histoire de la Guerre Mondiale* 4: 310-26.

World War II

Ballantine, Duncan Smith. *U.S. Naval Logistics in the Second World War*. Princeton: 1947.
Barthel, R. "Theorie und Praxis der Heeresmotorisierung im faschistischen Deutschland bis 1939." Ph.D. dissertation, University of Leipzig, 1967.
Boog, Horst. "Luftwaffe and Logistics in the Second World War." *Aerospace Historian* 35 (Summer 1989), pp. 257-68.
Bork, M. "Das deutsche Wehrmachttransportwesen—eine Vorstufe europäischer VerkehrsFührung." *Wehrwissenschaftliche Rundschau* (1952), pp. 50-56.
Burdick, Charles B. "'Moro:' The Resupply of German Submarines in Spain, 1939-1942." *Central European History* III (1970), pp. 265-84.
Busch, E. "Quartermaster Supply of Third Army." *The Quartermaster Review* (November-December 1946).
Bykofsky, J., and Larson, H. *The Transportation Corps*. Washington, D.C.: 1957.
Carter, Worrall Reed. *Beans, Bullets, and Black Oil: The Story of Fleet Logistics Afloat in the Pacific During World War II*. Washington, D.C.: 1953.
Carter, Worrall Reed. *Ships, Salvage, and Sinews of War: The Story of Fleet Logistics Afloat in Atlantic and Mediterranean Waters During World War II*. Washington, D.C.: 1953.
Central Statistical Office. *Statistical Digest of the War*. Official Civil Series. London: 1951.
Conniford, M.P. *A Summary of the Transport Used by the British Army, 1939-1945*. Bracknell, Berks: 1969.
Cuff, Robert D. "From the Controlled Materials Plan to the Defense Materials System, 1942-1953." *Military Affairs* 51 (January 1987), pp. 1-6.
Fanning, William Jeffress. "The German War Economy in 1941: A Study of Germany's Material and Manpower Problems in Relation to the Overall Military Effort." Ph.D. dissertation, Texas Christian University, 1983.
"General Marshall on Logistics." *Army Logistician* (January-February 1982), p. 49.
Goldberg, Alfred. "Air Logistics: Its Role in the European Theater in World War II." Ph.D. dissertation, Johns Hopkins University, 1950.
Golushko, I. "Razvitie Form I Sposobov Tekhnicheskogo Obespecheniia Po Opytu Voiny." *Vuenno-Istoricheskii Zhurnal*, 23, no. 7 (1981), pp. 42-49. (The development of Soviet doctrine of material supply based on the experience of the Great Patriotic War.)
Gowing, Margaret. "The Organization of Manpower in Britain During the Second World War." *Journal of Contemporary History* (January-April 1972).
Hall, H. Duncan. *North American Supply*. London: 1955.
Hall, H. Duncan, and Wrigley, Christopher Compton. *Studies of Overseas Supply*. London: 1956.
Hammond, P.Y. *Organizing for Defense: The American Military Establishment in the Twentieth Century*. Princeton: 1961.
Hammond, Richard James. *Food*. 3 vols. London: 1951-1962.
Holley, I.B., Jr. *Buying Aircraft: Material Procurement for the Army Air Forces*. Washington, D.C.: 1964.
Homze, Edward L. *Arming the Luftwaffe: The Reich Air Ministry and the German Aircraft Industry, 1919-1939*. Lincoln, Nebraska: 1977.
Howlett, W.P. "The Competition Between the Supply Department and the Allocation of Scarce Resources in the Second World War." Ph.D. dissertation, Cambridge University.

Jacobsen, H.A. "Motorisierungsprobleme im Winter 1939/40." *Wehrwissenschaftliche Rundschau* (1956), pp. 497-518.
Joubert de la Ferte, Air Chief Marshal Sir Philip. *The Forgotten Ones: The Story of the Ground Crews.* London: 1961.
Kreidler, E. *Die Eisenbahnen im Machtberich der Assenmächte wahrend des Zweiten Weltkrieges.* Göttingen: 1975.
Krumpelt, I. "Die Bedeutung des Transportwesens für den Schlachterfolg." *Wehrkunde* (1965), pp. 465-72.
Krumpelt, I. *Das Material und die Kriegführung.* Frankfurt am Main: 1968.
Leighton, Richard M., and Coakley, Robert W. *The United States Army in World War II; The War Department: Global Logistics and Strategy, 1940-43.* Washington, D.C.: 1955.
Leighton, Richard M., and Coakley, Robert W. *The United States Army in World War II; The War Department: Global Logistics and Strategy, 1943-45.* Washington, D.C.: 1968.
Maliugin, N.A. "Sovershenstvovanie Operativnogo Tyla." *Voenno-Istoricheskii Zhurnal*, no. 6 (1985), pp. 26-32. (Improvement of the strategic rear area during the Great Patriotic War.)
Marshal, S.L.A. *The Soldier's Load and the Mobility of a Nation.* Washington, D.C.: 1950.
Milward, Alan S. *The German Economy at War.* London: 1965.
Motter, David C. "Governmental Controls over the Iron and Steel Industry During World War II." Ph.D. dissertation, Vanderbilt University, 1959.
New Zealand War History Branch. Department of Internal Affairs. *Official History of the 4th and 6th Reserve Mechanical Transport Companies*, by J. H. Henderson, RMT. Wellington, New Zealand: 1954.
New Zealand War History Branch. Department of Internal Affairs. *Petrol Company*, by A. L. Kidson. Wellington, New Zealand: 1961.
New Zealand War History Branch. Department of Internal Affairs. *Supply Company*, by P. W. Bates. Wellington, New Zealand: 1960.
Overy, R.J. "Transportation and Rearmament in the Third Reich." *The Historical Journal* (1973), pp. 389-409.
Owens, Charles H., Jr. "The Logistical Support of the Army in the Central Pacific, 1941-1944." Ph.D. dissertation, Georgetown University, 1954.
Pottgiesser, H. *Die deutsche Reichsbahn im Ostfeldzug 1939-1944.* Neckargemund: 1960.
Rohde, A.G. *Das deutsche Wehrmachttransportwesen im Zweiten Weltkrieg.* Stuttgart: 1971.
Ross, W.F., and Romanus, C.F. *The Quartermaster Corps; Operations in the War Against Germany.* Washington, D.C.: 1965.
Ruppenthal, Roland G. *Logistical Support of the Armies, May 1941-September 1944. U.S. Army in World War II.* Washington, D.C.: 1953.
Ruppenthal, Roland G. *Logistical Support of the Armies, September 1944-May 1945. U.S. Army in World War II.* Washington, D.C.: 1959.
Schüler, Klaus Friedrich A. *Logistik im Russlandfeldzug. Die rolle der Eisenbahm bei Planunung, Vorbereitung und Durchführung des deutschen Angriffs auf die Sowjetunion bis zur Krise vor Moskau im Winter 1941/42.* Frankfurt: 1987.
Scott, John Dick, and Hughes, Richard. *The Administration of War Production.* London: 1955.
Spence, Ernest J. H. "Canadian Wartime Price Control, 1941-47." Ph.D. dissertation, Northwestern University, 1947.

Spielberger, Walter J. *Die Motorisierung der Deutschen Reichswehr 1920-1935*. Stuttgart: 1979.
Tarnovski, K. N. "Organizatsii Melkoi Promyshlennosti V Rosii V Gody Pervoi Mirovoi Voiny." *Voprosy Istorii*, no. 8 (1981), pp. 18-34. (Small industry organizations and the government's effort to mobilize them during the Great Patriotic War.)
Tischer, Glen L. "Research and Development in Military Subsistence During World War II." Ph.D. dissertation, University of Pennyslvania, 1947.
Ufficio Storico. *I Servizi logistici delle unita italiano al fronte russo (1941-1943)*. 1975.
Urner, Klaus. "La Suisse pendant la guerre: une mobilisation pour les besoins de l'economie de guerre." *Revue de l'histoire de la Deuxième Guerre Mondiale*, 31, no. 121 (1981), pp. 63-69.
U.S. Marine Corps. *Logistic Data, Marine Corps Matériel: Components, Spare Parts, Accessoiries and Contents of Chests, Kits, Outfits and Sets and Other Items of Property for Fleet Marine Force Units, with Reference Data for Loading and Stowing*. Washington, D.C.: 1942.
U.S. War Department. General Staff. *Unified Logistic Support of the United States Armed Services...Prepared Under the Direction of H. R. Lutes, Director of Service Supply and Procurement, War Department General Staff*. Edited by Robin Elliott. Washington, D.C.: 1947.
Windisch. *Die deutsche Nachschubtruppe im Zweiten Weltkrieg*. Munich: 1953.
Wothe, John W. "Logistics and the Battle of Schmidt." *Military Review*, 62, no. 3 (1982), pp. 19-28.
Zelenski, V.D. "Tylovoe Obespechenie 2-I Gvardeiskoi Tankovoi Armii V Berlinskoi Operatsii." *Voenno-Istoricheskii Zhurnal*, no. 4 (1985), pp. 47-52. (Concerns the flow of supplies to the front and rear area protection of the 2nd Guard Tank Army in its assault on Berlin in 1945.)
Zieb, Paul. *Logistische Probleme der Kriegsmarine*. Neckargemünd: 1961.

The Cold War Era to 1984

Adams, Valerie. "Logistics Support for the Falklands Campaign." *Journal of the Royal United Services Institute for Defence Studies*, 129, no. 3 (1984), pp. 43-49.
Anderson, Mary E., et al. *Support Capabilities for Limited War Forces in Laos and South Vietnam*. Santa Monica: 1962.
Banks, F. R. "The Importance of Time in Aircraft Manufacture." *Royal Aeronautical Society Journal* (January 1957).
Day, A.C.L. "Cost Benefit Analysis and Defence Expenditure." *Scottish Journal of Political Economy* (February 1963).
Demidovich, John W. "The Influence of Computer Assisted Instruction Experience upon the Attitudes of Logisticians in the Department of Defense." Ph.D. dissertation, Ohio State University, 1975.
Eccles, Henry Effingham. *Logistics in the National Defense*. Harrisburg, Penn.: 1959.
Franks, Oliver. *Central Planning and Control in War and Peace*. London: 1947.
Geneste, Elmon A. *Integrated Logistic Support: From Concept to Reality*. Washington, D.C.: 1969.
Harper, Gilbert S. "Logistics in Grenada: Supporting No-Plan Wars." *Parameters* (20 June 1990), pp. 50-63.

Heiser, Joseph M., Lt. Gen., USA. *Vietnam Studies: Logistic Support.* Washington, D.C.: 1974.

Hopkins, Charles K. *SAC Tanker Operations in the Southeast Asia War.* Offut Air Force Base, Headquarters, SAC 140, Nebraska: 1979.

Howard, Michael. "The Forgotten Dimension of Strategy." *Foreign Affairs* (August 1979).

Logistics: A Quarterly Forum Dedicated to the Effective Utlization of Our National Resources for Peace and Security. Washington, D.C.: Oct. 1945-July 1947.

Luttwak, Edward N. "The American Style of Warfare and the Military Balance." *Survival* (March/April 1979).

Montgomery, Lord. "Organising for War in Modern Times." *Royal United Services Institution Journal* (November 1955).

Morgan, John D. "Estimating Air Force Logistic Costs." Ph.D. dissertation, Georgetown University, 1971.

Precoda, Norman. *Logistic Support in Limited War.* Santa Barbara: 1958.

Smukul, Albert Ottovich. *Voenno-Morskikh sil.* Moscow: 1973. (Naval logistics.)

U.S. G.A.O. *Logistic Aspects of Vietnamization, 1969-72:* Report to the Congress [on the] Dept. of Defense by the Comptroller General of the United States. Washington, D.C.: 1972.

U.S. G.A.O. *Navy Logistic Support of the 7th Fleet in Southeast Asia: Continuing Logistics Issues and Constraints; Report to the Congress [on the] Department of the Navy by the Comptroller General of the United States.* Washington, D.C.: 1974.

U.S. Quartermaster Research and Engineering Center. *Notes on some evironmental conditions affecting military logistics in Thailand.* Natick, Mass.: 1962.

Zelenskii, V.D. *Tekhnicheskoe obespecheni tankovykhi motostrelkoykh podrazdelenii v souremeenom boiu.* Moscow: 1970.

About the Book

Mars must be fed. His tools of war demand huge quantities of fodder, fuel, ammunition, and food. All these must be produced, transported, and distributed to contending forces in the field. No one can doubt the importance of feeding Mars in modern warfare, and it takes no great effort to recognize that it has always been a major aspect of large scale armed struggle. Yet despite its undeniable importance, surprisingly little has been written about it. The literature of warfare is full of the triumphs and tragedies of common soldiers and the brilliance and blundering of generals. But logistics lacks the drama of combat. It can be expressed on balance sheets no more exciting than shopping lists; movement is not measured by the dashing gallop of charging cavalry but by the steady plod of draft horses.

Feeding Mars is an important contribution to the study of this essential aspect of warfare as practiced by Western powers from medieval times to the Vietnam War. It deals with logistics across a broader time span than that covered in any other work on the subject and emphasizes the various ways in which the essential materials of war have been produced, acquired, and transported to fighting forces in the field.

Feeding Mars makes an important contribution to military history and sheds new light on an important, but too often overlooked, aspect of warfare.

About the Contributors

Bernard S. Bachrach, professor of medieval history at the University of Minnesota, was elected a fellow of the Medieval Academy of America in 1986. He is author of more than seventy articles and eleven books, including *Merovingian Military Organization* and *Fulk Nerra: The Romanesque Consul*. Westview Press will publish his *The Anatomy of a Little War: A Diplomatic and Military History of the Gundovald Affair (568-585)*, in 1994.

Daniel R. Beaver, professor of history at the University of Cincinnati, is the author of several books and articles on American military organization and technology in the twentieth century. He has served as Harold K. Johnson Visiting Professor at the U.S. Army Military History Institute at Carlisle Barracks, Pennsylvania, and as Distinguished Visiting Scholar at the U.S. Army Center of Military History in Washington, D.C..

Robert V. Bruce is emeritus professor of history at Boston University. His major publications include four books: *Lincoln and the Tools of War* and *1877: Year of Violence*, both now in third editions; *Bell: Alexander Graham Bell and the Conquest of Solitude*, available in U.S., British, and Japanese editions; and *The Launching of Modern American Science, 1846-1876*, which won the Pulitzer Prize in History in 1988.

John F. Guilmartin, Jr., is an associate professor of history at the Ohio State University where he teaches early modern European history, military history, and maritime history. He is the author of *Gunpowder and Galleys: Changing Technology and Mediterranean Warfare at Sea in the Sixteenth Century* and was engaged by Encyclopedia Britannica to revise and rewrite its article on the technology of war for the 1990 and subsequent printings.

Walter E. Kaegi is professor of history at the University of Chicago. He has authored numerous articles on the history of Byzantium and several books, including the following: *Byzantine Military Unrest, 471-843*; *Army, Society, and Religion in Byzantium*; *Some Thoughts on Byzantine Military Strategy*; and *Byzantium and the Early Islamic Conquests*.

Edward N. Luttwak, of the Center for Strategic and International Studies, Washington, D.C., has been a guest lecturer at universities and war colleges in ten countries. He was 1987 Nimitz Lecturer at UC Berkeley and 1989 Tanner Lecturer at Yale. He serves on the editorial boards of *The Washington Quarterly*, *Journal of Strategic Studies*, *Geopolitique* (France), and *EJIA*, and *Orbis*. His books, which include *The Grand Strategy of the Roman Empire* and *Strategy: The Logic of War and Peace*, have been published in many languages.

John A. Lynn, professor of history at the University of Illinois at Urbana-Champaign, is the author of *The Bayonets of the Republic: Motivation and Tactics in the Army of Revolutionary France, 1791-94*, as well as numerous articles on French military history, 1610-1815. He also edited *The Tools of War: Ideas, Instruments, and Institutions of Warfare, 1445-1871*. Currently, he is completing *The French Army of the Grand siècle, 1610-1715*. He chairs the Midwest Consortium on Military History.

Joel D. Meyerson, is Chief of the Operational History Branch at the U.S. Army Center of Military History, Washington, D.C. An army veteran of Vietnam, his chief interest is modern strategy and policy. Among his publications is *Images of a Lengthy War: The U.S. Army in Vietnam*, a volume in the official army history. He is currently writing a second book in the U.S. Army in Vietnam series, *Logistics in the Vietnam Conflict*.

Timothy J. Runyan, professor and chairman of the Department of History at Cleveland State University, has published *European Naval and Maritime History, 300-1500* and with A.R. Lewis, *Ships, Seafaring and Society: Essays in Maritime History* for which he was awarded the K. Jack Bauer Prize. He is editor of *The American Neptune*, treasurer of the International Commission of Maritime History, past-president of the North American Society for Oceanic History, and president of the Great Lakes Historical Society.

George Satterfield is a doctoral student at the University of Illinois. He is currently finishing his dissertation, "Princes, Posts and Partisans: Small War in Flanders, 1654-1678." He has co-authored with John Lynn, *A Guide to the Sources in Early Modern Military History in Midwestern Research Libraries*.

John Shy is professor of history at the University of Michigan. He divides his research and teaching between early American history and modern military history. His published work includes *A People Numerous and Armed* and the chapter on Jomini in *Makers of Modern Strategy*, edited by Peter Paret.

Jon Tetsuro Sumida received his Ph.D. from the University of Chicago. Now an associate professor at the University of Maryland, College Park, he has been a fellow of the Wilson Center and the Guggenheim Foundation. His books include *The Pollen Papers: The Privately Circulated Printed Works of Arthur Hungerford Pollen, 1901-1916*, and *In Defense of Naval Supremacy: Finance, Technology and British Naval Policy, 1889-1914*.

Index

Abbasid caliphate: 52
Academy of Sciences, French: 204
   see National Academy of Sciences
Adams, Andrew J.: 280
Adams, Henry: 194
Adams, Peter: 171, 172
Admirals of the English fleet: 81
   Lord High Admiral, 81
Admiralty, British: 218, 219, 220, 222, 223, 224, 226, 228, 229, 230, 231, 232, 233, 234
Africa: 49, see North Africa
Agde: 141
Agincourt: 85, 95
Aircraft: 112
   aircraft as cargo carriers, 185
   as cargo carriers during Vietnam War 278
Aire: 153
Alard, Gervase: 82
Alba, duke of: 110, 130
Alcabala: 117
Alexander: 201
Alfred the Great: 63, 64
Algiers: 114
Allegheny Mountains: 172
Alps: 62
Alsace: 147, 148, 150, 152
Altmühl River: 67,
America:
   Central America, 117
   New World, 113, 116, 117, 129
   see United States
American Civil War: 184, 186, 191-212, 253
American Expeditionary Force (A.E.F.): 253, 258
American Revolutionary War: 161-76
Ammianus Marcellinus: 6
Ammunition:
   field artillery, 199, 219
   projectile production, 219, 227
   small arms, 199
   supply of, 11, 12, 21-22, 185-86

Anatolia: 40, 41, 42, 46
Angareia: 49
Anjou: 60
Annonae: 43
Antietam: 15
Antioch: 46
Antonine Wall: 66
Antwerp: 152
Appert, Nicolas: 192
Arabs: 42, 48, 52, 125
Aragon: 109, 114, 125
Archimedes: 192, 193
Archives Nationales: 145
Arles: 61
Arleux: 153
Arlon: 150
Armada: 14, 104, 110, 114, 126
Armenia: 42, 43, 45, 48
Armies, growth of:
   French, 105, 138
   Spanish, 112, 113
Armory: see Harper's Ferry, Virginia State Armory, and Enfield
Army Industrial College: see U.S. Army
Army of Flanders, Spanish: 24
Army of Italy, French: 146
Army of the Moselle, French: 24
Army of the North, French: 24
Arsenals: see Harper's Ferry, Springfield, and Washington
   naval arsenals, 119, 125-26
Articles of Confederation: 175
Artillery: see Ammuntion and Cannon
   motorization of: 257
Arx: 60
Asientistas: 120
Asiento: 120
Asser: 67
Assistant Secretary of War, U.S.: 255, 256
Atahuallpa: 114, 117, 127
Atarazanas: 119
Ath: 104, 148

Atlanta: 15
Atlantic Ocean: 163
Atom bomb: 191
Attrition:
    strategies of attrition and exhaustion, 47
Augsburg: 67
Augusta: 206
Augustus Caesar: 68
Aurelian: 62
Austro-Prussian War: 11, 15
Auto-Car, motor company: 263
Avars: 41, 43, 52
Avería: 117
Avignon: 61
Aviles, Juan Alvarez de: 111
Aztec: 109, 110

Bachrach, Bernard S.: 33, 26, 311
Bacon: 121, 124
Baden: 148
Baker, Norman: 161
Bakeries: see Ovens
Balfour, Arthur J.: 228, 229, 232
Balkans: 41, 43, 47, 52
Balsac, de: 35
Baltic Sea: 84, 265
Ban Me Thuot: 273
Barcelona: 125
Bartelmeu: 82
Bash, Louis H.: 260
Basingwerk: 67
Battle cruisers: 224, 225, 228, 229
Battle of Britain: 121
Battleships: 217, 224
Baudouin: 146
Baudry of Bourgueil: 72
Baxter, James Phinney: 211, 212
Beachy Head: 104
Beans: 121, see Garbanzos
Beaver, Daniel R.: 187, 311
Bede: 66
Beef: see Meat
Bell Helicopter: 278
Bendix corporation: 262
Bergues: 152
Berlin airlift: 185
Béthune: 153
Biederman Truck Company: 263
Bilbao: 125
Biscay, Bay of: 94
Biscuit: 45, 120-21, 124, 128, 130
Black Prince: 35, 90

Black Sea: 41, 47, 67
Blitzkieg myth: 265
Board of Trade, British: 223, 226
Bodle, Wayne: 168, 170
Bordeaux: 85, 90, 94, 141
Bordelais: 60
Borg-Warner: 262
Bosphorus: 40, 41
Boston: 170, 171
Bowler, Arthur: 161
Braudel, Ferdinand: 5, 130
Brazil: 114
Bread: 5, 20, 45, 120, 140-41
Bremen: 83,
Brétigny: 94
Briesach: 104, 148
Bristol: 87
Britain: 60, 66, 217-35, also see England
British Expeditionary Force, B.E.F.: 217
British Royal Navy: see Royal Navy
Brockway, motor company: 263
Brooke, John M.: 209, 210
Brown University: 194
Bruce, Robert V.: 186, 311
Brunswick, duke of: 21
Bulgaria: 50
    Bulgars, 52
Bull Run, 1st: 197, 198
Bull Run, 2nd: 199
Burghal Hidage: 63
Burgoyne: 170
Burgundy: 61, 141
Burma: 263
Burton, James H.: 206
Butler, Benjamin F.: 202, 210
Byzantine Empire, Byzantium: 7, 31-32, 39-53, 90

Cadiz: 125
Cahors: 63
Calabria: 90
Calais: 92, 95
Calcutta, India: 263
California, internment of Japanese-Americans: 258
Caligny: 152
Cameron, Simon: 197, 198
Campbell, Levin H.: 261
Canada: 167
Canning foods: 192
Cannon: 114, 116, 122, 125, 126, 130, 137, 210
    breech-loading: 203

Index

supply of: 126
Captain General of the Sea: 125
Carbines: 200, 201, 206
Caribbean Sea: 114, 117, 129, 163
Carlisle: 172
Carnegie Endowment: 218
Carolingians: 52
Carp, Wayne, *To Starve the Army at Pleasure*: 162
Cartagena: 125
Casa de Contratación: 124
Cassiodorus: 60, 61
Cassius Dio: 6
Castella, castra, castrum: see Fortifications
Castille: 109, 114, 125
Cateau Cambrésis, Treaty of: 129
Catholicism: 111
Catinat, marshal: 144
Catton, William: 85,
Caucasus: 41, 48
Central Ordnance Laboratory: 207
Central Steel Committee: 220
Cerdaigne: 141
Ceresole: 104
Chamlay: 148
Charlemagne: 33, 57, 64, 66, 67, 69, 70, 71
Charleroi: 24, 148, 150, 154
Charles V of the Holy Roman Empire, Charles I of Spain: 111, 114, 115, 130
Charles VIII, of France: 129
Charles the Bald: 69
Charleston: 196, 203
Chartoularios: 49,
Chastel-Marlhac: 62
Chattanooga: 15
Chaumont: 253
Cheese: 121, 124, 148
Cherbourg: 264
Chesapeake Bay: 168, 172, 173
Chevauchée: 35
Chevrolet, motor company: 261
Chief of Field Artillery: 257
Chief of Naval Operations: 276
Chief of Naval Ordnance, U.S.: 201
Chief of Ordnance, U.S.: 195, 259, also see Ripley
Chief of Staff, U.S. Army: 254, 255, 256
Chiers River: 150
Chilperic: 61
China: 185, 263, 273, 281
Chisbury: 63
Chu Lai: 283

Churchill, Sir Winston: 218, 228, 229, 230, 233
Chusma: 119
Cinque Ports: 80, 86, 87
Civilian Conservation Corps: 257
Civitas: 58, 59
Clausewitz, Carl von: 10, 24
Clay, Lucius D.: 266
Clermont: 183
Cog: 83
    Bremen cog, 83-84
Cohen, I. Bernard: 191, 192
Cold War: 186, 191, 205, 211
Combined Chiefs of Staff: 261
Comites: 61
Command and Staff College, U.S. Army: 276
Commander in Chief, Pacific: 278
Commines: 151, 152
Commons: 88, 89
Communications Zone (COMMZ): 263
Comptroller General, U.S.: 259, 260
Condé: 153
Condottierri: 6
Confederate States, Confederacy: 198, 201, 204, 208
    Army, 208
    efforts at research and development, 205-8
    Navy, 208
    Patent Office: 208
Congress, Confederate: 209
Congress, Continental: 106, 161, 163, 173, 174, 175
Congress, U.S.: 192, 194, 197, 199, 201, 259, 260, 282, 283
Connecticut: 168
Consejo de Aragón: 115
Consejo de Castilla: 115
Consejo de Estado, Spanish Council of State: 115
Consejo de Flandes: 115
Consejo de Hacienda, Spanish Council of Finance: 115
Consejo de Italia: 115
Consejo de la Guerra, Spanish Council of War: 115
Consejo de las Indias: 115
Consejo de Portugal: 115
Constantine I: 45,
Constantine VII: 39, 49
    Book of Ceremonies, 49
Constantinople: 31, 39, 40, 41, 42, 43, 48
Constitution, U.S.: 175, 176

Construction:
  high construction costs in Vietnam, 273
  materials as supply need in modern war, 22-23
Contamine, Philippe: 57
Contributions: 17, 138-39, 143-146
Convoys, in early modern land warfare: 21
Corbitt, motor company: 263
Cordova, Gonsalvo de: 110, 111
Corps of Engineers, U.S.: 262
Cortés, Hernán: 114
Council, King's, English: 85, 87
Courses (raids): 148, 150, 152
Courtrai: 148
Craig, Malin: 254
Crécy: 93, 94
Crete: 89, 95
Crimea: 40
Cruisers: 217, 224
Crusades: 46, 81
  first, 32
  fourth, 90
  third, 90
Crusnes River: 150
Crystal Palace Exhibition: 193
Cuba: 282
Curtis, Edward: 161
Cyprus: 90

Dagobert I: 63, 68
Dahlgren, John A.: 193, 195, 201, 202
Da Nang: 273, 278, 280, 281, 282, 283, 284
Danbury: 168, 172
Danevirke: 57, 66
Dangeau, marquis de: 145
Danube: 12, 18, 40, 41, 67, 143
Danzig: 85
Dardanelles: 40, 41
Dartmouth: 87
David: 209
Davis, Dwight L.: 258
Davis, Jefferson: 195
D Day: 264
Dead Sea: 48
Declaration of Independence: 174
Dee River: 67
Delaware: 167
Delaware Valley: 172
Department of Defense, U.S.: 272, 280, 281, 282, 284
Department of the Army, U.S.: 275, 282, 284
Desiderius of Cahors: 63

Destroyers: 224
DeWitt, John L.: 258, 259, 260
Deynze, conference at: 153
Diamond T, motor company: 263
Dickerson: 171
Dien Bien Phu: 272
Diest: 152
Dijon: 62
Dives-sur-Mer: 72, 73
Djerba: 120
Dodge: 261
Domesday Book: 68
Dorstein: 148
Dorystolon: 52
Douai: 153
Doughty, John W.: 211
Dover: 72, 80, 86, 92
Downing, Brian: xi
Draft animals: see Transportation
Duces: 61
Dunkirk: 148
Duras: 141
Dutch: 84, 109, 110, 111, 113, 131, 151
Dutch Protestantism: 129
Dutch War, 1672-78: 21, 137, 138, 144, 145, 151, 152, 153
Dyer, Alexander B.: 198

East Indies: 114
Easton: 168, 172
Ecuador: 117
Edward I: 84, 93
Edward III: 35, 79, 81, 82, 83, 85, 92, 93, 94
Edward the Elder: 63, 64
Egypt: 41, 43
Eighth Army, U.S.: 276
Eighty Years' War: 129
Eisenhower: 274
Elizabeth Jonas: 104
Elkton: 172
Enfield Armory: 206
  Enfield rifles, 206
England: 33, 36, 60, 67, 79-95, 111, 130, 79-95, 209
English: 109, 110, 111, 113
English Channel: 80
  control during Hundred Years' War, 92
Ericsson, John: 195, 196, 201, 203, 205, 209
Eshing: 63
Espenschied wagon company: 252
Espierres: 152
Étapes: 17-18, 143
Eugene of Savoy: 140

Index

Euphrates River: 40, 48
Europe, reinforcements during Vietnam: 282
European Theater of Operations (ETO): see World War II
Exmouth: 87
Extraordinaires des guerres: 145, 146

Fabricae, Byzantine: 51
Faciculus de Superioritate Maris: 81
Falaise Gap: 265
Fardas: 117
Farming, improvements in: 205
Fastolf, John: 35
Federal, motor company: 263
Felt, Harry D.: 276, 279
Feudalism: 32-33, 57, 68
   feudalism and supply, 33-34
Filipinos in Vietnam: 279
First Army, U.S., WW I: 254, 258
First Army, U.S., WW II: 264
Fish, as a foodstuff: 121, 124
Fisher, Sir John: 229, 232
Fishkill: 168, 171, 172
Flanders: 81, 129, 131, 144, 148, 152, 152
Flour: 168
Fodder: 11, 12, 22, 128, 139-40, 186
   availability of fodder determining operations, 52, 142
   distruction of fodder to deny it to enemy, 45, 142
   dry fodder, 16
   green fodder foraged near an army, 16, 141
   need for fodder to support American Revolution, 167, 171, 172
   supply of fodder by railroad in American Civil War, 15, 19
   supply of fodder in seventeenth century, 141-143
Folkstone: 92
Fonds, de la: 141
Food: 11, 12, 16, see Beans, Bread, Biscuit, Garbanzos, Meat, and Oil
Forage: see Fodder
Ford, motor company: 261
Fortifications:
   Byzantine, 43
   Early modern fortications and supply, 105, 146-54
   French fortified lines, 150-52
      lines of Brabant, 152
      lines of Cambrin, 153
      lines of Moder, 152
      lines of Stollhoffen, 153
      lines of Wissembourg, 153
   French fortresses, 137, 139, 146-49
   late Roman, early medieval, 58-59, 61, 62, 63, 64, 65, 69-70
   Ne Plus Ultra Lines, 153
   16th-century fortifications, 130
   see Hadrian's Wall, Antonnine wall, Offa's Dyke, Danevirke
Forzados: 121
Four-Wheel-Drive, motor company: 263
Fowley: 87
France: 33, 36, 60, 79, 81, 83, 87, 89, 91, 92, 93, 129, 137-53, 185, 221, 253, 254, 260, 265
   as competitor with Spain: 109, 111, 113
   military reform in, 17
Franco-Prussian War: 11, 15, 185
Franklin, Benjamin: 194
Frederick II, the Great: 6, 24
French Army:
   growth of, 105
   supply of around Newport, RI: 170
French Revolution: 10, 18, 21, 24, 161, 192
Frink, James L.: 262
Fuel, supply needs for: 12, 21-22, 183, 185-86
   naval needs for fuel, 186
   P.O.L., petroleum, oil, lubricants: 262
Fulk Nerra: 65
Fulrad of Saint Quentin: 70
Fulton, Robert: 183

Galeasse: 119
Galleon: 104
Galley: 82, 84, 90, 104, 114
   Galeras de lanterna, 121
   Galleys of Spain, 117, 122, 124, 125-26
   Spanish galleys, 119-22, 128, 130
Gallipoli: 14
Garbanzos: 121, 124
Gas, poison: 211
Gascon Roll: 81
Gascony: 83, 90, 93, 94, 95
Gasoline: see Fuel
Gates, Horatio: 170
Gattling, Richard and Gattling gun: 211
Gaul: 60
Geddes, Eric: 226
General Staff (G-4): 255
Genoa: 125
Gente de cabo: 121
German army, World War II: 184, 265-66

Germany: 141, 148, 211
Gettysburg: 198
Ghazis: 128
Gibbins, Henry: 260
Gibraltar: 112
GMC, General Motors Corporation: 261, 262
Gold: 117, 118, 125
Gordas, Josiah: 206, 207, 210
Gordon, G.A.H.: 233
Göttingen: 207
Gracedieu: 84,
Grain: 20-21, 106, 141, 148, 171, 172-73
Grand Fleet, British: 217, 231
Great Britain: 194
Great Depression: 259
Great Harry: 103
Great War: see World War I
Great Yarmouth: 87
Greece: 40
Greek fire: 194
Greek language: 42
Greene, Nathanael: 162
Gregory of Tours: 62
Gross, Charles P.: 262
Guanajuato: 117
Guderian: 6
Guerre de course: 129, 131
Guilmartin, John F., Jr.: 104, 311
Gulf War: 185
Gunpowder: 130
Gunpowder weapons, impact of: 113, 122
Gustavus Adolphus: 11

Hadrian's Wall: 66
Haguenau: 152
Haine River: 153
Hamble River: 85
Hamilton, Alexander: 175
Hanoi: 279
Hapsburgs, Austrian: 110, 114
Hapsburgs, Spanish: 111, 114, 115
Harbord Board: 255
Harper's Ferry: 198, 206
Hart, William H.: 256
Hastings: 72, 80, 86, 92
Haupt, Herman: 204
Havana: 125
Headquarters Support Activity: 276
Heemskerk, Jacob van: 112
Heilbron: 148
Helicopters: 185, 278
Henry I, of Saxony: 64

Henry V, of England: 85
Henry VI, of England: 35
Henry VIII, of England: 103
Henry, Joseph: 195-96, 204, 211
Heraclius: 42, 46
Hercules Motor Company: 263
Himcmar of Rheims: 69
Hitler, Adolf: 7, 266
Hodge, Courtney H.: 264
Holabird Quartermaster Depot, MD: 257, 258
Holland: 112
Holy Alliance: 114
Holy Ghost: 85
Holy Roman Empire: 147
Honolulu, headquarters of Pacific command during Vietnam War: 273, 275, 278, 279
Horses:
    as consumers of fodder, 16, 141-42
    as draft animals, see Transportation
    horse drawn transport and railroads: 15
    limitations of horse drawn transport: 15
    transporting horses at sea, 72, 89-90
Hospital of St. John of Jerusalem: 81
Howard, Oliver O.: 196
Hudson River: 168, 170, 171, 172, 183
Huger, Benjamin: 193, 194, 195
Hull: 92
Humber: 87
Hundred Years' War: 36, 79-95
Hunley: 209
Hurley, Patrick J.: 258, 259
Huston, John A.: ix
Hythe: 80, 86

Inca: 109, 110, 114
Inchon: 14
Industrial Revolution: 10, 14, 21, 183, 185, 186
Intendants: 141, 144, 146, 147
    French military intendants, 48
Internal combustion engine: 183, 184-85, 257
International, motor company: 263
Ipswitch: 87
Irmino of Saint-Germain-des-Près: 69
Ironclad war vessels: 202, 208, 209
Iron plates as armor: 205
Isabella of Castille: 115
Isherwood, Benjamin: 201
Islam: 42, 52, 90, 111, 114, 127
    Islamic conquests, 42, 57
Italian Wars: : 110, 111

Italy: 40, 60, 66, 72, 114, 129, 141

Japan: 274
Jeep: see Trucks
Jellicoe, Sir John: 220, 220
Jesus: 85
Jeumont: 152
John, king of England: 81
Johnson, Harold K.: 283
Johnson, Lyndon B.: 272, 280, 281, 283
John the Cappadocian: 45
Joint Chiefs of Staff: 261, 272, 279, 281, 283, 284
Jomini: 13
Jourdan: 24
Julian: 46
Julius Caesar: 72
Justinian I: 32, 42, 46, 47

Kaegi, Walter E.: 31, 32, 311
Kaiserwerth: 148
Kalm, Peter: 164
Kennedy, John F., administration: 275
Khaireddin Barbarossa: 114
King's Ferry: 170
King's Lynn: 87
Kingston-upon-Hull: 87
Kitchner, Lord: 217
Kontum: 273
Korat, Thailand: 274, 275
Korean War: 187, 276

La Bassée: 148
Labor supply for British war production: 220-23, 230, 233
  labor for ship production, 224, 227
  women in the labor force, 220
La Bourdonnaye: 141
La Fère: 150
La Grange: 148
Lake Champlain: 167
Lake George:167
La Kenoque: 151
Lancaster: 168, 172
Landau: 150, 154
Landric, abbot of St. Wandrille: 69
Landsknechts: 114
Languedoc: 141
Laos: 275, 277
Latin language: 42
La Trouille: 152
Laws of Oléron: 81

Ledo road: 263
Leo I: 47
Leo VI: 45
Lepanto: 104, 114, 120, 121, 127, 129
Le Quesnoy: 148
Le Tellier, Michel: 43, 106
Liège: 148
Lille: 104, 148, 153
Lima: 125
Lincoln, Abraham: 197, 202, 203, 204, 205, 210
Lines, fortified: see Fortifications
Lisbon: 125
Lithgow, James: 228
Little Yarmouth: 87
Living off the country: see Supply
Livingston, governor: 171
Logistical command, U.S. in Vietnam: 281
  9th Logistical Command, 275, 277
  origins, background, 276-77
  plans for logistical command in Vietnam, 277-80
Logistics, views of by professional soldiers:
  aristocratic views of: 3-7
  as of limited concern to Byzantines, 39-40
  U.S. Army view of, in low repute, 254
Logista: 39
Logistes: 39
Logistics: see Supply and Transportation
Logistike: 39
Logothete: 49,
London: 72, 83, 86, 87, 92, 193
London, Treaty of: 111
Lorge: 148
Louis XI: 33
Louis XII: 114
Louis XIV: 10, 21, 23, 105, 106, 137, 138, 139, 142, 143, 146, 148, 150, 151, 153, 154
Louis of Badden: 153
Louvois, marquis de: 43, 106, 142, 148, 150, 151, 152
Low Countries: 18, 144, 153, 154
Lowem, Thaddeus: 203
Loyalists, American: 164, 172
Ludwig I of Bavaria: 67
Luftwaffe: 121
Luttwak, Edward: 9, 311-12
Luxembourg, city and province: 142, 144
Lynn, John A.: 105, 312
Lys River: 151, 152

McClellan, George: 195

320

Machine gun: 192, 203, 208, 211
Mack: 263
Mackesy, Piers: 161
Maclay, Joseph: 226
McNair, Lesley J.: 263
McNamara, Robert S.: 277, 280, 283
McNeill, William: ix
Macon, Georgia: 207
Maestricht: 148
Magazines: 16, 17, 128, 140, 141, 142
    Byzantine, 32, 45
    in fortresses: 148
    naval, 124, 125-26, 128
    need for in early modern warfare, 19-21, 105, 106, 118
Magyars: 57, 64
Mahan, Alfred Thayer: 114
Malaga: 124, 125
Malhelem: 142
Mallet, John W.: 207, 208
Malta: 121
Maltby, William: 110
Malvern Hill: 199
Manhattan: 171
Mannheim: 148
Manpower procurement:
    for Spanish galleys, 120-22, 130
    impressment of English sailors during Hundred Years' War, 87-89
    Spanish soldiers, 126-27
Manses, mansi, as basis of military assessments: 70, 71
Manstein: 6, 7
Marine Corps: see U.S. Marine Corps
Marlborough, John Churchill, duke of: 153
    advance to the Danube, 1704, 18, 25, 143
Marmara, sea of: 40, 41
Marmon-Harrington, motor company: 263
Marsh gun: 200
Marshall, George C.: 255, 261, 266
Maryland: 171, 172
Mary Rose: 103
Massachusetts: 170
Materials and Priority Department, British Admiralty: 220
Maubeuge: 153
Maurice, Byzantine military writer of *Strategikon*: 44, 45
Maury, Matthew: 204, 208, 209
Maxwell, Russell L.: 276
Mazarin, cardinal: 150
Meat, provision of: 71, 121-22, 124, 141

Medina Sidonia, duke of: 119
Mediterranean Sea: 90, 104, 113, 114, 117, 119, 120, 125, 127, 128, 129, 130
Mekong Delta: 280
Mercia: 66, 67
Meros: 45
Merrimack: 209
Mesopotamia: 41, 43, 45, 48, 51
Messina: 125
Metz: 148
Meuse-Argonne Offensive: 253
Meuse River: 150, 151, 152
Mexico: 114, 125, 194, 258
Meyerson, Joel D.: 188, 312
Mézière: 148
Middle Ages, supply during: 16, 31-37
Middleton, NY: 172
Military Air Transport Service: 282
Military Assistance Advisory Group: 275
Military Assistance Command: 275
Military Assistance Program, U.S.: 272
    Assistant Chief of Staff for Logistics, 275, see Osmanski
Military manuals:
    Byzantine, 44, 45
    See *Strategikon, Tactica*
    Muslim, 44
Mines, naval: 192, 208-9
Minié Ball: 206
Ministry of Munitions, British: 218, 219, 220, 221, 226, 228, 230, 231, 232, 234
Ministry of Shipping, British: 226
Ministry of Supply, British: 232
Mississippi River: 209
Moctezuma: 117
Moltke, Helmut von, the Elder: 12
Moltke, Helmut von, the Younger: 12, 19
Monitor: 201, 209
Monitors: 224, 226, 228
Mons: 142, 148, 152
Montclar: 142
Montecuccoli: 6
Mordecai, Alfred: 193, 194, 195, 198
Morison, Samuel Eliot: 161
Morris, Robert: 161, 173, 175
Morris county: 171
Morristown: 172
Moscow: 12
Motor Transportation Branch, U.S.: 258
Motor Transport Service, U.S.: 261, 264
Moultrie, Fort: 196
Mumford, Lewis: 193

Index 321

Mummolus: 62
Muñido, Francisco-Felipe Olesa:
    La organización Naval de Los Estados Mediterraneos, 110
Munitionnaire: 138, 140, 141
Munitions of War Act: 223
Murphy wagon company: 252
Muslims: see Islam
Mutiny: 88, 118
    because of lack of supplies, 24

Namur: 152
Nancy: 148
Napier, John: 194
Naples: 125
Napoleon I: 10, 11, 12, 16, 17, 18,19, 23, 24, 25, 185
    advance to the Danube in 1805, 18, 24
Napoleon gun: 195
National Academy of Sciences: 204
National Advisory Committee: 211
National Committee for Aeronautics: 211
National Defense Act of 1920: 254, 255, 256
National Security Council: 283
Naval logisitics:
    British naval industrial logistics in WWI: 217-35
    in early modern Europe, 103-4, parameters of, 13-14
    in sixteenth-century Spain, 109-31
    van Creveld's exclusion of it, 10, 12
Navigation Acts:
    of 1380s, 89
Navy:
    British, see Royal Navy
    U.S., see U.S. Navy
Navy Department, U.S.: 204
Nef: 90
Netcong: 171
Netherlands: 118, 130, 143, 152, 153
Netherlands, Revolt of: 110, 114, 126, 129
New Brunswick: 172
Newcastle: 85
New England: 170, 171, 172
New Jersey: 167, 169, 171, 172
Newport: 170
Newton: 171
New Windsor: 168
New World: see America
New York: 170, 172, 173
Nha Trang: 273, 280
Nile: 40

Nimoue: 141
Nine Years' War: 137, 138, 144, 148, 151, 152, 153
Niter, experiments to produce it in U.S.: 203
Niter and Mining Bureau, Confederate: 207
Noailles, Adrienne, duc de: 141
Normandy invasion: 12, 264
Normans: 41, 90
North Africa: 10, 41, 43, 47, 51
North Sea: 67, 87
Norwich: 88
Nuntii: 61

Oak Ridge: 210
Offa: 66
Offa's Dyke: 33, 57, 66-67
Officers as a source of finance and supply: 138
Ohio: 205
Oil, cooking, eating: 121, 124
Oil, lubricant: see Fuel
Oise River: 151
Okinawa: 274, 275, 277
Operational Plan 32-59 (32 Plan): 274, 275
    1964 update of 32 Plan, 282
Operational Plan 37-64: 277
Operation Barbarosa: 265
Operation Cobra: 264
Ordnance Bureau, U.S. Army: 195, 202, 252, 253
Ordnance Bureau, U.S. Navy: 201
Ordnance Corps, U.S. Army: 193, 206, 262
Ordnance Department, Confederate Army: 206, 207
Ordnance Department, U.S. Army : 196, 197, 198, 203, 208, 261, 262
    Calibers Board: 257
Orwell: 88
Osmanski, Frank A.: 188, 275, 276, 277, 278, 279, 280, 281
Ostrogoths: 60
Ottoman Turks: 41, 50, 109, 111, 113, 114, 118, 127, 128, 129
Ovens: 16, 20, 125, 140, 141
Overlord, operation: 14

Palatinate: 154
Palestine: 43
Panama: 125
Papermaking: 205
Paris: 145, 264
Parker, Geoffrey: 24, 105
    Army of Flanders and the Spanish Road, 110

Parliament: 81, 88, 89, 93
Patton, George: 6, 12, 14, 16, 264
Pavely, John: 81,
Pearl Harbor: 261
Peekskill: 172
Pennsylvania: 171, 172
Pentagon: 282
Peppin I: 68
Perigueux: 58
Perjés, G.: 20-21, 140, 141
Permanent Commission: 204
Pershing, John: 258
Persia, Sassanid: 32, 46, 52
Persian Gulf: see Gulf War
Peru: 117, 125, 129
Pesos: 117
Petersburg: 211
Pevensey: 72
Peyssonel: 142
Philadelphia: 168, 170, 172, 175
Philadelphia Enquirer: 195
Philip II: 114, 115
Philip of Valois: 92
Philippines: 274
Philipsbourg: 150
Phillips, Carla Rahn, *Six Galleons for the King of Spain*: 110
Phu Bai: 284
Pignerolo: 148
Pitres: 69
Pleiku: 273, 280
Plutarch: 193
Plymouth: 87
Pochura: 117
Poitiers: 58, 94, 95
P.O.L., petroleum, oil, lubricants: see Fuel
Poland: 265
Polybius: 6
Polypychs: 69
Porte: see Ottoman Turks
Ports, 16th-century Spanish: 124-26
Portsmouth: 92
Portugal: 114, 125
Potosí: 117, 118, 131
Praefectus praetorio vacans: 46
Praetorian prefecture: 43, 45, 49
Praetorium: 60
Princeton: 171
Principle Supply Officers Committee: 233
Protective Mobilization Plan of 1937: 255
Protonotarios: 49
Prussia: 10

Puerto de Sant Maria: 124
Pulaski's Legion: 167
Pusan: 276
Puységur, Jacques-François de Chastenet de: 142

Quartermaster Bureau, U.S.: 252, 253, 256, 257, 258
Quartermaster Corps, U.S.: 259, 262
Quartermaster General, U.S.: 253, 254, 256, 258, 260
   during American Revolution, 170, 173
Quartermaster Motor Transport Service: 262
Quartermaster Technical Committee: 256, 261, 262
Qui Nhon: 273, 280

Ragusa: 114
Railroad:
   in the American Civil War, 14-15, 192
   as a means of transportation, 10, 12, 112, 184, 265
   van Creveld's evaluation of, 12, 14-15
Rains, George W.: 207
Raleigh, Sir Walter: 193
Ramsey, George D.: 202
Raritan River: 172
Raritan Valley: 171
Ratcliff: 85
Raymond, Morrison-Knudsen: 279
Reading: 168
Reconquista: 111, 119, 125
Red Ball Express: 264
Regensburg: 67
Reno, Jesse: 197
Research and development (R&D):
   in the American Civil War, 191-212
   vs. production: 186
Reybold, Eugene: 262
Rezat River: 67
Rhine-Danube canal: 57, 66, 67-68
Rhineland: 144
Rhine River: 18, 147, 148, 152, 153
Rhode Island: 173
Richard I: 80, 81, 90
Richmond: 208
Rifles: 186, 191, 196, 198, 206
   Breach-loading rifles: 192, 199-201, 202, 203, 211
   repeating rifles: 192, 203, 211
   see Carbines, Enfield, Sharps, Spencer, Springfield

Index

Ripley, James W.: 186, 196-202, 205, 210, 211
Risch, Erna: 162
River transport: 15, 40
    during the American Civil War: 184
Roads, during American Revolutionary War: 164-65
Rocketry: 191
Rocroi: 104, 148
Rodman, Thomas J.: 193, 195, 198, 204, 208
Rolling Thunder: 281
Rome:
    empire, 31, 50, 52, 57
    Roman logistical heritage, 57, 58-59
    Roman military and political heritage, 31, 32, 33, 40, 42, 43, 44, 68
    Roman roads, 44
Rommel, Erwin: xi, 7
Romney: 80, 86
Roos, Sir John: 88
Rousillon: 141
Royal Dockyards: 223, 224, 225, 228
Royal Navy: 217-35
    construction and repair of naval vessels in WWI, 223-31
Royster, Charles: 162
Runyan, Timothy J.: 36, 312
Rus: 52
Russia in WW II: 263, 265, 266
Rutland: 91
Rye: 80, 86
Ryukyu Islands: 274, 280

Saigon: 273, 274, 275, 280, 281, 282, 283
Saint Germain, comte de: 24
Saint-Mihiel offensive: 258
Saint Pouenge: 141
Saint-Valery-sur-Somme: 72
Saint-Venant: 153
Saint Wandrille: 69, 70, 71
Sambre: 151, 152, 153
Sandwich: 80, 86, 92
San Francisco: 274
Santa Crux, Mexico: 125
Sardinia: 51
Satterfield, George: 312
Sava River: 42
Saxons: 60, 64,
Saxony: 33, 57, 64, 70
Scheldt: 152, 154
Schlieffen Plan: 11, 12, 15
Schmalkaldic War: 130
Schuyler, Philip: 167

Scientific American: 196, 202, 204
Scotland: 88
Scott, Sir Percy: 232
Secretary of War: see U.S. Secretary of War
Seine River: 264
Seljuk Turks: 41, 53
Semoy River: 150, 151
Serbia: 41, 42
Sestas, Bernard de: 81
Severn River: 67
Seville: 118, 122, 125, 129
Sharp, Ulysses S. Grant: 278-79, 281
Sharps rifle: 200, 211
    Sharps cartridges, 199
Sheriffs: 91
Sherman, William T.: 15
Sherman tank: 262
Ships:
    arrest of during Hundred Years' War, 80, 82-83, 88, 89
    merchantmen as transports during Hundred Years' War, 89-90
    naval stores, 85, 122, 123
    ships as magazines, 128
    Spanish sailing vessels, sixteenth-century: 116, 122-24
    types during Hundred Years' War, 82-87
    see ship types by name
Shoe making: 205
Showalter, Dennis: 12
Shy, John: 106, 107, 312
Sicily: 47, 51, 72, 90
Sieges: 105,
    Supply demands of siege warfare, 11, 21
Sigillography: 45
Silistra: 52
Slavs: 41, 43, 52
Sluys: 92, 93, 94, 95
Smithsonian Institution: 195, 204
Society of Automotive Engineers (S.A.E.): 253, 258, 259, 260
Soc Trang: 278
Somerset Courthouse: 172
Somervell, Brehon B.: 261, 266
Somerville: 171
Somme: 151
Sorbs: 70, 71
Southampton: 84, 87
South Carolina: 173
Southeast Asia: 272, 274, 275, 277, 281, 282
Southeast Asia Treaty Organization: 275
South Koreans in Vietnam: 279, 282

Sovereign of the Sea: 104
Spain: 33, 51, 60, 66, 79, 91, 109-31, 137, 141, 153, 154
    Spanish war finance, 116-19
Spanish American War: 252
Spanish Road: 18
Special Logistic Actions: 275
Spencer repeating rifle: 203, 211
Spicer: 262
Spitfires: 121
Springfield Armory: 172, 196, 197, 198
    Springfield rifle: 196, 197, 200
Stalingrad: 185
Standard B: see Trucks
Standard Quartermaster Fleet: see Trucks
Stanton, Edwin: 210
State Department, U.S.: 272
Steam engine: 183
Steam power, supply needs for navies: 13
Steel: 226, 227, 230, 233
    production: 219
    see Central Steel Committee
Strasbourg: 147
Strassfurt: 70, 71
Strategikon: 44, 45
Strategos: 49
Strayer, Edgar S.: 258, 259
Studebaker, motor company: 263
    wagon company, 252
Subic Bay, Philippines: 274
Submarine: 209, 226, 230
    anti-submarine efforts in WWI, 218
Submarine Battery Service: 209
Succasunna, NY: 171, 172
Sumida, Jon Tetsuro: 186, 312
Summerall, Charles P.: 254
Supply, specific issues in addition to topics of chapters:
    acquisition during Hundred Years' War: 91-92
    ease of supply in base areas, 12
    living off the country: 10, 11, 12, 13, 15-19, 138, 139-43
    living off the country vs. supply from the rear: 10, 13
    supply as a weapon in the Middle Ages, 34-36
    supply from the rear: 10, 11, 12
    "umbilical cords" of supply: 10, 11, 12, 107
Surveys, medieval surveys of land, resources, and population: 68-70, see *Domesday Book*, Polypytchs

Sussex county: 171
Syrett: 161
Syria: 41, 43, 48, 50

Tactica: 45
Tacitus: 6
Tagmata: 49
Tank-Automotive Center, U.S.: see Trucks
Tanks: 184, 230, 263
Taurus passes: 50
Taxation, to support war in early modern France: 138
Taylor, Brainerd: 258, 259
Taylor, Maxwell D.: 284
Teamsters in American Revolutionary War: 163
    dangers to: 172
    problems of mobilizing, 164, 166, 172
Technology Review: 191
Telegraphy: 192
Thailand: 274, 275, 277
Thames River: 81, 87, 88
Thanet: 92,
Theme: 49,
Theodoric, the Great: 60, 61,
Theodosius I: 46,
Thessalonica: 41
Thibaut, Jacqueline: 168, 170
Thionville: 148
Third Army, U.S.: 264
Thirty Years' War: 10, 11, 17, 18, 24, 138
Thompson, James Westfall: 68
Thrace: 48
Thucydides: 5, 6
Ticonderoga: 167
Timber Creek: 210
Timken-Detroit: 262
Tonkin, Gulf of: 277, 279
Torgny: 150
Tories, American: see Loyalists
Torpedo:
    Torpedo Bureau, 209
    see Mines
Touldon: 39
Tournai: 148, 152
Transportation:
    draft animals in American Revolutionary War: 163
    early modern European transportation and supply, 105-6
    medieval technology of transportation, 36
    mules, 257

Index 325

oxen, 71, 163
pack animals, 42, 43, 44, 64, 112, 128
physics of air transport, 185
at sea, 13-14, 36, 112-13, 185
   vital to Byzantines, 40
   transportation and supply in the American Revolution, 106-7, 161-76
   see Aircraft, Trucks, Railroad, and River transport
Transportation Corps, U.S.: 262, 263
Tredegar works: 208
Trenton: 172
Trinity Royal: 85.
Trucks: 11, 12, 112, 184-85, 217
   choice and production of trucks for the U.S. Army, 187, 251-66
   deuce and a half, 2 1/2 ton truck, 260, 261, 262, 264, 265, 266
   Jeep, 260, 261, 263, 265, 266
   Standard B, "Liberty," 253, 254, 257, 258, 259
   Standard Quartermaster Fleet, 258
   Tank-Automotive Center: 261
   technological improvements of the truck, 257, 260
   U.S. Army truck types, 1940-45, 260
   U.S. need for heavy-heavy trucks, 264-65
   weapons carrier, 260, 261, 263, 265
Tunis: 114, 127
Tunisia: 264
Turenne, Henri de La Tour d'Auvergne, viscount de: 140, 148
Turgot: 147
Twelve Years' Truce: 111, 125

Udorn, Thailand: 274
Ukraine: 7, 265
Umayyad caliphate: 52
Umbilical cords of supply: see Supply
United States: 106, 161, 194
   during the U.S. Civil War, 191-212
   during the Vietnam War, 271-84
   during the War of the American Revolution, 161-190
   1920-45, 251-66
United States Air Force: 274
   Air Force Reserve, 282
   see U.S. Army Air Force
United States Army, 187, 251-66, 274, 276
   Army Air Forces (AAF), 261
   Army Ground Forces (AGF), 261, 262, 263

Army Service Forces (ASF), 261, 263, 266
U.S. Army Industrial College: 256, 257
U.S. Army Ordnance Department: 186
United States Marine Corps: 274, 284
United States Military Academy: 192, 193, 207
Unites States Navy: 276
   research and development during Civil War, 208-10
United States Secretary of War: 197, 256, 257, 258, 260
United States War Department: 192, 194, 197, 198, 199, 201, 253, 256, 257, 261, 276
Universities, colleges, as sources of research: 204
University of Virginia: 204, 207
Urbs, urbes: 58, 59, 60, 63

Valencia: 125, 130
Valenciennes: 153
Valley Forge: 162, 172
   supply problems at: 167-171
Valmy: 21
Van Creveld, Martin: ix, 9-25, 105, 140, 141, 142, 143, 154, 161
   Supplying War, 9-25
   views on military planning: 12, 14
Vandals: 47
Van Houtte, Hubert: 148
Vassalli dominici: 69
Vauban, Sébastien le Prestre de: 147, 150, 151, 152
Vegetius, *De re militari*: 61, 64,
Venice, Republic of: 32, 50, 114, 128, 130
Vera Cruz: 125
Verbruggen, J.F.: 57
Vicksburg: 203
Vienna: 114
Viet Cong: 271, 278, 281, 283
Viet Minh: 281
Vietnam: 7, 187-88, 271-84
   Central Highlands, 272, 273
   creation of a U.S. supply base in Vietnam, 187-88, 271-84
   North, 272, 281
Vietnam War: 185, 271-84
Vikings: 57
Villars, Claude: 144, 145, 146, 153
Villeroi, François: 142, 152
Virginia: 172
   Virginia Armory: 206

Virginia: 209
Visigoths: 60
Volmerange: 150
Vosges: 152
Vung Tau: 280

Wagons: 10, 11, 15, 19, 21, 40, 44, 45, 91, 92, 106, 112, 128, 163, 166, 168, 172, 173, 184, 252-53
Wales: 33, 67
Wallenstein, count Albrecht von: 11, 16, 17
War Cabinet: 223, 226, 228, 229, 231
War Department: see U.S. War Department
Ward-La France, motor company: 263
War of Devolution: 137, 138, 144
War Office, British: 218, 219, 220, 226, 228, 229
War of the Spanish Succession: 104, 137, 138, 150, 151, 152
War Powers Act: 261
War production: 187
 for the World War I Royal Navy, 217-35
 of trucks in U.S., 251-66
Wars of Italy: see Italian Wars
Washington, George: 163, 167, 170, 171, 173, 175
Washington, D.C.: 271, 275, 276, 277, 278, 281, 282, 283
Washington Arsenal: 202
Water, fresh, as a necessary naval supply: 120-21, 124
Watson, Peter H.: 210
Wavell, Sir Archibald: 251
Weapons carrier: see Trucks
Wehrmacht: 265
Weissenburg: 67
Welles, Gideon: 201
Wessex: 63
Westchester County: 170
West Indies: 114

Westmoreland, William C.: 278, 281, 282, 284
West Point: see U.S. Military Academy
Wetherill, Charles: 196
Wheat: see grain
White, motor company: 263
White House: 278
Widukind: 64
Wight, Isle of: 87, 92
William, the Conqueror: 14, 32, 33, 57, 68, 72
 invasion of England by, 1066, 71-73
Williams, D. R.: 208
Willys-Overland: 261
Winchelsea: 80, 86
Winchester: 63
Wine: 121
Wöhler, Friedrich: 207
Women in war production: see Labor
Works Progress Administration: 257
World War I: 5, 11, 15, 21, 185, 187, 211, 217-35, 252, 253, 254, 263
World War II: 11, 12, 13, 22, 185, 186, 187, 188, 191, 211, 235, 260-66, 276, 277
 British and U.S. army motorization during, 185
 German, French, and Russian dependence on horses at the start of, 184
 U.S. Army in the European Theater of Operations (ETO): 263-66
 U.S. Army supply figures for, 22
Wright, John: 172
Württemberg: 144-45, 148, 154

Yarmouth: 87, 92
York: 168
Yorkshire: 92
Yorktown: 174
Ypres: 150, 151, 152, 153

Zacatecas: 117

MARINE CORPS DETACHMENT
USAQMSCOL FORT LEE VA
RUC 54078 MCC K99

Printed in the United States
71504LV00005B/44